TELEVISION

— WITHOUT —

PiTY™

TELEVISION
— WITHOUT —
PITY™

752 THINGS WE LOVE TO HATE
(AND HATE TO LOVE) ABOUT TV

By TARA ARIANO and SARAH D. BUNTING

QUIRK BOOKS
PHILADELPHIA

Library of Congress Cataloging in Publication Number: 2006903875

ISBN-10: 1-59474-117-4
ISBN-13: 978-1-59474-117-3

Printed in Singapore

Typeset in Times New Roman and House Gothic

Designed by Doogie Horner
Illustrations by Kevin Sprouls

Distributed in North America by Chronicle Books
85 Second Street
San Francisco, CA 94105

10 9 8 7 6 5 4 3 2

Quirk Books
215 Church Street
Philadelphia, PA 19106
www.quirkbooks.com

To Ian Ziering

Introduction

A h, television. It s a constant presence in most of our lives, a comforting voice in the background, a familiar friend that does our thinking and feeling for us at the end of a long day. But ever since the very first cathode ray flickered to life more than half a century ago, TV has faced harsh censure, taking the blame at one time or another for every societal ill, from low high-school graduation rates to obesity to the electricity crisis. TV is bad, its critics say. TV is stupid. TV is crap masquerading as art. TV makes us fat. TV makes us dumb.

Television Without Pity doesn t disagree. And we ve watched enough TV to know.

We ve watched *much* more than TV s detractors have yes, even more than you, Focus on the Family which is why we appreciate all the good things about TV. Of course there are good things about it; if there weren t, would so many of us own TVs? And here in North America, we don t just own TVs; we re a little addicted to them. We keep them close by in case we need a fix, which is why we have them in the living room, and the den, and the kitchen, and the bedroom, and on the boat, and in the cottage, and in our cars, and cleverly tucked away in a hidden panel built into the hot tub.

We tell ourselves it s because we want to watch the news . . . but then how much of CNN is real news and how much is just telling us about the fortieth anniversary of some candy factory? We pretend we really don t even watch that much TV just PBS! but then we find ourselves mesmerized by the soothing voice and calmly static illustrations of *Reading Rainbow*. We act like reality TV is beneath us, but if the subject of *Survivor* comes up at a cocktail party, we end up in a vigorous debate with a stranger over whether there s been a really satisfying winner since Richard Hatch.

Television asks so little of us and gives us so much in return. It s a world of possibilities in a compact little box, offering instant access to crime-scene investigations, sassy robots, standup comics, dance-offs, and game shows older than we are. It can teach you things you never thought you wanted to know, or present you with programming so resolutely unchallenging that it actually does make you a little bit dumber. If you want to exercise, there are shows about that. If you want to eat chocolate, there s a channel where they show you what it looks like and tell you how awesome it is, and you can call them up, buy the chocolate, and someone *brings it to your house*. And if that doesn t work for you, turn your TV on at any hour of the day and you can probably watch *Law & Order*.

TV isn t always good for us, which is why we sometimes hate to love it: It seems like we shouldn t get that excited about, say, a *Small Wonder* marathon, but we do, and that s embarrassing. But TV isn t always bad for us, either, which is why it can be hard to admit that we re watching a show we know is awful because most of the fun comes from ripping on it loving to hate it.

Our relationship with TV is complicated . . . and so is yours. That s where this book comes in. Let s try to work through it together.

A

AAMES, WILLIE Perhaps you remember him as pint-sized Tommy Bradford on the large-family-wackiness dramedy *Eight Is Enough* (or as T. J. Latimer on the nearly identical *Family*). More likely, you remember him as pint-sized horndog sidekick Buddy Lembeck on *Charles in Charge*. He probably hopes you don t remember *Paradise*, the soft-core *Blue Lagoon* rip-off he starred in (naked aaaiiieeee!) with Phoebe Cates, because Aames is now a devout Christian who, until 2003, toured the country in character as Bibleman. Presumably he did this to atone for such sins as 1) lending his voice to the *Dungeons & Dragons* TV series, and 2) being very, very annoying. See also AFROS, IMPORTANT TV; BAIO, SCOTT; and *CHARLES IN CHARGE*.

A&E DAYBREAKS Time was, reruns of *Law & Order* aired not on TNT, but every afternoon on A&E. They were the center- piece of the cable network s Daybreaks block of programming comfort food that made a perfect diet for the self-employed. Granted, *Murder, She Wrote* is not for everyone, but that s why it aired so early, before the pajamaed home worker was even out of bed. However, a double shot of *NewsRadio* or *Night Court* at noon, followed by *L&O* and then *Northern Exposure*? Perfection. Many other cable networks have since followed A&E s lead on this, which may be why A&E phased out the Daybreaks in favor of true-crime programming. But we still miss watching that dang moose while eating mac and cheese at our desks. See also *LAW & ORDER* FRANCHISE; *MURDER, SHE WROTE*; *NIGHT COURT*; *NORTHERN EXPOSURE*; and TNT S PRIMETIME IN THE DAYTIME.

ABC AFTERSCHOOL SPECIALS Teenagers often behave recklessly, ignorant of the myriad dangers the world can pose to them. Fortunately for their anxious parents, ABC spent the mid- 70s and early 80s fearmongering with its series of *Afterschool Specials*, which aimed to scare the living crap out of its impressionable viewers while also (possibly incidentally) entertaining them along the way. A formative TV experience for members of Generation X, the *Specials* covered such explosive subjects as alcoholism, adoption, dead parents, hitchhiking, and boys who want to dance ballet yet may not actually be pansies. Watching in adulthood can be entertaining both for the caliber of writing and acting on display (low) and because the *Specials* feature some of today s stars in embryonic form, with great performances from Michele Greene, Malcolm-Jamal Warner, and in a rare hat trick Dana Plato, Nancy McKeon, *and* Rob Lowe in *Schoolboy Father*. See also ACTING, WOODEN; THE MORE YOU KNOW ; ONE TO GROW ON ; and TEEN SEX, CONSEQUENCES OF.

ABC's TGIF ABC wasn t always just the home of ostensibly scandalous yet actually quite tame nighttime soaps; the network used to set aside the first two hours of primetime on Friday nights to air family-friendly (read: drippy and saccharine) sitcoms. Alumni of the illustrious programming block include such luminaries as *Family Matters*, *Hope & Faith*, *Boy Meets World*, *Step by Step*, *8 Simple Rules*, and *Full House*, many of which live on in syndication, on ABC Family, and in the most secret crannies of your heart. (Yes, we thought Rider Strong was sort of cute, too.) See also *FULL HOUSE*; RIPA, KELLY; and URKEL.

ABRAMS, J. J. See *ALIAS* and *FELICITY*.

ACTING, WOODEN Although they get their starts on TV, some stars are just not des-

tined to stay there. They have charisma, magnetism, and above all, talent like George Clooney or Will Ferrell. But then there are those whose awkwardness on the small screen virtually guarantees that we will never see them on the big screen or, at least, not more than once. To these terrified heroes of the small screen, we say: Kudos. And lucky for you, there s still the CW. See also CRYING, FAKE/BAD; R H M, ELISABETH; and SCENERY, CHEWERS OF.

ADULT SWIM Cartoons aren t just for kids, you know! They re also for childish, poorly socialized adults! The Cartoon Network recognized this, and in response dubbed its late-night programming block Adult Swim. Airing daily starting at 11 PM, Adult Swim consists of such indispensable original series as *Aqua Teen Hunger Force*, *Space Ghost Coast to Coast*, *Samurai Jack*, and *Harvey Birdman, Attorney at Law*. There are also reruns of other networks animated genius, such as *Futurama* and *Mission Hill*; for some reason, a lot of anime, which . . . meh; and other networks embarrassing crap, like *Family Guy* and *American Dad*. As for the guilt factor well, we re not saying you *have* to be stoned to enjoy the adventures of a superhero who hosts his own bizarre talk show in space, but it doesn t hurt. See also *AQUA TEEN HUNGER FORCE* and STONERS, TV FOR.

AFROS, IMPORTANT TV Man or woman, young or old, we have at least one thing in common: *We all love Afros*. Seriously, they re the greatest. We treasure all the TV Afros God has seen fit to give us. The faint and fuzzy ones grown by blonds like William Katt, Willie Aames, and the dude who played Luke on *General Hospital*. The period-defining  late- 70s and early- 80s ones, like Tim Reid s on *WKRP*, and those of . . . everyone on *Welcome Back, Kotter* except Travolta and the principal. The Afros in flashbacks, like Chef s on *South Park*, George s on *Seinfeld*, and both Carl s and Dr. Hibbert s on *The Simpsons*. Even the fake ones, like Brandy s sewn-in Ronald McDonald number on *America's Next Top Model*, and the rainbow affair that became the John 3:16 Guy s signature. The only exception to our embrace of TV s many Afros? The thin, receding pouf that sat atop Ian Ziering s annoying head on *90210*. Get a haircut, Ian. See also AAMES, WILLIE; *AMERICA'S NEXT TOP MODEL*; GEORGE COSTANZA ; JOHN 3:16 GUY; KATT, WILLIAM; MUSTACHES, GREAT TV; SIDEBURNS, IMPORTANT TV; *SIMPSONS, THE*; SOAP OPERAS, DAYTIME; *SOUTH PARK*; *WELCOME BACK, KOTTER*; *WKRP IN CINCINNATI*; and ZIERING, IAN.

AGING OF MEN ON TV, UNGRACEFUL Evinced by the use of hair plugs or toupees (Ted Danson, Ian Ziering, William Shatner), girdles (Shatner again), or heroic holding in of abdomen (David Hasselhoff), abuse of self-tanner (Hassy, John Schneider), and eye lifts (John Fugelsang, Wink Martindale). These measures fool no one. See also DANSON, TED; HASSELHOFF, DAVID; MARTINDALE, WINK; SHATNER, WILLIAM; and ZIERING, IAN.

AIKEN, CLAY Ruben Studdard won the second season of *American Idol*, but it was the skinny, show-tune-belting redhead who won the hearts of female fans to an insane degree, given that on his best day he looks about thirteen years old (and on his worst he resembles a Fraggle a girl Fraggle) and is allegedly a big ol diva. Clay has had more success  than most *AI* contestants an album, constant touring, late-night TV appearances thanks to legions of women of all ages, whose single-minded support of him is as unwavering as it is creepy. The guy can sing pretty well, but we just don t understand the thinking he s cute part; it s like having a crush on Alfalfa. If Alfalfa lived in Chelsea. See also *AMERICAN IDOL* and UNIVERSALLY REVILED CHARACTERS.

AIRLINE Did you know that if an airline gate attendant thinks you re too drunk or otherwise chemically incapacitated, she can deny your boarding? Perhaps it s never come up in your life because you re not a chronic alcoholic whose financial means are so severely limited that your only option is to fly Southwest or because you never saw *Airline*. A&E s excellent reality show chronicled the utterly thankless job performed by the men and women of Southwest Airlines. The extremely low fares attract a colorful and eccentric clientele of mothers trying to claim their four-year-olds as babes in arms, seniors trying to board with burlap sacks full of stinky dried fish, and, of course, drunks aplenty. You cannot fathom the kind of rudeness, pigheaded ignorance, cheapness, and entitlement the poor Southwest staffers put up with. Occasionally, the show traded too heavily in such heartwarming storylines as a ballerina flying to Vegas to audition as a showgirl or a woman meeting her Internet boyfriend for the first time, but producers knew that drunks were their real bread and butter and rarely disappointed by denying us their drooling, belligerent antics. Good times. See also ALCOHOLISM.

ALCOHOLISM Problem drinking is such a television staple, you might even say TV is itself addicted to alcohol or,

really, to the automatic drama (read: Emmy nominations) alcoholic characters provide. Shows for teens can use it as a Public Service Announcement on the evils of demon rum; more mature dramas can wring a season s worth of subplots out of the hidden bottles, blackout adultery, abusive behavior, drunk-driving arrests, and rehab romances; even sitcoms go to the well of alcohol on occasion, giving the lead actors a chance to show more serious dramatic chops. The scripted version of alcoholism usually involves a rapid descent into the bottle, a single incident of driving drunk that doesn t harm anyone, an intervention presided over by Mackenzie Phillips (Dylan comforting his weeping inner child on *90210* comes to mind), and a complete and successful renunciation of liquor by the end of the ep (or the sweeps period). Meanwhile, over on reality TV, alcoholism is exploited and even encouraged on shows such as *The Real World* and *Blind Date*, which rely on ill-advised binge drinking in order to create good TV by which we mean sloppy hookups, bar fights, slurred shouting matches, and of course the heavily miked barf sessions. (Recall *The Real World* San Diego s Frankie, passed out in her own puke *on their first night in the house*.) We could try to give you a line about how it s messed up that TV manipulates alcoholism for its own selfish ends while raking in bucks from booze ads, but we enjoy watching and being scandalized by TV drunkards both real and fictional. We're not good people. See also DRINKING GAMES; DRUG ABUSE, PORTRAYALS OF; "DYLAN MCKAY"; *INTERVENTION*; PSAS; and *REAL WORLD, THE*.

ALEX: THE LIFE OF A CHILD Next to "maudlin" in the dictionary, you'll probably find a freeze-frame from this ultra-mawkish TV movie about Frank Deford's daughter's death from cystic fibrosis—but all we really remember about it is the heroic amount of fake hacking, borking, and wheezing Gennie James, who played Alex, had to do in almost every scene. That, and Bonnie Bedelia's exhortations that Alex "go to the light!" Craig T. Nelson, playing Deford, gets an honorable mention for spraying glycerin tears around the set like a lawn sprinkler. See also LIFETIME MOVIES; MOVIES, MADE-FOR-TV; and NELSON, CRAIG T.

ALIAS Meet Sydney Bristow: grad student by day, bewigged and ass-kicking secret agent by night. She was originally a double agent for the CIA and a shadow agency known as SD-6, whose members (other than Syd and her father, fellow double agent and bad-ass Jack) thought they *were* in the CIA, but series creator J. J. Abrams closed that chapter in Season 2. After that, there was only one continuing arc—the collection of devices created by Renaissance genius Milo Rambaldi, a fictional inventor half Leonardo da Vinci, half Nostradamus. The series was also notable for ignoring the laws of physics, biology, computer engineering, and plausibility—characters routinely posed as one another, switched sides, and came back from the dead—and for the off-screen romance between Jennifer Garner (who played Sydney) and Michael Vartan (who played Syd's love interest, Vaughn). Until the producers killed Vaughn off in the show's fifth- (and final-) season premiere, they still had to make out, for their job, when we at home all knew she cuckolded him with Ben Affleck! *Awkward!* See also FIGHTING, FEMALE CHARACTERS WHO ARE GOOD AT; GARNER, JENNIFER; "JACK BRISTOW"; and SCIENCE, IGNORANCE OF.

ALIEN SPECIES, DERMATOLOGICAL PROBLEMS OF Aliens as depicted on television, far from seeming alien or removed evolutionarily from humans in any way, inevitably seem to suffer from dermatological conditions like rosacea (Lt. Dax, *Deep Space Nine*); phrenological variations (Cardassian or Romulan forehead ridges); or various ear-related conditions easily corrected by plastic surgery (Spock, Quark, Odo, et al.). The only evident difference between alien species and humanity on television is a deeper commitment by aliens to perfecting prosthetic-latex and body-paint technology. Sci-fi shows use human actors, of course, but the fact that so many aliens resemble pre-Retin-A humans hardly contributes to a sense of realism. See also FUTURE ON TV, SIMILARITY TO PRESENT OF and *STAR TREK* FRANCHISE.

ALLEN, DAVE "GRUBER" Best known for his bravura turn as guidance counselor Mr. Rosso on NBC s cult hit *Freaks and Geeks*, Dave Gruber Allen has guested on such shows as *Mr. Show with Bob and David*, *Gilmore Girls*, *NewsRadio*, and *Frasier*, and he s never cut his hair for a role or altered his stoner intonation. (Instonation?) He always plays himself, and the dude is a big old hippie, period.

ALLEY, KIRSTIE First, there was the guilty pleasure of watching her train-wrecky Pier 1 commercials, where she flitted about like she was having a manic episode, perilously close to a *lot* of scented candles. We weren t supposed to notice that she was less Rebecca Howe than Rebecca House, even though her weird taffeta gowns made her look like she had landed the lead in the Camp Atkins production of *Camelot*. And then came the guilty pleasure of knowing she d be headlining a semifictional sit-com called *Fat Actress*, in which she played herself. But then the actual show

aired, and the pleasure dissolved. And now she s lost a bunch of weight again, so even the schadenfreude is gone. Ah, well at least we can still feel superior to her knowing she s a Scientologist. See also *CHEERS*.

ALTERNATIVE NATION/120 MINUTES Back when MTV still played videos, these two shows showcased the newest in alternative rock, or, in the case of *120 Minutes*, videos by too-weird-for-prime-time bands like Cibo Matto. The shows had various hosts over the years, but most fans from the 90s college kids who relied on *120 Minutes* and *AN* to tell them whether to bother with the new Soup Dragons disc remember Matt Pinfield (the bald dude built like a fire hydrant) and the loathsome queen-bee-ish Kennedy as the head nerds in charge. See also MTV VJs.

"AMANDA WOODWARD" *Melrose Place* s first season had *some* of the ingredients of a successful zeitgeist show (cuties, male and female; inter-apartment intrigue), but something was missing namely a credible villain in the Joan Collins mold. Enter Heather Locklear as Amanda Woodward (Parezi Burns McBride Blake McBride): backstabbing boss, ruthless landlady, manipulative man-stealer, and trashy-two-inch-dark-roots-sporter *par excellence* . . . and savior of the show. Questionable taste in men aside (*Billy?* blech), Amanda rocked as a bad guy because she wasn t just tiny, hot, and mean; she had *balls*, and she turned an earnest, beefcake-studded but dull show into a cultural touchstone. Oh, Mandy. You came and you  gave without taking. Well, actually you took a lot from your dimwitted apartment complexmates and work colleagues, but that s what made your character so bitchin . See also *MELROSE PLACE*.

AMERICAN IDOL We hardly remember a world without *American Idol* in it without the screechily horrendous auditions, without the androgynous Liquid Mercury Man in the credits, without Simon Cowell s acid comments and Paula Abdul s so-dumb-they re-deep koans, without I feel you, dawg, repeated violations of perfectly good Burt Bacharach songs, and the Ambiguous Horror of Ryan Seacrest. *AI* has become an O.J.-trial-esque part of our culture, a spectacle by which we re simultaneously disgusted and riveted as a society. And we do mean as a socie t y to find a person who *didn't* have an opinion on Justin lipping off to Simon, you had to go to Amish country. As of this writing, the show that claims to anoint

America s next great pop star each season doesn t have the greatest track record. Of the winners to date, only Kelly Clarkson has had any kind of real-world success, and we suspect that the recording contracts the winners sign with 19 Entertainment are the legal equivalent of that scene in *Zoolander* where Ben Stiller is capering around in a monkey suit and a fez, hooting and crashing a pair of cymbals. Still, it s grade-A schadenfreude for shower-singers across the land, and Seacrest announcing Ruben as the second-season winner, thereby forcing millions of Clay Aiken fans to eat it, may be reality television s finest hour. See also AIKEN, CLAY; AMERICAN IDOLS, PAST; DUNKLEMAN, BRIAN; REALITY TV, FOX TRAVESTIES OF; REALITY TV, HOSTS OF; SEACREST OUT! ; and SEACREST, RYAN.

AMERICAN IDOLS, PAST Once crowned, an Idol gets a recording contract, but that s no guarantee of future success. Famous original Idol Kelly Clarkson starred in the crapfest *From Justin to Kelly*, but recovered from that to chart a handful of singles. And creepy dinner-theater-diva Muppet Clay Aiken does pretty well for himself, although he didn t win, technically. As for everyone else, well, they ve got the Idol Tour, which exists mostly as a sop to fans whose favorites didn t get picked . . . and to the losers broken dreams. See also AIKEN,

CLAY and *AMERICAN IDOL*.

AMERICA'S MOST WANTED One of FOX s longest-running series, *America's Most Wanted* trades on an immutable law of human psychology: Secretly, everyone s a tattletale. *AMW* provides information on fugitives from justice and invites the viewing public to assist the authorities in apprehending them. Unlike its spiritual twin *Unsolved Mysteries*, *AMW* takes a newsy approach. Instead of having Robert Stack wander moodily toward the camera across a set meant to look like a clearing in the woods, *AMW* gives you an intense John Walsh on a set meant to look like a situation room. As Walsh will be the first to tell you, his career as a once-removed vigilante started because of the tragic death of his son Adam, so it s hard to make fun of him and his oversized, girly leather jacket. And his choice to call his autobiography *Tears of Rage*. (It s *hard*, not impossible.) *AMW* airs after *COPS*, which serves to make us feel guilty for laughing at and/or encouraging the flight of the criminals we watched in the previous hour. It also sobers us up and makes us scrutinize every fugitive photo in case it depicts that shady guy who sometimes works the counter at the deli and of whom we ve always been suspicious. As of this writing, *AMW* s Web site boasts that viewer tips have led to the capture of 867 fugitives, and you can t

argue with results like that. See also *COPS* and *UNSOLVED MYSTERIES*.

AMERICA'S NEXT TOP MODEL Combining the compulsively watchable bad performances of *American Idol* with the arbitrary judgments of an imperious, autocratic host allegedly assisted by a puppet quorum of advisors   la *The Apprentice*, UPN s *America's Next Top Model* plucks a dozen or so girls from obscurity (and, half the time, from the state of Oklahoma) with the goal of being . . . you know. To this end, the girls must submit to communal living; inhumane conditions on their photo shoots; only tangentially modeling-related activities, such as African dancing and Japanese tea ceremonies; bikini waxes; and, in the first four cycles, Janice Dickinson. At the end, one girl usually neither the prettiest, skinniest, tallest, nor least annoying gets the title gig and the opportunity to pose for the cover of *Psychology Today* or costar on *The Surreal Life*. See also *AMERICAN IDOL*; *APPRENTICE, THE*; BANKS, TYRA; DICKINSON, JANICE; and *SURREAL LIFE, THE*.

AMNESIA Extremely rare in real life, amnesia is epidemic among TV characters, particularly those on cop dramas (the writers need a device to drag a relatively simple case out over forty-seven minutes) and soap operas (the writers . . . well, work on soap operas). The most notorious case of amnesia in recent TV history: *24* s Teri Bauer (Leslie Hope) witnesses an explosion that she thinks killed her daughter, collapses, and comes to with amnesia. On the one hand, there s a perfectly good explanation for the writers decision to go that way (read: the actress was contractually bound to appear in every episode, regardless of how far-fetched her subplot), but on the other hand, if we wanted to watch a *telenovela*, we d change the channel to Univision. See also SOAP OPERAS, DAYTIME and *24*.

ANDERSON LEE ANDERSON LEE (ANDERSON), PAMELA   Most of us think of Pamela Anderson Lee Anderson Lee (Anderson) as a famous-for-being-famous celebrity, a tabloid kitten with drag-queen makeup and a goofy column in *Jane*. But before her *folie à "duh"* with M tley Cr eman Tommy Lee became the focus of her fame, Anderson Lee Anderson Lee (Anderson) had a nice little TV career going, first as Lisa the *Tool Time* Girl on *Home Improvement* and then as lifeguard/wank object C. J. on *Baywatch*. And much as we hate to admit it, we have to say in Anderson Lee Anderson Lee (Anderson) s defense that she s not bad. She s not Streep, but she s got decent comic timing, and we never watched *V.I.P.*, but we heard she did okay on that too and she isn t afraid to make fun of her trampy image, either, which makes us

like her. (Psst, Pam less mascara, more guest-star shots like Carmen Electra did on *House*. You can thank us later. Also, pick a last name and stick with it.) See also *BAYWATCH*.

ANGEL   It didn t seem like such a hot idea to spin *Buffy the Vampire Slayer* s resident broody love interest, Angel, off into his own show, because David Boreanaz s range consists of broody and broody with no shirt on. How could he carry a series as the central character? Fortunately, although Boreanaz never really conquered the whole smiling concept, the writing staff smartly made fun of the character s stiffness at every opportunity (the ten-second fantasy sequence in She that shows Angel doing the hustle is an all-time classic), and the supporting characters shouldered much of the acting load. *Angel* had its share of ridiculous plots: Connor, Angel s son, saddled the show with the acting of Vincent Kartheiser, a pouty, floppy-haired chunk of driftwood; the trip to alternate universe Pylea dragged; the Fred/Wesley/Gunn (Amy Acker/Alexis Denisof/J. August Richards) love triangle played like a spec script for *Duet*. But the show almost ran out of gas and then came roaring back a dozen times, sucking viewers back in with creepy ghost stories, touching plot twists, and Angel in Muppet form. Angel did spend kind of a lot of time in indirect sunlight, for a vampire, but *Angel* did a marginally better job adhering to its own internal logic than parent show *Buffy* did. We could have done without the addition of souled Spike in the final season, though. See also BABY, RUINATION OF SHOW BY ADDING; BOREANAZ, DAVID; *BUFFY THE VAMPIRE SLAYER*; CULT SHOW, DEFINITION OF; MAIN CAST MEMBER DEPARTURES, NOTORIOUS; SPIN-OFFS; and WHEDON, JOSS.

ANIMATED VERSIONS OF LIVE-ACTION SHOWS See LIVE-ACTION SHOWS, ANIMATED VERSIONS OF.

APPRENTICE, THE In following up *Survivor*, series creator Mark Burnett had to top a phenomenal, widely imitated success. So he did what the imitators had done: imitated his own formula. Debuting in January 2004, *The Apprentice* was almost exactly like *Survivor* sixteen type-A jerks were divided into teams and assigned a challenge. Each week, the losing team s project manager, plus two stooges of his or her choosing, faced off against host Donald Trump and two of his employees to account for their actions in the (tribal council-ish) boardroom, at the end of which Trump fired someone. The last contestant standing would get not a million dollars, but a job with Trump. (Yay?) The show was sufficiently successful to warrant a short-lived spin-off, with

Martha Stewart in the Trump role. Martha had TV experience and didn t require that every one of her telepromptered speeches be dubbed over later, *Don*, but it got canceled, anyway. See also BURNETT, MARK; REALITY TV, HOSTS OF; SPIN-OFFS; *SURVIVOR*; and TRUMP, DONALD, HAIR OF.

AQUA TEEN HUNGER FORCE The centerpiece of the Cartoon Network s Adult Swim line-up, *Aqua Teen Hunger Force* follows the generally pointless adventures of a collection of anthropomorphized foodstuffs superintelligent leader Frylock, an order of french fries; Master Shake, a simple-minded yet venal milkshake; and Meatwad, a moronic but sweet ball of (one presumes) ground beef who can assume nonwad forms, such as a bridge or a large hot dog who share a seedy house in suburban New Jersey. They are menaced by such enemies as a giant rapping spider in a diaper, invaders from the moon, and their gruff, sweat-panted, hot-rod-loving neighbor Carl. DVD commentary from the show s creators reveals that the trio were originally sold to the network as some manner of crime fighters, but that conceit never really comes up again after the first episode, and the whole incomprehensible mess is funnier if it s the TV equivalent of a non sequitur, anyway. See also ADULT SWIM.

ARRESTED DEVELOPMENT   See BATE-
MANS, JASON AND JUSTINE and CROSS,
DAVID.

ARTHUR, BEA   Bea Arthur starred in
Maude and *The Golden Girls*, and while
she s a formidable bad-ass with the best
frown-into-middle-distance reaction shot

in the business, at
some point her name
became synonymous
with   undesirable
butch older woman.
She has a deep voice,
and   *The   Golden
Girls'* wardrobe didn t do her any favors,
with those knee-length drapey layered
vests and giant *Battlefield Earth* shoulder
pads, but generations of babysitters
learned their comic-timing craft at the
knee of Dorothy Zbornak. So lay off our
girl B. Art, people. See also *GOLDEN
GIRLS, THE.*

"ARTHUR FONZARELLI"   We watched
Happy Days every afternoon in syndication. We were amused by the tough-guy
antics of Arthur The Fonz Fonzarelli
(as Golden Globe—winningly portrayed
by Henry Winkler). We imitated his
catchphrase aaaaaaaay! and may
have even owned T-shirts emblazoned
with it. We accepted the rebellion signi-
fied by his leather jacket, motorcycle, and
apparent lack of humor about himself,
and yet we also accepted that, being so
cool, he would hang out with a bunch of
dorks like Richie and Potsie. What the
hell was wrong with us? See also CATCH-
PHRASES, OVERUSED TV; COOL, TV SIG-
NIFIERS OF; and SITCOMS, UNFUNNINESS
OF SEMINAL.

"AS SEEN ON TV" PRODUCTS   Years of
watching reality TV have caused us to be
dubious about editing, cropped shots, and
too-convenient coincidences that further
the plot. But show us a pan with a lid that
flips over to become a second cooking
surface so we can make pancakes without
a spatula? *That* we totally believe. Turns
out the Perfect Pancake Pan broke after
about a week s worth of grilled cheese
sandwiches, but did that stop us from trying out the Wrap Snap & Go! Curling
System? You *know* it didn t. Then that
sucked, too, and we started keeping our
Visa a little farther away from the TV.
Direct-sell ads are all kind of the same:
The narrator is talking way too fast; the
product advertised seems to serve one
purpose and one purpose only (a machine
that cooks hot dogs? What was so wrong
with a saucepan and some boiling
water?); the voice-over s guess as to how
much we d be willing to pay for the item
is *way* higher than the amount we had in
mind, so that when we learn the much
lower actual price, we re not actually that
impressed; and but wait, there s more!

is a constant refrain. In general, the reason these products are advertised on television, amid quick cuts and muddy lighting, is that if we were confronted with them in stores we d see exactly how crappy they are (which is why the nonsensical As Seen on TV Store is such a depressing place). See also CHIA PET; CLAPPER, THE; INFOMERCIALS; and MRS. FLETCHER.

A-TEAM, THE This was the show universally mentioned by disapproving parents as proof that TV had gotten too violent, despite the fact that a tertiary character could flip a tank thirteen times, crash the bitch into an oil tanker, and *walk away* from the resulting fiery crash with only a cosmetic forehead smudge of soot *every week*. The hell? Anyway, Face, Hannibal, B.A., and Murdock got framed by the military and thrown in jail, and then they escaped and ran around helping people, all while allegedly in hiding. Because the best way to disappear into a crowd is to wear twenty-eight pounds of gold chains and a mohawk. How did the MPs not find these guys in about two seconds? Still, Mr. T rules. See also CANNELL, STEPHEN J.

AUTOPSIES The latest in procedural cop-drama chic, thanks to *CSI* and its spin-offs. Back in the day, viewers only *heard* about the results of autopsies on shows like *Law & Order* and *Quincy*; we never saw a bone saw or heard the sickening Foley squelch of a liver flopping onto a tray scale. But thanks to increased audience demand for blood-and-guts realism, technology that could better simulate a TMI-cam journey through the major blood vessels, and Court TV s need to fill programming hours with gory footage of famous murder victims, the autopsy is now a primetime staple. See also COURT TV; *CSI*; *CSI*, SPIN-OFFS OF; and *LAW & ORDER* FRANCHISE.

AWARD SHOWS, BAD HOSTS OF Once upon a time, you could get any old comic to emcee the Oscars and trust that he d acquit himself well; say what you will about Bob Hope (and God knows we have), but the man knew how to ad-lib. Nowadays, hosts are assigned to award shows based on their own promotable product (how else to explain that both Sarah Michelle Gellar and Kirsten Dunst have hosted the MTV Movie Awards?) as opposed to their ability to roll with the unscripted punches. Even an actual standup comic can t necessarily be trusted to keep things moving in an entertaining way but then again, Whoopi Goldberg is unfunny both on *and* off the Oscars stage. See also GELLAR, SARAH MICHELLE.

AWARD SHOWS, LEGENDARILY BAD SPEECHES ON We re not even talking about the dumb intros scripted for award-show presenters; those would be Award Shows, Ordinarily Bad Speeches on. No, we re talking about the times when an award recipient goes so badly wrong with his or her acceptance speech that it enters the annals of history. Sally Field? We don t like you that much. Marlon Brando? Leave Sacheen Littlefeather out of it. Jack Palance? The one-armed push-up is not so classy. Gwyneth Paltrow and Halle Berry? You just won an Oscar, so it s kind of unseemly for you to be sobbing as though you just watched a Dodge Dakota hit your dog. We would also like to give a little shout-out to perennial lefty event-dampeners Richard Gere (we d rather not meditate on Tibet right now, since *we have an Oscar pool to win*) and the Robbins/Sarandon delegation. Put on a ribbon if you must, but otherwise please save your politics until your next lunch with Graydon Carter.

AWARD SHOWS, OUTFITS IN HALL OF SHAME Celebrities have money, access to professional stylists, and, when award season rolls around, truckloads of gowns pressed upon them for free! by innumerable designers. And yet they can still show up on tele-vised red carpets looking like ass. The best part is that the worst sartorial disasters haunt their

wearers *forever*. We ll prove it with a little word association. C line Dion? Back-wards suit jacket/dyslexic pimp. Jennifer Lopez? Versace cabana robe. Lara Flynn Boyle? Demented ballerina. Bj rk? Swan dress. Cher? Take your pick. And truly, we thank them all for humiliating themselves so magnificently: Polished good taste is so *boring*.

AWARD SHOWS, THIRD-TIER The astounding ratings for the Oscars are probably to blame for the proliferation of all manner of televised award shows. While the big three Oscars, Emmys, and Grammys are awarded by perform-ers peers and carry some legitimate weight, the rest are of dubious worth, and it s come to the point where barely a week can go by without at least one award show airing. It s the very amateur-ishness of their production values that makes them so scrappily endearing. You just *know* no stars are showing up to the Nickelodeon Kids Choice Awards, the People s Choice Awards, the Blockbuster Entertainment Awards, or the *Billboard* Music Awards if they don t already know they won. But any event that could bring us the superhot clinch of Ryan Gosling and Rachel McAdams (at the 2005 MTV Movie Awards, celebrating their award in the category of Best Kiss) can t be all bad.

B

BABY, RUINATION OF SHOW BY ADDING
So your show is heading into its fifth, or sixth, or seventh season, and you ve run through every combination of characters sleeping together or otherwise having conflict among each other. Or your show started with a bunch of cute kids, but now they re getting old and awkward-looking. What can you do to continue generating new story ideas and keep things fresh? Knock someone up! Think of all the material you can mine out of morning sickness, arguments over baby names, mood swings, and the mother s fear of labor! The only problem is that as soon as there s a child in the midst of adults, it tends to pull focus from every single other thing in the world. This is why the addition of a baby, toddler, or child is the Hail Mary pass for an ailing show often attempted, seldom completed. The kid may catalyze a brief ratings bump or resurgence of interest in your show, but if you get sick of writing baby stories, you can t just send the kid back. Exceptions noted: *Sex and the City,* which gave Cynthia Nixon s Miranda a baby that didn t disrupt her life, allowing the show to continue revolving around lunch and whoring; and *Friends*, which found Ross fathering two babies many seasons apart, but without derailing the show s focus on . . . well, coffee and whoring. See also COUSIN OLIVER ; *FRIENDS; SEX AND THE CITY*; and SEXUAL TENSION, RUINATION OF SHOW BY RESOLVING.

BAD SITCOMS STARRING GOOD COMEDIANS Bonnie Hunt is funny; she s actually the only funny thing in *Jerry Maguire*. So how come her sitcoms keep bombing? Jim Gaffigan s standup is so crisp and dry; why did his sitcom turn out so limp and blah? How did Bob Saget, whose standup is pretty good (. . . no, for real), wind up on the diabetically sweet *Full House and* doing voice-overs of squirrel bloopers on *America's Funniest Home Videos*? Ironically, the sitcom genre isn t terribly kind to comedians. Paul Reiser s bits used to have snap, but then . . . *Mad About You*. For every Roseanne or Romano whose show didn t suck, there s a Cho or Negron who didn t translate. At least Denis Leary finally figured it out and switched to an hour-long drama. See also CANNED LAUGHTER, MANIPULATION BY/OF; COMMERCIALS, COMEDIANS IN;

LEARY, DENIS; *MAD ABOUT YOU*; and SAGET, ROBERT LANE.

BAD SITCOM, SURE SIGNS OF The leading indicator of a bad sitcom is, of course, that it just ain t funny but identifying secondary badness characteristics can lead you to that same conclusion without requiring you to watch the entire half hour. These attributes include, but are not limited to: an intrusive laugh track; an overly cute truth-telling child; a show premise involving either a blended family or a secret identity; a plot whose resolution is evident in the first thirty seconds; a sidekick whose entrance is heralded by a full minute of audience reaction; the presence of Dan Cortese, Gerald McRaney, or a *Seinfeld* alum; the sense that the producers chose the title of the show first and worked backward from there. See also CANNED LAUGHTER, MANIPULATION BY/OF; CHILDREN, OVERLY PRECOCIOUS; *SEINFELD*, ALUMNI OF; and THE ZIERING.

BAIO, SCOTT The Skeet Ulrich of his day, Baio played lovable Chachi on *Happy Days*, ran spin-off *Joanie Loves Chachi* into the ground, starred in well-meaning but hilarious *Afterschool Specials*, then made his real cultural mark as the titular *Charles in Charge*. While he s worked since then, on *Diagnosis: Boring* and as a director, these jobs do not require him to appear in his signature cut-to-the-midriff sweatshirt and skin-tight jeans, nor to costar with Ellen Travolta, and we must therefore deem them irrelevant. We hope that after his ex—*Happy Days* costar Ron Howard gave him a recurring guest slot on *Arrested Development* as lawyer Bob Loblaw, Richie found a brand-new Navigator in his driveway as a sign of Chachi s gratitude. See also *ABC AFTERSCHOOL SPECIALS*; *CHARLES IN CHARGE*; and SPIN-OFFS.

BALL, LUCILLE She produced a show in which her husband spanked her. She used Waaaaaaaaaaaaaaaaaah! as a punchline and she used it a lot. She apparently is the mother of physical comedy. She never once, in fifty-three years in show business, managed to apply her lipstick so that it followed her actual lip line. She. Was not. FUNNY. May she rest in peace. See also SITCOMS, UNFUNNINESS OF SEMINAL.

BANKS, TYRA One of the world s few supermodels of color, Tyra Banks has taken her exalted position in society and given back to the world by creating a reality show in which skinny, attractive young women may pursue their goal of being skinny and

attractive on a professional basis (known as *America's Next Top Model*). Banks both hosts and produces *Top Model*, in which capacity she wears a weave; interacts with the contestants alternately by nurturing them Oprah-ishly (which dovetails nicely with her work on daytime s *The Tyra Banks Show*) and screaming at them hysterically; gives her friends onscreen tasks they are not qualified for; and demonstrates how she can make her eyes dead and then, almost immediately, not dead. See also *AMERICA'S NEXT TOP MODEL*; REALITY TV, HOSTS OF; and WINFREY, OPRAH.

BARBARA WALTERS SPECIAL, THE Though she started out as a legitimate journalist, appearing on *Today* back when NBC still broadcast in black and white and becoming the first female anchor of any network s nightly news broadcast, over the course of her career Barbara Walters has gradually evolved into a renowned asker of ludicrous softball questions, delivered with her trademark, much-parodied, Elmer Fudd—esque speech impediment. This dubious skill is showcased in *The Barbara Walters Special*, an occasional ABC offering in which Babs sits down with newsmakers of all stripes, from Jamie Foxx to Monica Lewinsky. Of course, the reason Walters scores all these gets is that she can be counted on not to be too aggressive or pushy. You know

that clich of an inane interview question, If you were a tree, what kind of tree would you be? That was her. See also *INSIDE THE ACTORS STUDIO*; *TODAY*, WINDOW OUTSIDE; and *VIEW, THE*.

BARKER, BOB For years, Bob Barker showed up for work on *The Price Is Right* with a rich head of shoe-polish-colored hair an absurd fiction for a man older than dirt. Barker agreed, and he petitioned *TPIR* producers in the late 80s for permission to let his hair go white. Perhaps he thought the more grandfatherly appearance afforded him by his newly snowy locks would allow him to get grabby with the *TPIR* girls, because one of them charged him with sexual harassment in 1994. We still love him his gallant stifling of giggles at the crappy pricing skills of the show s contestants is admirable indeed but then again, we don t have to work with Ol Handsy. See also *PRICE IS RIGHT, THE*, SUCKY PRICING SKILLS OF CONTESTANTS ON.

BASIC CABLE, MOVIES ENDLESSLY AIRED ON Did you ever notice how much one weekend afternoon s worth of programming on WGN or FX or ABC Family resembles . . . the movies they air every other weekend? We understand that the same parent company owns both *Divine Secrets of the Ya-Ya Sisterhood* and TBS, but does that mean that TBS has to air that particular film an average of seventeen times a month? But that s just one example. Other movies whose rights sold, we suspect, for five dollars (Canadian) or less include *Dying Young*; *Aliens*; *Raising Arizona*; *Planes, Trains & Automobiles*; *Terms of Endearment*; *You've Got Mail*; and *City Slickers*. But we must not forget the movie without which this entry would not exist *The Shawshank Redemption*, which we ve watched on cable more often than we d care to admit. Get busy livin , or get busy dyin . That s goddamn right.

BATEMANS, JASON AND JUSTINE The Bateman siblings could give Kevin Bacon a run for his money in the Six Degrees game; between them, they ve appeared on approximately eighteen squillion sitcoms. Mind you, that s because, since their initial successes *Family Ties* for Justine, *The Hogan Family* for Jason they ve gone on to participate in a succession of made-for-TV movies (Justine) and shows that don t make it past one season (Jason), thus resulting in their never being committed to any one project for very long. The exception that proves the rule was Jason s critically acclaimed, Emmy-winning *Arrested Development*, which FOX is generally believed only to have renewed to expiate some of its psychic guilt over its exploitative reality shows. How close

are the Bateman kids? Between *AD* s first and second seasons, Jason facetiously suggested Justine could play his love interest, and then, in the third, she kind of did. See also FAMILY TIES; HOGANS, THE/HOGAN FAMILY, THE; and SHOW KILLERS.

BATTLE OF THE NETWORK STARS Exactly what it sounds like. Most people remember the show basically Game Night with Famous People as a relic of the Quaaludes-and-variety-show era, but it persisted well into the 80s and featured face-offs between such luminaries as Farrah Fawcett-Majors and Adrienne Barbeau in rounds of tug-of-war, Simon Says, relay races, and so on. What we wouldn t have given to see a Ken Olin/Philip Michael Thomas three-legged race entry! The networks exhume *Battle of the Network Stars* occasionally to fulfill the nation s dietary cheese requirements; Bravo recently revived it as *Battle of the Network Reality Stars*. See also BRAVO; *MIAMI VICE*; and *THIRTYSOMETHING*.

BAXTER (-BIRNEY), MEREDITH For years, she came into our living rooms as Keaton family matriarch Elyse on *Family Ties* . . . and feigned an attraction to Michael Gross, which frankly just ain t right. We also have Baxter to thank for helping to keep the Lifetime woman-in-peril movie pipeline full; her post-*Family Ties* C.V. consists almost exclusively of titles like *A Mother's Justice* and *She Knows Too Much*. Merry, love you, mean it, but: Taking a role as true-crime touchstone Betty Broderick is fine, once. Not twice. And what s with the guest shots on *7th Heaven*? Get a new agent, lady. At least she divorced human troll doll David Birney. See also *FAMILY TIES*; LIFETIME MOVIES; and PARENTS WHO ARE TOTALLY INTO EACH OTHER TO A CREEPY DEGREE.

BAYWATCH Everyone watched this jigglefest masquerading as a lifeguarding drama (heh); *nobody* admitted it. *Baywatch* spawned a good half-dozen spin-offs, launched the inexplicable careers of no-talent large-breast delivery systems like Carmen Electra and Pamela Anderson, and ushered millions of teenage boys into manhood. Lifeguard den father David Hasselhoff s Jet Ski didn t talk, more s the pity, but Hassy sang the end-credits theme. Come for the bouncing boobs; stay for the hysterical and every-one learned a valuable lesson subplots, like the one in which a young man comes to terms with his father s dwarfism. No, we re not joking. Best episode ever. Of anything. See also ANDERSON LEE ANDERSON LEE (ANDERSON), PAMELA and HASSELHOFF, DAVID.

BEAUTY AND THE BEAST *Beauty and the Beast* aired for two and a half seasons on CBS and followed assistant DA Catherine Chandler (Linda Hamilton) and her rela-tionship with Vincent (Ron Perlman), a feline-faced empath who lived in elabo-rately homey tunnels under New York along with a bunch of other social misfits who dressed like life below the earth s crust was a nonstop Ren Faire. If you came into the series late, you weren t sure if Vincent was some kind of mythic half-man, half-puma or just a dude with unfor-tunate facial birth defects (we *think* it was the latter). The whole thing was supposed to be extremely *romantic* because she was gorgeous and he had to hide himself away from judgmental human eyes because he s different, but in actuality it was just silly.

BEHIND THE MUSIC This addictive behind-the-scenes look at the meteoric rises and humiliating falls of various musical acts put VH1 back on the map after years of adult-contem-porary insignifi-cance. Despite a  predictable format early years, commer-cial, hitting the jackpot, commercial, descent into [insert substance or psy-chosis here], commercial, where are they now (or, as appropriate, death), credits a *Behind the Music* marathon is like Pringles: Once you pop, you can t stop. The much-imitated gossipy voice-over; the embarrassing stills of cadaverous rock-star addicts, clad in unfortunate fashions of the past; balding, crying Leif Garrett apologizing to the dude he put in a wheelchair for life . . . even bands you d never heard of became interesting under the *Behind the Music* lens. The show did start to scrape the bottom of the barrel at the end there (was Garbage really that scandalous?), but the Milli Vanilli episode never gets old. See also COURT TV and *E! TRUE HOLLYWOOD STORY*.

BELT, WHY MEN ON TV WEAR A TUCKED-IN SHIRT WITHOUT A Steve Sanders. Jerry Seinfeld. Peter DeLuise. These are just a few of the men on TV in the 80s and 90s who tucked their shirts into their jeans or pants but failed to wear belts, which caused unattractive pooching in some cases and just plain looked weird in others. We don t know the reason behind it; we just know it bugs. Wear a belt, dudes. See also *BEVERLY HILLS 90210*; FASHION, HILARIOUS ATTEMPTS OF TV GUYS IN THE 90S AT; *SEINFELD*; and *21 JUMP STREET*.

BENSON Mr. Robert Guillaume played Benson in both the eponymous sitcom and its progenitor, *Soap*. *Benson* a Witt/Thomas production and therefore a forebear of *The Golden Girls* followed Benson DuBois from butlering for Jessica Tate to the mansion of Governor Eugene Gatling (James Noble) in an unnamed U.S. state. The governor, of course, is a dimwit, which gives Benson plenty of opportunities to deploy his signature expression of silent disapproval, impatience, and loathing. Though it wasn t especially groundbreaking in its format or themes, it was notable for three things: featuring a nonwhite person holding a political office (Benson eventually gets elected lieutenant governor); featuring an extremely young Jerry Seinfeld (1980—81); and smoldering interracial sexual tension between Benson and Inga Swenson s housekeeper Gretchen. Rrrowr. See also *GOLDEN GIRLS, THE*; *SOAP*; and SPIN-OFFS.

BEN STILLER SHOW, THE Like so many shows ahead of their time, sparkling with wit and dicked around by FOX, *The Ben Stiller Show* burned brightly and then got snuffed. Basically a straight-up sketch show in the tradition of *Monty Python's Flying Circus* and *The Kids in the Hall*, *Stiller* starred Andy Dick, Janeane Garofalo, Bob Odenkirk, and the titular Ben Stiller before he got his front teeth capped and spent seven hours a day blasting his abs. It was also hilarious, satirizing Yakov Smirnoff, gangsta rap, and grunge music and, perhaps too often, FOX s other shows (as in *Melrose Heights 90210-2402* and *Skank*, a sitcom parody starring a profane sock puppet that reminded us of the profane cartoons on *Married . . . With Children*). The tragedy is not only that such a good show only lasted thirteen episodes, but that virtually nothing else any of the cast members ever did afterward was half as good. Okay, *Mr. Show*. And *Zoolander*. But that s it. Go buy the DVDs. See also FOX, SITCOMS PREMATURELY CANCELED BY.

BERNARD, CRYSTAL Oh, hypocrisy. Crystal Bernard star of the amazingly long-lived NBC sitcom *Wings* w a s a gospel singer before she was an actor and developed a reputation as a Christian. One of her pop albums is actually titled *Don't Touch Me There*. And yet the Internet tells a different story the story of *Chameleons*, a failed TV pilot in which Bernard wears a showgirl costume that gets torn off, revealing (for a few blurry frames) her naked boobs. Is that any way to celebrate the Lord? See also *WINGS*.

BERNSEN, CORBIN As of this writing, Mr. Corbin Bernsen has close to one hundred and fifty credits listed on his IMDb profile. Of those, he racked up more than a hundred (and counting) *after L.A. Law*. And yet, did you see any of them? *Inhumanoid*? *Kounterfeit*? *Bloodhounds* or *Bloodhounds II* both in 1996? You sure didn t. We can t say he only took a role on *General Hospital* in 2004 out of desperation, since he s worked enough that he really shouldn t be bored. What in the world *can* we criticize him for? Oh! How about his appearance on *both* seasons of *Celebrity Mole*? Bernsen did come on the show having seen the show s past (non-celebrity) seasons; that was evident from the way he obsessively monitored every setting he was ever in for clues. However, he apparently didn t watch the show closely enough to realize that the clues were primarily for the viewers at home, and that he should have saved his scrutiny for his fellow contestants in order to figure out *which one of them was the mole*, which is kind of *the purpose of the game*. Instead, he alienated everyone around him with the hypercompetitive, antisocial asshatery that forced fellow contestant Kathy Griffin to dub him superveiny hockey dad a name that s stuck to him so tenaciously that we ll still think of him that way even after some low-budget production casts him to play Gandhi or something. (We just have a feeling that s coming eventually; maybe that s why he s spent the past twenty years working so hard on his tan.) See also AGING OF MEN ON TV, UNGRACEFUL; GAME SHOWS, CELEBRITY EDITIONS OF; *L.A. LAW*; *MOLE, THE*; and SOAP OPERAS, DAYTIME.

BEST LITTLE GIRL IN THE WORLD, THE The very first of the eating-disorder TV movies and the North Star in the constellation of these extended PSAs, *Little Girl* starred Jennifer Jason Leigh as the titular anorexic (she starved herself down to ninety pounds for the role) and Charles Durning and Eva Marie Saint as her parents. If you ve never seen it, let s just say that Leigh s tendency to inhabit her roles to the fullest and twitchiest extent is already evident here. It s like the scene in *Georgia* where they won t let her on the plane, but with better hair. And laxatives. See also EATING DISORDERS, PORTRAYALS OF; MOVIES, MADE-FOR-TV; and PSAs.

BEVERLY HILLS 90210 The teen drama that began as an earnest look at the issues facing youngsters of the 90s and ended its run as a full-fledged soap opera, *90210* brought us, among many other things, sideburns, love triangles, PSAs on gun control and breast exams, cults, corrupt student government, the Brenda Stomp, the Summer of Deception, a cautionary tale from the front lines of both nepotism and botched boob jobs in the person of Tori Spelling, white-boy hip-hop, Reek, Donna Martin graduates!, *l'affaire Ohhhhhndrea*, and TV s first female lead with a cat butt for a mouth. *90210* stank up the joint after fabulous villainess Valerie (Tiffani Thiessen) left, Dylan (Luke Perry) returned, and Peach Pit mensch Nat (Joe Tata) started getting storylines, but the reruns are still good for a giggle. The gold standard for so-bad-it s-good TV. See also BRANDON WALSH ; BRENDA WALSH ; CULT SHOW, DEFINITION OF; DEAD SCOTT ; DYLAN MCKAY ; SIDEBURNS, IMPORTANT TV; SPELLING, AARON; SPELLING, TORI; THE ZIERING ; and ZIERING, IAN.

BEWITCHED A bait-and-switch sitcom, in that its opening credits are animated, so when you re a kid you think the show s a cartoon, and then it s just a run-of-the-mill old sitcom about a sassy housewife with magical powers and a dull husband who just wants her to be like every other damn housewife on the block. We re not saying that the premise of *Bewitched* expresses the aims of the patriarchy in allegorical form . . . or are we? See also *I DREAM OF JEANNIE.*

BIEL, JESSICA Biel s sole talent is looking pretty, so it s no surprise that *Gear* magazine wanted to avail itself of that talent by posing her in a gas-station bathroom, wearing heels, panties that gave her a wedgie, and a fuck you, Hampton smirk. And Biel s primary talent vehicle back then, *7th Heaven*, had started to suck ass, so it s also no surprise that Biel probably did the provocative spread (hee, we said spread) on purpose, to try to get fired. Well, it worked; *7th Heaven* creator Brenda Hampton assassinated Biel s character Mary in the most bizarre way possible and then punted her off the show entirely. Officially, Biel left the show, but really, she d deliberately provoked Hampton into firing her so she d have more time to devote to such fine films as . . . *Summer Catch*? Yeeeeeah. If she really did flash her dupa to piss off Hampton, that s rad, but still . . . *Summer Catch*. See also HAMPTON, BRENDA; MAIN CAST MEMBER DEPARTURES, NOTORIOUS; MOVIES-TO-TV/TV-TO-MOVIES CAREER PIPELINE/ARC; and *7TH HEAVEN*.

BIG BROTHER In 2000, *Big Brother* had already been a huge hit in every country with its own version of the show. Then it came to America and . . . not so much. The show, in its original iteration, is mind-numbingly simple: People are trapped in a house surrounded by cameras; all they can do is play cards, smoke, talk, and get on each other s nerves. Every week, two houseguests get nominated for eviction, and the viewers vote. But then America voted out the least likable people early, leaving only the nicest (and dullest), so that the eventual winner was a one-legged cancer survivor. Good for him, but, yawn. Then CBS figured out that though America may not want to give bad people financial rewards, they would rather watch them than people who are boring and well-adjusted. Out went the aimless sitting; now the houseguests had inane challenges. Starting in the second season, the contestants voted each other out. The most America could hope to influence was which kitchen appliance to give them. The show is now both baroquely complex and insultingly dumb. With nothing else to focus on, the contestants are free to plot against one another *all* the *time*. *BB* host Julie Chen is among the worst emcees in reality TV, with her stunning inability to cope with the challenges of live television, but now that she s married to CBS president Les Moonves, the only way she s leaving the show is toes up. Really, it s one of the dumbest reality shows on TV. Avoid watching even a little. It *will* suck you in. See also REALITY TV, HOSTS OF.

BIRTH CONTROL You may not think that something as pedestrian as contraception could be the high-larious basis for a sitcom episode. And that s exactly why you re not making your living as a sitcom writer, sucker! In fact, birth control turns up frequently in comic TV settings, as when Carlos switched out Gabrielle s pills with placebos on *Desperate Housewives*; when Rachel and Monica fought over the last condom (they shared a common supply? That s a little creepy) on *Friends*; and when Elaine stockpiled the Today sponge when it went off the market and forced her current boyfriend to prove himself spongeworthy before she d sleep with him on *Seinfeld*. See also *DESPERATE*

HOUSEWIVES; *FRIENDS*; and *SEINFELD*.

BLACKADDER   The Britcom is not for everyone, it s true the eleventeen seasons of *Are You Being Served?* notwithstanding and you may have sworn off Rowan Atkinson post-*Johnny English* and *Bean*, which we can understand, but never mind all that: *Blackadder* is brilliant. The show s four seasons followed Atkinson s Edmund through four periods in British history. In the first, Edmund is a prince in the medieval era who takes The Black Adder as his nickname. Then Edmund is Lord Blackadder under Elizabeth I, then a butler to Prince George, then a captain in the British army in World War I. Each season is peppered with period-appropriate touches witch hunts, Catholic-bashing, crooked elections, vaudeville. Really, the only theme common to all four seasons is that Edmund is forever hatching cunning plans in which he is nearly always thwarted. But to describe the show s nimble, obsessively quotable wordplay, history-nerd-friendly storylines, and fantastic cast particularly Hugh House Laurie as dim Prince George and then a barmy upper-class soldier is to drain it of its sparkle. Get your hands on the DVDs and prepare to scream bravo! at an annoyingly loud volume. See also LAURIE, HUGH.

"THE BLACK FAMILY"   The eighth season of *The Amazing Race* featured, among others, a family with the surname Black. The problem? The Blacks were African-American, so any time we referred to them, it sounded like we couldn t bother with their last name and were referring to them by their race instead . . . which was awkward enough, and then they didn t race very well and got eliminated first, but could we say, The Black family kind of sucked ? Not really, because: uncomfortable. See also KEOGHAN, PHIL.

BLACK, MICHAEL IAN   You either love Michael Ian Black, or you think he s a smug buffoon. We happen to love him. The studiously deadpan breakout star of VH1 s *I Love the [Decade]* series, Black is an alumnus of the comedy troupe The State who, through his connections to the various and sundry ex-Staters (of whom there are, like, seventy-three; they re the Polyphonic Spree of comedy), has also cracked up our shit on *Viva Variety*, *Reno 911!*, *Stella*, and in the brilliant and overlooked feature film *Wet Hot American Summer* (Black s the one with the slightly asymmetrical face, the coat-hanger grin, and, on *Reno*, the registered-sex-offender conviction on his rap sheet). And as if all of that wasn t enough to cement his place in pop-culture history, Black also played the hilariously demented Phil Stubbs on *Ed* (every crackpot promotion at Stuckey Bowl? His idea) and totally cleaned

Norm Macdonald s clock on *Celebrity Poker Showdown* in one of the awesomest comebacks ever. *And*, every single syllable he utters cracks us up on *Best Week Ever*. In fact, he can even make us laugh without saying anything. He s a national treasure. And he s hot! See also CELEBRITY POKER SHOWDOWN; ED; and VIVA VARIETY.

BLOSSOM A kind of spiritual heir to *Punky Brewster* (aaaaaand the sentence we never thought we d write award is officially claimed), *Blossom* chronicled the intermittently compelling adventures of Blossom Russo (Mayim Bialik), a teen whose love for wacky chapeaux and skirts made out of ties showed the world that you can be a confident, sassy young woman even if you happen to have a very, very large nose. The show s cast was filled out by *Soap* refugee Ted Wass as single father Nick; Michael Stoyanov as recovering drug-addict brother Anthony; Jenna von O as best friend and fellow hat enthusiast Six; and, of course, Danza-duplicate Joey Lawrence as borderline retarded hunk brother Joey. (Whoa!) Because *Blossom* couldn t compete with other sitcoms on a laugh-per-minute basis, producers decided it should distinguish itself by turning every episode into a forum for addressing some issue, thus rendering such episodes Very Special. And, okay, it was very special when Blossom did it with her boyfriend, or when Nick got married again, but we weren t so impressed by Joey s brave battle against dandruff. (Actually, we made that one up.) See also CATCHPHRASES, OVERUSED TV; PUNKY BREWSTER; SOAP; and VERY SPECIAL EPISODES.

BOCHCO, STEVEN The prolific TV series writer and creator Steven Bochco is responsible for some of TV s most critically acclaimed shows like *NYPD Blue* and *Doogie Howser, M.D.* as well as many of its dumbest, from *Cop Rock* to *Capitol Critters* to *Blind Justice*, the TV series about a blind cop. Who still carries a gun. Seriously. Bochco really came into his own as a TV producer with *L.A. Law*, in which capacity he hired a young lawyer with TV-writing aspirations by the name of David E. Kelley (and for which we assume Bochco will be paying quite the karmic debt in his next life). Though we long since stopped watching his series, we have fond memories of a *Politically Incorrect* in which he irritated Chevy Chase into losing his shit, which is awesome. See also CHASE, CHEVY; DOOGIE HOWSER, M.D.; KELLEY, DAVID E.; and L.A. LAW.

BOLD AND THE BEAUTIFUL, THE First of all, let s talk about the show s title, which is . . . well, *inaccurate* is putting it kindly, because nobody on the show is all that beautiful, to our minds. Okay, Jack Wagner is fairly beautiful, or at least he used to be, and Hunter Tylo has pretty hair, usually, but the lady who plays Brooke (Katherine Kelly Lang) wears *waaaaay* too much orange, and she s always pulling her lower lip down when she talks; Stephanie Forrester (Alex Hoover) is awesome, especially during the storyline where she goes bonkers (which one? Ex*act*ly), but she s a battleship with hair, basically; and Sally Spectra (Darlene Conley) . . . no. Just, no. And as for the *bold* part, well, we re all for punchy alliteration, but the show, unlike most daytime sudsers, is only half an hour. A serial on which it takes a year s worth of shows to get through two weeks of plot is not *bold*; it s narcotic. But oh, what a high. *Bold* is an incredibly dumb show, even for a soap, but the mustache-twirly scenery-chewing is the best in daytime. You should check it out, not least because Ridge (Ronn Moss) might put on a Speedo again. See also SCENERY, CHEW-ERS OF; SOAP OPERAS, DAYTIME; and WAGNER, JACK.

BONEHAM, RUPERT Rupert who first came to America s attention as a contestant on *Survivor* s Pearl Islands season is one of the most delusional reality-TV participants ever. (Do take a moment to let the magnitude of that statement sink in.) Recall Rupert s declaration, in the first episode of Pearl Islands, that he was a pirate, which is why he stole the opposing team s shoes to barter them for sup-

plies; his announcement that he wanted other players to get out of my adventure ; his response, to the temporary loss of a fishing spear he repeatedly called mine, of stomping into the ocean and

roaring his rage into the sky. The dude just . . . wasn t right. But he was colorful, which is probably how he managed to be the only Pearl Islands alumnus in the infamous All-Star season a few months later. It s also probably why the citizens of the United States awarded him with a million-dollar prize when CBS bullshittily decided to contradict the entire point of *Survivor* (that you win it by ingratiating yourself to your fellow players) by making another million dollars available to one contestant, awarded *American Idol*-style to the player the viewers liked best. Apparently, America would prefer that reality-show winnings go to those who play without strategy and hold grudges like seven-year-olds shooting marbles. See also *SURVIVOR* and UNI-VERSALLY REVILED CHARACTERS.

BOREANAZ, DAVID After playing Buffy Summers s soulmate Angel on *Buffy*, the aptly named *Bore*anaz followed the character to the spin-off, *Angel*. Boreanaz, who has a phobic fear of chickens, is often criticized for what might charitably be called an underplayed acting style and a hair-gel regime reminiscent of Reagan s second term, as well as for growing steadily fatter and more overtanned over the course of *Angel* s run, until he resembled a glazed ham in a black trench coat. He was cute once upon a time, but that time is behind us. See also ACTING, WOODEN; *ANGEL*; *BUFFY THE VAMPIRE SLAYER*; SPIN-OFFS; and STUNT DOUBLES, SADLY OBVIOUS.

BOSOM BUDDIES Looking for proof that Tom Hanks needs to maybe quit it with all the portentous Greatest Generation crap? Look no further than the sitcom that launched his career.

Hanks starred in a lot of bad film comedies back in the day, but this is the nadir. The short form: Kip (Hanks) and Henry (the bitty Peter Scolari) can t find an affordable apartment in New York City (credible), so they dress up as women in order to live in a women s residence hotel (not credible). The stupid part? The gambit works. They pass as women, despite evidently shaving with butter knives. The stupider part: The producers cast the indefensibly annoying Wendie Jo Sperber (may she rest in peace) and actually expected people to watch the show. It s utterly unfunny, and Hanks is chomping so much scenery, his wig keeps falling off. Scolari managed to avoid the blacklist, winding up on *Newhart*, and we all know what happened to Hanks. Run, Forrest! See also BAD SITCOMS, SURE SIGNS OF and DRAG, MEN IN/CROSS-DRESSING.

"BOSTON ROB" See MARIANO, ROB.

BOY IN THE PLASTIC BUBBLE, THE The notorious TV movie starring John Barbarino Travolta as Tod Lubitch, a boy whose immune system is so compromised, bacteria ate the second d in his name. Okay, not really, but he has to live in a plastic germ-proof bubble, which leads to the usual triumph-over-adversity, so-brave-yet-so-lonely, blah blah blah fishcakes plotting you d expect. At one point, Tod s girlfriend jumps over the bubble on horseback, which is supposed to make him feel like a normal kid but is actually incredibly dumb, and if we were Tod s mom we d have ripped the girlfriend a new one for pulling that shit on our kid. See also MOVIES, MADE-FOR-TV and *WELCOME BACK, KOTTER*.

BRADY BUNCH, THE It s treacly. It s predictable. The kids bathroom doesn t have a toilet. Even Barry Williams, who played Greg, admits that its badness bordered on the surreal at times. But after several movie spin-offs, ill-conceived forays into variety-hour programming and *thir-*

tysomething-esque drama, countless reunion shows, cartoons, speaking tours, where-are-they-now features in the entertainment press, and more than thirty years of reruns, it s probably the TV show most firmly rooted in the collective cultural unconscious.

The same American schoolchildren who can t find Washington, D.C., on a map have known what Marcia, Marcia, Marcia! means since before they could walk. See also BAD SITCOMS, SURE SIGNS OF; *BRADY BUNCH,* MUSICAL STYLINGS OF; COUSIN OLIVER ; LIVE-ACTION SHOWS, ANIMATED VERSIONS OF; REED, ROBERT; REUNION MOVIES; and SCHWARTZ, SHERWOOD.

BRADY BUNCH, THE, MUSICAL STYLINGS OF Never mind the benighted variety hour; the Brady kids could sing. Technically. Just, you know, not very well. Time to Change, starring Peter s breaking adolescent voice, pointed up that fact, but It s a Sunshine Day, which is supposed to be good . . . isn t. After the first season, the whole cast also sang the theme song, which is probably one of the most parodied ditties in history. See also *BRADY BUNCH, THE* and JOHNNY BRAVO.

"BRANDON WALSH" Supposedly the hero of *Beverly Hills 90210* its moral center. Actually an increasingly irritating, reactionary, sweaty, patronizing, chubby jackass who used too much butch wax. As the seasons came and went, Brandon s lecturing of other characters became more and more obnoxious and judgmental, his sexism less and less subtle. Brandon also walked like he had a porn career in his skin-tight Levi s. Jason Priestley s bitchface-y portrayal of Brandon didn t help, but fortunately, Priestley had the sense to take himself off the show before the last smoldering embers of relevance were stamped out by Vanessa Marcil. *Un*fortunately, he had already created a prototype for smug, not-that-cute teen-drama heroes bursting with self-regard and bad choices in pants. See also *BEVERLY HILLS 90210*; BRENDA WALSH ; and DAWSON LEERY.

BRAVO Bravo began its life as an artsy channel, the spot on the dial for high-fiber cultural programming like *Three Tenors* reruns and documentaries about Stradivarius violins. *Inside the Actors Studio*, often parodied, was a modest success, but eventually Bravo executives realized, Hey, the world already *has* a PBS, and started churning out reality shows. The network truly arrived in 2003 with *Queer Eye for the Straight Guy*, followed that up with the *[X] Moms & Dads* franchise, and never looked back. *Inside the Actors Studio* is well past retirement age Cameron Diaz? and Bravo should probably rename itself something more descriptive, like Schadenfreude, but it s now a basic-cable destination of note. See also *CELEBRITY POKER SHOWDOWN*; MARATHONS; *PROJECT RUNWAY*; *QUEER EYE FOR THE STRAIGHT GUY*; and *WEST WING, THE*.

"BRENDA CHENOWITH" A flibbertigibbet, a sex addict, a would-be therapist: How do you solve a problem like Brenda? L.A. native Brenda (Rachel Griffiths) daughter of two therapists and sister to Billy (Jeremy Sisto), a seriously effed-up guy with a severe incestuous crush on her arrives in *Six Feet Under* s pilot with authority, taking her seatmate on a plane (Peter Krause s Nate) into an airport broom closet and nailing him. She then embarks upon a fraught relationship with him that wends its way, over five seasons, through infidelity, attempted home tattoo removal, Nate s marriage to someone else, Nate s marriage to Brenda, a new career in the mental-health field, and, continuously, death. Volatile, self-involved, morose, a certified superfreak, but still somehow compelling, Brenda is the character who most divided fans of HBO s award-winning drama. See also RUTH FISHER.

"BRENDA WALSH" The distaff Walsh twin, and by far the more enjoyable to watch; most viewers date the show s decline to Shannen Doherty s departure, which was explained by the character going to England to study acting. (No comment.) Stubborn, impulsive, somewhat dense in matters of the heart, Brenda endeared herself to a nation with her crooked eyes and her willingness to pitch a fit (if necessary, while wearing a leather vest). On a show that, like so many teen shows, seemed to encourage female spinelessness and damsel-in-distressism, Brenda s brash approach was a breath of fresh air. We kind of couldn t believe she got back together with Dylan, though, even off-screen. That guy bugged. See also *BEVERLY HILLS 90210*; BRANDON WALSH ; DOHERTY, SHANNEN; and DYLAN MCKAY.

BRIDEZILLAS The kind of bride most of us dread way too caught up in the pretty-pretty-princess it s my day mythos of weddings, a screaming fascist about everything from flowers to the registry . . . in other words, a bridezilla is catnip to the WE channel, which showcases these hellcats as they prepare to walk down the aisle. The show s only reason for existing is to make the audience feel superior in matters of taste and manners, but boy, does it fulfill that promise, inevitably prompting a record number of oh my god SHUT UP s from the couch.

See also WEDDINGS, FAMOUS TV.

BRODY, ADAM Before Adam Brody became the It Boy of 2003 with his role as Seth Cohen on *The O.C.*, he kept busy playing pretty much that exact role on other shows. He was  Coop, the irresponsible, motormouthed friend to Shane West s Eli, on *Once & Again*. He was Justin, a comic-book geek crushing on Allison Mack s Chloe on *Smallville*. He was Dave, a sensitive musician and rock snob on *Gilmore Girls*. And then came Seth, the sensitive, motormouthed, comic-book geek cum rock snob on *The O.C.* If you think we re implying that Brody s parts seem to have an odd way of resembling both each other and his offscreen persona, you are totally right. We were charmed by both Seth and Brody when *The O.C.* hit, but then the show turned into this pop-culture phenomenon and much of its success was laid at Brody s feet. Brody started believing his own hype just as Seth started getting everything he d spent his life pining for, and both simultaneously became a lot less appealing. Adam Brody is just one vanity rock band away from being Jared Leto, and he should do some serious thinking about that and get his mind right, and fast. See also *GILMORE GIRLS* and *O.C., THE*.

BROOKS, JAMES L. Like Garry Marshall, but less mawkish, James L. Brooks has created some of TV s most beloved and enduring sitcoms *Taxi*, *The Mary Tyler Moore Show* and its spin-offs, and *The Simpsons* (not to mention movies like *Terms of Endearment* and *Broadcast News*). Unfortunately, he s also responsible for *The Tracey Ullman Show*, *As Good as It Gets,* and *Spanglish*. Eh, nobody s perfect. See also MARSHALL, GARRY; *SIMPSONS, THE*; and *TAXI*.

BUFFY THE VAMPIRE SLAYER That rarity among both teen shows and WB (and, later, UPN) fare: a well-written, often touching drama about a ditzy cheerleader type with vampire-killing superpowers, whose metaphorical premise physical demons standing for inner ones actually worked. The show provided an excellent  role model for young girls (Buffy [Sarah Michelle Gellar] kicked ass every week, literally), a long-running schmoopy love story, beloved supporting characters, and meditations on the nature of high school that never got too sticky. Once the characters contrivedly all went off to college together, the cracks began to show, but *Buffy* remained don t call me during appointment viewing for all of its seven seasons.

See also *ANGEL*; COLLEGE, UNREALISTIC PORTRAYALS OF; CULT SHOW, DEFINITION OF; FIGHTING, FEMALE CHARACTERS WHO ARE GOOD AT; GELLAR, SARAH MICHELLE; HIGH SCHOOL, UNREALISTIC PORTRAYALS OF; and WHEDON, JOSS.

"BULL" The bailiff Richard Moll portrayed on the long-running sitcom *Night Court*, Nostradamus Bull Shannon was sweet, dim, and *tall*. According to IMDb, the 6'7^{1}2" Moll was hired for the role both because he was funny and because he had to be taller than his tall costars John Larroquette and Harry Anderson. Bull shaved his head bald before everyone else was doing it. Bull could have put us in his pocket and carried us around all day. Bull was cool. See also *NIGHT COURT.*

BULLOCK, JM J. Best known for his role as Monroe Ficus, the extremely awkward boarder always running afoul of Ted Knight s crabby cartoonist on *Too Close for Comfort*, Jm J. Bullock is part of TV s long, not especially proud history of performers who are clearly gay playing characters who are clearly *written* gay but can t say they are. For instance, the big sexual secret Monroe was supposed to have been ashamed to admit was that he was a virgin. *The show was set in San Francisco!* Anyway, since Monroe, Bullock has gone on to appear in many gay-themed projects (such as the animated series *Queer Duck*

and the feature film *Kissing Jessica Stein*), and to add an i to his given name. We applaud both decisions. See also HOMOSEXUALITY, CODED.

BUNIM/MURRAY The production company behind seminal programming like *The Real World*, *Road Rules*, *Love Cruise*, and *Starting Over*. The late Mary-Ellis Bunim came out of soaps, teamed up with Jonathan Murray, and changed the face of MTV (and TV programming in general) forever when the first season of *The Real World* premiered in 1992. See also *REAL WORLD, THE*; *REAL WORLD/ROAD RULES CHALLENGE, THE*; and *STARTING OVER.*

BUNNELL, SHERIFF JOHN *World's Wildest Police Videos* is plenty of brainless, crashy fun on its own, but the enthusiastic narrative stylings of its host, Sheriff John Bunnell, make it irresistible. (What he was sheriff of? Never explained. Our guess: Shatnerville.) Bunnell s contempt for criminals both petty and serial, and his smugness at their stupidity and inevitable capture, imbues every overacted syllable. Frequently shown stalking toward a squad car to introduce a new clip, Bunnell also enjoys biting off punny summary judgments. For example, if a getaway car wrecks in a wooded area, Bunnell s disdainful pronouncement is something along the lines of, *This* crook learned the *hard* way . . .

by breaking the *law* . . . he s . . . barking up *the wrong tree*. The idea that Bunnell may in fact narrate his entire life in this fashion whether opening jars, having sex, or admiring a sunset is awesome. Call us, Bunny! See also REALITY TV, HOSTS OF and SHATNER, WILLIAM.

BURNETT, MARK If you throw out the phrase reality TV producer in a word-association game, what s the most likely response? Mark Burnett, the evil genius behind *Survivor*, *The Apprentice*, and *The Restaurant*. He started out with the Emmy-nominated *Eco-Challenge*, but it wasn t until voted off the island entered the American lexicon that Burnett himself became a household name, and for several years, it seemed like we wanted to see whatever he thought to put on TV, no matter how outlandish the premise. Umpteen strangers sit around on an island, backstabbing each other and eating bugs while prodded by a slick host (*Survivor*)? Brilliant. A Vespa-riding, pretty-boy celebrity chef opens his own restaurant and annoys his investors, his staff, and America (*The Restaurant*, prematurely canceled but still tasty in reruns)? Awesome. Celebrity divorc and mediocre real-estate financier Donald Trump chooses a tyro (*The Apprentice*)? Irresistible. But then Burnett began to falter. *The Casino* was by turns depressing and (mostly) dull. *The Contender*, which aimed to pick the next boxing champ, got undercut by a competing (and equally uncompelling) boxing show that debuted earlier. The assy sitcom based on the Burnett family s unorthodox child-care provider, *Commando Nanny*, got sacked before it ever aired, and *Rockstar: INXS* just seemed kind of morbid. We watched *Boarding House: North Shore* once, and we ll never get that hour back. See also *APPRENTICE, THE*; PROBST, JEFF; *RESTAURANT, THE*; *SURVIVOR*; and TRUMP, DONALD, HAIR OF.

C

CABLE CHANNELS, UNWATCHED Service providers like Comcast and Time Warner Cable act like they re doing you a big favor when they give you six hundred channels to choose from but how many of those channels do you actually watch? Maybe a dozen, right? Meanwhile, the Speed Channel and AmericanLife TV (we have no idea, sorry) languish, unloved, because there is absolutely no need for them. Nor would each individual body part seem to merit its own Discovery Channel, but that s the world we live in, where one good C-SPAN deserves another. Aaaaand another. Shut up, televised government. See also BRAVO and GAME SHOW NETWORK.

CAGNEY & LACEY It doesn t seem like any big whoop now, but back in the 80s, when the women s movement was still wrestling with the ERA and floppy-bow-tied power suits, a cop show whose two detective protagonists were *both* women was a big deal. The show starred Sharon Gless as hard-ass Christine Cagney and Tyne Daly as married-with-kids Mary Beth Lacey. Lacey did a little too much knitting on stakeouts for some people s tastes, but the chicks-with-badges twist aside, it was a good police procedural and way more realistic than *Charlie's Angels*. The show also costarred Martin Kove, aka Cobra Kai sensei John Kreese from *The Karate Kid*, as a fellow detective. Sweep the leg, Johnny! See also HANDCUFFS, CLICH S ASSOCIATED WITH and *NYPD BLUE*.

CALIFORNIA RAISINS After making their debut singing I Heard It Through the Grapevine in a 1987 TV spot for . . . you know, dried grapes grown in the most populous American state, the Claymation-animated California Raisins somehow grew into an enormous cultural phenomenon. There were plastic figurines, T-shirts, not just one but *two* albums, and several TV specials including *Claymation Christmas Celebration*, which first aired in 1987. (The show featured Carol of the Bells with little Clay-mated bells that struck themselves in the head with hammers.) Apparently the campaign also boosted raisin sales, which just proves what a genius idea it was, because raisins are gross. See also *DAVEY & GOLIATH*; HOLIDAY SPECIALS; and NOID, THE.

"CAMDENS"   See *7TH HEAVEN*.

CAMERON, KIRK   Kirk Cameron might have been just another former child star. But Jesus had something different in mind for old Kirk. Cameron was merely the costar of the *ABC Afterschool Special Andrea's Story: A Hitchhiking Tragedy* when he won the role of eldest brother Mike Seaver on *Growing Pains*, a *Family Ties* rip-off. During the run of the amiable but unimpressive sitcom, Cameron became a born-again Christian and according to the *E! True Hollywood Story* of *Growing Pains* turned into a right pain in the ass, objecting to storylines he found immoral and judging his costars for such offenses as swearing and not appreciating his ministry. In this century, Cameron has eschewed participating in such secular entertainments as *Like Father Like Son* or the remake of *The Computer Wore Tennis Shoes* to appear exclusively in Christian-themed projects like the *Left Behind* series and . . . in two *Growing Pains* reunion movies. See also *ABC AFTERSCHOOL SPECIALS*; *E! TRUE HOLLYWOOD STORY*; *FAMILY TIES*; *GROWING PAINS*; and REUNION MOVIES.

CAMP, JESSE   Once upon a time, MTV had a users-pick-the-new-VJ contest, and it came down to Dave Holmes, a cuddly and knowledgeable music geek, and Jesse Camp, a beanpole white-belt hipster with crazy hair and the intellectual horsepower of a boiled potato. Dave Holmes knew his stuff in the trivia challenge, looked comfortable on screen, and just generally rocked that bitch. Who won? Jesse Camp, because some git put his voting number on speed-dial. Camp was rumored to have a drug problem, and despite a certain cute-but-dumb, Kelso-esque charm, he quickly dropped out of sight after MTV realized its mistake. Holmes still hosts various shows around the dial, including the occasional *Real World* reunion; Camp was last seen in *Crossroads*. Enough said. See also HOLMES, DAVE and MTV VJs.

CANNED LAUGHTER, MANIPULATION BY/OF   Some sitcoms tape in front of a live studio audience usually primed by a warm-up comedian but many shows use canned laughter instead. It s insurance. If a punchline or pratfall isn t funny, the laughing, groaning, or happy hooting of others may fool the audience into believing otherwise. Emotions teased out by prefab soundtrack sounds include: joy at the entrance of a sidekick (Wooooo!); appreciation of a good snap (Oooooh); relief that a problem has been solved with hugging

("Awwwww"); confusion at the sight of a man wearing a dress (*uncomfortable titter*). Use of this humor crutch is a sign that the writing staff has—correctly—no confidence in its ability to earn laughs on its own. See also BAD SITCOM, SURE SIGNS OF.

CANNELL, STEPHEN J. Long before there was Spike: Television for Men, there was Steven J. Cannell, producing ever so many shows that would be just perfect for it. Characterized by car chases, black-and-white morality, and mavericks who play by their own rules, Cannell's oeuvre makes for relaxingly unchallenging TV viewing. Unless what you're trying to do is fall asleep in front of one of them on a Saturday afternoon, in which case a challenge may be posed by the many very loud explosions (from which you may be sure your hero will walk away unscathed). See also *A-TEAM, THE*; *GREATEST AMERICAN HERO, THE*; *HUNTER*; and *21 JUMP STREET*.

CANTONE, MARIO Standup comedian Cantone, a veteran of comedy clubs and one-man shows, is probably most famous for his role as Charlotte's wedding planner/gay BFF on *Sex and the City*. But children of the '80s may also remember him as the host of the culty kids' variety show *Steampipe Alley*, an hour of TV that in many ways resembled Cantone himself— sometimes fun, sometimes headache-inducing, always hyperactive and screechy. Cantone is an acquired taste, and many TV viewers are relieved that the theater has "acquired" him, at least for the moment. See also CHILDREN'S SHOWS, HOSTS OF and *SEX AND THE CITY*.

CAPTAIN CAVEMAN AND THE TEEN ANGELS Captain Caveman, a supposedly (except not really) "cute" Neanderthal accessorized with a gaggle of cooing girls, has the most annoying signature catchphrase *in the world* . . . provided you can even call screaming one's own name a catchphrase: "Captaaaaaain CAAAAAAVE-maaa-eeee-aaaa-eeee-aaaaaan!!" And he uses the "catchphrase" a lot. And five-year-olds who watch the show will then use it a lot also. And older sisters of five-year-olds who watch the show will come to despise Captain Caveman and everything he stands for. It's typical Hanna-Barbera fare: grating, asinine, lots of vibraphone on the soundtrack. Shut up, Messrs. Hanna and Barbera. See also CARTOONS, HANNA-BARBERA.

CAPTAIN KANGAROO Captain Kangaroo, TV's longest-running kids' show, rocked. First of all, Bob Keeshan, who played the Captain, had *the* most amazing sideburns back in the '70s, and a preternaturally shiny bowl cut. Like, *really* shiny and bowl-y. The show also had lots of cool characters (like Word Bird) and a bunch of fancy guest stars like Imogene Coca and Doug Henning not that we really knew who Coca was when we were little, and Doug Henning was sort of a weirdo, but whatever, we were five. But the best part about the show? It aired before school, so you could sort of ease into a tough day of carpool and cursive lessons by checking out some baby skunks with Mr. Green Jeans. The Captain himself, in retrospect, seems like maybe a little bit of a druncle, but we loved the show at the time. See also CHILDREN S SHOWS, HOSTS OF; MR. GREEN JEANS ; and SIDEBURNS, IMPORTANT TV.

"CAPTAIN STUBING" See *LOVE BOAT, THE.*

CARD SHARKS A game show in which contestants basically had to guess whether the next card turned over would be higher or lower simple odds-playing livened up by the lupine host Bob Eubanks and by the giant cards used in play, which kids in the audience wished were sold commercially because they looked really fun. Imagine trying to stuff one of those bad boys in your bike spokes. See also GAME SHOW NETWORK.

CAROL BURNETT SHOW, THE We ve never really gotten why the classic *Gone with the Wind* parody skit where Carol wears a curtain rod is so hilarious, and we only watched the show in the first place because it came on right after the afternoon *Brady Bunch* rerun but we still watched it, because the skits weren t very good, but it was pretty funny when the grown-ups couldn t hold it together and started cracking up. (Did Harvey Korman ever get through a *single* line without giggling? How drunk *was* that guy?) Plus, we kind of wanted to see it in person someday so we could ask Carol Burnett a question when she came out to talk to the audience. See also CHARACTER, BREAKING OF.

CARTOONS, HANNA-BARBERA It s not that we hate *all* Hanna-Barbera cartoons. We loved old-school *Tom and Jerry* (the newer ones from the 70s must have used a different drawing team, because Tom looked a lot like Rosalind Russell, and it creeped us out), and we dig the more recent offerings such as *Samurai Jack* and *The Powerpuff Girls*. It s that the cartoons we *do* hate all happen to come from Hanna-Barbera: the odious *Top Cat*, whose eponymous hero shot for Dean Martin cool but missed by an adenoidal mile; crappy C-list cartoons *Captain Caveman* and *Grape Ape*; marketing tie-ins like *Monchichis*, *The Dukes*, and *Partridge Family, 2200 A.D.* (. . . no, seriously); and of course *Scooby-Doo*, the most enduringly charmless cartoon of all. As kids, we craved cartoons in any form, but more often than not, the Hanna-Barbera offerings just got on our nerves; the characters did a lot of bellowing, it seemed like, and had a lot of body hair; and the feeble sitcommy plotting looked threadbare even to our grade-school eyes. And Scrappy-Doo? Is a dick. The Shmoo is still supercute, but it in no way makes up for *Laverne & Shirley in the Army* or (*shudder*) *Trollkins*. See also CAPTAIN CAVEMAN AND THE TEEN ANGELS; CARTOONS PRIMARILY DESIGNED AS PROMOTIONAL TIE-INS; DUKES OF HAZZARD, THE; and PARTRIDGE FAMILY, THE.

CARTOONS PRIMARILY DESIGNED AS PROMOTIONAL TIE-INS In the 1980s, toymakers discovered what breakfast-cereal manufacturers had known for years: the best way to sell something to a kid is to dress up your marketing plan in animated form. Thus, our Saturday morning cartoon hours were taken over by shows based on Transformers, He-Man, G.I. Joe, and the Care Bears. These days, the Saturday morning cartoon has become a relic of a bygone age, with the proliferation of cable networks that air cartoons round the clock. Which is just as well those shows were pretty bad. (Not so bad, though, that Michael Bay wouldn t attach himself to a big-screen Transformers movie!) See also CARTOONS, HANNA-BARBERA and LIVE-ACTION SHOWS, ANIMATED VERSIONS OF.

CARTOON VERSIONS OF LIVE-ACTION SHOWS See LIVE-ACTION SHOWS, ANIMATED VERSIONS OF.

CARUSO, DAVID, AS GO-TO REFERENCE FOR CAREER SUICIDE David Caruso s now long-ago decision to leave *NYPD Blue* partway through its second season made his name pop-cultural shorthand for a doofus who didn t know what a good gig he had until he quit and turned into an instant has-been. (One of the most beloved jokes of the *South Park* pilot comes when Kyle begs his brother to jump from a signifi-cant height by exhort-ing him, Ike! Do your impression of David Caruso s career!) Since then, Caruso s had to eat a lot of crow  for his early bad career moves including several unremarkable films and a failed TV series before he landed on *CSI: Miami* and clung to it for dear life. But the stench of failure won t wash off him until another TV star makes an *even worse* career move. See also *CSI*, SPIN-OFFS OF; HORATIO CAINE ; *NYPD BLUE*; and *SOUTH PARK*.

CASSIDYS, THE David and Shaun Cassidy shared not just a father but also remarkably similar *Tiger Beat*—driven careers. *Partridge Family* star David toured a lot in his tight sequined overalls (you heard right), basically disappeared in the early 80s, then resurfaced in a cheesy Vegas show and in the *Behind the Music* devoted to him, in which he sported crappy hair plugs and a humorless attitude. Hardy Boy Shaun, several years younger, also released a bunch of records (primarily covers), starred in one of the funniest TV movies ever made (*Like Normal People*), and then turned to creating and producing TV shows. Shaun is pretty cool now; David, based on his self-aggrandizing memoir, is kind of a dink and really in love with himself. See also *BEHIND THE MUSIC*; HARDY BOYS, SAD SLOW DECLINE OF; *LIKE NORMAL PEOPLE*; and *PARTRIDGE FAMILY, THE*.

CATCHPHRASES, OVERUSED COMMERCIAL Too often, a line of ad copy can be so well turned that it becomes a part of the cultural lexicon, and thus becomes divorced from the product it was originally intended to sell. Today alone, we've told loved ones to drop the chalupa, accused smelly subway riders of having that not-so-fresh feeling, and teased a pet for acting as though he were built Ford tough. And that's just among friends. Where's the beef? was used in a presidential debate, for heaven's sake. And how long did we suffer through the dark years of There is no step three, Dude, you're getting a Dell, and (we hate even to mention it, but we must) WHAAAAASSSSSS-SAAAAAAAAAAAAP?! You can probably more easily place the source of I can't believe I ate the whole thing (Alka-Seltzer!) than the source of It was the best of times, it was the worst of times (. . . the Bible?). And maybe that means we're culturally bankrupt, but there are a lot of TV spots that have more relevance and immediacy than some of what we read to earn our English degrees. That's right, Sir Edmund Spenser: *Can you hear me now?* See also COMMERCIALS, CAREFULLY EUPHEMISTIC; COMMERCIALS, SUPER BOWL; and COMMERCIALS, VINTAGE.

CATCHPHRASES, OVERUSED TV Ah, the catchphrase the lazy writer's crutch. A good (or, rather, enduring) catchphrase only *really* has to hit once to work; every subsequent use is just a callback to that very first time, so that instead of laughing at the catchphrase itself upon its eightieth repetition, what the viewer is really laughing at is the memory of the time, in the distant past, when the line was still fresh and new sort of like the way we don't actually see the stars themselves when we gaze at the night sky, but rather the light they gave off thousands of years ago. In fact, divorced from their contexts (by which we mean: yelled between hipsters across a crowded bar), most catchphrases are so banal that you can scarcely imagine a screenwriter even using them once, much less dozens of times: How *you* doin ? Whoa! Seacrest out! Did I do thaaaaat? D oh! We were on a break! Don t be ridiculous. . . . for me to poop on. Is that your final answer? See also BAD SITCOM, SURE SIGNS OF; *BLOSSOM*; CANNED LAUGHTER, MANIPULATION BY/OF; *FRIENDS*; *FULL HOUSE*; *PERFECT STRANGERS*; ROSS GELLER ; SEACREST OUT! ; *SIMPSONS, THE*; TRIUMPH, THE INSULT COMIC DOG ; URKEL ; and *WHO WANTS TO BE A MILLIONAIRE*, REGIS EDITION.

CAULFIELD, MAXWELL Vintage 80s beefcake. Scottish cutie Caulfield first surfaced in *Grease 2*, and also did time on *The Colbys* and in various made-for-TV Judith-Krantz-originated mediocrities. Somewhere in there, he married a much older woman. Never really lived up to his promise, *except* for his hammy turn in the *90210* pilot as sexually aggressive, weird-kissing lawyer Jason Croft. See also *BEVERLY HILLS 90210* and MOVIES, MADE-FOR-TV.

CELEBRITY POKER SHOWDOWN Riding the wave of America s love affair with Texas Hold Em, Bravo s *Celebrity Poker Showdown* takes five stars of stage, screen, and sport, puts them around a poker table in front of a live studio audience in Las Vegas s Palms Casino Resort, places cameras in the table so we can see their hands (and, therefore, when they re bluffing their asses off), and pretties up the whole affair by having them play for charity. The emcees are dry-witted, very tall poker expert Phil Gordon and former Kid in the Hall Dave Foley, who has aged rather poorly since *NewsRadio* and, in each episode, gets visibly drunker over the course of taping. The show is generally only as good as its guests are entertaining, which is why it s a good thing its alumni include Nicole Sullivan, Amy Poehler, Seth Meyers, half the cast of *Arrested Development*, and our personal favorite, Michael Ian Black. When he beat Norm Macdonald, we cheered out loud. See also BLACK, MICHAEL IAN and BRAVO.

CENTRAL PARK WEST In the early 90s, it seemed like Darren Star creator of *90210* and *Melrose Place* (and later *Sex and the City*) could do no wrong, so CBS handed him a primetime slot and a blank check. The result wasn t so much a soap opera as a dog s breakfast of publishing-intrigue plotlines, hasty recasting, and . . . fat Mariel Hemingway. The show got a buttload of press before it aired and was then savaged by the critics, but it wasn t awful (and its fans still defend it zealously); it just felt cobbled together out of spare parts from other soaps. Even the overhyped catfight between Raquel Welch and Lauren Hutton was old hat we d seen fighting ladies wind up in the pool before, several times. An extensive revamp didn t help; the show bit the dust in the summer of 1996. See also ACTING, WOODEN; *BEVERLY HILLS 90210*; *MELROSE PLACE*; OVERHYPED SERIES THAT BOMBED; RECASTING, NOTORIOUS; *SEX AND THE CITY*; and STAR, DARREN.

CENTURY CITY They called it *Century City*, but we always preferred *Space Lawyers* and when we say always, we mean for the four episodes CBS aired before yanking it unceremoniously as too crappy *even for a midseason replacement*. It was just your basic legal drama, only it happened to be set in the year 2030 . . . the fuuuuuuuuuuuuuuture! Except the cases were all just barely more technologically complex than what might be argued in a contemporary courtroom, revolving around cybernetic body parts, cosmetic surgery of all kinds, cyber-stalking, cloning, yada yada yada. And apparently, in the future, lawyers will be just as smarmy and amoral as they are now only then, they ll argue cases before judges who are *holograms*! The fuuuuuuu-uuuuuuuture! See also FUTURE ON TV, SIMILARITY TO PRESENT OF.

CHARACTER, BREAKING OF Back when they were both on *Saturday Night Live*, Jimmy Fallon and Horatio Sanz could be counted on for one thing. No, not that they d consistently make us laugh! Oh, heavens no. No we could be sure that whenever they were in a sketch together, they would prove utterly incapable of staying in character. Instead, they d just crack each other up as though they were undergrads goofing around during seminar presentations and not actors on a national live television show. We kept hoping they d get fired over it, or at least cast in fewer sketches, but then *Entertainment Weekly* took leave of its senses and published an appreciative item on their laughing in the middle of sketches, which . . . no. It s funny when it happens rarely and the actors involved are doing their best to regain control; when it s built into the sketch and totally not a surprise, it s annoying and unprofessional. But at least Fallon and Sanz had the (kind of) excuse that the show was live and they couldn t ask for another take. The cast members on *That 70s Show* couldn t say the same, and yet they giggled through so many scenes that we had to wonder whether the pot that was only ever suggested in those spinning fish-eye scenes was, in fact, an integral element of the actors Method. Because, MY GOD, get it together! Having Kurtwood Smith call you a dumb-ass for the fourteenth time *this episode* is just not that funny. See also *SATURDAY NIGHT LIVE*; STONERS, TV FOR; and *THAT 70s SHOW*.

CHARLES IN CHARGE Who ever heard of

a college boy getting hired as a house-keeper? And not only did Charles (Scott Baio, doing his best with dreadful material) get hired he got hired *twice*. First he worked for the Pembrokes, minding their three children, and then, when the Pembrokes moved away (read: the show got retooled due to toilet-bound ratings), they just left him in the house for whomever moved in next. Enter the Powells, the family everyone remembers, and the Powells teenage daughters and they just adopted Charles as *their* house-keeper/kid-minder. Does this seem like the smart play when Charles is a straight guy and one of said daughters is Nicole Eggert? No, it doesn t, but that s how the Powells rolled. And they didn t lock their doors, either, so humpy sidekick Buddy (Willie Aames) was free to barge in day or night and ogle the Eggert. (We always felt sorry for Josie Davis, who played the other, ungainlier sister, Sarah Powell. She turned out really pretty, but back then . . .) The show inflicted irritation on a generation of real-life Charleses, who to this day have the nails-on-a-chalkboard theme song sung at them moments after introducing them-selves. Charles in Charge of our days and our nights / Charles in Charge of our wrongs and our rights / and I sing, I want / I want Charles in Charge of me! Kind of porn-y given that he s the nanny, no? See also AAMES, WILLIE; BAD SITCOM, SURE SIGNS OF; BAIO, SCOTT; NEIGHBORS, INTRUSIVE; and THEME SONGS.

CHARLIE'S ANGELS See SPELLING, AARON.

CHARMED See SPELLING, AARON and TNT s PRIMETIME IN THE DAYTIME.

CHASE, CHEVY, UNMITIGATED LOATH-SOMENESS OF When we used to watch reruns of old-school *Saturday Night Live*, we didn t love Chevy Chase as the anchor of Weekend Update ; he just seemed like one of those guys who s funny and yet has no sense of humor. His signature I m Chevy Chase, and you re not line came off as if he actually meant it, instead of cute and jokey. But we didn t have any *proof* that Chase was a horse s ass until 1993, when *The Chevy Chase Show* aired and detonated the Fat Man of late-night bombs. His disastrous hosting perform-ance awkward pauses, flaccid ques-tions, flop sweat hinted rather strongly at a profound difficulty relating to other human beings. Confirmation came at last in the book *Live from New York*, which outed Chase as a dickhead nonpareil who wrote only for himself and not for the group, dismissed the show as going nowhere after he left it, suggested an AIDS sketch to a gay staff writer, and screamed at people when he returned as a guest host. In his own interviews in the book, Chase comes off as an even *bigger* asshat, boohooing that he wouldn t have left the show if Lorne Michaels *had given him a hug and begged him to stay*, and shrugging that he didn t give a flying fuck about the show. Pretty big talk from the star of *Cops and Robbersons*. Even for Hollywood, that level of narcissism is rare. We almost have to admire it . . . but we don t. We hope he Gerald Fords butt-first onto a brown recluse. See also MOVIES-TO-TV/TV-TO-MOVIES CAREER PIPELINE; *SATURDAY NIGHT LIVE*; *SATURDAY NIGHT LIVE,* WEEKEND UPDATE HOSTS ON; TALK SHOWS, LATE-NIGHT; TALK SHOWS, NOTORIOUS EPONYMOUS FAILED; and UNIVERSALLY REVILED CHARACTERS.

CHEERS The Hallmark-y maudlinity that attended the series finale notwithstanding, *Cheers* was a great show. The trick, when watching it in reruns, is to catch an episode during the show s post-Coach, pre-Rebecca-Howe peak, when the cast of just-wacky-enough secondary characters is firing on all cylinders and Carla s love life isn t getting too much screen time. Forget how sweaty Kelsey Grammer got during the *Frasier* years; forget the embarrassing Danson-in-blackface incident; forget Woody Harrelson s hemp advocacy. Before any of that, during the Shelley Long years, *Cheers* did ensemble comedy and sexual tension better than any other sitcom, and in spite of a few creaky Reagan jokes and Danson s toup-pouf, most of the writing holds up . . . including the endless variations on a theme of Norm!, which you would think we d have gotten sick of, but to the writers credit, we never did. See also ALLEY, KIRSTIE; CATCHPHRASES, OVERUSED TV; DANSON, TED; *FRASIER*; and RECASTING, NOTORIOUS.

CHIA PET Probably tied with the Clapper and the Ginsu knife as the most famous As Seen on TV product ever. (Note: A grown-in Chia Head looks like Richard Simmons, which freaks us out.) Ch-ch-ch-chia! See also AFROS, FAMOUS TV; AS SEEN ON TV PRODUCTS; and SIMMONS, RICHARD.

CHICAGO HOPE In 1994, two TV series premiered concerning the fraught personal lives of doctors and nurses against the background of their medical cases, both set in Chicago hospitals. *Chicago Hope* is the one no one remembers, because the other one was *ER*. At the time, *Hope* s marketers tried to claim that it was possible to like both, because the two shows were so different. But they weren t, really, except that *Hope*, as a David E. Kelley production, came to rely so heavily on the interesting (read: annoying) tics of its characters emotionally stunted, crooning heart surgeon Jeffrey Geiger (Mandy Patinkin); reflexively sexist surgeon Billy Kronk (Peter Berg); stuttering freakazoid house counsel Alan Birch (Peter MacNicol); and so on. *Hope* started out an engrossing character drama but gradually got overwhelmed with outlandish cases and plot twists, making it the *L.A. Law* of doctor shows, with all that that implies. See also *ER*; KELLEY, DAVID E.; *L.A. LAW*; and MEDICAL DRAMAS, TROPES OF.

CHILDREN, OVERLY PRECOCIOUS   On TV, children grow up so fast! And not just on soap operas, where a baby can be born in April and make it to its first day of kindergarten in September of the same year. On sitcoms and dramas, too, children are clever, stoic, or wise beyond their years. Babies wear sunglasses and roll their eyes at their parents antics; toddlers do the macarena; elementary school—aged children have their own catchphrases (Whatchu talkin bout, Willis? How rude!); teenagers are mature enough to offer sage advice on their single mothers love lives. And that s just on sitcoms; dramas are full of kids suffering bravely with terminal cancer, making nary a self-pitying remark; they have keen insights into their parents very adult problems; they handle disappointments and setbacks better than the grownups around them. What a bunch of smug little pukes they are. See also BAD SITCOM, SURE SIGNS OF; CATCHPHRASES, OVERUSED TV; *FULL HOUSE*; and SOAP OPERAS, DAYTIME.

CHILDREN'S SHOWS, HOSTS OF   Sunny, patient, suspiciously enthusiastic about learning, children s show hosts often acted *in loco parentis*—and we do mean loco. Mister Rogers seemed like a normal guy, except for the puppets maybe, but Captain Kangaroo . . . may have had some problems. I mean, we loved the guy, but *what* was going on with those suits? And it s pretty obvious what the hippie ladies from *The Magic Garden* were *really* growing, if you know what we mean. And you totally do. (Mushrooms. And pot.) All of them were way better than Barney, but watching the shows as an adult, you can sometimes sense an underlying despair. And pot. See also *CAPTAIN KANGAROO* and ROGERS, FRED.

CHINA BEACH   After what seemed like a decade of tacit cultural agreement not to talk about it, the 1987—88 TV season saw not one but two dramas set in the Vietnam War: *Tour of Duty* and *China Beach*. The former had more of a battle focus, but the latter concentrated more on women s experiences of the war, whether as nurses (Dana Delany, in her only really good role), USO performers (Chloe Webb, aka *Sid & Nancy* s Nancy Spungen), Red

Cross volunteers (Ricki Lake), or working girls (Marg Helgenberger as K.C. Koloski). Sounds kind of cool; didn t really work, given the tendency of the writing to yaw into preachy (or broody-montage) waters nearly every episode. We watched it anyway, though, because in the 80s, everything 60s was in, and we liked the music as much as we disliked K.C. s self-righteous I am *not a whore* snit-fits. If you re not a whore, stop sleeping with dudes for money, *K.C.* God, hate. See also *CSI*.

CHiPs California Highway Patrolmen Ponch (Erik Estrada) and Jon (Larry Wilcox) solved problems, dogged chicks, expressed bafflement at French food and UFOs, endangered countless stuntmen, and faced off against guest star Danny Bonaduce several times while Erik Estrada s gigantic Chiclet teeth hypnotized viewers unable to change the channel. Estrada and Larry Wilcox clearly hated each other and clearly could not really ride the bikes, and if the average episode is anything to go by, California had an epidemic of runaway vehicles on its hands back in the day. But the show is a rad 70s time capsule. Come for the profusion of recognizable guest stars (Bruce Jenner! Michelle Pfeiffer!), stay for the Dolphin shorts and the wacky subplots involving supporting character Grossman. See also ESTRADA, ERIK.

"CHRIS IN THE MORNING" When you re a certain age (say, a high school senior), and a quirky, likable TV show presents you with a character who s an artist, a self-taught philosopher, a DJ, and did time, it s going to take all your willpower to resist being swept up by his charms. When he also happens to look about seventeen feet tall and have long, soulfully tousled hair . . . just give up. Our older selves can look back at our younger selves and be amazed and slightly ashamed that they were so taken with John Corbett s Chris in the Morning on *Northern Exposure*, but our younger selves were totally smitten, dreaming of a time when we d have our own philosophy-spouting ex-cons to read the Bhagavad Gita to us. Then we actually got to college and realized those guys are all self-important dinks who d just cheat on us anyway. See also *NORTHERN EXPOSURE*; *SEX AND THE CITY*; and TV BOYFRIENDS AND GIRLFRIENDS.

CHRISTMAS COMES TO PAC-LAND This holiday special s across-the-board suckitude remains seared into our memories like a brand. The crappy animation made the Pac-family look like squashed grapefruits and didn t sync up to the voice acting. But never mind the pathetic production values, or the disturbing subtext of Pac-Baby s existence, namely that Pac-Man and Ms. Pac-Man clearly . . . er . . . Pac-Chicka-Bow-Wow, if you know what we mean. Why is Pac-Man wearing boots, a scarf, and a hat but no pants? For that matter, why does Pac-Man have legs in the first place? And a nose? Why is Ms. Pac-Man all girled up with fake lashes and a spit-curl instead of just rocking her signature bow? Oh, right: She can t rock the bow; she s wearing a winter hat. (And no pants.) It didn t stop at the holidays, either; the non-Christmas series version of the cartoon ran for a couple of years on Saturday mornings. Trying to capitalize on Pac-Man fever is one thing, but not when the characters look nothing like the original. How hard is it to animate a circle with a pie piece cut out of it? See also CARTOONS PRIMARILY DESIGNED AS PROMOTIONAL TIE-INS and HOLIDAY SPECIALS.

"CHRISTOPHER MOLTISANTI" Tony Soprano s nephew-slash-wannabe-son is a nasty piece of work. We know this. We know he cheated on his fianc e Adriana, like, a billion times, and we know he sat on her dog and killed it while junked out on heroin. He s obsessed  with his Lexus, he s got a crazy short temper and a butt-ugly Jersey blow-dry, he s jealous of any other guy who asks Tony the time, and he way overdoes it

with the screenwriting aspirations and, now that he s out of rehab, the twelve-step-speak. But we can t help it: We love him. And it s not the malapropisms (we still giggle every time he calls that Emil guy E-mail), or the old-hen bickering with Paulie Walnuts, although we love that too. No, it s that giant schnozzola. Chrissy is foxy. See also TV BOYFRIENDS AND GIRLFRIENDS.

"CHUNG CHUNG" At least, that s our phonetic rendering of the distinctive sound you hear over the black location screens on all installments of the *Law & Order* franchise a sound that s become so iconic in pop culture that TNT built an entire *L&O* promo around it. Could it possibly be the best thing the prolific TV scorer Mike Post ever composed? Yes. Yes, it could. See also *LAW & ORDER* FRANCHISE; POST, MIKE; and TNT S PRIMETIME IN THE DAYTIME.

CLAPPER, THE A gadget that allowed you to turn lights and appliances on and off by clapping your hands, and that nobody has ever actually owned. The commercial featured a catchy yet strangely dirgelike song. Clap on! [*clap clap*] Clap off! [*clap clap*] Clap on, clap off the Clapper! Then, at the end, an elderly woman who had fallen asleep with the lights on clapped sort of violently in the direction of her bedside lamp, then flopped over on her side, and it was . . . kind of upsetting, actually. See also As SEEN ON TV PRODUCTS.

CLIFFHANGERS TV cliffhangers seldom leave characters literally hanging from cliffs. (Exception: the episode of *The O.C.* called The Cliffhanger, which ended with the death of a tertiary character from, yep, falling off an actual cliff.) But there is scarcely a show on TV now even sitcoms that can resist hooking viewers for the next season by leaving a huge, unanswered question at the end of its season finale. Not all of them can be as momentous and shocking as Who shot J.R.? (partly because overly explanatory network promos and nonstop entertainment journalism have rendered us incapable of surprise), but some can still propel us to the proverbial water cooler to debate the questions they raise. Will Luke accept Lorelai s proposal? When that road-ragey driver shot at Chen and Pratt, did he hit them? Did Jack and Will just sleep together, or did they really have sex? Will Zach shoot Mike? Will Abe and Joan get together? Will Emily still marry Ross after he said I take thee, Rachel ? And for God s sake, if he s not Michael Vaughn, *just who in the hell is he?!* See also *ALIAS*; *CLONE HIGH*; *DALLAS*; *DESPERATE HOUSE- WIVES*; *ER*; *FRIENDS*; *GILMORE GIRLS*; *O.C., THE*; and *WILL & GRACE*.

CLARKSON, KELLY See *AMERICAN IDOL.*

CLONE HIGH One of the most quotable animated series of all time, MTV s brilliant *Clone High* answers the question of what might happen if a secret government experiment cloned various important historical figures and timed their births so that they d all end up in high school together. Well, you d get Freud critiquing the school film festival, Abraham Lincoln and John F. Kennedy running against each other for class president, and Joan of Arc founding a teen crisis line, all overseen by a mad-scientist principal, Cinnamon J. Scudworth, and his robot servant, Mr. Butlertron. Obviously. The show was canceled prematurely, amid protests against the character of Gandhi, and given that the reimagined Mahatma was shown suffering from ADD and its hyperactive cousin, ADHD and uttering lines like If Gandhi stands for one thing, it s revenge, you can kind of see the protestors point. Still, the show is awesome. Wesleeeeeeeeey. See also CATCHPHRASES, OVERUSED TV and *MR. BELVEDERE.*

CLOONEY, GEORGE He didn t have the most auspicious beginnings a recurring role as George Burnett on *The Facts of Life*, a turn as an orderly on sitcom *E/R*. He just bumbled along through the rest of the 80s and the early part of the 90s in crappy films (*Return of the Killer Toma-*

toes!) and even crappier TV (on *Sunset Beat*, in which L.A. cops went undercover as bikers, he played a character named Chic Chesbro . . . guess Clooney really hates to wait tables) until he nabbed the Doug Ross role on *ER*. Despite Clooney s tendency to confuse head-tilting with acting, Carol Hathaway (Julianna Margulies) couldn t resist Dr. Ross, a Rat-Packy rou with commitment issues, and neither could we he screwed up a lot, but he looked like George Clooney, so we didn t mind. The show blew up huge, so Clooney used his newfound stardom to . . . star in movies just as crappy as the ones he d done before, but with higher-profile directors (Robert Rodriguez) or in collapsing franchises (*Batman & Robin*). So when he left the show for the silver screen, it didn t seem like a smart move. We had a feeling he d come crawling back to *ER* with some soap-operatic excuse about how the job in Seattle didn t work out, blah blah. Didn t happen. He did return, in Hathaway s farewell episode, which was sporting of him, but by that time he d pretty much completed his transformation into the twenty-first century s heir to Cary Grant dry as a good champagne, wears a Hollywood tan like nobody s business, charisma out the wazoo. We hear he s kind of a ho, but we don t care. The man has an Oscar now. Come over, Cloon! The pink champers is already on ice! See also

E/R; *ER*; *FACTS OF LIFE, THE*; MOVIES-TO-TV/TV-TO-MOVIES CAREER PIPELINE/ARC; and TV BOYFRIENDS AND GIRLFRIENDS.

COACH We didn t like football. We didn t think the coaching of it was all that interesting. And yet we watched *Coach*. We don t know why. It wasn t Craig T. Nelson s portrayal of the titular college football head coach Hayden Fox. Hayden was as predictable and wearying in his intolerance and prickliness as his lieutenants, played by Bill Fagerbakke and Jerry Van Dyke, were in their intractable dopiness. It certainly wasn t Shelley Fabares, as the WASPy, poodle-permed love interest Christine, that kept us coming back. The only thing we can guess is  that we were interested in Clare Carey s Kelly, Hayden s daughter, inasmuch as we were aspirationally interested in all depictions of cool late-adolescence. Or that, in the manner of *Wings*, it happened to air in a time slot in which nothing else was on that we ever watched like 4 AM, a time we routinely used to see when we were first self-employed, sleeping all day and working into the wee hours of morning. And there s nothing like a good dose of Craig T. Nelson bellowing to make you realize, seriously, it s time for bed. See also

NELSON, CRAIG T. and *WINGS*.

"COACH McGUIRK" If we ever stop being amused by fictional authority figures who hold children in contempt, we will know we have really gotten old. Coach John McGuirk, of the late Cartoon Network series *Home Movies*, is one such authority figure an overweight children s soccer coach with minimal knowledge of sport, a Bryan Adams fixation (including a hot rod with RECKLESS scrawled across the top of its windshield), and kind of a serious drinking problem. In a voice that sounds like a fatter, more dissolute version of Dr. Katz s son Ben (no coincidence both are supplied by comic genius H. Jon Benjamin), McGuirk is wont to give his eight-year-old charges advice like Brendon, there s nothing wrong with lying to women. Or the government. Or parents. Or God and Life sucks, Brendon. That s your lesson. Go enjoy it and commenting, on a physically challenged player, I love this kid. He s like a chipmunk with a disease. McGuirk also has no compunction against spending walk-a-thon pledges on lunch and a movie or forfeiting a game due to his own drunkenness. He s totally irresponsible and actually seems to hate kids. He s our kind of people. See also ADULT SWIM.

COLD OPEN ZINGER LINE Cops like gallows humor. And there is no better time to deploy such humor than when you ve spent juuuuust enough time at the crime scene to be cursorily apprised of the facts of the case. The late, great Jerry Orbach s Lennie Briscoe, of *Law & Order*, inaugurated this tradition, often with a wry reference to one of his several ex-wives. But it was Gil Grissom of *CSI* who took the ball and ran with it, making the cold open zinger line an opportunity for situation-specific puns. We like to use the time wasted on Who Are You? to one-up each other with alternate puns the writers may have rejected and the writers, by the way, have never improved upon the zinger that followed the discovery of a body with a rodent in her mouth: Looks like she ratted herself out. [*Slow clap.*] See also GIL GRISSOM and LENNIE BRISCOE.

COLLEGE, UNREALISTIC PORTRAYALS OF First, all the main characters in a high-school show just *happen* to get into the same college . . . the same *local* college. And they all go there, even the ones who got into Ivy League schools, because UC Sunnydale is the ninth Ivy. Not. They live in *huge* dorm rooms; they only go to class, study, or sit for exams when the writers need a *contrivance ex machina* to serve some other plot point; they never have trouble getting booze; the book they re reading for class always parallels the problem *du jour* in some way (failing that, watch for falling chemistry puns); and they sleep with their professors and/or RAs. Like, constantly. You have to give *Felicity* credit; at least those kids had regular homework and knew the word registrar. See also *BEVERLY HILLS 90210*; *BUFFY THE VAMPIRE SLAYER*; *DAWSON'S CREEK*; *FELICITY*; HIGH SCHOOL, UNREALISTIC PORTRAYALS OF; and REAL ESTATE, VASTNESS OF.

COMEBACK, THE   After making several movies during the run of *Friends* that were completely terrible (*Lucky Numbers*, *Marci X*, *Hanging Up* we could go on, but why be cruel?), Lisa Kudrow decided instead to produce a sitcom vehicle for herself. She sold it to HBO, presumably so that it could contain swears, and called it *The Comeback*. The overly complicated idea is that Kudrow's character, Valerie Cherish, used to be on a sitcom years ago, but hasn't worked much until she gets cast as the tracksuited, middle-aged busybody Aunt Sassy on the twentysomething sex sitcom *Room and Bored*, partly by agreeing to have the process filmed for a reality show called *The Comeback*. What the viewer sees is supposedly the raw footage of the reality show. *The Comeback* allows Kudrow not only to satirize reality TV (which all TV actors must either hate or say they hate, at the risk of getting bounced out of SAG), but also to use Valerie's many daily humiliations to

mock everything she apparently thinks is pathetic about aging sitcom actresses their outdated hair, their recollections of playing teenaged hookers on *Magnum, P.I.*, their inflated sense of their own importance as TV veterans. For a sitcom, it actually wasn't that funny, which may have been why HBO didn't pick it up for a second season. But it was extremely mean-spirited, and . . . we kind of loved that about it. See also *FRIENDS* and SELF-REFERENCING BUSINESS, CLOYING.

COMEDY CENTRAL, EARLY PROGRAMMING OF   In the pre-*Daily Show* era, Comedy Central's slate consisted almost entirely of *Short Attention Span Theater*, a standup clip show hosted by the resolutely unfunny Marc Maron; *Bill Cosby: Himself*; and endless selections from the *Police Academy* catalog. Handy if you needed a *Johnny Dangerously* fix on the weekend (and hey, who doesn't?), but not good for much else. See also MARATHONS.

COMMERCIAL CATCHPHRASES, OVERUSED See CATCHPHRASES, OVERUSED COMMERCIAL.

COMMERCIALS, AMATEURISH LOCAL With the software advances we've seen in recent years, you'd think local TV ads might have improved. Think again. Porn has better production values (and acting) than the average suburban car-dealership spot, and any local commercial will include a combination of the following nuisances: slack-jawed, droning children; paper cut-outs; a voice-over that is either screamed or recorded underwater; still photos of jaundiced-looking food, dying plants, and brides in desperate need of powder; a barrage of different *WarGames*-era typefaces (preferably in illegible neon colors and/or flashing). Crazy Eddie may have been insane, but those ads looked like Kubrick compared to this stuff. See also PUBLIC/CABLE ACCESS TV.

COMMERCIALS, BAD PERFORMANCES BY PRO ATHLETES IN Even the least talented professional actor, slumming it for a quick buck in a TV commercial, can probably acquit him- or herself reasonably well and with a minimum of embarrassment hence Lindsay Wagner s heartfelt testimonials for her mattress, or Cher s for Equal. But when it comes to professional athletes, it s a different story. For every Michael Jordan comfortable enough in front of the camera that one of his Nike spots actually got promoted into the feature film *Space Jam* there are a dozen less talented athletes crapping up ads for Buick (Tiger Woods), Sprite (LeBron James, Jerome Williams), or Campbell s Soup (Donovan McNabb). Exceptions noted: Joe Namath for Beauty Mist pantyhose, and that Ironhead guy

from the ad for Zest Body Wash who was all, But *Iiiironhead*! What s with this *thingy*?! They rocked. See also COMMERCIALS, SUPER BOWL.

COMMERCIALS, CAREFULLY EUPHEMISTIC Wetness. Upset stomach. That not-so-fresh feeling. What do they have in common? They re the code words you use to describe sweat, diarrhea, and vaginal odor if you live in a commercial. Now, granted, no one s really agitating for Preparation H advertisements to spell out in great detail precisely what the product does, but using cutesy terms to talk around a phenomenon that happens in every life for instance, the trots is sort of ridiculous in this day and age. (Props go to Imodium, which has advertised its antidiarrhea medication by having people ask How s your diarrhea? to a guy with a girl s face pressed against his butt playing Twister; a guy in a hot tub with a bunch of other people; and the front half of a two-man horse costume.) And honestly what s with the blue water all the time?

COMMERCIALS, COMEDIANS IN We don t begrudge comedians the right to make a living it s a tough business, and if they need to take commercial gigs to pay the bills, hey, we don t judge them. Eeeeexcept for the don t part, because when comedians star in commercials, they don t get to write their own material the ad firms do. So not only do the comedians seem a little bit like sellouts (as if anyone believed Dennis Miller actually used 10-10-220 or whatever the hell in his daily life), but people who *don't* already know their work get annoyed by them and blow them off as unfunny. Occasionally, the ad is actually good (we liked the Sierra Mist spots with Michael Ian Black and Jim Gaffigan), and when it isn t, it can be kind of fun to watch the comedian in question gritting his teeth through some of the brand-name puns as though it physically pains him. Which it should. See also BAD SITCOMS STARRING GOOD COMEDIANS; BLACK, MICHAEL IAN; LEARY, DENIS; and MILLER, DENNIS.

COMMERCIALS, SUPER BOWL Super Bowl spots can cost upward of a million dollars per minute, and a lot of non—football fans (and professional media watchers) tune in just for the commercials, which makes it especially puzzling that so many of them suck. Some years, lightning strikes (the cat-herding ad from a few years back; a CGI Christopher Reeve walking; the many variations on Budweiser s Whaaaaasssssssaaaaaaaaaaaap? theme), but more often, it s dull insurance campaigns, or the rape of classic rock by chronically unhip car companies. See also CATCHPHRASES, OVERUSED COMMERCIAL and COMMERCIALS, BAD PERFORMANCES BY PRO ATHLETES IN.

COMMERCIALS, TALKING CGI ANIMALS AND BABIES IN The Quiznos baby gets a pass; he s a supercutie, and for some reason a baby saying Come to Papa is pretty funny. But nine times out of ten, a CGI mouth on an infant or a cat who s freaking out about its stinky litter box isn t cute or funny. It s creepy, because the technology isn t good enough yet for it to look real. Dogs aren t supposed to 1) have lips or 2) know fuck-all about GMAC financing. It s messed up. Leave the pets out of it.

COMMERCIALS, VINTAGE We miss a lot of the catchy commercials we grew up with the Chiquita Banana Song, sometimes you feel like a nut, Choo-Choo Charlie b u t  thank *God* the I m a Pepper campaign finally got killed. That freakwad in the rainbow suspenders needed a handful of Valium and a kick in the slats. And Where s the beef? is *sort* of funny again, now, but back in the 80s, it got old just as fast as Can you hear me now? did. We kind of miss tastes great/less filling fights, though. *Kind of.* See also CATCHPHRASES, OVERUSED COMMERCIAL.

COMPUTERS, CLICHÉS ASSOCIATED WITH Computers provide writers particularly those working on suspenseful shows with the handiest plot device imaginable. When our hero is in a big old hurry and racing ahead of evil henchmen, computers cooperate beautifully: Passwords are overridden, directories are easy to navigate, and an entire hard drive s worth of data can be copied to a portable device in a matter of seconds (and all on a totally unfamiliar operating system no one on TV runs Windows?). But when our hero is in jeopardy, passwords get a lot more intractable, files are hidden with nonintuitive names, and processors are much more sluggish. Really, that s the only way to make a shot of someone keyboarding look exciting even if they re typing really, really fast. But no single show has done more to violate what we actually know about the way computers work than *24*. Yeah, okay, Chloe is some kind of computer savant, but still: She routinely performs programming tasks that no one else on the floor can do and has skillz a hacker would sell his thumbs for. We just want to know where the government buys computers that can move a satellite from Minsk to Reseda in eleven seconds, because we know it ain t no Best Buy. See also *ALIAS*; INTERNET, CLICH S ASSOCIATED WITH; and *24*.

COOL, TV SIGNIFIERS OF An hour of TV time is actually not very long, so when you have to let the viewer know that a character is cool in as economical a fashion as possible, there are several clich s at your disposal: smoking; wearing sunglasses, pointedly (often indoors); not being a great student, but not caring or, alternatively, not trying much in class but doing lots of independent reading, especially of Hemingway or the Beats; leather jacket; disdain of organized extracurriculars; being a musician or having a band; having a job involving manual labor; driving a vintage convertible; sassing teachers; cutting class; giving other people faintly derisive nicknames; having sideburns. Hacky TV writers who will use this list to invent the next Dylan McKay or Ryan Atwood: You re welcome. See also ARTHUR FONZARELLI ; DYLAN McKAY ; and *O.C., THE*.

COOLEY, TONYA, KIDNEY OF Most seasons of MTV s *The Real World* feature seven roommates. However, the show s eleventh season, set in Chicago, included an eighth: Tonya s kidney. Tonya was a former foster child who, when that sob story failed to bend people to her will, reached into her bag of tricks as a borderline Munchausen syndrome case by whining about her kidney disease while not doing anything to take care of herself (i.e., spending time in the hot tub although dehydration is contraindicated).

Tonya eventually required surgery to deal with her kidney stones but didn t have the money, so she asked some sketchy platonic male friend to pay for it while running him down on the show as a geek with no social interaction. And did we mention that she might have had more money to deal with her excretory system if she hadn t bought herself some big fake boobs? Obviously Tonya s kidneys sucked. They were in Tonya. See also REAL WORLD, THE and UNIVERSALLY REVILED CHARACTERS.

COOPER, ANDERSON We miss Anderson Cooper. We know we can still see him every weeknight on CNN, but in that context, he s just reporting the news (or, actually, he seems to spend more time lashed to a lamppost with bungee cord in the middle of a tropical storm Coop, honey, we really will just take your word for it that it s raining). No, we miss the Anderson Cooper of *The Mole*. As the host of ABC s ratings-challenged but diabolically addictive reality  show, Cooper was a treat. He knew the show was kind of dumb, and that he was supposed to act all self-serious around the contestants, but he just couldn t help being sarcastic about it. The man had a fabulously dry deadpan and a great smirk and the fact that he s a total silver fox didn t hurt. (Would you expect any less from Gloria Vanderbilt s son?) But ultimately, there s nothing sexier in a reality TV host than a sense of humor, and Cooper has that in spades (even as a newsman, thank God). Cooper left *The Mole* after its second season, turning hosting duties over to the far inferior Ahmad Rashad. But Cooper s smirky spirit lives on in *The Amazing Race* s Phil Keoghan. See also KEOGHAN, PHIL; *MOLE, THE*; and REALITY TV, HOSTS OF.

COPS Starting with its infuriatingly addictive theme song (Bad boys, bad boys, whatcha gonna do?), *COPS* will suck you in and make you feel really bad about yourself for finding it entertaining. Some have criticized the show for its pro-cop bias, but they are pinkos. Seriously, the show definitely isn t winning any Peabodys by airing footage of drunken rednecks being escorted unwillingly out of various Arkansas bars pantsless, of course but in our experience, the viewer s allegiance naturally attaches not to the predator, but to its prey. In much the same way you might, while watching nature programming, root for the gazelle to outrun the lion, so does *COPS* make you cheer on the drunken joyrider . . . before he runs into a highway median and gets dragged out of the car by fourteen angry police officers, during which scuffle his pants fall off. Of course. See also *AMERICA'S MOST WANTED* and THEME SONGS.

COSBY SHOW, THE The sitcom that saved NBC and made its Thursday-night lineup a must-see destination, *The Cosby Show* was revolutionary in the mid- 80s for portraying an African-American family headed by two (2!) professionals: Bill Cosby s Cliff, an obstetrician, and Phylicia Ayers-Allen/Rashad s Clair, a lawyer. Somehow, in the midst of earning their advanced degrees, Clair and Cliff found the time to have five (5!) children, ranging in age, at the start of the series, from college student Sondra (Sabrina Le Beauf) down to five-year-old Rudy (Keshia Knight Pulliam). The series was also revolutionary in its portrayal of a bunch of kids who, most of the time, were pains in their parents asses and routinely got punished and reprimanded for it. As the years went on, Dr. Cosby apparently started to take his position as a leader among African-American entertainers a little too seriously, using the show as a forum for raising political issues (was there *any* seminal event in the civil rights movement that *none* of the kids grandparents attended?) or a make-work project for aging jazz musicians like Dizzy Gillespie, Lena Horne, and Tito Puente. In the early 90s, FOX took on the aging *Cosby Show* (which by then had replaced nearly all the Cosby kids with various cousins, adoptees, and foundlings) by scheduling *The Simpsons* in the same time slot; the competition killed *The Cosby Show* dead, apparently scrambling Cosby s brains to such a degree that he s never recovered, erasing his legacy as a beloved entertainer by using college commencement speeches to complain that black kids today wear their pants too big, or something. See also BABY, RUINATION OF SHOW BY ADDING; COSBY SWEATER ; DADS, TV; DENISE HUXTABLE ; *DIFFERENT WORLD, A*; PARENTS WHO ARE TOTALLY INTO EACH OTHER TO A CREEPY DEGREE; and *SIMPSONS, THE*.

"COSBY SWEATER" As Dr. Cliff Huxtable, Bill Cosby modeled a series of hideous pullovers known thenceforth as Cosby sweaters. Bright, clashing colors and chaos-theory patterns and textures contributed to an overall impression of vomit in knit form. Still favored by dads around the country. See also *COSBY SHOW, THE*.

"COSMO KRAMER" His livelihood mysterious, his free time apparently limitless, Cosmo Kramer (Michael Richards) was the apotheosis of TV s wacky neighbor archetype: Mrs. Poole was nosy, true, but she was also managing to function reasonably well in society and understood the rules of same. Kramer didn t understand that it s not acceptable to do such things as tell a near-stranger to her face that she d be pretty if she got a nose job; prepare salad in his bathtub, while showering; feed canned pasta to a carriage horse; take a karate class with nine-year-olds; and . . . well, if you ve ever seen *Seinfeld*, you know Kramer s weird. Why Jerry never locked his apartment door is the real mystery. See also MRS. POOLE ; NEIGHBORS, INTRUSIVE; *SEINFELD*; and *SEINFELD*, ALUMNI OF.

COURIC, KATIE Longtime anchor of NBC s *Today*, Couric is known for two things: unrelenting perkiness and a segment on colorectal cancer awareness in which she gave America a guided tour of her digestive tract. But from where we sit, all the espresso-fueled perk in the world can t conceal the fact that Katie s a bit of a rag. And her legs aren t that great, either. Perhaps that s why, in 2006, she accepted a gig as permanent anchor of *CBS Evening News*, where her famous gams wouldn t be on such prominent display. See also CURRY, ANN; LAUER, MATT; and *TODAY*, WINDOW OUTSIDE.

COURT TV If umpteen *Law & Order* and *CSI* spin-offs don t satisfy your bloodlust, Court TV is willing and able to fulfill all your true-crime needs live trial coverage and commentary all day, *I, Detective*

and *Forensic Files* all night. It s like Ann Rule in cathode-ray form trashy and embarrassing, but addictive. Dominick Dunne s show (*Power, Privilege, and Justice*) is a rip-off although he s barely in it himself, which is a plus but *Forensic Files* is a good time, if only for the narrator, who tears into each line with hamtastic gusto and has a really strange Snidely Whiplash way of pronouncing murder as *mur-ther*. His name is Peter Thomas and we d like to shake his hand. See also *CSI* and *LAW & ORDER* FRANCHISE.

"COUSIN OLIVER" The Cousin Oliver character (played by Robbie Rist) joined *The Brady Bunch* in the show s final episodes, basically because the Brady kids themselves had gotten too old for the adorable antics a family-hour sitcom relies on for market share. It s probably the first example of a  show plunging an EpiPen of cute into its own heart to revive itself, but certainly not the last; nor is it the last time it didn t work. The term Cousin Oliver, which can also be used as a verb, is now synonymous with desperate but futile endgame moves designed to stave off cancellation. See also BABY, RUINATION OF SHOW BY ADDING; *BRADY BUNCH, THE*; and CHILDREN, OVERLY PRECOCIOUS.

CROSS, DAVID Although we don t really know anything at all about him in real life, we feel as if we probably would get along well with David Cross just because he is at the center of the Venn diagram of so many of the TV shows we like. In addition to his membership in the casts of such legendarily great TV series as *Arrested Development* and *Mr. Show with Bob and David* (which would be enough to make himself a nice little legacy), Cross has also written for the TV series *Tenacious D* and guested on some of our favorite cult shows, such as *Strangers with Candy*, *Aqua Teen Hunger Force*, *NewsRadio*, and *Home Movies*. He also rocked *Celebrity Poker Showdown*. In an episode in which the players were made up of four *Arrested Development* stars plus Peter Facinelli (randomly), Cross was the most openly (and hilariously) hostile to and dismissive of The Fatch, ultimately beating the poseurish pants off him. But all his other work on TV pales in comparison to his first guest-starring appearance on *Just Shoot Me!* as Elliott s slow brother Donnie, who turns out just to be faking his mental disability so that his mother will coddle him and he won t have to get a job. *Just Shoot Me!* was a pretty crappy show, but David Cross made the first Donnie episode (there was a second that wasn t as good, after Donnie has to go back to acting like he s of normal intelligence) an instant classic. See also *AQUA TEEN HUNGER FORCE*; *CELEBRITY POKER SHOWDOWN*; FACINELLI, PETER THE FATCH ; and GUEST STARS, FREQUENT/FAMOUS.

CROSS, MARCIA Don t we all remember the shock we felt when Marcia Cross, as *Melrose Place* s crazy-ass Dr. Kimberly Shaw, took off her wig to reveal that giant scar on her head? It wasn t enough: She then decided to secure her place in TV history by playing berhomemaker Bree Van De Kamp on *Desperate Housewives*. (In between, she showed up as Linda Abbott, Treat Williams s HIV-positive love interest on *Everwood*, but that was a respectable job; let s not dwell on it.) Bree is an anal-retentive dynamo, exerting the same drive for perfection on her children that she does on her osso bucco; also, you have to respect a woman who can make a twinset look so sexy. Unfortunately, a May 2005 *Vanity Fair* profile of the *Housewives* stars made Cross come across as a demanding, unhinged bitch on wheels, actually making us feel sorry for her irritating costar Teri Hatcher. Pity. See also *DESPERATE HOUSEWIVES* and *MELROSE PLACE*.

CROSSOVERS It s a shame that crossover episodes so often seem, you know . . . desperate, like the time *ER* s Susan Lewis (Sherry Stringfield) headed to New York City to track down her sister Chloe via a *Third Watch* episode, in an obvious (and fruitless) attempt to boost the latter show s ratings. The ones that work can give both series a shot in the arm, like the *Law & Order*/*Homicide* one that featured Briscoe and Munch sniping at each other like the world s crustiest (and, since it involved Munch, pockiest . . . sorry, Belzer) married couple. And the *Buffy*/*Angel* crossovers always came as something of a relief we d rather see spin-offs do joint eps with their parent shows than characters pretending to have just gotten off the phone with various former characters that aren t on the parent show anymore. We get it. But what we d *really* like to see is more crossovers of the wacky variety, like *The Amazing Race* meets *The Sopranos* or something. We don t know. Just go for broke, network VPs in charge of cross-promotion! See also *ANGEL*; *BUFFY THE VAMPIRE SLAYER*; *ER*; *HOMICIDE: LIFE ON THE STREET*; and *LAW & ORDER* FRANCHISE.

CROUSE, LINDSAY, MENTALLY UNBALANCED THERAPISTS PLAYED BY On film, Lindsay Crouse is an accomplished performer, playing strong, unflappable women. On TV, the lady is bonkers. Well, not always she played a cop on *Dragnet* and a doctor on *ER* but she s also made herself the go-to choice to play therapists or psychologists who are kind of disturbed themselves. On *Buffy*, Crouse was Dr. Maggie Walsh: ball-busting psych prof by day, government-contracted demon researcher by night. Maggie s pet project was Adam, a superdemon Frankensteined together from parts of various dead beasties who surprise! awoke to life and instantly killed her. On her first *Law & Order* appearance, she was therapist to a murdered girl s boyfriend who essentially talked him into killing her and, also, was sleeping with him. And on one of *CSI* s many people who have sex in any way other than the heterosexual missionary position have mental problems and want to kill you plots, Crouse played a transsexual therapist with a sideline in performing unlicensed gender reassignment surgery. We really hope all of these characters would have been in jeopardy of losing their American Psychological Association memberships. See also *BUFFY THE VAMPIRE SLAYER*; *CSI*; and *LAW & ORDER* FRANCHISE.

CRYING, FAKE/BAD There s always a handful of good criers on T V *ER* s Julianna Margulies, *Buffy* s Sarah Michelle Gellar, and the queen of naturalistic weepers, Claire Danes of *My So-Called Life* women (and a few men) who can call it up when they need it and aren t afraid to get a little red-lipped and puffy. And then there s . . . everyone else. You d think, for all the angsting they did on *thirtysomething*, the cast would have mastered the crying thing, but only Patricia Wettig, who played Nancy, really had the hang of it; Mel Harris looked like she d eaten a large jalape o, and Ken Olin, who probably sobbed the most frequently, consistently sounded like he had an actual frog in his throat. Some actors just don t have the tools to summon up tears on command; others (i.e., soap actors) have so much makeup on that messing it up with a genuine bawl isn t the smart play. So in an emotional scene, the viewer is enjoying a close-up, and then there s a weird cutaway shot so the makeup lady can skulk in and work her glycerin magic, and then it s back to the close-up, in which a cosmetically perfect tear is now rolling at a stately pace down the exact middle of the actor s cheek. Cue the constipation faces; it s Cry City, and Luke Perry s the mayor. See also ACTING, WOODEN; *BEVERLY HILLS 90210*; *ER*; GELLAR, SARAH MICHELLE; *MY SO-CALLED LIFE*; SCENERY, CHEWERS OF; and *THIRTYSOMETHING*.

"CRYING PAM" It s hard to communicate how completely awesome Crying Pam is without a video feed, but we ll do our best. So there was this episode of *Trading Spaces*. One couple Pam and . . . her husband, whose name is forgotten by history and doesn t matter anyway was getting a living-room makeover, and left a note on the (ordinary, unspectacular) fireplace that it wasn t to be touched.

Unfortunately, their designer was Doug, for whom a don t touch sign is like a red cape to a bull. Over his own team s strenuous objections, Doug built a wooden fireplace surround basically, a fa ade to conceal the fireplace s ugly brick. Upon the reveal, Pam noted the fireplace and told host Paige Davis, You guys are going to be fixing that in a little bit. Paige tried to get her to see more of what she liked, but Pam was having none of it and left the room. So she s offscreen, except her body mic is still on, so when she starts *crying* about the state of her living room, it s totally audible to the viewer at home. In the aftermath of the episode s airing, Pam visited *TS* message boards online and defended her juvenile behavior by saying that she had been distressed throughout the episode s filming due to a sick relative even though in all the footage we d seen of her while she was working on her neighbors house, she was in a perfectly jocular mood, joking with designer Frank and henpecking her husband. So, nice spin, Pam, but we re not buying it, and now you ve been on national (cable) television acting like an asshole. We hope the free slipcovers were worth it. See also HOME MAKEOVER SHOWS.

CSI Sure, you can watch *CSI: Crime Scene Investigation* as a straight-up police procedural but why? First of all, it isn t really straight-up : The crime-scene investigators don t just process evidence, they also interrogate suspects and Take! It! Personally! just like real cops. Second of all, there s so much to mock on the show starting with CSI Sara Sidle s (Jorja Fox) on-again, off-again, back on-again, off-and-drunk-again crush on her boss, Gil Grissom (William Petersen); Sara s bitchfaced competition with Nick Stokes (George Eads) and Catherine Willows (Marg Helgenberger) for the honor of Gil s Favorite; and Sara s desperate need for a hot oil treatment. It probably sounds like we re picking on Sara, but at least she managed not to blow up the lab, *Catherine*, or insert herself into literally dozens of conflict-of-interest-y cases involving her father, *Catherine*, or get so much Botox that she can t frown anymore, *Marg Helgenberger*. (Although, in Marg s defense, if she doesn t have the prettiest hair on TV, she s at least in the top five.) The show rode America s interest in criminology to the top of the ratings and never looked back, spawning two reasonably successful spin-offs (*CSI: Miami* and *CSI: NY*) and introducing the world to the yumminess that is Gary Dourdan. But that doesn t mean it s always good, or that it couldn t afford to be a bit less judgmental of alternative lifestyles and single women who enjoy sex. And whoever s in charge of Foley design on that show needs to turn the mics down; we get that human tissue is squishy. We don t have to hear the bullets squelching through it every single time. . . . It s weird, but every time Archie Kao is on screen, we forgive the show all its sins. See also AUTOPSIES; *CSI*, SPIN-OFFS OF; GIL GRISSOM ; RED HERRING, TOOLS FOR IDENTIFICATION OF ON COP SHOWS; SCIENCE, IGNORANCE OF; and TAKING! IT! PERSONALLY!.

CSI, SPIN-OFFS OF   *CSI: Crime Scene Investigation*, which premiered on CBS in the fall of 2000, has turned into a real hit machine. After *CSI*, set in Las Vegas, there came *CSI: Miami* in 2002 and *CSI: NY* in 2004. (A guest star—heavy episode of *CSI* set in Los Angeles toward the end of the 2004—5 season caused widespread speculation that before long there would be a fourth *CSI: LA* but as of this writing it hasn t happened.) While *CSI* captured TV lightning in a bottle with a likable, nicely balanced cast, unusual cases, and a refreshingly little-used setting, the series that came afterward have been cynical carbon copies of the original; as well, the addition of two more forensic procedurals in primetime has meant they keep cannibalizing one another s ripped-from-the-headline story ideas. See also *CSI* and HORATIO CAINE.

"CULT SHOW," DEFINITION OF   Sometimes a cult show does okay in the ratings (*Buffy the Vampire Slayer*); sometimes (read: usually), it doesn t, and gets canceled quickly (*Wonderfalls*). Sometimes a cult show is an artistic triumph that nobody watched (*Freaks and Geeks*); sometimes it s more of a campy thing that viewers found endearing, or just plugged into for whatever reason (*Star Trek*). Sometimes it s a case where the network didn t know what to do with the show, stuffed it into various bad time slots, then gave up on it and pulled the plug (*My So-Called Life*). But regardless of their relative quality, or what critics thought of them, the characteristic that all cult shows share is the fierce, bordering-on-monomaniacal loyalty the audience has for them (thus the cult comparison). *Star Trek* is, of course, the gold standard of cultiness; long before the Internet was a gleam in some Defense Department Spock-ear-wearer s eye, Trekkies (or Trekkers, as some of them prefer to be called . . . or nerds, as they are actually called) gathered for conventions and delved into the minutiae of their beloved program. If a show has gatherings devoted to it; if its fans have special names for themselves; if the fans have organized, over the Internet or otherwise, elaborate mail-in campaigns involving plot-related tokens in order to save the show; or if the show spawns a higher-than-normal amount of fan fiction, filk, needlepointed representations of its stars, et cetera, then it s probably a cult show. And you should probably criticize the show in question extreeeeeemely gingerly. *Doctor Who* may be dippy, but it s not worth losing an eye over. See also ACTING, WOODEN; *ANGEL*; *BEVERLY HILLS 90210*; *BUFFY THE VAMPIRE SLAYER*; *MY SO-CALLED LIFE*; and *STAR TREK* FRANCHISE.

CURRY, ADAM An extremely tall MTV VJ with poofy hesher hair that vaguely resembled a bonnet, Curry started out hosting *Top 20 Countdown* and *Head-bangers' Ball*, then sort of became the face of the network for a while in the 80s. Curry went on to found an Internet company, then sold it, then starred in a Dutch *Osbournes*-style reality show about himself, and . . . is still really, really tall. See also MTV VJs.

CURRY, ANN If Ann Curry has ever made it through an entire *Today* broadcast without flubbing at the teleprompter, asking a subject a pointless question (or one he s already answered), or starting a sentence without knowing how it s going to end, we haven t seen it. She once teased a segment about a presidential  biography by saying it contains evidence that Bill Clinton may have been gay; she meant *Abraham Lincoln*, as Al Roker was quick to correct her. *Radar* magazine named her one of the dumbest people in news, and we were gratified to have our view corroborated in the press. We love to hate her incompetent ass. See also COURIC, KATIE; LAUER, MATT; and *TODAY*, WINDOW OUTSIDE.

D

DADS, TV Although TV can be revolutionary and world-changing in many ways, its depiction of dads still tends to be steadfastly traditional: TV dads are disciplinarians (*The Cosby Show*), seldom interact with their kids (Ross on *Friends*), have a hard time accessing their emotions (Luke Danes on *Gilmore Girls*), and favor advice riddled with platitudes (Mike Brady of the *Bunch*, Jim Walsh of *90210*, and Jonathan Kent of *Smallville*). When fathers deviate from the 50s model, it s usually to scare the hell out of us, whether because they re bringing their daughters to work with them at their incredibly dangerous government intelligence jobs (Jacks Bauer and Bristow, of *24* and *Alias*), or performing in a transsexual Las Vegas cabaret act (Chandler s dad on *Friends*), or dangling their chicken-resembling babies over the mouths of hungry crocodiles (Steve Irwin, *Crocodile Hunter*), or . . . anything

Homer Simpson has ever done. But despite all the TV scribes who ve apparently made it their life s work to dramatize their view that no father can ever be trusted or relied upon (*Joss Whedon*), some contemporary shows are trying to expand the definition of what it means to be a father on TV. We like Jason Bateman s Michael Bluth, who though a pushy Type A who s turned his son into a little clone of himself, only so screwed up that he has a crush on his cousin always acts out of love. (Scary love.) See also BATEMANS, JASON AND JUSTINE; *BEVERLY HILLS 90210*; *BRADY BUNCH, THE*; *COSBY SHOW, THE*; *FRIENDS*; *GILMORE GIRLS*; IRWIN, STEVE; JACK BAUER ; JACK BRISTOW ; PARENTS/PARENTING, BAD; ROSS GELLER ; *SIMPSONS, THE*; and WHEDON, JOSS.

DALLAS Everything s bigger in Te x a s even primetime soap operas. The glamorous exploits of the oil-millionaire Ewing clan so captivated audiences that its run spanned a remarkable *three decades*. (Okay, it barely made it into the 90s, finally giving up the ghost in 1991, but still.) For the most part, the plots revolved around the usual primetime soap material shady financial dealings, marital infidelity but is remembered for a couple of key elements: 1) Who Shot J.R.?, still among TV s legendary season-finale cliffhangers; 2) that thing where a entire season s worth of events, including the death of Patrick Duffy s Bobby, was totally negated when it all turned out to be a dream on the part of Pam (Jhirmack spokesmodel Victoria Principal). The show directly spawned *Knots Landing* and indirectly spawned *Dynasty* when Esther and Richard Shapiro, ably assisted by Aaron Spelling, blatantly ripped it off. See also CLIFFHANGERS; *DYNASTY*; and SPELLING, AARON.

DALY, CARSON   Despite a well-known lack of charisma, talent, or even good looks, Carson Daly has been fortunate to land a succession of  notable broadcasting jobs; first, he presided over the afternoon squeeeeee! -fest *TRL*, cheerfully sucking up to celebrities in all media and with varying degrees of cred; he was also deployed to emcee all manner of MTV specials, from *Blow the Boat: Isle of MTV Summer Launch* to *A Very Busta Christmas*. When he tried to branch out with a new challenge on another network, it was, unfortunately, to host his own talk show, *Last Call with Carson Daly*, on NBC; fortunately, the show airs at 1:35 AM, where it is seen only by high-rise security guards and actual vampires . . . when *Maury* is a rerun. Daly has also evinced some luck with the ladies having been engaged to Tara Reid and dated Jennifer Love Hewitt though not any ladies you d want to spend more than nineteen seconds with. See also HEWITT, JENNIFER LOVE; MTV VJs; TALK SHOWS, LATE-NIGHT; and *TRL*.

DANCING WITH THE STARS   It shouldn t have worked. We saw the promos for the first season and laughed up our urban-sophisticate sleeves, mocking the dorkiness of ballroom dancing generally and of ABC s reality-show variant specifically, with its D-list stars and its Bedazzled costumes. Then we watched the first episode just out of curiosity, just to make fun of it! and came face to face with Joey McIntyre s ass, and dear reader, we were hooked. That boy could move! And the black trousers he wore for his Latin numbers clung to him in all the right places. The rest of the dancers were okay, t o o particularly *Seinfeld* s John O Hurley, who took to ballroom dancing like a natural but we only planned to watch as long as Joey was on. And then we got sucked in and started talking like we knew a *paso doble* from a *merengue*. The entire thing is so earnestly cheesy, from the self-serious judges to the ridiculous faces the dancers make to further sell their routines, that it would take a real churl not to be charmed by it. However, the first season was marred by a finale in which underdog (and ABC soap star) Kelly Monaco got triple 10s the only perfect score of the season for a routine in which even laymen (us) could tell she tripped over her feet, while her fellow finalist O Hurley tripped the light fantastic and got robbed. Viewers cried fix! and the entire debacle left us suspicious of the show going forward. Plus we could never be all that interested in a season that lacked a Joey McIntyre.

"DANNY PARTRIDGE" The ur-wisecracking sitcom kid. Danny Bonaduce s chunky, freckled wisenheimer blazed the trail for generations of preternaturally insightful sitcom spawn, horndoggy younger brothers, and substance-abusing former child stars. This precocity is usually played for cuteness today, but The Dooch and his *Partridge Family* costars seemed to know he was annoying and made Danny s campaign to drive Reuben crazy into a running gag. See also CHILDREN, OVERLY PRECOCIOUS and *PARTRIDGE FAMILY, THE*.

DANSON, TED Washed-up ballplayer Sam Malone, of *Cheers*, was supposed to be the hottest thing on TV, but even when we were kids, we were like, . . . Him? Sam the role that made his career was annoyingly fratty, but Ted Danson was pretty funny playing him, especially considering he had to do so opposite an insufferably pretentious nag (Shelley Long) and a screeching, neurotic mess (Kirstie Alley). Considering that he s known in actuality to be a toupee-wearer, the jokes about Sam s hair obsession suggest a man who can laugh at himself. Danson went on to headline the short-lived *Ink* (opposite wife Mary Steenburgen) and the bizarrely tenacious but critically unloved *Becker*, but no matter: In *Cheers*, he left a fine legacy. See also AGING OF MEN ON TV, UNGRACEFUL; ALLEY, KIRSTIE; and *CHEERS*.

DARK SHADOWS It was a soap opera. That aired during the day. About vampires. And lasted, like, five seasons. These are the sorts of pitches that could actually make it into production back when there were only three channels. Still, it remains an enduring cult classic. Really, there s no accounting for taste. See also *ANGEL* and *BUFFY THE VAMPIRE SLAYER*.

DAVEY AND GOLIATH Generations of American children awakened early on Sunday mornings and, hoping for the same embarrassment of animated riches that awaited them on Saturday mornings, turned on their televisions to find a stop-motion-animated series sponsored by the Lutheran Church, in which suburban square Davey and his talking dog Goliath (prone to disappointed utterances of *Day*-vee!) learned valuable moral lessons through the magic of talking Play-Doh. And also the Lord. Allegedly. A poor substitute for *Muppet Babies*, but at that hour on a Sunday, it was that or a test pattern. See also CALIFORNIA RAISINS.

"DAWN SUMMERS" For the first four seasons of *Buffy*, our titular heroine was an only child. Then, suddenly, in Season 5, she had a kid sister named Dawn. At least, due to the show s supernatural plotlines, the blatant Cousin Oliver -ing could be wedged into the plot: The Key, some kind of mystical energy source, was turned into a fourteen-year-old girl (Michelle Trachtenberg) and assigned to the slayer s care for protection from Glory, an evil god. Everyone around Dawn was programmed to think they d always known her, much as she was loaded up with counterfeit memories. Like all younger siblings, Dawn was a pill, always trying to tag along with Buffy. Eventually, everyone (including Dawn) figured out what she was; her mother s death caused her to act out in inappropriate but all too predictable ways (oooh, shoplifting *and* breaking curfew? Call the feds!). But on the whole, Dawn bugged less than a lot of *Buffy* characters did, *Anya*. See also *BUFFY THE VAMPIRE SLAYER* and COUSIN OLIVER.

"DAWSON LEERY" We defy you to name a less likable lead character. Show creator

Kevin Williamson named *Dawson's Creek* after his so-called hero because Dawson really did think he owned the creek and everyone who lived near it. Dawson s unpleasant traits include, but certainly are not limited to: a con-descending attitude; cheesy directorial aspirations and the selection of middle-of-the-road *not-teur* Spielberg as his film-making hero; consistent rudeness to and patronization of his parents; smugness; a sense of entitlement whose basis remains a mystery; owning a stuffed E.T. doll; judging those who have had more sex than he (i.e., anyone at all); wrecking an expensive boat because he couldn t think of another way to manipulate or control Joey Potter emotionally; constant sneering at the problems of Pacey Witter, ostensibly his best friend; wearing XXXXL khakis; flapping his arms like a junior-high drama club vice president; a by-turns poofy and greasy zipperhead hair-don t; and a drive-in movie screen—sized forehead. In later seasons of *DC*, it seemed like the writers had *finally* caught on to what we d known all along: Dawson is an asswad (and interviews with James Van Der Beek, who played Dawson, in which the Beek blathered on pretentiously about top-shelf tequilas and complained about getting recognized, suggested that the role might have been type-

cast). And when Joey finally, *finally* ankled The Fivehead in favor of Pacey, we cheered. See also CRYING FAKE/BAD; *DAWSON'S CREEK*; FASHION, HILARIOUS ATTEMPTS OF TV GUYS IN 90S AT; PACEY WITTER ; SOULMATE ; TEENAGERS, BRATTY; and UNIVERSALLY REVILED CHARACTERS.

DAWSON'S CREEK Even for a teen melodrama, this effort is overcooked and underseasoned. It started with too few characters, so that we were sick of their predictable love triangles even before the first season was out. There s also Dawson (James Van Der Beek): judgmental, self-centered, pompous, smug, already balding even though he was playing a high school sophomore. Dawson s wide-ranging loathsomeness was all the more noticeable due to the show s likable core supporting cast Joshua Jackson, Michelle Williams, Mary Beth Peil who all did what they could to make Kevin Williamson s pretentiously overwrought prose sound natural. Katie Holmes, as Joey, the female point in the show s central love triangle, became less of a tomboy and more of a doormat over the run of the series, getting passed around among the show s various himbos (including a prof, ew), and by the time she emerged on the other side to make bad movies and get engaged to Tom Cruise, we d forgotten why we d ever liked her (although marriage to a barking-mad Scientologist isn t even in the top ten meanest fantasies we ever entertained with regard to her future). In general, the show gave you exactly what you expected Jen (Williams), as a teenage girl who enjoyed sex, never really found true love and got killed off with a mysterious heart affliction in the series finale, to name but one example but the show got one thing right, ending with Joey and Pacey (Jackson) happily together, leaving Dawson alone to come up with the fortieth fictional gloss on his dull-ass adolescence. See also DAWSON LEERY ; HIGH SCHOOL, UNREALISTIC PORTRAYALS OF; JACK MCPHEE ; LOVE TRIANGLES; PACEY WITTER ; TEEN SEX, CONSEQUENCES OF; and UNIVERSALLY REVILED CHARACTERS.

DAY AFTER, THE Remembered by millions of 80s kids as the single most terrifying universal formative event of their childhoods (until the *Challenger* disaster two years later), *The Day After* dramatized the aftermath of a nuclear strike on American soil. Critics complained both that it was too sensationalistic a topic to be covered on such a vapid medium as TV and that it soft-soaped some of the catastrophic effects of nuclear warfare. The lasting effects of the film on us include a somewhat irrational terror of all apocalyptic events; a certainty that if we were among the few survivors of any major extinction-level event, humanity would be in a lot of trouble, since we d have no real skills to contribute; and a horror of any depiction, however absurd, of radiation sickness, which forced us to cover our eyes when a scene in *Alias* s fourth season included what we still hysterically term floppy fingers!!! *The Day After* is available on DVD now, but even as adults, we may be too chicken to watch it again. See also *ALIAS* and MOVIES, MADE-FOR-TV.

DEAD EYES See BANKS, TYRA.

"DEAD SCOTT" The first season of *Beverly Hills 90210* concerned the attempts of two pairs to break into the school s ruling clique: Brandon and Brenda Walsh (Jason Priestley and Shannen Doherty), as sophomores, succeeded; David Silver (Brian Austin Green) and his best elementary-school friend Scott Scanlon (Douglas Emerson), as freshmen, did not. In the second season, however, it became advantageous to the plot for David to break into the show s core clique, by way of his father s marriage to the mother of Jennie Garth s Kelly. The dorky, corn-fed Scott could not follow David into the promised land, however. After spending the summer at a relative s ranch, he appeared back at school sporting a cowboy hat. As he and David drifted apart, he threw a party, invited the cool kids, and,

when he could tell he was losing the room, tried to show off by demonstrating the facility he d learned with firearms. Naturally, the punk ended up accidentally shooting himself in the stomach and dying. Thereafter, Scott was swiftly forgotten, except when the plot required a reminder of the fragility of human life, in which case poor old Dead Scott s corpse was very briefly invoked. Eh, he was kind of a chump anyway. See also BEVERLY HILLS 90210; BRANDON WALSH ; BRENDA WALSH ; and DORKINESS, TV SIGNIFIERS OF.

DEAN MARTIN CELEBRITY ROASTS, THE, **COMMERCIALS FOR** Aired in an unbroken paid-programming loop on some basic cable stations, the half-hour ads for *The Dean Martin Celebrity Roasts* are inexplicably addictive; everyone s drunk (except Dino, whose highball of bourbon is actually apple juice), falling off chairs, and teasing each other horribly while wearing caftans and Lew Wasserman glasses. It s a window into another time, when what we call substance abuse was considered nighttime and folks like Lucille Ball and Don Rickles hadn t passed out face-down on their laurels yet. The infomercial ran all the best parts (particularly the crackling sexual tension between Phyllis Diller and Ruth Buzzi), so you needn t have bothered buying the whole thing and if you did, you were disappointed. If the combination of celebrities; bad, double-entendriffic one-liners; and booze in evidence here didn t give producers the idea for *Match Game*, it s the greatest coincidence in history. See also *MATCH GAME*.

DEGRASSI JUNIOR HIGH There wasn t anything like this on American T V a *Saved by the Bell/Afterschool Special* hybrid starring kids who looked and talked like real kids with real pores and real butts (which they were) so when *Degrassi Junior High* came to PBS, we ate it up. *Degrassi* dealt with Issues large and small pregnancy, suicide, wet dreams, how to shoot a video, parental divorce in an earnestly dorky but not condescending way. The sincerity v rit could make it squirmy to watch, like when Claude woos Caitlin, fails, and kills himself, or when Erica goes all PTSD bitchface on Heather, or any time keyboard-guitar-heavy band the Zit Remedy is on screen. Everybody wants something they ll never give up, indeed starting with Wheels going *up a size*, oh my God. See also *ABC AFTERSCHOOL SPECIALS*; *DEGRASSI: THE NEXT GENERATION*; and *SAVED BY THE BELL*.

DEGRASSI: THE NEXT GENERATION More of the same, but with (duh) a new generation of junior high and high schoolers and recurring roles for Joey Jeremiah and Snake (both a bit thin on top), Spike, and Mr. Raditch. All the way with Paige Michalchuk doesn t have quite the same ring to it, but the new version is just as cringily awesome as the original and covers the same breadth of PSA-worthy topics at least, in its Canadian incarnation. (An episode dealing with a character s abortion wasn t permitted to air in the States boo!) See also *DEGRASSI JUNIOR HIGH* and HIGH SCHOOL, UNREALISTIC PORTRAYALS OF.

"DENISE HUXTABLE" Lisa Bonet s Denise, second-eldest Huxtable offspring, was the height of sophisticated teenagerhood. She had an inexhaustible supply of large, geometric earrings and huge, unwieldy blouses that she wore with the sleeves rolled and  the collars up, accented with a brooch over the top button, a belt slung over them around her hips, and leggings. (It was cool at the time!) Then she starred in *Cosby* spin-off *A Different World*, in which Denise did other glamorous olderperson things like live in a dorm and get hit on by Dwayne Wayne. But in fact, Bonet was blank-eyed most of the time and delivered her lines either in a monotone or in a screeching whine. But lots of young girls couldn t see those faults when looking at Denise with the eyes of love. Which happen to have a lot in common with the eyes of dumb preteens who don t have any older teenaged role models and don t know any better. See also ACTING, WOODEN; COSBY SHOW, THE; and DIFFERENT WORLD, A.

DESIGNING WOMEN The Golden Girls + Workplace — Bad Hips = *Designing Women*. The long-running CBS sitcom brought us all into the intimate inner workings of an Atlanta interior-design firm headed by Julia Sugarbaker (the badass Dixie Carter) and her flighty sister Suzanne (Delta Burke) and employing mousy designer Mary Jo (Annie Potts) and slightly dim Ozarks refugee Charlene (Jean Smart). The sassy ladies often playing out social-policy debates as written by the show s feminist producer, Linda Bloodworth-Thomason were tended in their seldom industrious workplace by company eunuch Anthony (Meshach Taylor), who was a handyman or something. Toward the end, original cast members Burke and Smart bailed, leaving two slots to be filled by a succession of lesser lights (yes, lesser than Delta Burke) including Julia *Newhart* Duffy, Jan *SNL* Hooks, and Judith Who? Ivey. If you catch it on Lifetime, stick to the pre- 91 episodes. See also *GOLDEN GIRLS, THE* and RECASTING, NOTORIOUS.

DESPERATE HOUSEWIVES It s hard to say that *Desperate Housewives* is the most overrated show in TV history. But if you downgraded that to most overrated show since *Ally McBeal*, you d have it about right. *Housewives* exploded onto the scene in the fall of 2004 and became an instant hit for ABC, offering viewers a campy take on the primetime soap (starting with the grabby series title, suggestive of midafternoon assignations and trashy lingerie stashed between orderly stacks of cashmere sweaters). The storylines for the first season were straight out of the soap playbook: drug abuse, closeted homosexuality, spying, suicide, dubious paternity, extramarital affairs, a baby sold for cash . . . yawn. So since producers couldn t grab us with their groundbreaking plots, they went for a quasi-satiric tone which was, admittedly, a bit more arch than anything on *Dallas* or *Dynasty*, but still hardly qualified it as the *comedy* it kept billing itself as at awards time so it wasn t competing with *Six Feet Under* or *Deadwood*. And anyway, the funny moments most of which seem to revolve around the clumsiness of Susan (Teri Hatcher), the obsessive Martha Stewartitude of Bree (Marcia Cross), the petulant childishness of Gabrielle (Eva Longoria), the open hatred toward her children of Lynette (Felicity Huffman), and the boobs of Edie (Nicollette Sheridan) are . . . not that funny. Don t get us wrong the show is okay, and God knows its first season sucked us in and wouldn t let go but the more overpraised it is by rapturous critics, the worse it looks when you actually watch it. The show also loses points for having obviously been headed toward the revelation that Bree s husband Rex (Steven Culp) wasn t sleeping with her because he was gay, but then pulling its punches by making him an S&M devotee instead. We expect better from a show created by a gay man, even if he does call himself a Republican. See also CROSS, MARCIA; DRUG ABUSE, PORTRAYALS OF; HOMOSEXUALITY, CODED; HUFFMAN, FELICITY; MOTHER-DAUGHTER RELATIONSHIPS, OVERLY CLOSE; SMALL TOWNS, HIDDEN DEPRAVITY OF; and TEENAGERS, BRATTY.

DEVANE, WILLIAM   Runty, toothy veteran of *Knots Landing* and many, many TV movies, Devane, like Shatner and Hasselhoff, is not a great thespian but gives 130 percent every second he s on screen. Devane turned up most recently on *24* as the secretary of defense, a hawkish hard-ass who authorized the torture of his own son to get information. Frankly, we prefer the mean neocon Billy D to the one we were expected to buy as a sex symbol, because as much as we love the guy, he looks like that short dude in the Beach Boys. That is to say: not so much with the hot. See also HASSELHOFF,

DAVID; SHATNER, WILLIAM; and *24*.

DICK CLARK'S NEW YEAR'S ROCKIN' EVE   The fact that Rockin is part of the title makes it a little awesome, but in actuality the annual variety show which cuts between musical acts in a standard TV studio and beleaguered, ever older Dick Clark bundled up in Times Square, giving us updates on how soon the ball is going to drop for those of us who have TVs but not clocks kind of blows. Tends to be the default program to which TVs are turned, just before midnight, at New Year s Eve house parties; otherwise, it s programming fit only for pubescent babysitters. An era ended on New Year s Eve 2004 when, after suffering a stroke, Clark missed New Year s Rockin Eve for the first time in thirty-two years; both Carson Daly and Regis Philbin were poor substitutes. See also DALY, CARSON and PHILBIN, REGIS.

DICKINSON, JANICE   Author, personality, defiant plastic-surgery advocate, and self-declared World s First Supermodel, Janice Dickinson is . . . well, crazy. Though in her younger days she was a renowned drunk, cokehead, and Studio 54 fixture (but we repeat ourselves), Dickinson is known to this generation primarily as the subject of an absolutely scorching *E! True Hollywood Story* and as the awesomest judge on *America's*

Next Top Model. Dickinson is brutally honest to the point of frank tactlessness which made her the perfect housemate for Omarosa Manigault-Stallworth on the fifth season of *The Surreal Life* and on *Top Model*, she always championed the tallest, skinniest girls, who never won. At the end of *Top Model* s fourth season, the show announced that Dickinson would no longer be a judge. Jumped or got pushed? It s a mystery. See also AMER-ICA'S NEXT TOP MODEL; E! TRUE HOLLY-WOOD STORY; OMAROSA; and SURREAL LIFE, THE.

DIFFERENT WORLD, A *A Different World* is to college what *The Facts of Life* was to private boarding school an unrealistically sunny portrait of scholarship that, when imbibed in one s youth, sets one up for crushing disappointment later in life. When Denise Huxtable (Lisa Bonet) left Brooklyn Heights for college, she ended up at Hillman (a barely fictionalized version of Spelman College, a historically African-American school), where she made friends, ran out of money, earned crappy grades for essays she didn t work hard enough on, and left after one year. Hey, maybe it wasn t that unrealistic after all. We lost interest in *World* following the first-season departures of Bonet and Marisa Tomei and the arrival of Sinbad, but the show went on for a staggering total of six seasons, at the end of which

Jada Pinkett was Cousin Olivered in as a sassy freshman. See also COLLEGE, UNRE-ALISTIC PORTRAYALS OF; *COSBY SHOW, THE*; COUSIN OLIVER ; DENISE HUXTABLE ; *FACTS OF LIFE, THE*; and SPIN-OFFS.

DIFF'RENT STROKES See *FACTS OF LIFE, THE* and ORPHANS.

DISNEY SUNDAY MOVIE, THE See EISNER, MICHAEL, HOST OF *THE DISNEY SUNDAY MOVIE*.

DOGS, TV Used for their comedic (read: saccharine, but cheaper than human actors) effect on commercials, dogs also appear on sitcoms; when a human character has just delivered a spazzy, deluded, or otherwise dramatically ironic thinking-out-loud monologue, what better punctuation than a cut-away shot to a dog, humorously barking, whining, or slumping down with its head on its paws and heaving a defeated growly sigh? This is Happy the Dog s primary function on *7th Heaven*, and we don t know who owns that dog, but we think a set visit from the ASPCA is overdue. Dogs also appear in dramas, usually to underscore symbolic upheaval in the human characters personal lives, like when Felicity found the doomed Lucky, or Carrie lost Aidan s dog in the rain on *Sex and the City*. (And went out looking for him wearing four-inch heels, coochie-cutter gym shorts, and a see-through peasant top. Shut up, Carrie.) For some reason, a TV dog is usually a superhairy mutt who peers winningly through his Olsen-twin-esque bangs; we don t know why. Our favorite TV dog is Wishbone, the Jack Russell terrier who dressed up as various literary figures. No, he didn t rescue anyone trapped in a well like Lassie did, but how many times did Lassie or Rin Tin Tin dress up as Homeric heroes? None, that s how many. So there. See also *FELICITY*; *7TH HEAVEN*; and *SEX AND THE CITY*.

DOHERTY, SHANNEN The third Heather, but first in our hearts. Ol Crooked Eyes rocks, if only because Alyssa Milano (allegedly) got her fired from *Charmed* for (allegedly) having a more popular character and getting more screen time. But she also rocks because she patented the Brenda Stomp. If your boyfriend cheats on you with your best friend, don t bitch him out yourself; hire Doherty to do it, because nobody can rip a strip the size of the Autobahn off somebody, say innything a bunch of times, and clomp angrily away quite like she can. She s apparently an acid-flashback nightmare to work with (or get married to boy-band reject Ashley Hamilton lasted only seven months), which got her fired from *90210*; she s rude to interviewers; the producers of *90210* had to digitally remove her from the series-end retrospective; she s

appeared in *Playboy* and gotten sentenced to anger-management classes.

 She is, it s safe to say, a very angry lady, and we can see why, because she doesn t get nearly enough credit for her work in one of the most awesome TV movies ever made, *Friends 'til the End*. Doherty s singing is wretched, Stevie Wonder did her eye makeup, and Jason London looks terrified of her every time they re in a scene together. Genius, we tells ya. See also *BEVERLY HILLS 90210*; BRENDA WALSH ; LONDONS, JASON AND JEREMY, DISTINGUISHING BETWEEN; and MOVIES, MADE-FOR-TV.

DOOGIE HOWSER, M.D. Much as Ed Asner will always be Lou Grant and Sarah Michelle Gellar will always be Buffy Summers, so will Neil Patrick Harris live out the rest of his life as Doogie Howser, M.D. The premise of the show was patently absurd: A genius kid our Doogie graduates from college ridiculously early, goes to medical school, and gets licensed as a doctor at the age of fourteen. You d think any lawsuit-minded hospital would have the foresight not to hire a physician to do such things as pelvic exams before he s old enough to vote, but Doogie does get work as a doctor. He also pursues Wanda (Lisa Dean Ryan) and ignores the advice of best friend Vinnie (Max Casella), who not only doesn t have Doogie s genius IQ but may not even tip the scale with triple digits. You d never know that the show only ran for four seasons if all you had to go on was the widespread use of the Doogie sobriquet elsewhere in pop culture. Fortunately for Harris, he seems to have a sense of humor about himself; we still fondly recall his cameo in a *Roseanne* fantasy sequence, where she goes into the hospital for breast-reduction but instead  gets implants, courtesy of Doogie; and his performance as a horny, balls-tripping version of himself in *Harold & Kumar Go to White Castle* was just adorable. See also BOCHCO, STEVEN; DORKINESS, TV SIGNIFIERS OF; GELLAR, SARAH MICHELLE; *ROSEANNE*; and THE ZIERING.

DOOLEY, PAUL Casting directors had better start looking for a sufficiently crusty replacement for Dooley now, because he s not getting any younger and they re not making TV dads any crustier than this guy. Dooley played a sensitive, helpful dad in Brat Pack film *Sixteen Candles*, but on TV, he s usually dadding it up the surly way: as Patty Chase s grumpy, stubborn dad on *My So-Called Life*; as Susan Lewis s selfish,

grouchy dad on *ER*; and as crazy, gruff Judge Swackheim on *The Practice* a n d while a judge isn t *technically* a dad, in a courtroom setting? Same diff. Who will fill his crusty slippers when he s gone? See also DADS, TV; *ER*; *MY SO-CALLED LIFE*; PARENTS/PARENTING, BAD; and *PRACTICE, THE*.

DORKINESS, TV SIGNIFIERS OF Any actor good-looking and charismatic enough in reality to actually land on TV in the first place probably has only a vague understanding of what dorkiness is. So in order to dramatize a character s supposed lack of cool, a lot of writing, costuming, and prop work is required to really sell it. Standard signifiers of TV dorkiness include: the wearing of glasses; acquisition of/enthusiasm for comic books; ill-fitting trousers; contrasting clothing patterns; participation in less glamorous extracurriculars such as debate club, Model UN, or yearbook; facility with science; easy mental access to a wide range of trivia; composition of unpopular music; awkwardness with the opposite sex; sycophancy toward authority figures; and especially snooty correction of other characters grammar. See also BRODY, ADAM; COOL, TV SIGNIFIERS OF; DEAD SCOTT ; *DOOGIE HOWSER, M.D.*; DUNKLEMAN, BRIAN; MR. FURLEY ; ROSS GELLER ; SAGET, ROBERT LANE; and URKEL.

DOUBLE DARE A game show for kids that alternated questions and physical challenges (read: Slip n Slide obstacle courses involving copious amounts of green slime). What everyone seems to remember about *Double Dare* is that one of the hosts,  Marc Summers, suffered from severe obsessive-compulsive disorder ironic, in light of the heavy slop fire he took for a living. See also CHILDREN S SHOWS, HOSTS OF.

DOUBLE TROUBLE We may have hallucinated this sitcom about a pair of twins who move in with their cool artist aunt in New York City and have twinny, switcheroo-ish adventures, because nobody we ve ever mentioned it to has heard of it. It only lasted a season and a half (the first half season featured the girls living in Des Moines with their widowed father), and the twins (Jean and Liz Sagal, playing Kate and Allison Foster) couldn t really act very well. But we never missed a single episode, because we idolized Kate, the wacky twin or, really, Kate s *ne plus '80s* wardrobe of neon lace fingerless gloves, tiny plaid minis, Chuck Taylors that didn t match, off-the-shoulder Esprit sweatshirts with paint splatters on them, gigantic Madonna-esque hair bows, and so on. Oh, and her superstraight shoulder-length bob, which Kate would sometimes wear with the bottom part straight and the top part crimped. But would our moms let us cut up our clothes that way, or do our hair like that? Nooooo. They said it looked trashy. Allison studied hard and got picked on by her design-school professor, which, boring. We only wanted to see how Kate made a pair of gauchos out of pillowcases. See also BAD SITCOM, SURE SIGNS OF and TWINS IN COMEDIES, FORCED HILARITY OF.

DRAG, MEN IN/CROSS-DRESSING Nothing will stop a sitcom dead for three minutes of audience (or laugh-track) hooting and hollering like the sight of a man in a dress a reality to which Martin Lawrence owes a significant portion of his career. Odd, then, that it . . . isn t that funny. Or edgy. See also BAD SITCOM, SURE SIGNS OF and *BOSOM BUDDIES*.

"DR. DAVE MALUCCI" *ER* has been the home of many hotshot docs over the years starting with the original hotshot, George Clooney s Doug Ross but Dr. Dave Malucci (Erik Palladino) was . . . actually the least hot. Most of the time, he came off as an incompetent boob (the character detail that he d attended medical school in Grenada did nothing to change this impression), and whenever he took dangerous risks in the service of his patients, he was generally wrong. In the end, he misdiagnosed a rare condition, killing a patient not enough in and of itself to do him in professionally, since after all, who at County *hasn't* erroneously killed someone? but when he decided to follow up that brilliant move by screwing a paramedic in her rig, Weaver (Laura Innes) fired his ass on the spot. Suggesting that the writers hated the character as much as most viewers did, Dr. Dave s final words on *ER* consisted of a homophobic slur. Smell ya later, ass. See also CLOONEY, GEORGE and *ER*.

DRINKING GAMES Often, the only way to get through a particularly miserable show without busting a Presleyan cap in the TV set s ass is to fashion a drinking game around the more frequent (or maddening or both) aspects of said show, and let alcohol ease your pain. Games vary according to programming genre, but watching, say, a reality show, you could drink each time there s a reference to integrity or trueness to oneself; a tic of the host; pixelation or a bleeped curse word; or a suspicious edit. For dramas, opportunities to drink might include obvious parallel plotting; violation of the real-time format (*24* only); use of technobabble; or overused transitions (the overhead shot of the hospital on *House*). Sitcoms let you drink on the entrance of the wacky neighbor, the utterance of the signature catchphrase, and so on. The booze helps, don t get us wrong, but TV drinking games really work best when you ve surrounded yourself with like-minded friends and associates who share your shut *up*, Mischa Barton! pain. It s like a support group, but with margaritas. Drink! See also BAD SITCOM, SURE SIGNS OF; CATCHPHRASES, OVERUSED TV; NEIGHBORS, INTRUSIVE; PIXELATION; REALITY TV, LOYALTY AND INTEGRITY ON; and *24*.

DR. PHIL Dr. Phillip C. McGraw man, myth, builder of a psychobabble catchphrase empire met Oprah while consulting on her beef trial, scored a regular slot on her show, and spun it off into his own syndicated tough-love program, *Dr. Phil*. At first, with his giant mustache and down-home phrase-ology, Dr. Phil seems like a refreshingly folksy dispenser of commonsense advice . . . but after a while, the show seems like  it s more about 1) shilling Dr. Phil—branded workbooks and weight-loss products, and 2) reinforcing Dr. Phil s sexist ideas about hearth and home. Dated attitudes, a wife who fell out of the plastic-surgery tree and hit every branch on the way down why do we keep watching? Because *Dr. Phil* guests are a traveling circus married couples who obviously hate each other, moms who still breast-feed their grade-schoolers, sociopathic teens who fondle their little sisters, the neuroticized-beyond-repair Dr. Phil Phamilies and, right or wrong, Phil isn t afraid to yell at them, which is vicariously enjoyable in the extreme. Less enjoyable: his boring infomercially primetime specials. See also DR. PHIL PHAMILIES ; TALK SHOWS, DAYTIME; and WINFREY, OPRAH.

"DR. PHIL PHAMILIES" Screwed-up families agree to undergo the *Dr. Phil* treatment on an ongoing basis, and the show features them once each week. And when we say screwed-up . . . dude. The inaugural Phamily consisted of serial cheater and lack-of-affect poster boy Marty; his ber-controlling, helmet-haired wife, Erin; and their teen daughters, pregnant moron Alex and overlooked Katherine. They were way beyond help, really, as was the next family, headed by another serial cheater, the weepy buck-passer Stacy, but the home audience got to feel smugly superior, which is really the point of the entire enterprise. See also DR. PHIL.

DRUG ABUSE, PORTRAYALS OF Hey, TV characters: Thinking of experimenting with drugs? Think again. Smoking too much pot will kill you (*90210*), or you might take a puff from a doob laced with PCP and jump out a window (the brilliantly named and overacted Just Say No propaganda artifact *Angel Dusted*, starring a pre-Oscar Helen Hunt as the jumper). Cocaine? Oh hell no you ll get addicted in, like, a week (*90210* again), then join a cult after rehab. And don t try meth instead, or your lank-haired boyfriend will flip shit and open fire at your roommates Christmas party (*Felicity*). Prescription drugs forget it. Either you ll get dependent on them, freak out at your daughter for hiding them, then freak out again when she takes a Vicodin thinking it s candy and ODs (*Rescue Me*), or you ll get dependent on them, try to wean yourself off them on a dare, get bitched out by your entire staff, wind up going back on them, and get mocked every episode because you can t deal with chronic pain (*House*). The good news is that your downward spiral will be accomplished over the course of, tops, two hours (less, if you re in a TV movie); the bad news is that networks Standards and Practices departments won t permit any nuance in portrayals of drug use, much less abuse, so expect to be vilified, dead, or both by the end of the story arc. See also ALCOHOLISM; *BEVERLY HILLS 90210*; *FELICITY*; and MARIJUANA, CLICH S ASSOCIATED WITH.

DUCHOVNY, DAVID After kicking off his TV career by playing transgendered FBI agent Denise (formerly Dennis) on *Twin Peaks* and a homely woman he made, too Duchovny landed his big break as narrator Jake Winters on *Red Shoe Diaries*. Ha ha! You thought we were going to say *X-Files*! And that was nice for him, of course, but the man did a lot of *RSD*. Duchovny was fine on *The X-Files,* too: His understated mien served him well in playing FBI agent Fox Mulder, whose belief in UFOs is measured and informed, rather than crazed and wild-eyed. After eight years of whining about how much he hated shooting in Vancouver, he got the show moved to Los Angeles, and then quit, returning for a few scattered episodes and the season finale. While we were annoyed by the show for most of the last five seasons, we have to confess that the eighth-season finale, in 2001 in which Mulder and Scully finally kiss totally gave us the shivers. Duchovny also showed up as one of Carrie s many swains on *Sex and the City* (boo!), and in a recurring guest role on *The Larry Sanders Show*, playing a fictionalized version of himself that happened to have a stalkerish crush on Larry (yay!). Duchovny took a lot of shit for his part in the downward spiral of *The X-Files*, but most of that blame belongs to series creator Chris Carter. Marrying T a Leoni, however well, that s the Duke s

bad, and he just has to live with it. See also ACTING, WOODEN; DRAG, MEN IN/CROSS-DRESSING; MAIN CAST MEMBER DEPARTURES, NOTORIOUS; *SEX AND THE CITY*; TV SERIES, FILM ADAPTATIONS OF; *TWIN PEAKS*; and *X-FILES, THE*.

DUFF Loathsome MTV VJ from the early 90s turned loathsome Almay pitchwoman. Born Karen Duffy, Duff broke two cardinal rules: 1) don t give yourself a nickname, and 2) don t confuse perkiness with cocky self-regard. See also MTV VJs.

DUKES OF HAZZARD, THE How this show stayed on the air for six seasons is beyond us the premise practically defined low-concept (tight-jeaned bootlegger cousins outrun corrupt local law in hot car whose doors don t work; Daisy [Catherine Bach] helps out by wearing coochie-cutter shorts). Plus, the emergency casting of third-generation copies Coy (Byron Cherry) and Vance (Christopher Mayer) when John Bo Schneider and Tom Luke Wopat held out for more money made an already bad show even worse. It certainly didn t merit a Saturday-morning cartoon, much less the feature-film nostalgia treatment twenty years later, but apparently wrecking more than three hundred Dodge Chargers and giving America a guided tour of the bottom half of Catherine Bach s butt cheeks gives you a place in the cultural pantheon. See also LIVE-ACTION SHOWS, ANIMATED VERSIONS OF; RECASTING, NOTORIOUS; and TV SERIES, FILM ADAPTATIONS OF.

DUNKLEMAN, BRIAN When *American Idol* premiered in the summer of 2002, its producers for some reason believed that one host would be insufficient to manage the complicated logistics involved in having kids sing songs and get critiqued. In fact, hosting *AI* is a pretty easy job. So when the show was a huge hit and it came time to get all the talent back on board, maybe Dunkleman short, gawky, wooden in front of the camera, not funny should have realized that one of the hosts would be redundant, and that maybe he shouldn t make a big power play during his negotiations. Alas, he didn t, which is why the producers went with Seacrest, and Dunkleman has been lost to the mists of time. More like Duh-nkleman, right? HA HA! Yeah. See also *AMERICAN IDOL*; REALITY TV, HOSTS OF; and SEACREST, RYAN.

DVD, WATCHING AN ENTIRE TV SEASON IN ONE WEEKEND ON We try to ration the *24* episodes, one or two at a time, but we can t if we don t *have* to wait until next week to see whether Jack disarms the device or Kim gets eaten by that cougar, why should we? So one or two becomes four; then four puts us in the heart of sweeps suspense; then the next thing we know it s Sunday night, and we re sitting in adult diapers or on wee-wee pads on the couch, surrounded by forty-eight hours worth of snack bags and empty Diet Coke cans, heads pounding, cracked out on Kiefer, the Scooby gang, or whatever other show we foolishly opened the plastic on with a na ve Let s just watch a couple episodes, eh? See also MARATHONS and *24*.

"DYLAN MCKAY" Of *90210* s two shelf-haired male leads, Dylan (Luke Perry) was the one who wasn t a conservative, crotch-stuffing snot. Credited for making the world safe for sideburns again (for which we thank him), Dylan had rich, absent parents, lived in a hotel suite and later in his own beachside bungalow, and drove a really cool classic convertible. All those things are good. He also ostentatiously read Lord Byron, claimed to be similarly mad, bad, and dangerous to know (like, ooh, we re so scared of someone who s as big a bad-ass as a *Romantic poet*), and cheated on Brenda with Kelly when Brenda was in France. All those things are bad, although Brenda could be a real nag, and we might have cheated on her, too. Dylan was generally as close as anyone West Beverly High ever got to being even a little bit nonconformist, and his money allowed him the freedom not to care what anyone thought of him (fortunately, since it s doubtful anyone thought well of that sleeveless Baja top he so often sported). Unfortunately, he then used his money to bankroll a pair of grifters, and then later married a mobster s daughter, who was accidentally assassinated instead of Dylan himself. Then Perry left the show, and should have stayed gone, but . . . eh, the opportunities to play Riff Raff in Broadway revivals of *The Rocky Horror Picture Show* evidently aren t what they used to be. We thought Dylan was totally dreamy back in the day, although when we watch *90210* now, we re embarrassed to admit it: Luke Perry made one hell of a craggy high-school sophomore. See also BEVERLY HILLS *90210*; BRENDA WALSH ; COOL, TV SIGNIFIERS OF; and SIDEBURNS, IMPORTANT TV.

DYNASTY   The primetime soap that defined the 80s, *Dynasty* followed the activities of the super-rich Blake and Krystle Carrington (John Forsythe and Linda Evans); their antagonist, and Blake s ex-wife, Alexis Colby (Joan Collins); and the many bratty-ass Colby/Carrington offspring. A recent behind-the-scenes TV movie (to which we ascribe the absolute gospel truth of a Bar-

bara Kopple documentary) implied that the show s genesis came when ABC contracted married TV writers Esther and Richard Shapiro to come up with their own take (read: carbon copy) of CBS s runaway hit *Dallas*. Enter superproducer Aaron Spelling to tart the whole thing up, and *Dynasty* was born. It was so obvious a copy that the super-rich family at its center was even in the oil business, just like the Ewings. Shameless! And yet, millions became addicted to all the shoulder-padded intrigue. People were dumber back then. See also *DALLAS* and SPELLING, AARON.

E

E! You wouldn t think that a channel that employs Tara Flash Whoredon Reid (as host of *Wild On* and *Taradise*) is a channel whose programming we d have much use for and, for the most part, you d be right. E! is a smorgasbord of celebrity coverage, most of it slavishly uncritical and therefore quite dull, and we couldn t care less about Howard Stern or specials about famous people s yachts. But in spite of a certain randomness to the schedule (what s with the *Saturday Night Live* reruns? Did Comedy Central lose them in a poker game or something?), E! does have the occasional stroke of genius: *Talk Soup*, *E! True Hollywood Story*, and that celebrity breakups show, which can be fun to watch if you make a bet with yourself beforehand on how many times Liz Taylor s on the list. See also *E! TRUE HOLLYWOOD STORY* and *TALK SOUP*.

EATING DISORDERS, PORTRAYALS OF Perhaps because so many actresses are anorexic or bulimic in real life, comparatively few very special episodes dare to tackle the touchy subject of eating disorders. Infamously skinny Calista Ally McBeal Flockhart actually played the title character in the The Secret Life of Mary Margaret: Portrait of a Bulimic episode of HBO s *Lifestories: Families in Crisis*, and probably still hasn t quite lived it down (she stored her *barf* in *jars*, people!); many girls who watched *Kate's Secret* are still haunted by Meredith Baxter-Birney s sensitive and nuanced (not) portrayal of bulimia, in which she binged on every comestible item in her house, stopping just short of scarfing down the family dog. But generally speaking, TV s anorexics and bulimics overcome their complex diseases by suffering a minor health scare (usually heart palpitations), realizing they re beautiful on the inside, cheerfully eating a slice of pizza, and never speaking of their body-image issues again. And then the actresses who play them eat half a Fig Newton from craft services, followed by three hours on the StairMaster. See also BAXTER (-BIRNEY), MEREDITH; *BEST LITTLE GIRL IN THE WORLD, THE*; *KATE'S SECRET*; and *VERY SPECIAL EPISODES*.

ED He s a *lawyer* in a *bowling alley*! Really, that should have been the whole show in a nutshell, but no. Instead, *Ed* was saddled with a drippy romantic-comedy plot: Manhattan lawyer Ed Stevens (Tom Cavanagh) loses his wife and his fancy job pretty much at the same time, so he decides that all he needs to get his life back on track is to return to his hometown of Stuckeyville and reunite with his unrequited high-school love, Carol Vessey (Julie Bowen). The only problems are that Carol s already in a relationship with someone else, and Carol is mind-bendingly annoying. Oh, wait the latter is only a problem for the audience, since we are meant to see her, as Ed does, as an object of unbridled perfection. And, no. The show predictably ran through its several seasons of will-they-or-won t-they, as various other guest stars (Kelly Ripa, John Slattery, Rena Sofer, Sabrina Lloyd) crossed their paths, but ultimately they did though it s not clear which of Ed s many stunts was the one that finally wore Carol down: interrupting her wedding on a white horse, or showing up at her classroom in a suit of armor? When the show wasn t focused on Ed and Carol s tiresome antics, it was really good; Ed sets up his law practice in an office at Stuckey Bowl, where he is assisted by the awesomely weird Shirley (Rachel Cronin), Phil (Michael Ian Black), and Kenny (Mike Starr, who left the show much too soon). Ed also strikes up a friendship with Warren (Justin Long) pretty much Ed Jr.

whose high-school-aged crises are much more compelling than the graceless Ed and Carol tango (and kudos to the producers for being the first to recognize the talented Long, who went on to rock *Dodgeball*, among other projects). If you ve never seen it, just record it in syndication and fast-forward through the Carol scenes. Did we mention that we hate her? We do. See also BLACK, MICHAEL IAN; OFFICE WEIRDO; SEXUAL TENSION, RUINATION OF SHOW BY RESOLVING; and SMALL TOWNS, QUIRKINESS OF.

EISNER, MICHAEL, HOST OF *THE DISNEY SUNDAY MOVIE* Under Michael Eisner s chairmanship, the Walt Disney Company grew from a $2 billion venture to one worth more than $50 billion. Which is certainly a most impressive achievement. But was he really so desperate to raise his Q rating with the under-fifteen crowd that he had to make himself the host of *The Disney Sunday Movie*? Even as kids we could tell how stiff his ass was in front of the camera. The Disney company already has a pretty recognizable mascot he s called *Mickey Mouse*. Quit trying to horn in on his action, Mike.

ELDARD, RON Eldard first came to our attention as sexy-but-tortured paramedic (and Carol Hathaway love interest) Shep on *ER* . . . and promptly joined our lengthy roster of TV and Movie

Boyfriends. We ve patiently watched every show he appeared in thereafter. Since his attention-grabbing debut, he s appeared in *Men Behaving Badly*, the Americanized version of a British import, which also starred Rob Deuce Bigalow Schneider, Justine Human Flatline Bateman, and the mute button on our remote; and *Blind Justice*, in which Eldard had to deliver several awkward monologues on overcoming his disability each week, every last one photocopied straight out of *The Great Big Book of Oy, Who Talks Like This?* Eldie did the best he could he s had several high-profile theater gigs, so if anyone s going to pull crap like that off, it s him, even with hella ugly chunky ash-blond highlights but the show just stank. We still believe in him, though. See also BATEMANS, JASON AND JUSTINE; *ER*; PHYSICALLY CHALLENGED PERSON/CHARACTER, CLICH S ASSOCIATED WITH; and TV BOYFRIENDS AND GIRLFRIENDS.

ELECTRIC COMPANY, THE This children s educational programming staple, which often aired in a block with *Sesame Street* and *Mister Rogers' Neighborhood*, featured a then-fetal Morgan Freeman as Easy Reader and used various skits and songs to teach kids to read and add. It also introduced the world to the universally beloved we are out of sweet rolls sketch, in which a guy orders coffee and a sweet roll, and the waitress tells him they re out of sweet rolls, so the guy asks for orange juice and a sweet roll, and the waitress repeats patiently that they re out of sweet rolls, so the guy asks for tea and a sweet roll, and the waitress is like, dude, out of sweet rolls over here, and it goes on and on and on like that until finally the guy shrugs, Okay, then I ll . . . just have a sweet roll, and the waitress runs screaming from the room in frustration. Good times. See also CHILDREN S SHOWS, HOSTS OF; ROGERS, FRED; and *SESAME STREET*.

ELEVATOR, CLICHÉS ASSOCIATED WITH Although the elevator is a fairly unremarkable conveyance to most of us, TV characters should avoid them. Sure, there s the occasional scene of hot elevator sex, as Christopher had with the red-headed D-girl on *The Sopranos*, but that s comparatively rare. Sitcom characters share awkward rides with someone malodorous or otherwise unpleasant, or get caught on the security camera doing something embarrassing, like picking a wedgie or nostril. One unlucky attorney on *L.A. Law* stepped heedlessly through a pair of elevator doors and straight into an empty shaft, to her death. Then there was that dude on *Six Feet Under* who tried to crawl through parted elevator doors when the car got stuck between floors, only to get cut clean in half when it started moving. But if you are a TV character about to get onto an elevator containing a pregnant woman, *don't*: It is definitely going to get stuck, she is definitely going to go into labor, and you are definitely going to have to deliver her baby. See also *L.A. LAW* and PREGNANCY, CLICHÉS ASSOCIATED WITH.

"ELLIOT STABLER" The genius idea of taking the *Law & Order* franchise and adding to it a guaranteed lurid sex crime *every week* gave the world the precious gift of *Special Victims Unit*, anchored by its male lead detective, Elliot Stabler (Christopher Meloni). If the purpose of every *SVU* episode is to pair up the week's crime with the cop with whom it will resonate most and it is then Elliot, as the rage-aholic father of a large brood of children, must take the following very personally: a child's death; a child's molestation;

a child's kidnapping; some mishap befalling the child of a broken home (added after Elliot and his wife split up in the 2004—5 season); the separation of a child from its siblings; a child's mutilation; a child's skinned knee; a child's hurt feelings; a bruise on a child that the child didn't actually notice until Elliot got right up in the child's grill to demand, WHO DID THIS TO YOU?!!!!?!!?! See

also *LAW & ORDER* FRANCHISE and TAKING! IT! PERSONALLY!

END CREDITS, FREEZE-FRAME Remember when every show's end credits screens scrolled or flashed over a montage of frozen frames of the episode's key moments? And we'd sit there, because we didn't have TiVo then and couldn't fast-forward them, and watch what the show's producers apparently thought were the episode's greatest moments? Watching older shows now and not even *very* old shows, but just drama series from the early 90s it's impossible not to make fun of them. Remember when Brandon smirked at Jim? Remember that time Brenda was standing in a hallway? Ooh, remember when Ohndrea smiled too hard and her eyes were completely obscured by her leathery wrinkles? Since then, the networks have figured out how to squeeze the credits no one reads to one side of the screen and use the other for promos, and sitcom producers have figured out how to prevent that by running one last scene as the credits flash by in the bottom eighth of the screen. And who needs credits, anyway? If you want to know who played 'Thug #3,' that's what the damn Internet is for. See also *BEVERLY HILLS 90210*.

E/R Not to be confused with *ER* (except it totally could be, since George Clooney was on both shows). Here s how to tell them apart: *E/R* is a sitcom, while *ER* a drama; *E/R* starred Elliott Gould and Conchata Ferrell, while *ER* thankgodfully did not; *E/R* featured occasional guest appearances by Sherman Hemsley as George Jefferson, while *ER* unfortunately did not; *E/R* got sacked after two seasons, because it sucked, while as of this writing *ER* continues to putt along on fumes of goodwill. See also CLOONEY, GEORGE and *ER*.

ER The first time Michael Crichton and Steven Spielberg hooked up, the result was the entertaining film adaptation of *Jurassic Park*. So why wouldn t the product be as good when they collaborated on a medical drama? Two words: Anthony Edwards. Two more: Noah Wyle. Actually, the first several seasons of *ER* f e a-turing Edwards and Wyle, both original cast members, among others were good. We were interested in the characters portrayed by its likable cast (including a pre—Lake Como George Clooney) and compelled by the v rit grittiness of the cases they handled. Then Edwards s Mark Greene got beaten up by an unknown assailant, suffered post-traumatic stress, and became an insufferable prig, dragging the show down to his portentously moralizing level. Once Edwards left the show his character was killed off by the slowest-progressing brain tumor e v e r Wyle s John Carter took on the

mantle of the ER s conscience, judging every ER staffer and patient for everything, all the time. And then he left the show, but the damage was done. *CSI* had overtaken *ER* as TV s top-rated drama, and we had long since stopped watching current episodes, sticking to the soapier early seasons on TNT. (Cloooooney.) See also *CSI*; CLOONEY, GEORGE; DR. DAVE MALUCCI ; *E/R*; *ER*, HIGHER THAN NORMAL CONCENTRATION OF *TOP GUN* ACTORS ON; MEDICAL DRAMAS, TROPES OF; SCHLAMME, TOMMY; and TAKING! IT! PERSONALLY!

***ER*, HIGHER THAN NORMAL CONCENTRATION OF *TOP GUN* ACTORS ON** In its infancy, *ER* featured a weirdly high number of actors who had also been in the seminal Navy pilots drama/homoerotic Tom Cruise vehicle *Top Gun* Anthony Edwards, of course, played emergency-staff moral center Mark Greene and had played doomed RIO Goose; Rick Rossovich played Carol Hathaway s erstwhile fianc John Tag Taglieri and had also played snotty Iceman s equally snotty sidekick Slider; and Michael Ironside lent his distinctive voice to the roles of ER chief Wild Willy Swift and Jester, the Top Gun school s second-in-command. Once the *ER*/*Top Gun* Venn diagram made itself apparent, we couldn t help but hope for a hamtastic guest shot from Val Kilmer (or, better yet, foxy John Stockwell), but it hasn t happened . . . although, at the current cast turnover rate, it s probably only a matter of time before Tom Cruise himself turns up on the show. As a psychiatrist. See also *ER*.

"ERIC CARTMAN" In any ensemble cast, our affection naturally goes, always, to the character with the least developed sense of ethics, morality, scruples, or occasion; it s why we love *NewsRadio* s Bill McNeal, *Arrested Development* s GOB, and *South Park* s Cartman. He loves Cheesy Poofs. He hates poor people. He s not fat, he s big-boned. He once made chili out of his enemy s parents, and then made the kid eat it. (Well, the kid *did* sell Cartman his pubes.) Cartman isn t the kind of person we d want to hang out with, but we envy the consequence-free world he lives in. Also, when you want to get your way with anyone, the fastest way is to put on your squeakiest Cartman voice and shriek, But Mooooooooooom! Try it, it works! See also *SOUTH PARK*.

ESPN Admit it: Every time the World s Strongest Man Competition is on ESPN2, you say out loud, God, how many times a day do they *air* that shit? but you watch a few minutes of it before changing the channel anyway, because a guy the size of the house you grew up in is clean-and-jerking a warthog. Yeah, we do that, too. It s a warthog! We like famous original

ESPN fine *SportsCenter*, the channel s flagship show made famous in part by the legendary nicknaming gifts of Chris Ethel Berman, is well written enough that even people who don t like sports (or only care about one sport) can enjoy it. But does that mean we need a second ESPN, or ESPNews, or ESPN *Classic*? Because, seriously: Nobody cares about softball. If you really need to fill airtime, show a gag reel of Harold Reynolds rolling his eyes at John Kruk. See also SPORTSCASTERS, MOST ANNOYING; SPORTS COVERAGE, FATUOUS; SPORTS COVERAGE, HALLMARK-Y BACKGROUND STORIES IN; SPORTS COVERAGE, HORRIFYING CLOSE-UPS IN; and SPORTS COVERAGE, SADLY INEPT USE OF CHALKBOARD TECHNOLOGY IN.

ESTRADA, ERIK The very, very toothy star of *CHiPs* (and, more recently, *The Surreal Life*), Estrada is the North Star in the constellation of self-proclaimed TV mack daddies. (Other lights include Larry of *Three's Company*  and *Night Court* s sexaholic Dan.) Estrada got into a salary dispute with the network during the run of *CHiPs*, thus indirectly inflicting the acting stylings of Bruce *Can't Stop the Music* Jenner on the world, but he went on to star in *telenovelas* and seems pretty willing to make fun of himself. So despite the fact that his Chicletty chompers are probably also responsible for the epidemic of poorly fitted caps in Hollywood, we ll forgive him. See also *CHiPs*; *NIGHT COURT*; *SURREAL LIFE, THE*; and *THREE'S COMPANY*.

E! TRUE HOLLYWOOD STORY Behind the Music s broader-ranging cousin, *E!THS* covers not only musical acts (their two-hour New Kids entry is a classic), but also actors, TV shows, movies, porn stars, Hollywood urban legends (one 2002 episode explored The Curse of *Poltergeist*), and anyone or anything with a reading on the fame-o-meter. Like the channel that spawned it, *E!THS* is somewhat undiscriminating in selecting subjects for coverage; Bruce Jenner is a weird enough choice, but at least he had a couple of film and TV roles. Mary Kay Letourneau, on the other hand, seems like she s better left for Court TV s original-movie division, and was the world really begging for an in-depth bio of Rudy Galindo? *E!THS* isn t quite as good as *BtM*, using lots of pick-up shots and interviews with random flunkies, but the eps about the Monkees, Liza Minnelli, and Corey Haim more than make up for a certain slapped-together and overly fannish quality at times. See also *BEHIND THE MUSIC*; *CAMERON, KIRK*; *CHiPs*; *E!*; and *MONKEES, THE*.

EXPOSITION, CLUNKY What s that? You say there s a big concert down in the town square? And Davy Jones is *there?* Well, of course I ll be right down! There must be nothing more annoying than phoning a TV character, since a TV character has that annoying habit of repeating back to you everything you just said, as if for the benefit of some unseen audience. But the one-sided phone call is just one of the myriad clumsy methods used to introduce information into a dramatic situation. Other, equally graceless means include: characters getting out of a car together, their conversation setting up whatever s about to happen, as though they hadn t spoken to each other throughout their car ride; new characters who have to be brought up to speed on what the audience has already seen in past episodes; amnesiacs who ve conveniently forgotten everything the audience most needs to know and thus require it to be retold to them; a situation where several people meet each other for the first time, so they all share their backstories upon introduction. If there were a Lifetime Achievement Award in the category of Clunky Exposition, *24* would win it in a walk. See also PILOTS and *24*.

EXTREME MAKEOVER: HOME EDITION
See HOME MAKEOVER SHOWS.

F

FACINELLI, PETER "THE FATCH" The Fatch s first role was a smug, fratty sociopath on trial for running a sex-for-points ring on *Law & Order*, and he played the role so well that we hated his poor-man s-Tom-Cruise ass immediately. We continued to scoff contemptuously at The Fatch as he made his way through various movies, some of them sort of okay (*Can't Hardly Wait*), most of them unseen (*Calm at Sunset*? Did the world really need a *Great Santini* knock-off starring Michael Moriarty? . . . Actually, that sounds campily awesome, so forget we said anything). We scoffed even louder when he got married to Jennie Garth, with whom he has two incredibly stupidly named daughters. Luca Bella? Lola *Ray*? He couldn t have done something about that shit? Anyway, he eventually landed a leading role on *Fastlane*. Created and often directed by McG, *Fastlane* was a short-lived show about undercover cops, and we only watched it because we love Tiffani-Amber Thiessen. The Fatch spent a lot of time with his shirt off, it seemed, and he usually paired that freshly waxed chest with a cowboy hat, but he threw himself into the musical montages *con queso* with such zest that he won us over. He s a smarmy dicksmack *and* sort of charming, and when he surfaced again on *Six Feet Under*, showing up at the Fisher family dinner table in his underpants while tripping in one episode and ripping Claire a new one at her gallery opening in another, we had to give it up for The Fatch. But the best part of The Fatch, obviously, is that we can call him The Fatch. If his last name were Smedley, he wouldn t be in this book. See also BEVERLY HILLS 90210; CROSS, DAVID; LAW & ORDER FRANCHISE; McG; and SCENERY, CHEWERS OF.

FACTS OF LIFE, THE You take the good, you take the bad. You take them both, and then you have . . . four snitty private-school girls and their querulous, warbling housemother. Few remember the legendary sitcom s confused first season, which featured like a million girls (including Molly Ringwald!) and no source of conflict other than that they were probably all on the rag at the same time. It s just as well, since the show didn t hit its stride until its second-season retooling, which found first-season cast members Blair

(Lisa Whelchel), Natalie (Mindy Cohn), and Tootie (Kim Fields) hooking up with rough-edged scholarship student Jo (Nancy McKeon), breaking curfew, and being punished indefinitely with a room over the school cafeteria and a job in same under the watchful eye of *Diff'rent Strokes* spin-off-ee Mrs. Garrett (Charlotte Rae). The plots were standard teen-sitcom fare fighting over boys, mainly and once Mrs. G. left, to be replaced by Cloris Leachman and an Astin, the magic was gone, leaving only lingering questions about whether Jo was a lesbian or what. See also HIGH SCHOOL, UNREALISTIC PORTRAYALS OF; HOMOSEXUALITY, CODED; REUNION MOVIES; and THEME SONGS.

FAME It shouldn t have worked. Viewers will *barely* accept it when characters randomly stop talking and start singing in musical *movies* for such a thing to be attempted in a TV series was unheard of! And yet, the TV series adaptation of the 1980 film musical *Fame* lasted five seasons. Sure, it looks cheesy *now*, but it was the 80s! That s what pop music sounded like, and that s how kids dressed. Seriously, it was. Plus, Right here is where you start paying. With sweat is a catchphrase with many real-life applications. See also CATCHPHRASES, OVERUSED TV and MOVIES, TV SERIES ADAPTATIONS OF.

FAMILY BONDS See HBO PROGRAMMING, LESSER-KNOWN.

FAMILY FEUD, **CLASSIC** Current *Feud* sucks the big one the set is all teched up, and the families don t pose family-portrait-style during the opening anymore. Give us classic *Feud* every time, not just for the *hi*larious vintage fashions on the contestants or the questions that occasionally posed an actual challenge, but for the beyond-awesome hosting. First Richard Dawson, fat and drunk and equal-opportunity leching on every female contestant regardless of age; then Ray Combs, whose bright smile and poofy blow-dry did little to mask the empty-eyed despondency that led to his suicide in 1996. And no, we won t be dignifying alleged sexual harasser and full-time sphere Louie Anderson with a comment, because: ew. See also GAME SHOW NETWORK.

FAMILY MATTERS See URKEL.

FAMILY TIES This long-running NBC series was one of the first family sitcoms to feature baby boomers as the parents, and Steven and Elyse Keaton (Michael Gross and Meredith Baxter-Birney) were boomier than most. Not only were they full-on ex-hippies, but Steven spent the series working at PBS. PBS! Why not just go the whole nine and make him a Communist? That, of course, was the central conflict of the series that two hippie-ish parents could produce a Republican son in Alex (Michael J. Fox). Why they put up with his Reaganite bleating when he was 4'3" and Steven could have just stepped on him is a mystery. Though Fox became the show s breakout star, meaning that most episodes revolved around his character, the Keatons also had two other children shallow clotheshorse Mallory (Justine Bateman) and doughy lump Jennifer (Tina Yothers) but all they ever did was date a monosyllabic troglodyte (Scott Valentine s Nick) and act like a bimbo to impress some popular girls, respectively. But amid all the intergenerational political wrangling, the Keatons also found time to deal with serious issues, like whether they should get a gun for home protection, or when Mallory should sleep with her college-aged boyfriend. And then, when interest in the show started to wane,  Elyse conveniently got pregnant. Shocker! Oh, and along the way, the show picked up pre-famous guest stars like Tom Hanks (as Elyse s alcoholic brother, Ned), Geena Davis (as incompetent yet statuesque housekeeper Karen), and Courteney Cox (as Alex s girlfriend Lauren). Oh, and remember when Alex s

friend killed himself that time? Sha la la la! See also BABY, RUINATION OF SHOW BY ADDING; BATEMANS, JASON AND JUSTINE; BAXTER (-BIRNEY), MEREDITH; COUSIN OLIVER ; FOX, MICHAEL J.; PARENTS WHO ARE TOTALLY INTO EACH OTHER TO A CREEPY DEGREE; and SHA LA LA LA!

FANTASY ISLAND Admit it all you *really* remember about the show is the troubled Herv Villechaize standing next to Ricardo Khan Montalban and shouting, Da plane, da plane! Yeah, us too. It s the show you begged the babysitter to let you stay up for, then fell asleep during, so don t front.

FASHION, HILARIOUS ATTEMPTS OF TV GUYS IN THE '90S AT The early 90s were a dark time for men s fashion on TV. Frequent offenses included: brightly colored Hanes Beefy Ts, tucked into jeans or slacks which in turn were worn without a belt; lingering acid-wash; double-dyed black roadie jeans worn with blinding white sneakers; plaid shirts over white T-shirts, often with the sleeves cut off; woven Baja tops, also frequently sleeveless; David-Byrne-inspired oversize jackets with gigantic shoulder pads, paired with wristwatches the size of salad plates; mullets; too much hair gel; ill-advised suspenders worn by individuals not in ska bands. See also BELT, WHY MEN ON TV WEAR A TUCKED-IN SHIRT WITHOUT A.

FAT GUY/SKINNY WIFE MARRIAGES
The model-perfect women who populate today s sitcoms sure aren t shallow. How else to explain why so many conventionally attractive, slender women seen in real life on the arms of hunky producers and Latin dancers willingly yoke themselves to big fat lumps? Okay, Carrie and Doug Heffernan (Leah Remini and Kevin James) on *The King of Queens* we ll allow: he is lovable, and she, while physically attractive, is kind of crusty, so she s not the perfect package her own self. Also, the show is hilarious. And we can make some sense of *Still Standing* (starring Mark Addy and Jami Gertz), because there s got to be an episode coming where it comes out that she s into him because he s obviously British (and could a brother learn to fake that, please?), and because . . . again, she s no prize herself. But there s no excusing *According to Jim*. On any front. Shut up, Jim. See also *KING OF QUEENS, THE* and REMINI, LEAH.

FEAR FACTOR The premise of this gross-out-fest: Perform feats of derring-do (or disgusting-do), get money. Contestants must complete tasks like lying in a tank filled with tarantulas for five minutes; crossing high wires stretched between two apartment buildings; eating various unpleasant organ meats (the boiled ungulate testicle is a popular *Fear Factor* dish); jumping out of planes; et cetera. There s a lot of shrieking, wailing, and gagging in the average episode, but you have to give the show credit many reality shows dress up the greed principle inherent in these game shows, but *Fear Factor* puts the how low will you go for a cash reward principle right out there. See also REALITY TV, QUITTERS OF.

FELICITY One of the few good things The WB ever did, *Felicity* is the understated, underplayed, underrated story of our titular heroine (Keri Russell) and her college career at the fictional University of New York. Marked by extremely naturalistic performances from  the show s uniformly excellent (once Amy Jo Johnson left) cast, including Scotts Speedman and Foley, Greg Grunberg, Amanda Foreman, and Donald Faison all of whom went on either to successful runs on other shows, in movies, or among *Felicity* creator J. J. Abrams s repertory company *Felicity* managed the rare feat of dramatizing a college experience that actually felt true to life. The one bad thing we can say about it, in fact (other than that Amy Jo Johnson was ever on it) is that there was perhaps a little too much dithering in the Felicity/Ben/Noel love triangle, especially since Felicity and Ben were always the better couple. His love really is better than ice cream, y all! See also COLLEGE, UNREALISTIC PORTRAYALS OF; JULIE EMRICK ; and NEW YORK CITY, CLICH D/INACCURATE TV PORTRAYALS OF.

FICHTNER, WILLIAM We were too young to have seen him on *As the World Turns*, and too uninterested in drug-addicted abused women to have seen him on *Grace Under Fire*. And though we did see him on the big screen in movies like *Heat*, *Contact*, and *Virtuosity*, none of those roles really affected us all that much. Then came *The Perfect Storm*, in which William Fichtner was mulleted and generally drenched in sweat and fish guts while wearing waders, and somehow that and not the scene in *Go* when he s stripped down to his tighty-whities was the one that hooked us. Sooooooo hot, you guys. Maybe it was the accent? Anyway, after that, we were William Fichtner s bitches forever, following him to *MDs* and the miniseries *Empire Falls* and the *Lost* rip-off *Invasion*. He s going to make a hit eventually, and we ll be able to say we got in on the ground floor. Maybe he ll know how devoted we ve been this whole time and invite us to join him in his waders so that we can make out. It could happen! See also SHOW KILLERS; SOAP OPERAS, DAYTIME; and TV BOYFRIENDS AND GIRLFRIENDS.

FIGHTING, FEMALE CHARACTERS WHO ARE GOOD AT Why is it cooler when a woman beats someone up than when a guy does it? Is it because she has the greater challenge in chasing down bad guys on her high heels? Or because half the women who really kick ass on TV are 5'3" or shorter, and are therefore the underdogs we naturally root for? Or because their opponents underestimate them just because they re women, and therefore it s all the more satisfying when sexist jerks get their teeth kicked in? We don t know. It just is. See also *ALIAS*; *BUFFY THE VAMPIRE SLAYER*; GARNER, JENNIFER; and GELLAR, SARAH MICHELLE.

FOX, EARLY YEARS OF Nowadays, FOX has a reputation as a ruthless, and sometimes foolish, exploiter of programming trends (not least the willingness of reality-TV contestants to debase themselves), but in the network s infancy, that exploitiveness read as a refreshing readiness to try anything. Facing off against the three established networks, FOX had to throw a lot of shows at the wall and hope some of them would stick in a hurry and some of those shows peeled off fast (and rightfully so good Lord was *Duet* awful), but a lot of them hung in there and gave the netlet a foothold. Shows like *21 Jump Street*, *The Tracey Ullman Show*, and *Married . . . with Children* seemed cutting-edge back then, if only because the other networks didn t have hunky undercover cops, or sitcoms where all the characters were assholes and even the shows that didn t pull great ratings often turned into still-well-regarded cult hits (*Get a Life*, *Parker Lewis Can't Lose*). *The Simpsons* and *90210* let FOX tell the big three to eat its shorts permanently around 1990. See also *BEVERLY HILLS 90210*; FOX, SITCOMS PREMATURELY CANCELED BY; *GET A LIFE*; *SIMPSONS, THE*; and *21 JUMP STREET*.

FOX, MICHAEL J. You don t see Michael J. Fox on TV much anymore, unless he s testifying at a congressional hearing on stem-cell research, but twenty years ago, that Platonic ideal of bear-claw haircuts graced the covers of *Teen Beat*, *People*, or *TV Guide* every week. Fox had a pretty good movie gig going with the *Back to the Future* franchise in addition to his star-making role as Reaganophile Alex P. Keaton on *Family Ties*. The claw got steadily gellier, poufier, and more lead singer of the Hooters -y as his career wore on, but Fox s pint-sized panache never diminished; *Spin City* never recovered after his departure. And every time we watch that *Clone High* episode where he plays a kidney (. . . we know; just watch it) and never fails to crack us up with *one line*, we miss him a little bit. See also *CLONE HIGH*; *FAMILY TIES*; MOVIES-TO-TV/TV-TO-MOVIES CAREER PIPELINE/ARC;

and *TEEN BEAT*, COVER BOYS OF.

FOX, SITCOMS PREMATURELY CANCELED BY FOX has a truly impressive track record when it comes to picking up comedy shows, airing them just long enough for critics and die-hard fans to get personally invested, and then yanking them and leaving fans with no closure. *Andy Richter Controls the Universe*, *Futurama*, *Get a Life*, *Undeclared*, *Flying Blind*, and even *The Ben Stiller Show* all felt Rupert Murdoch s ax too soon, while *That 70s Show* was allowed to linger on like skunky pot fug, even after its two biggest stars decided to haul ass out of there. Some pointed to the three seasons of *Arrested Development* and the resurrection of *Family Guy* as signs that FOX is actually starting to respond to its fans; we say, *AD* was an Emmy winner for Best Comedy and *Family Guy* sucks. We re still not over *Futurama*. [*Pout.*] See also *BEN STILLER SHOW, THE*; FOX, EARLY YEARS OF; and *GET A LIFE*.

FRASIER Of all the characters who earned a place in your heart on *Cheers*, would Frasier have been the one you d peg to carry a spin-off for eleven seasons? And yet, that s what happened, as Frasier (Kelsey Grammer) moved from Boston to Seattle and into an apartment with his recently injured father, Martin (John Mahoney). The spin-off also introduced us to Frasier s brother Niles (David Hyde Pierce), every bit as pompous and persnickety as Frasier, and thus a polar opposite to the working-class retired cop Martin. The show labored for half its run to keep the married Niles away from his oblivious crush, Martin s home-care worker Daphne (Jane Leeves), and once they finally did get together, producers had to find new and clever ways to write stories around Frasier s social climbing and poor luck with women. The series gets a lot of credit for its writing, and rightly so the best episodes work like French farce, with just a touch of slapstick, like a classed-up *Three's Company*. The series also became reliant, as the years went on, upon stunt-casting to drive its ratings, casting as Frasier s love interests such illustrious talents as Jean Smart, Patricia Clarkson, and Laura Linney. Rarely laugh-out-loud funny (except when Harriet Sansom Harris stops by to portray Frasier s loony agent, Bebe), the show is pleasantly droll and stands up well in syndication. Just skip the Very Special tenth-season episodes when Niles undergoes heart bypass surgery; we promise, he lives. See also *CHEERS*; FRASIER CRANE ; HOMO-SEXUALITY, CODED; SEXUAL TENSION, RUINATION OF SHOW BY RESOLVING; SPIN-OFFS; STUNTCASTING; *THREE'S COMPANY*; and VERY SPECIAL EPISODES.

"FRASIER CRANE" Psychiatrist Frasier Crane is a comparatively rare animal among TV characters, especially on sit-coms: He s really smart. Or, at least, he s really snooty and pretentious, which on TV generally stands for intelligence. Kelsey Grammer embodied the character across two series (*Cheers* and *Frasier*), three decades, and innumerable cocaine  benders. Given the reputation America has for cheerful igno-rance (insert your own Dubya joke here), it s somewhat surprising that it would clasp a pompous, subtextually gay aesthete like Frasier to its bosom for so many years; it s not like the bulk of the audience was tuning in for the Greek tailor-themed Euripides, Eumenides puns. Maybe we all just didn t want to miss the episode when the vein in Frasier s forehead finally burst. See also *CHEERS*; *FRASIER*; and HOMOSEXUALITY, CODED.

FRIENDS *Friends* followed the adven-tures of six attractive twentysome-things Jennifer Aniston, Courteney Cox, Lisa Kudrow, Matt LeBlanc, Matthew Perry, and David Schwimmer and their misadventures in dating and careers, set against a Manhattan back-drop. The show became a hit, and then a cultural phenomenon, influencing everything from Gen Xers slang cadences to their hairstyles. Even once the backlash kicked in, and it became cool to sneer at it, *Friends* was still a hit show, spending its last five years on the air as TV s number one sitcom. It s easy now to joke about the show s ubiquitous cast, its cutesy episode titles (all of which are The One with _____), and its departure from the airwaves marked by a send-off so emphatically maudlin that you d think the callow sextet had spent the last ten years storming the beach at Normandy instead of delivering increasingly hoary wisecracks belying their advanced ages. But the truth is that it was a pretty great show, worthy of inclusion in the pantheon of TV s classic sitcoms. Should it have wrapped things up sometime around Monica and Chandler s wedding? Perhaps. But a bad *Friends* is much more watchable than the best *Yes, Dear*, so on balance we re glad there are ten seasons to treasure, and then to endure, and eventually to shun in syndication. See also *Friends*, Failed Clones of; New York City, Clich d/Inaccurate TV Portrayals of; Real Estate, Vastness of; and Ross Geller.

Friends, Failed Clones of If you re one of the rare TV producers to hit upon a successful formula no one s used before, you can be sure of one thing. No, not that your show will continue airing until you decide to pull the plug! The audience is far too fickle for that! No, you can be sure another network, or maybe even your own, will rip it off. So it was with *Friends*. There are some who ve observed that its premise was already a rip-off aimless New Yorkers hanging out and talking a lot about inconsequential crap had already been done, several seasons earlier, with *Seinfeld* but once *Friends* made the sitcom safe again for hugging and learning, paired with attractive, eligible young urbanites, the door was opened for *The Single Guy*; *It's Like, You Know . . .*; *The Drew Carey Show*; *Partners*; and *Alright* [*sic*] *Already*. And then, when those all tanked, derivative TV producers moved on to ripping off *Ally McBeal*. It s the circle of life. See also *Friends*.

FRYE, SOLEIL MOON See *PUNKY BREWSTER*.

FULL HOUSE You know, one could *say* that one watched so much *Full House* because one had a sister who was five when it started. But if one was thirteen when it started, and capable of reading or . . . leaving the room, one s excuse kind of falls flat. *Full House* is such a terrible show it s saccharine and twee, and no one on it is cute. (Stamos is cute now, but back in 87, rocking that fluffy mullet? Not so much.) It s basically *Three Men* *and a Baby*, changed just enough from the movie storyline that the producers wouldn t get sued. Danny (Bob Saget) loses his wife and, unable to cope with parenting his three daughters on his own, invites his brother-in-law (Stamos) and meathead friend (alleged standup comic Dave Coulier) to come live with him and help out. And even though they re single and have no experience with children that would be at all helpful, they . . . do. Anyway, the parenting team runs into the usual challenges the kids get caught shoplifting, lip off, and have annoying friends (GIBBLER!) but wrap up every episode with a gentle talking-to and a reassurance that the kids are loved. Yeah, that s exactly what happened to us when we went joyriding in a vintage convertible not. When it went off the air in 1995, after a shocking eight seasons, dentists across America mourned the loss of such a reliable source of cavities. See also ABC s TGIF; BAD SITCOM, SURE SIGNS OF; CHILDREN, OVERLY PRECOCIOUS; DADS, TV; FASHION, HILARIOUS ATTEMPTS OF TV GUYS IN THE 90S AT; OLSEN, MARY-KATE AND ASHLEY; PARENTS/PARENTING, BAD; SAGET, ROBERT LANE; STAMOS, JOHN; and TEENAGERS, BRATTY.

FUTURE ON TV, SIMILARITY TO PRESENT OF When Steven Spielberg directed *Minority Report*, he consulted with numerous prominent engineers, designers, and critics, so they could flesh out his futuristic vision with elements based on technologies we live with now. The future, on TV, is just like that, except crappy. Characters on the various *Star Trek* series even *Enterprise*, which only wrapped in 2005 routinely use PDAs larger and more cumbersome than the Treos viewers may be fiddling with even as the show airs in front of them. Characters drink out of skinny little glasses we may know as IKEA bud vases. Ships are controlled with levers and throttles and the like, similar to our standard jets. As for fashion, producers avoid the issue completely by throwing the cast into nondescript, androgynous, jumpsuity uniforms. And what s with the computers talking to everyone all the time? Are we to believe that, in the future, humans will enjoy conversing verbally with some know-it-all computer? Because that sure seems annoying now. See also CENTURY CITY and STAR TREK FRANCHISE.

G

GALLAGHER, PETER, EYEBROWS OF The fine actor Peter Gallagher has always had an impressive pair of eyebrows, going all the way back to *sex, lies, and videotape*. But now that he s entered his fifties, they are *out* of *control* big, bushy, black as the darkest night.  They re almost too much eyebrow for TV, and when he was cast as the Cohen family patriarch on *The O.C.*, producers should have anticipated that there would be many scenes in which Gallagher s eyebrows would be more expressive than Mischa Barton, Benjamin McKenzie, and the awesome yet over-Botoxed Melinda Clarke combined. Peter Gallagher s eyebrows are, frankly, a national treasure, and the mere suggestion that he tweeze or wax them should be punishable by death. See also *O.C., THE*.

GAME SHOW NETWORK It seems like such a dumb idea for a cable channel: nothing but old game shows. We re talking shows so old that if they have a trivia element, you may not be able to play along, since actual facts have changed and there s no longer any such thing as a Soviet Union. And yet the Game Show Network (or, as we in the know call it, The G) is one of the few cable channels you can turn on at nearly any time of the day and find something you wouldn t mind watching Dawson-era episodes of *Family Feud*, Kato Kaelin on *Weakest Link*, or Chuck Woolery on any one of an approximately eighty-seven different series. In recent years, the network has started airing more original programming (such as *Friend or Foe?* and *Lingo*), vaguely game-ish acquisitions from other networks (such as *The Amazing Race* and *Kenny vs. Spenny*), and the inescapable casino twosome of blackjack and poker; the result has been to consign all the classic game shows to daylight hours. Hey, it s their network, but we do kind of miss the days when *Match Game* was considered viable primetime programming. And by that we mean 2002. See also CABLE CHANNELS, UNWATCHED; *CARD SHARKS*; *FAMILY FEUD*, CLASSIC; GAME SHOWS, CELEBRITIES ON; *LINGO*; *MATCH GAME*; and *WEAKEST LINK, THE*, BRITISH LADY EDITION.

GAME SHOWS, CELEBRITIES ON The 70s were chockablock with series on which common folk depended on celebrities to focus, answer questions, and not be drunk in order for the civilians to win cash and prizes. Fortunately, some shows were rigged to give contestants a fighting chance: On *Hollywood Squares*, you always had the option to disagree with whatever idiotic crap Nanette Fabray had to offer, and on *Match Game* you could handicap yourself by at least trying to think like Charles Nelson Reilly. But on *Password*, unless your partner was Betty White, it was a crap shoot. And we can t be the only ones who get irrationally enraged whenever a celebrity blurts out the forbidden word on *Pyramid*. Dammit, Soupy Sales, get it together! See also GAME SHOW NETWORK; *HOLLYWOOD SQUARES*; and *MATCH GAME*.

GAME SHOWS, CELEBRITY EDITIONS OF Putting celebrities in high-tension settings where regular folks have succeeded has one objective: to make the stars look dumb. And the results seldom differ from that objective. Celebrities have gamely embarrassed themselves on *Who Wants to Be a Millionaire*, *Fear Factor*, *Weakest Link*, and *The Mole*, generally for charity (which is also fun you can revile or, rarely, improve your opinion of a given star based on his or her cause of choice); rumors of a planned celebrity version of

Survivor (and fantasy teams) have been kicking around the Internet almost since the show s premiere. But the all-time greatest place to see celebrities humiliated in a competitive setting is still celebrity *Jeopardy!* The famous *Saturday Night Live* skit exaggerates the stars lack of trivia knowledge . . . a little. Like, a recent Beltway Insider week kicked off with an answer, the question to which was What is *All the President's Men*? Bob Woodward was on. *And did not answer the question.* See also *FEAR FACTOR*; GAME SHOWS, CELEBRITIES ON; *JEOPARDY!*; *MOLE, THE*; and *WEAKEST LINK, THE*, HIP-HOP CELEBRITY EPISODE.

GARNER, JENNIFER The lissome, sensitive Jennifer Garner has a well-earned reputation for romantic involvement with her costars she married Scott Foley after playing opposite his Noel on *Felicity*, and later left him for her *Alias* love interest Michael Vartan. Then, after she worked with Ben Affleck during their joint film bomb *Daredevil*, the seeds were planted for her to throw Vartan over for him; she eventually got impregnated by and married to the former Jennifer Lopez swain. Garner gets a lot of guff in the tabloids, and rumor has it that she s not so bright, but she seems sweet and well-meaning, and we still like her. Though given that she s married the only person in Hollywood with a jaw and forehead bigger than her own, it s too bad she and Ben didn t have a boy. See also *ALIAS*; *FELICITY*; and FIGHTING, FEMALE CHARACTERS WHO ARE GOOD AT.

GELLAR, SARAH MICHELLE We have heard that she lied about having a brown belt in karate in order to get the part of Buffy Summers. We have heard that she got the *Buffy the Vampire Slayer* stunt coordinator and his wife, Gellar s stunt double fired because she didn t want anyone else taking credit for her fight scenes, and that the rest of the cast didn t really like her. And we have heard that she s actually a bot. Okay, we haven t heard that last thing, but, while we liked her okay in the first few seasons of *Buffy*, she got so scary thin during the fourth season that the fight scenes went into the toilet anyway. Slayer powers, schmayer powers a vampire in a diaper could have snapped her like a twig. The more weight Gellar lost, the more self-absorbed and less likable the Buffy character became, and Gellar s semi-bitch-face didn t help. But again, we loved her back when she had baby fat, before Riley showed up. Pity she s spent all our good-will on a string of cynically shitty franchise films like the *Scooby-Don't* movies . . . and that she s so fake, canned, and concerned with letting us all know how smart she is in her media appearances. She made a great Buffy, for a few years,

but when she s not trying to impress Conan O Brien, who *went to Harvard*, with how she *reads the classics*, like, we re so sure, we suspect that she s hanging upside-down Batman-style in a recharging bay. See also *BUFFY THE VAMPIRE SLAYER*; FIGHTING, FEMALE CHARACTERS WHO ARE GOOD AT; and MOVIES-TO-TV/TV-TO-MOVIES CAREER PIPELINE/ARC.

GENERAL MILLS INTERNATIONAL COFFEES, COMMERCIALS FOR Ladies, you know how when your best girlfriend comes over for an afternoon visit, all you want to do is put the kettle on, dump some powder in a couple of mugs, and make some instant coffee you can nurse on the couch for a few hours while you reminisce about your trip to Paris and that dude you met . . . what was his name? Ah, yes: JEAN-PIERRE! That never happened to you in real life, though, because 1) no one who s any kind of a host actually serves instant coffee to a guest, and 2) if you and a friend are going to sit around drinking coffee and chatting in the middle of the day, you re doing it at a caf . We ve seen some pretty asinine techniques used to sell women crap they don t need, but the General Mills International Coffee ads of the late 80s displayed some of the dumbest. Kudos. See also CATCH-PHRASES, OVERUSED COMMERCIAL.

"GEORGE COSTANZA" It s the rare TV character who would choose to engage in a little impromptu onanism with his mother s copy of *Glamour*, and do so *in his mother's house*, but George is that character. The short, stocky, balding loser of *Seinfeld* s fab four, George (Jason Alexander) is such an idiot, makes such bad decisions, and is so reliably *wrong* that it s almost as great a pain to watch him as it is a pleasure. In

fact, the combination of glee and horror one feels in watching George s many moments of social retardation tailing a date into the restroom to see if she s refunding his meals, because it s a waste of his money, or his attempts to prove to his African-American boss that he has black friends prefigure intentionally awkward sitcoms like *The Office* and *Seinfeld* cocreator Larry David s *Curb Your Enthusiasm*. And the episode where he gets a toupee still cracks us up. See also DORKINESS, TV SIGNIFERS OF; *OFFICE, THE*; *SEINFELD*; and *SEINFELD*, ALUMNI OF.

GET A LIFE The *Plan 9 from Outer Space* of sitcoms, *Get a Life* is a cult favorite that s often unwatchable, starring Chris Elliott as a thirty-year-old paperboy who still lives with his parents. Elliott, a *Late Night* featured player for many years, shared Letterman s gift for variations on a comedy theme of Un! Comfortable!, and while we admire that in theory, in practice it can be difficult to sit through especially when the production values suggest that the show was shot for public access. In prison. How it lasted two seasons, we can t begin to speculate, but if you re curious, watch *Stella* instead; it s a similar type of show (from the minds a few of the guys from sketch show *The State*), but the execution is far superior. See also CULT SHOW, DEFINITION OF and FOX, SITCOMS PREMATURELY CANCELED BY.

GIBB, ANDY Gibb, a recording and stage star when he was sober enough to show up, also hosted *Solid Gold*, *also* when he was sober enough to show up; his tendency to be unreliable eventually got him fired. We didn t know any of the gory details back when he died in 1988, but we know them now, thanks to the spellbinding episode of *Behind the Music* devoted to Gibb, which we really can t recommend highly enough. Gibb is such a late- 70s/early- 80s relic, fashionwise, that you can t help giggling at the dead, and then of course he s *such* a train wreck that you can t look away like, a he overdoses, he s taken to the hospital, and he s guzzling rubbing alcohol no-survivors Amtrak-derailment-level train wreck. The episode also features these blackly humorous interviews with his mother, who is *laughing* about how crazy he got with the drinking and the cocaine in a very British well, what can you do sort of way, *and* interviews with the Bee Gees, who sit before the camera wearing blue-tinted sunglasses. All three of them. Indoors. You couldn t maybe respect the memory of your kid brother, who basically drank and drugged himself to death because he d never measure up to your successes, by *removing your shades that don't even do anything*? And what s with the hair, *Barry*? It s like your entire head became a dime-store lion costume. Anyway, we miss you, Andy. See also BEHIND THE MUSIC; SOLID GOLD; and TV BOYFRIENDS AND GIRLFRIENDS.

GIFTS, SEPARATE BOTTOM AND TOP WRAPPING OF Oh, you know *exactly* what we re talking about. When a character on a TV show gets a gift, it s not in a box with wrapping paper all the way around it that she has to tear up; it s in a wrapped box bottom, covered with a separately wrapped box top, and she just lifts it off to get to the gift within no muss, no fuss. How much damn time do people have in TV World that they can double their gift-wrapping time? (Okay, yes, we know: The props department does it that way so that there can be multiple takes without matching the actor s paper-rip pattern. But it s still annoying.)

"GIL GRISSOM" Played by William Manhunter Petersen, Gris is the paterfamilias of the *CSI* team, in spite of apparent difficulty relating to other people as easily as he does to bugs . . . and, for several seasons, he was the joy of coworker Sara Sidle s (Jorja Fox) mopey desiring. Fine, we thought, so she s got some daddy issues but it isn t just Sara who finds the silver forensic fox irresistible. Despite a rather large and feminine posterior, Grissom moves many of the show s female fans to write X-rated fan fiction involving Petersen and judiciously applied chocolate sauce, if you know what we mean, and we fear that you do. Back in the day, when Petersen starred in baseball cult flick *Long Gone*, we could kind of see it. Now, with that Beardo the Weirdo facial hair? We just don t get it. Nor do we want to, frankly. See also *CSI*.

GILLIGAN'S ISLAND Okay, first of all, if it s a three-hour tour as claimed by the theme song, how did the *Gilligan's Island*-ites get blown so far off course that they didn t get rescued for three years? And what in the Sam Hill were a millionaire and a movie star doing on the crappy old *Minnow* anyway don t rich people have their own boats? And if the castaways spent all that time building themselves living quarters elaborate enough to pass for the Tiki Lounge, why couldn t these idiots like perhaps the so-called Professor build a raft sturdy enough to get them home? And speaking of the Professor, it s called a radio, dude. And functioning genitals. If the show had ever been even a little bit funny, we could maybe let some of this stuff go. It wasn t; we can t. *Three years*, people. What was that guy a professor *of* c o n-trivance? See also BAD SITCOM, SURE SIGNS OF; CANNED LAUGHTER, MANIPU-LATION BY/OF; SCHWARTZ, SHERWOOD; and SITCOMS, UNFUNNINESS OF SEMINAL.

GILMORE GIRLS The WB s popular dramedy follows the lives of Lorelai Gilmore (noted show killer Lauren Graham) and her daughter Rory (Alexis Bledel), whom Lorelai had at sixteen. When the show started, *Rory* was sixteen, and the exact opposite of her mother at that age an overachieving nerd whose terminal shyness and inappropriately friendlike relationship with Lorelai left her confused and awkward around boys. For added drama, Lorelai s parents (Edward Herrmann and Kelly Bishop) wealthy, tight-assed WASPs weren t that psyched when she got pregnant back in the day, and haven t entirely accepted her life apart from them. But Lorelai needs them to pay for Rory s education, so she has to swallow a lot of their pas-sive-aggressive abuse for the sake of the greater good. Rory and Lorelai talk a lot, and fast (and mumbly, in Rory s case,

which is a challenge for the viewer to fol-low), and about everything. Like so many long-running shows, *Gilmore Girls* ran out of decent story-lines before it ran out of episodes, and the strain of contriv-ing new scrapes for them to get into meant that the characters real-seeming charac-teristics grew ever more cartoonish, with Lorelai turning into a selfish, flighty monster and Rory letting every guy she dates walk all over her. Once Rory lost her virginity to her married ex-boyfriend Dean (Jared Padalecki) and Lorelai finally consummated her long-standing, unacknowledged crush on diner owner Luke (Scott Patterson), it was clear the show wasn t going to recapture its old charm. Not that we stopped watching, but . . . we did so bitterly. See also MOTHER-DAUGHTER RELATIONSHIPS, OVERLY CLOSE; SEXUAL TENSION, RUINATION OF SERIES BY RESOLVING; SHOW KILLERS; SMALL TOWNS, QUIRKINESS OF; and TEEN SEX, CONSEQUENCES OF.

GOLDEN GIRLS, THE Picture it: Sicily, 1904. *The Golden Girls* is a seminal sit-com for several reasons first, it depicted women over fifty as complete people with goals and desires; second, it didn t apologize for the trampalicious behavior of Rue McClanahan s Blanche; third, it rewarded faithful viewing with lessons on bitchy comic timing; and fourth, it contained Bea Arthur, who is awesome even when costumed in curtains from Graceland, which she frequently was. The girls ate cheesecake, talked about sex, teased each other rudely, slammed doors, and generally acted more like actual women (and roommates) than sitcom characters usually do. Also, in case you ve been living under a rock since the 80s: Estelle Getty is actually younger than Bea Arthur. See also ARTHUR, BEA and SENIOR CITIZENS, CLICH D PORTRAYALS OF.

GOLDEN GLOBES   The Golden Globes recognize extraordinary achievement in both film and television. Because they have separate categories for Motion Picture Drama and Motion Picture Musical or Comedy, there are twice as many nominees as at the Oscars, which is how someone like Jim Carrey can win for *Man on the Moon*. The Globes have clawed their way to the top tier of showbiz kudosfests even though the voting body is all fifty-something members of the Hollywood Foreign Press Association. And yet! It is broadcast with pomp enough to make you think it actually means something, and it can be more fun to watch than the Oscars: Producers jettison all those crappy technical categories like Best Sound Effects Editing ; the winners are so random that a pool is harder to win; and they serve booze *during* the ceremony. And apparently no one there is driving. See also AWARD SHOWS, LEGENDARILY BAD SPEECHES ON.

"GOPHER"   See *LOVE BOAT, THE*.

GOOD COP/BAD COP   A classic clich of the procedural drama, good cop/bad cop reveals why detectives come in pairs. Here s how it works: Bad Cop comes at the perp really hard, screaming in his face that the whole department knows he s guilty, maybe begging, Gimme a reason to mess you up! Then Good Cop pulls Bad Cop off the perp and shoves him out of the box. Alone with the perp, Good Cop sits, offers a drink, and gently says that if the perp has done something, he should be honest so they can get this straightened out. (Alternative: Start with Good Cop, but bring in Bad Cop to put the fear of God in the perp.) *Law & Order* loved to show us Bad Cop really going nuts, then strolling to the other side of the two-way mirror, smirking at his lieutenant. Lennie Briscoe (Jerry Orbach), may God rest his soul, was old, and therefore a better fit as Good Cop, so when he got his Bad Cop on, it was actually a little scary, like if a Macy s Santa suddenly started acting like he might kill you. See also *LAW & ORDER* FRANCHISE and LENNIE BRISCOE.

"GRAPE APE" Grrrrape-ape! Grrrrape-ape! Uch. We already have a Magilla Gorilla; shut up, Grape Ape. You too, Beegle Beagle. See also CARTOONS, HANNA-BARBERA.

GREATEST AMERICAN HERO, THE It never really got off the ground; the network kept changing its time slot, or preempting it, or changing the lead character s last name (the show debuted in 1981, which, after John Hinckley Jr. s attempt on President Reagan s life in March of the same year, was not a great time to name a character Hinkley). And the concept is pretty ridiculous Ralph Hinkley (William Katt) is given a superhero suit by aliens in the desert; the suit has special powers; dude loses the instruction manual (yeah, we don t know either); wacky hijinks ensue, some of them involving Connie Sellecca as Hinkley s girlfriend, some of them not involving her because Sellecca got pregnant during the second season. *GAH* (heh) eventually bit the dust (in spite of having an outstanding theme song) because an action show with an even more ridiculous premise a guy with a new face and a talking car got programmed opposite it on Friday nights, and *Knight Rider* kicked its ass. We still can t figure out why Katt never got more famous; no, he s not the greatest actor, but neither is Lorenzo Lamas, and we re still stuck with *that* guy. See also CAN-NELL, STEPHEN J.; KATT, WILLIAM; *KNIGHT RIDER*; and THEME SONGS.

"THE GREAT PUMPKIN" When we were kids, the TV calendar contained certain hallowed event programs the annual airing of *The Wizard of Oz*, for example, and the Charlie Brown specials at Christmas and Halloween. *It's the Great Pumpkin, Charlie Brown* encouraged kids to stick to their beliefs, as Linus did when insisting on the Great Pumpkin s existence; even better, it was a cartoon that aired *at night*. Heaven! Or so it seemed at the time; watching it now, we wonder why we liked it. The pacing is glacial, and the precocious cynicism of the kids actually kind of depressing. And Snoopy s Red Baron shtick is just as unfunny now as it was then. See also HOLIDAY SPECIALS.

GREY'S ANATOMY Finally, a medical drama that depicts the experience of a first-year intern from the female perspective! And apparently, what female interns do is carry on secret affairs with hot attending physicians who turn out to be married. Bolstered by its phenomenally successful lead-in, *Desperate Housewives*, *Grey's Anatomy* became the capper for ABC s amazing 2004—5 comeback season (joining *Housewives* and J. J. Abrams s *Lost*). Much was made in the press of its strong female characters, which (as is usually the case) was a load of crap. Cristina (Sandra Oh) is a socially maladjusted brown-noser; Izzy (Katherine Heigl) worked her way through medical school as an underwear model; and the titular Meredith Grey (Ellen Pompeo) the aforementioned attending-nailer wanders through the hospital with all her hair hanging in her face, hoping to skate by on her rabbity nose and flinty giggle. Fortunately, what the show does have going for it is a passel of gorgeous dudes in Isaiah Washington, Justin Chambers, and Patrick Dempsey, so much cuter in his forties than he was circa *Can't Buy Me Love*. As feminists, we should be disgusted that the female interns are such a bunch of spineless, stereotypical *girls*, but as women, we enjoy watching them sex up all that beefcake. See also *DESPERATE HOUSEWIVES* and MEDICAL DRAMAS, TROPES OF.

GROSSMAN, LESLIE As the deranged Mary Cherry, a Texan sorority girl with no filter and a devotion to the Lord, the amazingly hilarious Leslie Grossman was, bar none, the funniest thing on *Popular*. *Popular* s cancellation left the world a little darker and a little colder for her sudden absence from the airwaves. Someone needs to put this genius on her own sitcom, and if no one can come up with one worthy of her talents, we might have to. See also *POPULAR*.

GROWING PAINS Making Alan Thicke the father on a family sitcom seems like a crazy gamble for a TV network to undertake, and yet it happened, and it yielded the seven-season marvel *Growing Pains*. One of the most cynical *Family Ties* rip-offs in TV history, *Growing Pains* chron-icled the lives of the Seavers, but quickly turned into the Kirk Cameron Show. The actor s role as eldest Seaver sibling Mike became a hit with mid- 80s TV audiences, even though he was a douche with an unshakable shit-eating grin who couldn t stop making fat jokes at the expense of his normal-sized sister Carol (Tracey Gold, who was later anorexic). *Pains* further aped *Family Ties* when Seaver matriarch Maggie (Joanna Kerns) became pregnant midway through the run of the series to distract from the fading cuteness of youngest Seaver Ben (the actually quite homely Jeremy Miller), but then it pulled a *Cosby Show* when the Seavers took in a homeless teenager named Luke (Leonardo DiCaprio) who Taught Them All How Lucky They Are to Have Each Other. Whether the Luke year was more or less poignant than the story of Carol s boyfriend Sandy (a pre-*Friends* Matthew Perry) and how he got killed in a car crash is a matter of personal preference. ABC has so overrated the world s continuing interest in *Pains* that it has produced not one but *two* reunion movies in the twenty-first century (that s two as of this writing). Neither movie included Andrew Koenig s Boner, which we blame on super-Christian Kirk Cameron and his ostensible disapproval of erection-themed humor. See also BAD SITCOM, SURE SIGNS OF; CAMERON, KIRK; CHILDREN, OVERLY PRECOCIOUS; COUSIN OLIVER ; *FAMILY TIES*; PARENTS WHO ARE TOTALLY INTO EACH OTHER TO A CREEPY DEGREE; REUNION MOVIES; and TEENAGERS, BRATTY.

GRUNBERG, GREG Grunberg is our very favorite sidekick, whether as Sean Blumberg on *Felicity* or Agent Weiss on *Alias* h e s funny and obviously a really good sport as well (e.g., the ass-less pants he sported in one *Felicity* episode). And? Sexy! Especially when he s rocking the vintage-Bobby-Kennedy brush cut and sideburns. For years, we thought it was just us who secretly wanted to marry Grunberg, but every woman to whom we confessed our Grunberg-philia also thought he was a tasty dumpling with a sexy voice. He s the crush sensation that s sweeping the nation, but totally on the down-low. Grunberg s brother, Brad, is also an actor who works under the *nom de Hollywood* Johnny Cocktails, which is awesome. See also *ALIAS*; *FELICITY*; and TV BOYFRIENDS AND GIRLFRIENDS.

GUEST STARS, FREQUENT/FAMOUS Some actors just like to work, it seems, and they ll do anything. They ll even do *Two and a Half Men*. Or a doughy defense lawyer. Don t get us wrong, we love Holland Taylor, but why can t she do more Brad Anderson movies and less . . . Jimmy Berluti? Then there s that whole class of actors who keep showing up over and over on *Law & Order*, who once they ve shown they can cut it in a procedural get drafted into *CSI*, *Without a Trace*, and *Cold Case* (Robin Weigert, among about eight jillion others). And speaking of *CSI*, how damn many shows is Aisha Tyler going to have to guest on before she gets her own sitcom? See also *LAW & ORDER* FRANCHISE and STUNT-CASTING.

GUNS ON TV, UNRELIABILITY OF It s weird how guns don t shoot straight on TV; a professional marksman or trained assassin, equipped with notoriously good aim and the finest automatic weapon money can buy, will *still* miss any main character he or she fires upon. Either a hail of gunfire allows our protagonist to run through it unscathed or shelter from it behind a flimsy piece of furniture, or the bullet will wing the hero in the shoulder instead of killing him outright. Meanwhile, the cast members important enough to appear in the credits can somehow shoot a chandelier out of the ceiling and onto a villain from around a corner, in the dark, using the nondominant hand, and sometimes guns will just randomly shoot tertiary characters in the stomach and kill them, even though nobody has actually died of a gut-shot since the Civil War. Darn guns. See also DEAD SCOTT and *21 JUMP STREET*.

H

HAMLIN, HARRY *L.A. Law* sex symbol Hamlin isn t just a graduate of the Log with Lips Acting Academy; he s also the founder. He s attractive, if you like that sort of thing, and we re sure he s a very nice person; it was good to see him getting some work in *Veronica Mars*. But he had more chemistry with Pegasus in *Clash of the Titans* than he ever did with Susan Dey on *L.A. Law*, and we don t wish to slander the man, but it does seem like Botox may have reduced his range of two expressions smoldering and, uh, smoldering angrily to one. See also ACTING, WOODEN and *L.A. LAW*.

HAMPTON, BRENDA *7th Heaven* started out earnest and treacly, but at least it was endearing occasionally. As time went on, though, The WB s top-rated show (and seriously, what was *that* about?) got more and more socially conservative, judgmental, antifeminist, uptight, and just plain creepy. And who do we have to blame for the increasingly fundamentalist adventures of the Cam fam? Executive producer Brenda Hampton, who is pro-marriage (and, apparently, pro-buttinsky) but militantly against just about everything else sex before marriage between consenting adults, drinking of any kind, children s privacy, birth control, career women, questioning the U.S. government, driving too slowly, and giving characters names that don t derive from the 1940s. Viewers came to dread seeing Hampton s name next to written by in the credits, and we re all for family-values programming, but how does banishing your oldest daughter to Buffalo for drinking half a beer fit into that agenda? Hampton is also responsible for the Kirstie Alley neurosis-fest *Fat Actress*. And when she was a writer on *Blossom*, she was credited as Brenda Hampton-Cain. Coincidence? *We* don t *think* so. See also ALLEY, KIRSTIE; BIEL, JESSICA; *BLOSSOM*; and *7TH HEAVEN*.

HANDCUFFS, CLICHÉS ASSOCIATED WITH Someplace maybe where all the odd socks go there is a huge pile of keys that belong to TV s novelty handcuffs. Those things are always getting locked onto characters wrists and then stuck there through all sorts of wacky doings. Feuding characters get locked together to work out their quarrels, only to fight all the harder when escape is impossible due to a lost key. Characters are made to stay in one spot by getting cuffed to some kind of bathroom fixture, and get stuck there because, yes, the key is lost. The all-time sitcom classic: A groom is entertained at his bachelor party by a stripper dressed as a police officer, gets cuffed to her, can t find the keys, and has to free himself before his wedding the next day! Why can t strippers just dress as insurance claims adjusters? See also BAD SITCOMS, SURE SIGNS OF and ELEVATORS, CLICH S ASSOCIATED WITH.

HARDY BOYS, SAD SLOW DECLINE OF Okay, so *The Hardy Boys Mysteries* isn t exactly a dizzying height from which to fall, but still. Since the show, the gloriously 70s-coiffed Parker Stevenson married and divorced known Scientologist Kirstie Alley, and starred in a string of craptastic TV movies with titles like *Shadow of a Stranger* and *Not of This Earth*. He also appeared on *Melrose Place* as Alison s Steve Jobs-ian love interest, and he s done some directing, but he s all leathery now, and did we mention the Kirstie Alley? Shaun Cassidy has fared slightly better, going on to produce and write for series such as *American Gothic* and *The Agency*, and he also starred in the TV version of *Breaking Away* (which, huh?) and in one of the most hilarious TV movies ever, *Like Normal People*. Actually,

Shaun kind of rocks, now that we think about it. Stevenson . . . has some problems. (Scientology!) See also ALLEY, KIRSTIE; CASSIDYS, THE; *LIKE NORMAL PEOPLE*; and *MELROSE PLACE*.

HARRISON, CHRIS, INDISTINGUISHABILITY FROM MARK L. WALBERG OF If the host of *The Bachelor* (Chris Harrison) and the host of *Temptation Island*, *Russian Roulette*, and *On the Cover* (Mark L. Walberg) were standing side by side in front of you, we swear, you would not be able to tell them apart. Both broadcast the same dorky neediness, both cover it with the same waxy, smarmy jocularity. They both even have the same nose. It s spooky, actually. See also REALITY TV, HOSTS OF.

HASSELHOFF, DAVID Dandelion-coiffed David Hasselhoff was the star of not one but two formative programs: *Knight Rider*, the story of a man who does not  exist and his closeted talking car; and the *Baywatch* franchise. Hasselhoff is not a master thespian, but he gives 100 percent to whatever role he s in, whether it s muttering urgently into a two-way-radio watch that his car needs to rescue him from a pack of short-browed henchmen (again) or dashing grimly down the beach to save a drowning swimmer, stomach sucked valiantly in. Hasselhoff is allegedly a recording star overseas, and all five fans of his music can hear his musical stylings over the closing credits of most *Baywatch* episodes and in the *Knight Rider* episode Let It Be Me, in which he goes undercover in a rock band (and models a too-tight Benataresque jumpsuit instead of his customary too-tight jeans and Members Only pleather jacket). Beloved by many in spite of the distinct odor of cheese that attends his every movement, The Hoff is enough of a cultural icon to have scored himself a role in *The SpongeBob SquarePants Movie*. The Hoff doesn t take himself too seriously, either, which is refreshing. KITT, come get us! See also AGING OF MEN ON TV, UNGRACEFUL; *BAYWATCH*; *KNIGHT RIDER*; SCENERY, CHEWERS OF; and TV SERIES, FILM ADAPTATIONS OF.

HATCH, RICHARD If *Survivor* occupies an elevated position on TV for being the first to enslave America in front of a competitive reality show, then Richard Hatch will forever reign in infamy for being its first winner. When we watched *Survivor* s series premiere, in which a chubby, bearded know-it-all ground his team to a halt by sitting in a tree and bossing everyone around, we thought surely he would be the first to get voted off. Clearly, we knew nothing about game theory. Even though no one liked him not even those

in his own alliance he avoided ejection, largely because everyone thought that if they went up against him in the final two, no one on the jury would award him the million. Sadly, taking Richard to the final two was the last mistake Kelly Wiglesworth made in the game. In subsequent seasons, many players have tried variations on Richard s strategy, and it s virtually impossible now for anyone to last in the game without making an unbreakable alliance. Richard rode his victory pretty far, getting a deal for a self-help book based on his televised ability to screw people over to his own advantage. And then he came back to *Survivor* for the All-Star season and completely undid his own legacy by acting like a total jackass. And *then* the genius was convicted of tax evasion charges for never having declared his million-dollar *Survivor* booty. Did he not realize all those cameras were actually on? See also *SURVIVOR*.

HBO PROGRAMMING, LESSER-KNOWN We love *The Sopranos* too, but HBO isn t just about quality drama. It s also about sketchy documentary programming like the *Real Sex* series, which has about twenty bazillion chapters by now and is clearly a counter-programming strike designed to lure the Skinemax soft-core audience over to the classier precincts of HBO. Or like that crazy documentary about the hit man who looked like a warthog and kept ickily licking his lips during the interview segments while he talked about offing people. Probably the best HBO series nobody really paid attention to, though, is *Family Bonds*, a reality show about a Long Island family that ran a bail-bonds business. Midnight manhunts, barbecues in Flushing, the birth of a grandchild the audience witnessed it all. And speaking of warthogs . . . Flo, we mean this in the nicest possible way, but get thee to an orthodontist. See also CABLE CHANNELS, UNWATCHED.

HEAD OF THE CLASS Do you like *Welcome Back, Kotter* but wish the students getting schooled in life lessons by their cool teacher weren t all . . . special? Then *Head of the Class* may be the show for you. ABC s long-running sitcom took the *Kotter* formula but replaced the Sweathogs with a passel of Poindexters in a special class for gifted students. And yet, for a group of brainiacs, the *Class*ers didn t conform to TV s stereotypes for smart kids. Aside from Arvid (Dan Frischman), a straight-up dork in the *Revenge of the Nerds* mold, and Janice (Tannis Vallely), a child genius, the students were diverse, and, in some cases, even a little cool (by TV standards). Brian Robbins s Eric, with his leather jacket and surly attitude, was practically the second coming of The Fonz. Also, the girls were all attractive and well-dressed and generally didn t pre-

tend they were dumb to get male attention. Of course, when they did, they had the gentle and mellow advice of permanent substitute teacher Charlie Moore (Howard Hesseman) to set them straight; Charlie s job was to help the un-Sweathogs keep their noses out of their books and live real life, to learn street smarts as well as book smarts, blah blah blah. Those of us who earned good marks and read a lot may have bristled at the show s message that smart kids were naturally social rejects (even if that was . . . often true), but we also may have watched it for its wish-fulfillment elements, such as the notion that sensitive teen poet girls all eventually find Fonz manqu s to love them (even if said sensitive teen poet girls insist upon not cutting their hair and wearing gigantic Shaker-knit sweaters). See also ARTHUR FONZARELLI ; COOL, TV SIGNIFIERS OF; DORKINESS, TV SIGNIFIERS OF; and *WELCOME BACK, KOTTER*.

HETEROSEXUAL MEN, ODDLY EFFEMINATE See HOMOSEXUALITY, CODED.

HEWITT, JENNIFER LOVE She wasn t that bad, at first; when she showed up as Bailey s girlfriend Sarah on *Party of Five*, we kind of liked her, although she did that look at me, I m so skinny and cute thing where she pulled her sleeves way down over her knuckles too much . . . and we didn t really get where the Audrey

Hepburn comparisons were coming from, but whatever. Then came the derivative horror movies, and the dating of the Carson Daly, and the recording career, and then the Sarah character spun off into the corrosively saccharine *Time of Your Life*. Billed as a coming-of-age drama, *ToYL* actually functioned almost entirely as a Love-fluffing vehicle. Love starred and produced, you see, which required the other characters to heap her with unearned praise (la Tori Spelling as Donna Martin). The show got sacked midseason, but Love had bought into her own hype and went on to produce and star in a miscarriage of TV biopics known to the world as *The Audrey Hepburn Story*. That gentle breeze you feel? The real, non-rat-faced Audrey Hepburn, spinning like a top in her grave. Love returned to series TV with *Ghost Whisperer*, but if she thinks she can live down the *Garfield* movies, she should think again. And she should shut up. Forever. She sucks. See also DALY, CARSON; MOVIES, MADE-FOR-TV; *PARTY OF FIVE*; and SPIN-OFFS.

HIGH SCHOOL, UNREALISTIC PORTRAYALS OF We wish *we'd* attended high school in TV Land. Television high schoolers don t do much in the way of schoolwork or, really, anything else to do with school besides have contrivedly awkward moments in the hallway and go to the prom. They don t do much homework, or study for tests, unless it s in the service of a plot contrivance; they don t worry about the SATs unless it s part of a PSA about learning disabilities (Donna on *90210*) or the perils of cheating (Andie McPhee on *Dawson's Creek* n o t that there were any consequences that we saw, but whatever). And why should they focus on academics? If the show  stays on long enough, they ll all wind up at the same college anyway, and we can forgive Buffy Summers for having a couple of other things on her mind. On the other hand, TV high school has two major drawbacks: 1) you always have to read a book for English class that exactly parallels your tortured romantic situation, and 2) the teachers will get inappropriate with their students at the drop of a hat. Seriously: Pacey and Ta-MAH-ra on *Dawson's*, Paige and Matt on *Degrassi: The Next Generation*, fill-in-the-blanks on *Boston Public*. High school on TV isn t realistic; it s just a framework to get all the young cuties in the same place and force them to interact, and it s not like we need to see them posing for yearbook photos or cringing through the Human Sexuality unit in health class. We get that. But real kids don t just ditch class and get away with it, or hang out in a coffee shop on a school night, or carry backpacks with, like, one textbook and one Trapper Keeper in them. It s telling that two of the shows that got most of the little things about day-to-day high school life right, *Freaks and Geeks* and *My So-Called Life*, both got sacked before their time. See also BEVERLY HILLS 90210; BUFFY THE VAMPIRE SLAYER; COLLEGE, UNREALISTIC PORTRAYALS OF; DAWSON'S CREEK; DEGRASSI: THE NEXT GENERATION; MY SO-CALLED LIFE; PACEY WITTER ; and PROMS.

HOGANS, THE/HOGAN FAMILY, THE The Rasputin of sitcoms pure evil, and nothing could kill it. Not the recasting and repeated name changes, not the horrendous acting and scary outfits, not the formulaic writing, not even a change of network. The show first aired as *Valerie*, but star Valerie Harper got herself fired, and producers brought in hyper Wheat Thins pitchwoman Sandy Duncan as Aunt Sandy and renamed the show *The Hogan Family*. It trundled along in that form for several years, featuring Jason Bateman as the chunky, bear-claw-haired David; scrawny Jeremy Licht and beefy Danny Ponce as twins Mark and Willie, respectively; Josh Jack McKay Taylor as absentee father/airline pilot Michael; and Edie McClurg as ur-abrasive neighbor Mrs. Poole. Neither Licht nor Ponce could act worth a damn (and neither of them

really worked again), Duncan s wonky eye worked against any touching scenes in which she appeared, and . . . God, Mrs. Poole, get a hobby. Why didn t they just lock the damn side door? Apparently, *The Hogan Family* was the first sitcom to utter the word condom, but the idea that any of the Hoganlets could have gotten some action while clad in those retina-searing acid-washed *and pleated* jeans is absolutely preposterous. See also BAD SITCOM, SURE SIGNS OF; BATEMANS, JASON AND JUSTINE; MRS. POOLE ; NEIGHBORS, INTRUSIVE; RECASTING, NOTORIOUS; and TEENAGERS, BRATTY.

HOLIDAY SPECIALS How do you know it s Christmastime? The Christmas specials and winter-holiday spectaculars cluttering the primetime airwaves, from the stop-motion *Rudolph the Red-Nosed Reindeer* to *A Very Brady Christmas* to *Nick & Jessica's Family Christmas* to the worst holiday programming ever aired, *The Star Wars Holiday Special*. (Second worst: *Christmas Comes to Pac-Land*. Words cannot begin.) The players change it s always whoever s popular that year or can capitalize best on cross-promotion but the slapped-together sets, droned renditions of Silent Night, and forced hokey cheer of a winter special taped on a soundstage in August remain the same. Save yourself and change the channel to one of the myriad reairings of *A Christmas Story* or *It's a Wonderful Life*. At least George Bailey knows the difference between tuna and chicken. And doesn t have a man-perm. See also BRADY BUNCH, THE; CARTOONS PRIMARILY DESIGNED AS PROMOTIONAL TIE-INS; CHRISTMAS COMES TO PAC-LAND; THE GREAT PUMPKIN ; HOLIDAYS, SPECIAL EPISODES BASED AROUND; and STAR WARS HOLIDAY SPECIAL, THE.

HOLIDAYS, "SPECIAL" EPISODES BASED AROUND TV characters are stupid. That s the only explanation for why they have to keep relearning what Christmas is about charity, family, forgiveness, yada every damn year. How many times do the Simpsons have to lose all their gifts to get it through their heads? Doesn t Santa have to deliver presents instead of making like a hobo and handing out gifts to the Walshes before slipping out to, apparently, walk on their roof? Then there are the countless kids shows that carefully (and with maximum use of Yiddish phlegm) educate us about Chhhh-hchhhchanukkkhhkchkah. Less often exploited holidays include Thanksgiving (it doesn t matter if the meal got ruined; what s important is that we re together!); Valentine s Day (secret admirers, show yourselves!); Independence Day (America is great!); and Easter (. . . um, chocolate is yummy?). Looking to learn the true meaning of Martin Luther King Day?

Sorry, your only option is *The Cosby Show*. (For a deadly accurate parody of every lame-ass clich of special holiday episodes, track down the Snowflake Day episode of *Clone High*. It s got an egalitarian conflation of all religions winter celebrations: the challenge of tracking down a perfect gift; a girl learning the true meaning of the occasion; and, of course, a homeless angel.) See also BEVERLY HILLS 90210; CLONE HIGH; COSBY SHOW, THE; HOLIDAY SPECIALS; and SIMPSONS, THE.

HOLLYWOOD SQUARES It s remarkable that a concept this lame could have made it through three iterations (the one with Paul Lynde and Peter Marshall, from the 60s; the one with Joan Rivers and John Davidson, from the 80s; and the one with Whoopi Goldberg and Tom Bergeron, from the 90s). It s tic-tac-freakin -toe! And, as is always the problem with game shows that rely on celebrities to populate them, the caliber of stars who are willing to turn out for an entire afternoon of pretending to care about regular people is . . . well, you re not getting Catherine Zeta-Jones; you re getting ALF. It took a long time before we figured out that the celebrities jokey answers the ones the contestants were meant to disagree with were scripted in advance. Give us a break, we were dumb kids. See also GAME SHOWS, CELEBRITIES ON.

HOLMES, DAVE We re *still* annoyed that Dave Holmes lost that I Want to Be an MTV VJ contest to Stupidville, Population: Jesse Camp! Dave knew a crapload about music, but not in a music-fascist way, and he s cute, too, in the slightly doughy Greg Grunberg style. Fortunately, he got work elsewhere, but we feel that gigs like *DVD on TV* don t take full advantage of his sarcastic wit, which is formidable. And we suspect that he feels the same way, because we might best describe his hosting of *Fire Me, Please* as sheepish. No wonder, really. Free Dave! See also CAMP, JESSE; GRUNBERG, GREG; and MTV VJs.

HOME MAKEOVER SHOWS Back when Bob Vila was the only person on TV messing with anyone s duct work, the point of a home renovation show was practical to show the idiots at home how to repair their foundations, put in new linoleum, or what have you. And even in the first season of *Trading Spaces*, they still spent a significant amount of time on instruction. But once producers figured out that there was drama to be wrung out of the possibility that the makeover recipients might hate what they got (that means you, Crying Pam), all that learnin went out the window. Enter *While You Were Out*, *Surprise by Design*, *Clean Sweep*, *Clean House*, and many more reveal-reliant shows that demonstrate, more often than not, that design on a budget generally means shoddy paint job and maybe a new IKEA lamp, suckers! At the other end of the spectrum is *Extreme Makeover: Home Edition*, where all you have to do to get a lavish, full-house renovation is survive nineteen simultaneous heart attacks or give birth to a kid whose bones are made of dry spaghetti. See also CRYING PAM.

HOMICIDE: LIFE ON THE STREET It s probably a little weird to call it a cult show, given that it lasted six years, but *H:LOTS* spent most of that time lounging on the cancellation bubble, and its fans still talk about its demise like it s a breakup that just happened last week. It s not hard to see why.  *H:LOTS* blended the grit and the personal-lives focus of *NYPD Blue* with the businesslike cynicism of *Law & Order*, then threw in a handful of hotties (Kyle Secor, Andre Braugher) and a too-large pinch of Richard Belzer for a tasty cop-drama Chex Mix. And as satisfying as it is as a straight police procedural, it s just as satisfying from a love-to-hate standpoint; any given episode features an actor or character to hate and yell at from the couch, starting with Jon Seda and Daniel The Fat One Baldwin and ending with . . . well, Belzer.

And Belzer's sunglasses. Shut up, Belzer's sunglasses. Unfortunately, although watching it in reruns is fun, it's also sad, because it makes us wish Michelle Forbes would get another starring role . . . or that they'd do a reunion movie in which her character flicks Reed Diamond's character in the head . . . What? Kellerman is annoying. See also "CULT SHOW," DEFINITION OF; *LAW & ORDER* FRANCHISE; and *NYPD BLUE*.

HOMOSEXUALITY, CODED In less enlightened times, it made sense for male characters who were maybe a little flamboyant (*Bewitched*'s Uncle Arthur, *Too Close for Comfort*'s Monroe) or female characters who were maybe a little butch (*The Beverly Hillbillies'* Miss Hathaway, *The Facts of Life*'s Jo) to be cagey. We understood what they were into, and anyway, their private lives were none of our business. But even into the present day—when we've all lived through countless Very Special Episodes in which we learned that it's actually okay to be gay—there are still allegedly straight characters who display signs of latent homosexuality. Joey and Chandler are clearly in love with each other; Kip and Henry may have arrived a little too readily at the "let's try drag" solution to their housing crisis; and Frasier . . . well, no straight guy is that heavy into sherry. Not that there's anything wrong with that. See also *BEWITCHED*; *BOSOM BUDDIES*; BULLOCK, JM J.; *FACTS OF LIFE, THE*; FRASIER CRANE, and *FRIENDS*.

"HORATIO CAINE" The putative moral and ethical center of *CSI: Miami*, Horatio Caine (David Caruso) is in actuality one of the most odious cops TV has ever produced. The man is a snitty bitch with nothing but contempt for everyone he deals with—not just perps, but his colleagues as well. We choose to believe that the character as written is actually okay, but that it's Caruso's spin that makes Horatio so objectionable. Every line he delivers sounds as though it ends just a split second before he adds, ". . . stupid!" That's how he treats everyone. He's a tool. An ugly tool. See also CARUSO, DAVID, AS GO-TO REFERENCE FOR CAREER SUICIDE and *CSI*, SPIN-OFFS OF.

HUFFMAN, FELICITY In David Mamet films, Felicity Huffman has a flinty, WASPy presence that's sort of likably brittle. As a TV actress, it's a different story. Her Dana on *Sports Night* was saddled with a bitchy attitude and a ridiculous story arc that had her arbitrarily delaying consummation of a mutual attraction between herself and Peter Krause's Casey. And on *Desperate Housewives* . . . oy. Lynette Scavo is like a horrendous caricature of all of Huffman's previous "strong woman" characters. As a former executive who somehow wasn t high-powered enough to resist her husband s request that she stay home with their four children, she used every possible pretext to complain about her station in life how her kids are uncontrollable (her fault), how she can t even manage her time well enough to take a shower (her fault), how her husband isn t interested in sexing her up when she stinks (her fault), how she misses working (her fault), how her dowdiness is driving her husband into the arms of a woman who s basically her from when she had a job (her fault), how the nanny she hired had to be let go after her husband accidentally saw her naked (. . . her fault for being so jealous). You get the point. Lynette sucks. She sucks even harder now that she s back at work, since we can t help vicariously sympathizing with the coworkers who have to put up with her unprofessional ass. And her suckiness and the cheerfulness with which Huffman has confessed to how much she has in common with Lynette has made us rethink everything we ever may have liked about Huffman. It s just one more way that *Desperate Housewives* has ruined everything for everyone everywhere. See also *DESPERATE HOUSEWIVES*; SITCOM, MOVIE ACTRESSES ATTEMPTS TO PROP SAGGING CAREER BY MEANS OF; and *SPORTS NIGHT*.

HUNTER *Hunter* is like the Hootie & the Blowfish of TV nobody admitted to watching it, but it somehow stayed on the air for seven years. A fairly run-of-the-mill cop drama, *Hunter* starred former pro footballer Fred Dryer as Rick Hunter and Stepfanie Kramer as his partner (and orange-lipstick connoisseur) Dee Dee McCall. It was a good show, if by good you mean you re home babysitting your little bro and there s nothing else on. But . . . that was the bulk of the show s ratings, right there. We don t think anyone was learning to program the VCR timer for the sake of *Hunter* completism. Dryer shows up now and then in *Hunter* reunion movies and straight-to-video stuff, but we feel that he should work more; he s very tall and kind of a bad-ass. And did you know he was almost Sam Malone on *Cheers*? See also CANNELL, STEPHEN J.; *CHEERS*; and REUNION MOVIES.

despite the power imbalance of their relationship from its very start. We just hope Jeannie had her own savings account in case she ever had to flee a drunken Master in the night. See also *BEWITCHED* and THEME SONGS.

"I FEEL YOU, DAWG" See *AMERICAN IDOL*.

I LOVE LUCY See BALL, LUCILLE and SITCOMS, UNFUNNINESS OF SEMINAL.

I DREAM OF JEANNIE When people talk about the golden age of television presumably when competitive eating wasn t broadcast as a sport are they really talking about shows such as *I Dream of Jeannie*? Like *Bewitched*, Jeannie kicked off with adorable animated credits (and, granted, the *Jeannie* theme song still rocks); like *Bewitched*, it featured a woman with  magical powers in the service of a generally befuddled and un-fun mortal dude. However, at least on *Bewitched*, the couple was married, and therefore nominally equals; Jeannie s (Barbara Eden) Major Nelson (Larry Hagman) had freed her from her bottle, and therefore she was in his service and called him nothing but Master. Um, ew. Worse yet, the series eventually had them getting married,

INFOMERCIALS Infomercials: everything you hate about regular-sized commercials, and so much more! Nowadays, most channels schedule real programming around the clock, but post—1 AM time slots used to be the exclusive domain of half-hour blocks in which advertisers shilled exercise machines, diet pills, skin-care systems, knife sets, non-FDA-approved cleansers, and any other product that might require a lengthy demonstration. Some infomercials spotlighted a D-list celeb and her girlfriends who just *happened* to be sitting around a tackily decorated living room chatting about Victoria Jackson s No Makeup Makeup ; others showed Stain-B-Gon—type products cleaning everything from a marinara-stained rugby shirt to the carpet at the scene of a triple homicide. All of them tried to make it seem as if they weren t *trying* to sell you anything; they just wanted you to *know* about the product. Which is very nice of Chuck Norris and Christie Brinkley, but we re still not buying that Bodyflex or whatever it s called. It s just gonna sit in the garage next to the Ginsu knives. See also AS SEEN ON TV PRODUCTS and RONCO.

INSIDE THE ACTORS STUDIO The idea behind Bravo s long-running chatfest is to show the intimate interviews our generation s greatest actors give to students at the New School for Social Research s Actors Studio Drama School. The reality is that they ran out of good actors about twenty episodes in, which is why they ve more recently played host to the likes of Meg Ryan, Melanie Griffith, Nathan Lane, and, most notoriously of all, Ms. Jennifer Lopez. The show is characterized by the spectacularly sycophantic questions dished out by *Studio* host James Lipton (nary a hardball in the bunch seriously, What s your favorite word? is a common query), and the even more brown-nosey behavior of the Drama School students, who seem less interested in asking probing questions than they are in making Juliette Binoche smile at them. If nothing else, the show makes excellent fodder for drinking games: If Lipton ever gives a guest cause to cease thinking she s a total genius, CHUG! See also BRAVO; DRINKING GAMES; and LIPTON, JAMES.

INTERIOR MONOLOGUE, USES OF A cousin to the cloying protagonist voice-over (as in *Grey's Anatomy* or *Doogie Howser, M.D.*) as an expository tool, the interior monologue is a boon for lazy writers and actors alike. Deployed poorly, as on *Ally McBeal*, it can ensure that the viewer understands that what a character may say aloud to others doesn t necessarily line up with her actual feelings or thoughts and saves the actor having to *act* as though that were the case. (E.g., The Biscuit: You don t mind, do you, Ally? Ally: Oh, no. Ally s mind: Yes! Maybe Calista Flockhart accompanies the yes with a sharp facial expression; maybe not.) Deployed well, as on *Scrubs*, it becomes almost a supporting character the audience comes to depend on to deepen the humor of a situation. (E.g., J.D. s Mind: Oh no! If she knows it was me who screwed up her date she ll give me the evil eye and rip off my nipples.) Somewhere in the middle is Homer Simpson s interior monologue, which once got so disgusted at Homer s stupidity that it left, slamming a door behind it. Tee hee. See also *DOOGIE HOWSER, M.D.*; EXPOSITION, CLUNKY; *GREY'S ANATOMY*; and *SIMPSONS, THE*.

INTERNET, CLICHÉS ASSOCIATED WITH As of this writing, most people we know in life including those who are senior citizens and retired from the workforce have access to the Internet at home and use it for all sorts of banal purposes, like checking e-mail, reading snarky Web sites, and shopping for books. But on TV, the Internet is invariably portrayed either as a bastion for inveterate (and potentially dangerous) nerds (like the trio who terrorized Sunnydale in the sixth season of *Buffy*), or for sex-crazed (always dangerous) predators (*Degrassi: The Next Generation*'s pilot episode). Whole episodes of the *Law & Order* franchise are devoted to pedophiles who use the Web to recruit underage nude models, stalkers who track their quarries through their innocuous message-board posts, or identity thieves who live high on the hog by harvesting credit-card information through illegal hacks. Bottom line as far as TV is concerned, there's no one on the Internet that can possibly be trusted. In real life, of course, we can't live that way. Because *everyone uses the Internet*. Live in the now, TV writers! See also *BUFFY THE VAMPIRE SLAYER*; COMPUTERS, CLICH'S ASSOCIATED WITH; *DEGRASSI: THE NEXT GENERATION*; and *LAW & ORDER* FRANCHISE.

INTERVENTION Real people battling serious addictions deserve our sympathy and our support not our mockery. But if A&E is going to put them at the center of a TV series, then it's really A&E's fault if we watch the show solely to judge and heckle them. *Intervention* shows us a meth and sex addict calling out for a new friend to hang with for a few hours; a self-mutilation addict cutting a bloody triangle into her torso; and one especially memorable woman hooked on pills, horse racing, *and* bingo. Most of the time, we're glad when the addicts sob into the camera and get tough love from their relatives, because their addictions have made them such assholes that we really wish them ill. See also ALCOHOLISM and DRUG ABUSE, PORTRAYALS OF.

"IN THE BUTT, BOB" A TV urban legend . . . *or is it?* According to lore, Bob Eubanks opened a round of *The Newlywed Game* by asking, What's the strangest place you've ever made whoopee? The show's writers used that question frequently and usually got answers like on top of a piano, but in this case, the contestant interpreted the word place a little differently, and responded, In the butt, Bob. For every viewer over the years who swears she's seen the infamous episode, there's a denial from Bob Eubanks that it ever happened. But according to the urban-legend investigations site Snopes.com, a 1977 episode in which Olga Perez tried to match her husband Hank's answer by blurting out, Is it in the ass? might be the source of the myth. The ep has aired on the Game Show Network at some point (with the last three words bleeped) and was included in

Confessions of a Dangerous Mind (entirely unbleeped), but she doesn t say butt, or Bob, so . . . who knows. And, really, who cares, because the word butt is funny, and the phrase is really handy for yelling out when a present-day game-show contestant is spacing on an answer. See also GAME SHOW NETWORK.

IRON CHEF Two chefs walk in; one chef leaves. Well, sort of. *Iron Chef* pits two chefs, each a master in a different type of ethnic cuisine, against each other; the chefs must cook an entire meal based around a theme ingredient, within the allotted time, and then submit the meal to a panel of celebrity judges. It s a Japanese show, with Japanese chefs and Japanese celebs, presided over by a Japanese Liberace named Chairman Kaga . . . but when it airs Stateside, everything is voiced over in English, including the commentators remarks. Often the voice-over has nothing to do with what the audience sees (one judge pulls an awful face when presented with a peanut butter puttanesca; the voice-over murmurs, Hmm, quite good). And yet, somehow, it works the cameramen will dive side-ways into the woks to get a good shot if they have to, and the dishes always amaze and delight. *Iron Chef America* is, in our opinion, a pale copy of the original, which is like watching *Big Night*, only sweatier.

IRWIN, STEVE Though he comes across as your standard braying Aussie loon, Steve Irwin is apparently a qualified zoologist. He owns the Australia Zoo and is the host of several series for Discovery and Animal Planet (most famously, *The Crocodile Hunter*), in  which he takes very stupid risks in the name of documentary television. We ll give him his props you really do have to love animals to basically stick your head in their jaws and the footage of him fleeing a komodo dragon is some of the funniest shit we ve ever seen. But his unshakable enthusiasm for the entire animal kingdom makes him an exhausting talk-show guest, and we re hoping he s learned why it s not cool to feed a crocodile a chicken while holding your chicken-like month-old baby in your other hand. And *get filmed doing so*. Dumb-ass. See also DADS, TV.

"I'VE FALLEN AND I CAN'T GET UP!" See MRS. FLETCHER.

J

JACKASS *Jackass* proved, once and for all, that the only thing cooler than seeing someone pull off a really difficult skateboard stunt is seeing someone biff it and injure himself. *Jackass* had a glorious two-year run on MTV, during which time host (and series cocreator) Johnny Knoxville and his fellow idiots were videotaped covering themselves with bees; loudly farting through a yoga class; kidnapping Brad Pitt off the street (Pitt was complicit in the prank); getting their butt cheeks pierced; and (squeamish folk, look away!) eating the ingredients of an omelet, vomiting them up, and then cooking the regurgitated food and eating it. Still, our favorite segment wasn t physical at all: The crew traveled to Mianus (pronounced My Anus), Connecticut, and talked to locals about the town. So is there a lot of crime in Mianus? Oh look, there s a little Jack Russell terrier in Mianus! The series was adapted as a movie in 2002; we re still crossing our fingers for a sequel, despite Knoxville s new fame as a legitimate actor (*Dukes of Hazzard*, y all) and rumored Jessica Simpson defiler. See also SIMPSONS, ASHLEEEEE AND JESSICA and STONERS, TV FOR.

"JACK BAUER" In spite of a growly voice that could melt polar ice caps and the magical ability to get anywhere in Los Angeles by car in under ten minutes (even at rush hour), the protagonist of *24* doesn t have very good luck with the ladies. His late wife, Teri, rocked the house but he cheated on her with global-village sociopath and mole Nina Myers and wound up more or less getting Teri killed at the end of the first season. The second season saw him building a flirtation with the haplessly clammy Kate My Sister Is NOT a Terrorist! . . . Oh, Hold on a Sec Warner, but we never saw it consummated, and by the beginning of Season 3, he d already dumped her. Great, we thought. Jack could use some time on his own, to work through a few issues. Alas, his affinity for sticky love triangles wasn t among the issues getting dealt with, as Season 4 saw The Velvet Fed doing the Posturepedic polka with the boss s daughter. Did we mention that William Devane played dear old Dad? Because if we re Jack, we re avoiding that shit like the plague. But if you think we re saying that to his face, think again. We don t want him cutting our heads off and bringing them to terrorist meets in bowling-ball bags. Or breaking our fingers one at a time. The man can go twenty-four hours without taking a pee; he kind of scares us. Looks great in a bulletproof vest, though. See also DADS, TV; DEVANE, WILLIAM; and *24*.

"JACK BRISTOW" Watching the promos for or press coverage of *Alias* probably made you think that Jennifer Garner was the star of the show. And maybe she was, in the sense that every story revolved around her and she got top billing. But watching the show in a more compressed way, the viewer s impression of the show is quite different specifically in that it tends to highlight how unfailingly awesome Garner s TV dad, Jack Bristow, actually is. Veteran Broadway and character actor Victor Garber was, in his distinguished middle age, handed one of the all-time great TV dad roles: Jack Bristow was not only supersmart (an expert in game theory hot!), but also a total badass. When a troublesome quarry had to be eliminated off the books and without a lot of muss or fuss, Jack Bristow was the man for the job. He d put on a pair of fingerprint-concealing all-purpose black leather gloves and garrote a mole in the CIA. Hell, he d even make a special trip to off his own ex-wife. And yet, for all his enforcing, Jack was still totally refined; he favored four-button suits with high lapels, kept his hair in a perfectly marcelled wave over his forehead, and just looked like someone who knows a lot about wine. All of that, plus his gift for qualm-free murder, made him one of *Alias* s most interesting characters; not for nothing did we wish for a spin-off called *Jack & Sloane*. See also *ALIAS*; DADS, TV; and GARNER, JENNIFER.

JACKÉE Jack e is annoying for two reasons. (Well, three, if you count the fact that she dropped her last name because . . .  Harry was creating too much wind resistance? We don t know.) The first reason is her gin-soaked, baby-voiced giggle: blech. The second reason is actually not her fault; the sassy-black-woman Hollywood stereotype is sort of a problem, and it s, like, the only kind of part Jack e ever seems to play. And we have a sneaking suspicion that, given something to do besides suck her teeth, bug her eyes out, and mince along in high heels like the floor is on fire, she . . . might rock that shit. Enough with the *Sister, Sister*; put her on *CSI: 227*. See also *227*.

"JACK McPHEE" We really wanted to like Jack McPhee. We could have done without the nude-portraiture subplot (don t ask), and the goopy poem he wrote and Pacey read aloud in English class that led to his reluctant declosetation. But once that story arc fiiiiinally got rolling, we thought he d become a groundbreaking character on *Dawson's Creek* an uplifting example for gay teens, on a network aimed squarely at their demographic. Yeah, not so much. The character never really lived up to his potential, partly because of the show s customary clumsy writing, but mostly because Kerr Smith played the gay teen in question. Smith does have certain talents fratty handsomeness, decent comic timing but portraying a gay adolescent without breaking character to look nauseated isn t one of them. In any scene that called for Smith even to smile at, much less French, another guy, the actor could not disguise his utter panic. And not only could he not act like he dug guys onscreen, Smith couldn t keep his trap shut off-screen either; he d already accepted a GLAAD award for his portrayal of Jack when *Entertainment Weekly* quoted him as saying he didn t think viewers needed to see two dudes kissing on TV. All of which made it a little hard to care about Jack s storylines. What a waste. Shut up, Kerr. See also *DAWSON'S CREEK* and HOMOSEXUALITY, CODED.

JAG If *Hunter* is the Hootie & the Blowfish of procedural drama, *JAG* is the mac and cheese it s not prime rib, just starchy, filling comfort food. Set in the U.S. Navy s Judge Advocate General s Corps, with blandly attractive leads and solidly conventional plots, *JAG* was hardly the stuff of passionate water-cooler debate, but sometimes pretty good is enough to keep you on the menu for ten years. That, and the unresolved heat between Mac (Catherine Bell) and Harm (David James Elliott), which the show smartly refused to act on until the series finale. And David James Elliott is pretty cute in a fratty sort of way, although it s strange that he never seemed to age. Like, at all. See also *HUNTER* and SEXUAL TENSION, RUINATION OF SHOW BY RESOLVING.

JEM We know at least one thing about this cartoon heroine: She was truly outrageous. No, truly: truly, truly outrageous. On TV, *Jem* dramatized the adventures of Jerrica Benton, the frontwoman of an all-girl rock band who happened to possess magic earrings that allowed her to change into superheroine Jem to battle the evildoings of rival rock band the Misfits (not to be confused with the existing punk band of the early 80s). Off TV, Jem was at the center of a line of twelve-inch fashion dolls (read: off-brand Barbies), which were actually a pretty good value, since each one came with an outfit for the girl s real identity *plus* accessories that could be used to change her into her superhero alter ego. In the case of the Jem doll, that actually just amounted to a fringe belt that could be turned inside out, but still. See also CARTOONS PRIMARILY DESIGNED AS PROMOTIONAL TIE-INS and THEME SONGS.

JENNINGS, KEN As of this writing and, probably, for all time Ken Jennings has the longest winning streak in *Jeopardy!* history. Through its first nineteen years on the air, the rule was that an undefeated contestant could return until he or she had earned $100,000 or played on five episodes, whichever came first. But in the show s twentieth season, the rule changed: As long as you kept winning, you could keep playing. The producers probably thought this would freshen the show and provide additional suspense; they surely never counted on a Ken to come along and win $2,520,700 over seventy-four consecutive games. But that he did, going out on a comparatively easy Final Jeopardy question : Most of this firm s 70,000 seasonal white-collar employees work only four months out of the year. Ken said FedEx, but duh, it s H&R Block. Increasing the ignomity of Ken s defeat, he was beaten in 2005 s Ultimate Tournament of Champions by relative unknown Brad Rutter. Who s younger than we are and has earned $3.2 million from *Jeop-*

ardy! Rutter may hold the earnings record, but we ve still got to give it up for Ken. See also *JEOPARDY!* and TREBEK, ALEX.

JEOPARDY! Feeling superior to *Wheel of Fortune* contestants is easy (No, you fools, the expression they re looking for is not That s All, Yolks) but not especially satisfying. No, to really get your smug on, you need a tougher show. What could have been a fairly dull trivia show is jazzed up (somewhat) by an arbitrary twist: The show supplies the answers, and contestants must phrase their responses in the form of a question (and when the players get excited and forget this fairly straightforward rule, it s schadenfreudelicious). *Jeopardy!* s contestants test is notoriously difficult, which may be why so many of the people who make it onto the show are such nerds. *Jeopardy!* is one of the few game shows where trivia buffs can really earn some serious money (as Ken Jennings could tell you), although the show has, in recent years, been dumbing down the answers, phrasing them in a way that clearly telegraphs the question. Still, that change hasn t done anything to dull the thrill of our favorite *Jeopardy!* play-along guessing the Final Jeopardy! question based on the category alone. See also GAME SHOWS, CELEBRITY EDITIONS OF; JENNINGS, KEN; TREBEK, ALEX; and *WHEEL OF FORTUNE.*

JERRY SPRINGER SHOW, THE The *Jerry Springer Show* was originally a serious talk show in the style of *Donahue*, and Springer himself the former mayor of Cincinnati was a respected local news anchor. But the original iteration of *Springer* got terrible ratings and was in danger of cancelation, whereupon the format was revamped to be more lurid and trashy, saving it from the ax. Springer apparently hasn t stopped selling out since. We confess that *Springer* made for fine viewing, once. But when the chair-throwing, midget-baiting, and baby daddy disputes became the rule instead of the exception, we got bored; there are only so many I m really a man reveals you can sit through before you start to question how Bobby Joe didn t notice Sharon s enormous Adam s apple. And penis. See also TALK SHOWS, DAYTIME.

"JOHNNY BRAVO" Greg Brady s obnoxious rock-star alter ego. (Not to be confused with *Johnny Bravo*, the Cartoon Network series, which we know nothing of because it looks really dumb.) Barry Williams, who played Greg, released an album a few years back called *The Return of Johnny Bravo*, and while we commend Williams s continuing (if somewhat fame-whorish) willingness to make fun of himself in this manner, what s with the cover version of Hip to Be Square ? See also *BRADY BUNCH, THE* and *BRADY BUNCH,*

THE, MUSICAL STYLINGS OF.

JOHN 3:16 GUY The John 3:16 Guy was a fixture in the background of televised sporting events through much of the 80s. Then he went crazy. Originally just a garden-variety attention-seeker, and then a Christian attention-seeker (the Bible verse to which his signs referred reads, For God so loved the world that He gave His only begotten Son, that whosoever believeth in Him should not perish but have everlasting life), Rockin Rollen Stewart escalated his missionary work in the 90s, choosing to spread the word of God through a series of bombings including a church and a Christian bookstore in the L.A. area, culminating with a final effort on September 22, 1992, which he believed was six days before the Rapture. Long story short, it ended in a hostage situation with a maid at an airport hotel, and although no one was hurt, the John 3:16 Guy is now serving a life sentence for kidnapping. So the next time you re out at a game, keep an eye on those guys who ve spelled out BEARS in body paint across their chests; they might have bigger plans . . . See also AFROS, IMPORTANT TV.

JOHNSON, DON He s a lot better at modeling the latest in artful stubble, or posing next to a penis-substitute car of some sort the Barracuda he drove on *Nash*

Bridges, or one of the Ferraris from *Miami Vice* than he is at acting. (The studio execs agreed, and initially opposed casting him in *Miami Vice*; at the time, he had a reputation as a show killer.) Or picking scripts, for that matter *Miami Vice* is now largely viewed as a garish 80s time capsule, and *Nash Bridges . . .* well, we didn t actually watch *Nash Bridges*, using it instead as our go-to punchline for jokes about crappy weekend-night TV nobody actually watches. But we didn t watch *Harley Davidson and the Marlboro Man*, either, and we still know it sucked. And as bad as he is at identifying quality projects (his music video/crappy movie vanity project, *Heartbeat*, is a nonstop gigglefest), he s even worse at selecting quality spouses. Marrying Melanie Moonbeam Griffith is bad enough once; twice, it s unacceptable. And yet, in spite of all of this, and in spite of the fact that he s an arrogant jackass (he once claimed to be a better actor than Robert De Niro), we love him. Why? 1) He insulted David Cassidy at a party one time, and 2) a Finnish rock group named itself Don Johnson Big Band. Hee. See also ACTING, WOODEN; CASSIDYS, THE; *MIAMI VICE*; and SHOW KILLERS.

JUDGING AMY How does a TV producer girl up a typical legal drama? If she s Barbara Hall, she teams up with Amy Brenneman to create a show about a divorced female family-court judge (so that her cases involve troubled children and/or abusive parents) living with her social-worker mother (more abused kids). *Judging Amy* wasn t always the slyest when it came to disguising its gynocentric mission, but when the cases were sufficiently lurid (a suspenseful hour about Munchausen Syndrome by proxy actually did keep us guessing as to whether the mother really was abusing her daughter or not she was), we didn t really care. A supporting cast of beefcake like Reed Diamond, Chris Sarandon, Adrian Pasdar, and John Slattery (Amy s love interests), Dan Futterman (Amy s brother), and Richard T. Jones (Amy s court services officer) didn t hurt, either. But special mention is due Jillian Armenante, as Amy s hilariously weird clerk Donna, and Tyne Daly, as Amy s stalwart and awesomely prickly mother Maxine. We hope we have that gorgeous a head of silver hair when we re that age. And can cut down our foes with her force and economy of expression. Love her. See also OFFICE WEIRDO.

"JULIE EMRICK" Julie Emrick s (Amy Jo Johnson) melodramatic departure from UNY and *Felicity* is possibly the most satisfying midseason exit in TV history. Julie elected herself mayor of Bitchville the minute she hooked up with Ben Covington in the first season, and reigned unchallenged from then on going out with Ben even though she knew Felicity was obsessed with the guy; acting like a snot about it when Ben chose Felicity over her; writing and singing a mean song about Felicity at an open-mic night; repeatedly and obliviously breaking Sean s heart (she did him a favor, because he so deserved better, but still); refusing her birth father a kidney *and thereby killing his ass*, then sniping at Elena when she tried to be supportive; and did we mention all the singing? Because she did a lot of singing breathy Lilith Faux crap full of lyrics about wings and hearts and blah, and she accompanied herself on a twee painted guitar (sure, why not mess up the acoustics of the instrument by covering it in gouache?) while wearing a buttload of cutesy multicolored butterfly clips in her hair. Yeah, yeah, she helped get the morning-after pill at the health center, but she still sucked. Haaaaaaate! See also *FELICITY* and UNIVERSALLY REVILED CHARACTERS.

K

KATE & ALLIE The 80s thought up dozens of variations on the nonbiological-family-unit sitcom premise: three dads for one set of kids (*Full House*); two possible dads for one kid (*My Two Dads*); male nanny as father/older brother figure (*Charles in Charge* and, to an extent, *Who's the Boss?*); half-human, half-alien kid raised by earth mother and ball-of-light space father (*Out of This World*) you get the idea. And most of them focused on men thrown into unexpected parenting roles, because a man plus a loaded diaper or a teenage girl s first period equals instant gender-bending comedy, apparently. But *Kate & Allie* featured two divorced moms (and their three collective kids) sharing a house in New York City. Cue the learning, sharing, and jokes about the subway, right? Well, yes, but cue also the taste this, I think it s rotten acting of Allison Smith as Allie s daughter Jennie with her cool barretted-on-one-side hair, frosty pink lipstick, and sulky demeanor, she reminded us of the bitchy popular girls at school. Ditto Ari Meyers as Emma, who delivered every line as though she had just eaten a large, active bug. We liked Susan Saint James as Kate; she seemed like a cool mom, and we wouldn t have minded sharing a sweet Greenwich Village pad with her if we could have gotten rid of the kids . . . and of Allie, played by Jane Curtin as an uptight shrew with a voice that could reshape diamonds. See also BAD SITCOM, SURE SIGNS OF; *CHARLES IN CHARGE*; *FULL HOUSE*; NEW YORK CITY, CLICH D/INACCURATE TV PORTRAYALS OF; *OUT OF THIS WORLD*; and *WHO'S THE BOSS?*

KATE'S SECRET Next to TV-movie camp classic in the dictionary, there s a picture of Kate (Meredith Baxter-Birney) shotgunning Mallomars in a grocery-store parking lot. *Kate's Secret* intended to enlighten the viewing public on the dangers (and the secret shame) of bulimia, but succeeded primarily in the unintentional-hilarity department, filled as it was with snack product placements, screechy soundtrack cues, horror-movie camera angles, and Fellini-esque shots of wads of cake disappearing into the Baxter-Birney . . . er, cakehole. Also contributing to the hee hee atmosphere: Shari Belafonte as Kate s best friend and personal trainer yeah, seriously. *Kate's Secret* is probably the most entertaining in the anorexia-bulimia-PSA genre not as titillatingly gross as the Calista Flockhart one where she saves her barf in jars in the closet, but still fun. See also BAXTER (-BIRNEY), MEREDITH; EATING DISORDERS, PORTRAYALS OF; and MOVIES, MADE-FOR-TV.

KATT, WILLIAM The size of William Katt s hair is directly proportional not only to his own hotness but also to the quality of the project he s appearing in. Check it out: In *Carrie*, a horror-film classic directed by American master Brian DePalma, Katt s hair is heeee-*yuge*, and he s playing the romantic lead, kicking it with Sissy Spacek *and* Amy Irving. By the time he hits *The Greatest American Hero,* the fro is toned down, and while the show has possibly the best theme song *ever* so good it had a renaissance on *Seinfeld* it got sacked after two seasons. (Our theory: Nobody watched the show itself; they d just listen to the theme song and then change the channel to *Dallas*.) Fast-forward ten years to Katt s guest-star turn on *Models Inc.* He s playing a married man who s having an affair with the Carrie-Anne Moss character (as if), the show is a dog, and Katt has modestly cropped hair and looks like fried hell. Kattsie: Grow out that crazy mane and start wearing stronger sunscreen. Thespionics alone won t get it done. See also AFROS, IMPORTANT TV; *DALLAS*; *GREATEST AMERICAN HERO, THE*; *MODELS INC.*; *SEINFELD*; and THEME SONGS.

KELLEY, DAVID E. In 1999, something remarkable happened at the Emmys. The series that won in the two biggest categories Outstanding Drama Series and Outstanding Comedy Series were both created by the same guy. Those series were *The Practice* and *Ally McBeal*, and that guy was David E. Kelley. (An aside: In a year that also included nominees like *The Sopranos* and *Friends*, Kelley gets the two-peat?!) Kelley, a former lawyer, got his start as a staff writer on *L.A. Law*, where he was responsible for penning some of the most sensationalistic episodes of the series (such as Blood, Sweat, and Fears, in which one of McKenzie, Brackman s associates defends a doctor who refused to operate on an AIDS patient). He then built on his early success by bringing his special brand of fetishistic sexist tripe to series he created, including *Picket Fences*, *Chicago Hope*, *Snoops*, *Boston Public*, *girls club*, and *Boston Legal*, as well as the aforementioned award winners. Kelley is also married to lovely movie star Michelle Pfeiffer, which either speaks well of him or poorly of her. See also *CHICAGO HOPE*; *FRIENDS*; *L.A. LAW*; and *PRACTICE, THE*.

KEOGHAN, PHIL *The Amazing Race* is often credited as one of the smartest, most suspenseful, most satisfying reality competitions on TV and rightly so. And maybe it still would have been as good if someone like Tom Bergeron or Paige Davis had been tapped to host . . . but probably not. Phil Keoghan is the perfect host for a show like *TAR*: His hot Kiwi accent makes him seem glamorous and debonair in a way that suits a show involving thrilling international travel, and he seems to have some sense of how

ridiculous his job is. Keoghan also recognizes what offensive boors the show s contestants often are telling Jonathan Baker, in Season 6, to go see to his wife when she was sobbing and panting after he shoved her, was one of Phil s finest moments but also seems to like all the same contestants we do. Our only objection is the way the producers have, in recent years, made Phil perform elaborate pantomimes, all Let me shade my eyes and point at the horizon to see which team is about to approach the mat and confer with the colorful local charged to greet them! And yet as silly as that is, Phil still sells it. That s a pro. See also THE BLACK FAMILY and REALITY TV, HOSTS OF.

KEPCHER, CAROLYN We don t know that we d want to hang out with Carolyn, the distaff Trump henchperson on *The Apprentice*; she seems like a bit of a pill. And how exactly does running Trump s golf courses qualify her to comment on the business acumen of others? . . . Oh, wait. We comment on the business acumen of the Apprenti all the time. When Carolyn turns those flat, icy blue eyes on an inept contestant (or, more specifically, on a female contestant who s using her so-called feminine wiles to score a cheap victory, *Ivana and Heidi*), we thrill with anticipation. She s usually a little clumsier with the takedowns than we d like, but she wields a lot of influence on Trump, and she s honing that disgusted eye-roll to a more razorlike sharpness with every episode. See also *APPRENTICE, THE*; REALITY TV, HOSTS OF; and TRUMP, DONALD, HAIR OF.

KIDS IN THE HALL, THE One of the only Canadian-produced comedy series worth watching, *The Kids in the Hall* starring Dave Foley, Bruce McCulloch, Kevin McDonald, Mark McKinney, and Scott Thompson was sketch comedy the way it was meant to be: short, profane, absurd, and smart. Unlike that other show run by the Kids producer, Lorne Michaels, *Kids in the Hall* seldom used recurring characters and almost never relied on catchphrases at which audiences laugh out of sheer familiarity. Most critical commentary on the show focuses on the matter-of-fact way the guys would play female characters as opposed to the screechy cartoonishness of Monty Python drag which the Kids explain by saying that they got bored of writing skits that were only about men. But in terms of using comedy for revolutionary purposes, we have greater admiration for the show s mainstreaming of gay themes in sketch comedy, due largely to the homo sensibility of gay Kid Scott Thompson. Sadly, none of the Kids has gone on to the superstardom he deserves, although at least Dave Foley had a great run on *NewsRadio* and Scott Thompson donned hot pants for the latter seasons of *The Larry Sanders Show*. But Bruce McCulloch shouldn t be directing *Stealing Harvard*, Kevin McDonald shouldn t be cameoing in *Sky High*, and Mark McKinney shouldn t . . . be on the kind of Canadian-produced sitcoms we would never, ever watch. See also *MONTY PYTHON'S FLYING CIRCUS* and SKETCH COMEDY ENSEMBLES, FORGOTTEN MEMBERS OF.

KILBORN, CRAIG Because Jon Stewart ended up being such a perfect fit, we often forget that he hasn t always been the host of *The Daily Show*; before him, the show s founding host was ESPN anchor—meathead Craig Kilborn. Stewart s opposite in nearly every way tall, self-aggrandizing, strawberry blond, Gentile Kilborn s tenure on *The Daily Show* was largely unmemorable but for the inclusion, in each celebrity interview segment, of 5 Questions (random questions that usually had some tangential relevance to the guest), and for the time Kilborn was suspended in disgrace for calling the show s cocreator and head writer, Lizz Winstead, a bitch in *Esquire* magazine. When he came back, she quit; he left the show a few months later. Kilborn went on to take over *The Late Late Show* from Tom Snyder in 1999, bringing the 5 Questions with him, but no one we knew ever watched him, because he was a fratty wanker. Kilborn mysteriously and suddenly left his CBS berth in 2004, possibly to spend more time on his feature-film acting career. We saw him in *Old School*, and . . . well, good luck with that, Craiggers. See also ESPN and TALK SHOWS, LATE-NIGHT.

"KIM BAUER" Elisha Cuthbert is a lovely young woman and a decent actor. But man, she was saddled with some thankless material on *24*, and no one could have made that character likable. The daughter of the show s superspy protagonist Jack Bauer (Kiefer Sutherland), Kim spent the first season with crimped hair and in a skanked-up football jersey. Oh, and kidnapped. Plus, she basically got her mother killed. In the second season,

Kim made a more practical wardrobe choice (chinos and a sweater) as a nanny in an abusive household, but all anyone actually remembers about that season is when Kim abandoned her boyfriend in a car wreck (after which he had to have a leg amputated), stepped in an animal trap, and got menaced by a passing cougar because how much less hap could a character have? The third season found non-college-graduate Kim working at CTU as a desk agent, which was obviously absurd; fortunately, the producers wrote her out of the series before she could turn up in the fourth season as the president of the United States or something. Unfortunately they ve since brought her back. Why?! See also *24* and UNIVERSALLY REVILED CHARACTERS.

"KIMBERLY SHAW"   See CROSS, MARCIA.

KING OF QUEENS, THE   We know the fat guy/skinny wife marriage is a kind of absurd TV convention, and generally the only reason it occurs is so that a fat male standup can have a sitcom built around his comic persona, and a cute woman can get a job being cute. So *The King of Queens* should bug the crap out of us for being such a big old clich , but in fact, it is awesome. Kevin James is the titular King, Doug Heffernan a driver for the fictional courier service IPS. Veteran show killer Leah Remini plays his wife,

Carrie, an ambitious administrative assistant. Filling out the show s ensemble is Jerry Stiller as Arthur, Carrie s father, a failed salesman living out his retirement in the Heffernans basement. Episodes usually revolve around the usual marital conflicts Carrie gets a new hairstyle Doug doesn t like; Doug is sneaking unhealthy food behind Carrie s back but sharp writing and superlative comic timing from the show s leads really make it work. Special mention goes to Victor Williams as Deacon, Doug s best friend and coworker, who provides so much of the show s racial and noncarnally homoerotic humor. Furthermore, Carrie is a total rageaholic, and since we are too, we adore her. See also FAT GUY/SKINNY WIFE MARRIAGES; REMINI, LEAH; and SHOW KILLERS.

KLUM, HEIDI   See *PROJECT RUNWAY*.

KNIGHT RIDER   Nobody really cared about the premise of *Knight Rider*. Detective Michael Long (David Hasselhoff), shot in the face and left for dead, is adopted by dying millionaire Wilton Knight, given a new face and identity (Michael Knight), and is sent out to fight crime under the aegis of the Foundation for Law and Government. No, we cared about his car: the Knight Industries Two Thousand (KITT), a talking Trans Am. Most of us assumed, back then, that by now we d *all* be driving chatty cars that could break us out of jail, jump over warehouses and vats of acid, and drive us around at Super Pursuit Mode speeds while we read magazines. Alas, the halcyon days of self-parking cars remain in the future. Hasselhoff earns himself a Golden Chompers Lifetime Scenery-Chewing Achievement Award when he plays both Michael Knight *and* his clone-enemy Garthe, who drives an evil eighteen-wheeler named Goliath and has a soul patch. And let s not forget the gut-wrenching face-off between KITT and *his* evil twin, KARR  (Knight Automated Roving Robot), voiced with Snidely Whiplash enthusiasm by Peter Cullen. The skin-tight jeans and Members Only jackets! The revolving door of overly made-up love interests! The oh, *Alice* eye-rolls of stuffy British boss Devon! The numerous queeny but Michael! s, perfect for drinking games! See also ACTING, WOODEN; DRINKING GAMES; HASSELHOFF, DAVID; HOMOSEXU-ALITY, CODED; and SCENERY, CHEWING OF.

KUDROW, LISA See *COMEBACK, THE* and *FRIENDS*.

KURTIS, BILL Kurtis who needs to start spelling his last name with a C like a normal person started out on a CBS morning show, which we kind of can t imagine. Maybe we ve just gotten too used to him intensely narrating the majority of the A&E true-crime lineup to envision him doing puff pieces on the Atkins Diet. With his steel-gray side-parted hair, plummy Troy McClure voice, and generally dad-like demeanor, he gently guides viewers into the ninth circle of serial murder and lurid small-town contract killings. A little birdie has told us that his pompous much-older-boyfriend tone isn t a put-on, and that he s actually exactly the professorial blowhard you d expect in person, but weirdly, that makes us like him more if you have to deliver an overwrought voice-over about Jos Menendez allegedly abusing his sons with a pencil, you might as well do it from a firmly entrenched position of self-seriousness. See also BUNNELL, SHERIFF JOHN; SMALL TOWNS, HIDDEN DEPRAVITY OF; and *UNSOLVED MYSTERIES*.

KUTCHER, ASHTON See *THAT '70S SHOW* and TV PRODUCERS, UNQUALIFIED CELEBRITIES AS.

L

actors and characters, proving that some series could rely more on writing than on star power. Which was fortunate for a show that never could manage to shake Corbin Bernsen. As an irresistible ladies man. Yes, you read right. Look, it wasn t reality TV, okay? See also BERNSEN, CORBIN; BOCHCO, STEVEN; *DALLAS*; HAMLIN, HARRY; KELLEY, DAVID E.; MENTALLY CHALLENGED PERSONS, ACTORS OF NORMAL INTELLIGENCE WHO VE PLAYED; and SMITS, JIMMY.

L.A. LAW Anchoring NBC s legendary Thursday-night lineup through much of the 80s and about half the 90s, *L.A. Law* did for law firms what *Dallas* had done for oil. The gelled, shoulder-padded litigators of the Los Angeles—based firm McKenzie, Brackman were attractive, passionate, and apparently oversexed, as they fit rounds of musical beds between their titillating legal cases. Say what you will about David E. Kelley, but the man knew how to spin taboo material into watchable TV. Over the course of the series, we had recovered memories of sexual abuse, stalkers, date rape, bisexuality, and the mainstream employment of mentally challenged adults all of which is old hat now, but was pretty groundbreaking then. Also groundbreaking and pre—*Law & Order*, no less was the show s habit of revitalizing the cast every few seasons by bringing in entirely new

LATE NIGHT WITH CONAN O'BRIEN, STARING CONTESTS ON Andy Richter s 2000 departure from his sidekick gig on *Late Night with Conan O'Brien* left a gaping hole in the show s roster of recurring bits: It meant there could be no more staring contests. Like so many *Conan* bits, it was so dumb that it somehow came back around to being smart; the very notion of a staring contest is inane enough, but elevating it to the echelon of activities worth televising is sort of brilliant. Anyway, they all went pretty much the same way: Conan and Andy would stare into each other s eyes Conan haughtily, Andy intensely for a few seconds. Then disturbing shit started happening behind Conan that would make it hard for Andy to continue staring at him a guy biting tinfoil, another wringing out his head for skull juice, etc. Andy lost every time, until his final episode, when disturbing shit happened behind *him* people labeled Conan s Parents and Conan s Grandparents came out, stripped naked, and started making out; then bandleader Max Weinberg joined in until Conan couldn t take it anymore and, for the first time ever, Andy was the Staring Contest Winner. It was a great day for underdogs everywhere. See also TALK SHOWS, LATE-NIGHT.

LATE SHOW WITH DAVID LETTERMAN, THE See WILL IT FLOAT?

LAUER, MATT When we first started watching NBC s *Today*, we didn t think there was all that much about cohost Matt Lauer to recommend him. Granted, he was better-looking than any other male morning-show host,  but that was about it. And when we learned that he was a golf buddy of President George H. W. Bush, we figured we could never be fans. But then, the more we watched, the more we saw the appeal. Lauer is a surprisingly tough interviewer: His refusal to cave in under the rockslide of Tom Cruise s antipsychiatry ranting in Cruise s infamous *Today* appearance in June 2005 impressed us mightily. We admired his commitment to completely ridiculous Halloween costumes, often partnered with *Today* weatherman Al Roker (the two have portrayed Simon and Garfunkel and Siegfried and Roy, among others). But most of all, we lived for the moments when Lauer s latent hostility toward cohost Katie Couric blazed into sarcastic sniping disguised as friendly joking. She never could give it back as good as she got it and ended up looking like the giggling twit she was. See also COURIC, KATIE; CURRY, ANN; and *TODAY*, WINDOW OUTSIDE.

LAURIE, HUGH Anarchic sketch comedy? Weird yet hilarious historical sitcom? Superserious medical drama? Hugh Laurie can do all that and more. Having come up through the generation of university-trained British comic actors that also includes Emma Thompson and Stephen Fry, Laurie went on to rock *Blackadder* (as a witless Prince Regent in *Blackadder the Third*, and an even more witless Peer of the Realm—cum—army private in *Blackadder Goes Forth*). But it s as the eponymous hero of FOX s *House* that Laurie has finally attracted the U.S. fandom he has always so richly deserved. House is a bitter, misanthropic doctor turned Vicodin addict (as a result of a bum leg). Normally, such characters behave hatefully toward other people because they re concealing deep emotional hurt and are just praying that someone will scratch that surface animosity and discover the pussycat within. But House totally does just hate every living person as much as he seems to, and we admire that. See also BLACKADDER and MEDICAL DRAMAS, TROPES OF.

LAVERNE & SHIRLEY Lord, what a terrible show. The theme song is fun to sing along with, but the fun ends when the opening credits do, and the kitschy coolness of Laverne s L sweaters (and L pajamas, and L car . . . no, seriously) does nothing to alleviate the migraine caused by Laverne s nails-on-a-chalkboard speaking voice (Shhiiirrrrrrl?!). Plus, it s . . . just not funny. Wacky neighbors Lenny and Squiggy, and Lenny s fist-biting shtick, never failed to bore and annoy, and if someone could explain to us why Shirley tolerated Carmine The Big Ragoo Ragusa s crap for so many seasons he s a walking, talking, cheating, Italian-love-song-badly-singing pelt of back hair with feet, for God s sake or why the writers thought it would be a neat idea to relocate the entire show and all the characters to Los Angeles, we d appreciate it. See also BAD SITCOM, SURE SIGNS OF; CANNED LAUGHTER, MANIPULATION BY/OF; MARSHALL, GARRY; NEIGHBORS, INTRUSIVE; SPIN-OFFS; and THEME SONGS.

LAW & ORDER **FRANCHISE** It all began with an overly complex ripped-from-the-headlines Mob plot, a gritty filmic quality, and of course that famous scene-change audio cue, Chung chung! A lot s changed since then: Michael Moriarty moved to Canada and went bonkers, Angie Harmon got religion, and the patron saint of precredits quippery, Jerry Briscoe Inferno Orbach, passed away. But the show endures, in a variety of flavors for every police-procedural taste, and for every spin-off that bombs (*Law & Order: Crime and Punishment*), there s one that works (*Law & Order: Criminal Intent* succeeds for one reason and one reason only: D Onofrionics). For every casting change that seems like a disaster, there s one that breathes new life into the series; everyone still misses Jill Hennessy, and of course Briscoe, but you know who *nobody* misses? Elisabeth R hm. Or Dianne Why Yes, This *Is* Yet Another Mao Jacket I m Wearing Wiest. Or . . . George Dzundza. Today, countless detective teams, assistant prosecutors, spin-offs, and drinking games later (it s a Sorvino episode chug!), Dick Wolf s juggernaut is the cop-drama standard, and no matter what time it is, or what day of the week, an episode of *L&O* is airing somewhere. See also CHUNG CHUNG ; DRINKING GAMES; ELLIOT STABLER ; GOOD COP/BAD COP; *LAW & ORDER* FRANCHISE, REUSE OF ACTORS IN; *LAW & ORDER/HOMICIDE/OZ* CASTING OVERLAP; *LAW & ORDER*, IMPATIENT WISECRACKING ARRAIGNMENT JUDGES ON; LENNIE

BRISCOE ; ROBERT GOREN ; R H M, ELISABETH; and TAKING! IT! PERSONALLY!

LAW & ORDER FRANCHISE, REUSE OF ACTORS IN You d think that, with all the aspiring actors in New York City, the *Law & Order* franchise would have no shortage of talented, available performers to fill out its many episodes. But apparently, that s not the case or so one would surmise from the way the show s producers recycle actors from episode to episode, playing entirely unrelated characters. Not only that, but there s a kind of progression to it: Lauren Ambrose (of *Six Feet Under*) first cut her teeth on the show as the two-line friend of a murder suspect s daughter (Skin Deep); she then graduated to being a defendant s sister (Pride and Joy); and finally got to play the mentally challenged victim of a sexual assault (Damaged). Other actors are only ever on the show to play perps: As soon as you see Denis O Hare (Volunteers, Pro Se, Nullification, Under God), you can be pretty sure any other suspects will turn out to be red herrings. The series has also used one-off guest shots to audition actors who ll later join the permanent cast: Before she was Lieutenant Anita Van Buren, S. Epatha Merkerson was the young shooting victim s mother in Mushrooms. Keep your eyes peeled for The Wages of Love in syndicated reruns, in which Jerry Orbach plays the kind of defense attorney his yet-to-be-invented Lennie Briscoe character would compare unfavorably to one of his ex-wives. See also *LAW & ORDER* FRANCHISE; LENNIE BRISCOE ; and RED HERRING, TOOLS FOR IDENTIFICATION OF ON COP SHOWS.

LAW & ORDER/HOMICIDE/OZ CASTING OVERLAP Why do so many of the same actors turn up on at least two, and sometimes all three, of these acclaimed shows? And why is one of those actors Richard The Thing That Wouldn t Die Belzer? In the case of *Homicide: Life on the Street* and *Oz*, it s because Tom Fontana produced both programs, and he has his favorites in the acting stable. And Fontana is old pals with Dick Wolf, the grandpappy of the *L&O* franchise. All three shows shoot, or shot, mostly on the East Coast, so a carpool from the *Oz* set to the *Law & Order: SVU* set might have included Dean Winters (Ryan O Reily on *Oz*, Brian Cassidy on *L&O: SVU*), Christopher Meloni (Chris Keller/Elliot Stabler), and B. D. Wong (Ray Mukada/Dr. Huang), with a stop to drop off J. K. Simmons (Vern Schillinger/Emil Skoda) at the *L&O: Mothership* set. Most of *Oz* s inmates have turned up on at least one *L&O* and/or *H:LOTS* episode as a guest star some of them (like Robert Clohessy) on many of each. One of the exceptions to the rule, Michelle Forbes, should really pop up on an *L&O* sometime soon maybe as a love interest for D Onofrio? That would be hot. See also *ER*, HIGHER THAN NORMAL CONCENTRATION OF *TOP GUN* ACTORS ON; *HOMICIDE: LIFE ON THE STREET*; *LAW & ORDER* FRANCHISE; and *OZ*.

LAW & ORDER, IMPATIENT WISECRACKING ARRAIGNMENT JUDGES ON   Not that we plan to get arraigned, but if we ever are, we will surely be disappointed that the presiding judge isn t as quick with a quip as those on *Law & Order*. Once each episode s main trial gets underway, the presiding judges are all business, but the arraignment judges perhaps because they only get three lines in which to make memorable impressions use their paltry screen time to advantage. A not-guilty plea will make one reply, with withering sarcasm, Life is beautiful. All God s children are innocent. The show s arraignment judges also seem to be anxious to get out of the courtroom and on to lunch of course, coming up with new variations on Let me guess: Not guilty? is hungry work.

LEACH, ROBIN   Robin Leach hosted *Lifestyles of the Rich and Famous*, a program that in many ways kicked off the celebutainment genre we ve come to take for granted. But the show would never have worked without Leach or, specifically, Leach s accent, which is a gaudy, plummy, totally fake-sounding version of British upper crust. Endlessly imitated in *SNL* sketches and standup routines (Oim smiling . . . and Oi don t know whoiiiyyyy), Leach s over-the-top narration never flagged in its amazement at the spendthrifty achievements of the wealthy, but managed to imply at the same time that he found excesses like Donald and Ivana Trump s Mar-a-Lago mansion as tacky as we did. Leach also took the opportunity to poke fun at himself in a series of Honda commercials in the 90s. See also *SATURDAY NIGHT LIVE* and TRUMP, DONALD, HAIR OF.

LEARY, DENIS   A lot of his standup is affected (the smoking onstage, the raspy yelling), a lot of the writing on *Rescue Me* is deeply misogynistic, and on the first season of *RM*, Leary had a bungled bleach job that turned his hair pee-yellow. And yet, we find him hot. Why? Maybe it s the hint of a Boston accent that peeks through when he s speaking, or that his short-lived sitcom *The Job* rocked, and everyone loves an underdog. Maybe it s that no other pee-yellow-blond on TV can wear a pair of wheat-colored jeans quite like Leary. Whatever the reason, he can come put out a fire at our house any time. See also TV BOYFRIENDS AND GIRLFRIENDS.

"LENNIE BRISCOE" He isn t the alpha of *Law & Order* detectives; that honor is shared by Mike Logan (Chris Noth) and Max Greevey (George Dzundza). But he is the omega, the be-all and end-all, and all other *L&O* detectives must suffer by comparison. When Phil Big Daddy Cerreta gets shot midway through the third season and  decides to retire from street duty, enter Lennie Briscoe divorce veteran, recovering alcoholic, unapologetic pomade abuser to win our hearts. And so it went for a few years, Briscoe cracking wise in an anti-marriage fashion and busting out awesome you ve got to be kidding me rubber-faced frowns until Logan got disappeared to Staten Island (read: Chris Noth and series creator Dick Wolf had a catfight). When Rey Curtis (Benjamin Bratt) joined the squad, Briscoe really came into his own; he started giving Rey crap immediately (I got ties older than him) and never really stopped. And we thought Rey was kind of a whiny bitch with bad hair ourselves, so we loved Briscoe for that . . . and for every bad pun, every lie he greeted with an eye-roll, every time he wandered through a scene eating a dirty-water dog or drinking crappy deli coffee, every alimony joke. He had a little too much blush on his cheeks toward the end there, and we love Dennis Farina (as Briscoe-replacement Det. Joe Fontana), don t get us wrong, but . . . we still miss Briscoe. Thank God for reruns. See also GOOD COP/BAD COP; *LAW & ORDER* FRANCHISE; and NOTH, CHRIS.

LEX VAN DEN BERGHE See VAN DEN BERGHE, LEX.

LIES, OBVIOUS If you re thinking about getting up a poker game, you should try to include a sitcom character he ll be your ATM. Because sitcom characters can never tell when someone is lying, even when the lie is completely absurd (Where were you two? Uh . . . planning your surprise party! Yeah!) and the liar is not even trying to disguise it, and is shifty-eyed, stammering, and taking long pauses to think of what he s going to say next. We should all have such gullible audiences for our mendacity. See also BAD SITCOM, SURE SIGNS OF.

LIFETIME MOVIES A Lifetime movie is more or less a Mad Lib of C-list acting, bad relationship choices, and physical perils. The variables in the equation might change Nancy McKeon + abusive husband + sexist police officers = *A Cry for Help: The Tracey Thurman Story*; Valerie Bertinelli + sister murdered by brother-in-law + custody fight over infant

+ Michael Ontkean = *In a Child's Name* but they always add up to a Lifetime movie. Other ingredients of the average Lifetime movie may include, but are not limited to: Meredith Baxter (-Birney); a child with a rare and/or deadly disease; stalking; physical, sexual, or emotional abuse; Melissa Gilbert; a subplot involving gaslighting the heroine; a kidnapped child; an addiction or eating disorder; amnesia; cults; a husband or lover with a double life/hidden identity/second family in Utah/last name Bluebeard ; Chris Sarandon; Dale Midkiff; a title along the lines of *In [X's] Name, [Past Participle]: The [Name] Story, Deadly [Noun Having to Do with Eating or Sex],* or *[Preposition] Two [Nouns]*; Louise Fletcher; a real-life fourth-tier feminist icon about whom nobody really cares anymore; Joanna Kerns. See also BAXTER (-BIRNEY), MEREDITH and MOVIES, MADE-FOR-TV.

LIKE NORMAL PEOPLE A late- 70s TV movie starring Shaun Cassidy and Linda Purl as Roger and Virginia, a developmentally disabled couple who want to get married and live . . . well, like normal people. The film, which also stars a very stoned Zalman King, aims to teach viewers a valuable lesson about acceptance, but the lesson *actually* learned is threefold: 1) mentally challenged people are super-nice and good at poetry and swimming, but have trouble cooking sausages; 2) mentally challenged people walk strangely and have speech impediments; 3) mentally challenged people are either profoundly annoying or unintentionally hilarious . . . or both. Casting then teen idol Cassidy as a special person works in theory, but in practice, he gives his lines more ham than an Easter buffet, and Purl s abrasive Virginia isn t exactly an argument for mainstreaming either. This well-meaning idea fails on just about every level except giving black-hearted viewers like ourselves a severe case of the church giggles. See also CASSIDYS, THE; MENTALLY CHALLENGED PERSONS, ACTORS OF NORMAL INTELLIGENCE WHO VE PLAYED; and MOVIES, MADE-FOR-TV.

LINGO Lingo combines the fun of spelling with the tedium and crappy prizes of bingo. Two pairs of contestants are confronted with a five-by-five square, in the top line of which are four blanks and one letter. So if they got T_ _ _ _, they might guess Track T-R-A-C-K. Then host Chuck Woolery might tell them that C was right but in the wrong place, so they d have to guess again and, if they were smart, use a word that didn t have any of the same letters other than the correct T and C. (For the record, the word we were going for was TUNIC. Did you get it?) The bingo element comes into play as each team gets to reach into a bowl under its podium and pull out balls that correspond to yet another bingo-sized card, but since a year s supply of Turtle Wax is a prize too rich for *Lingo* to offer (the show is so cheaply made that even the studio lighting sucks), that part is irrelevant: The reason to watch is to yell out which words players *should* be guessing and to make fun of them when one of their five-letter-word guesses is Through T-H-R-O- . . . uh. Whoops. See also GAME SHOW NETWORK and WOOLERY, CHUCK.

LIPTON, JAMES   If there were an award for TV s all-time greatest sycophant, James Lipton would win it in a walk. First a failed actor (who studied with Stella Adler), then dean of the Actors Studio Drama School at the New School for Social Research, Lipton didn t let his inability to carve out a career as a thespian stifle what were apparently dreams of fame. He became the host of *Inside the Actors Studio*, where Lipton s singular pop-culture niche has made him something of a personal-ity he s been parodied on *Saturday Night Live* and *Mr. Show*, and has played himself, or versions of himself, on *Late Night with Conan O'Brien*, *Arrested Development*, and in the film version of *Bewitched*, opposite his *SNL* portrayer Will Ferrell. The man just never learned the difference between good and bad attention. Please someone teach it to him. See also INSIDE THE ACTORS STUDIO and *SATURDAY NIGHT LIVE*.

LITTLE HOUSE ON THE PRAIRIE   Some of the best and most satisfying TV comfort food you re likely to find in this world, *Little House on the Prairie* (adapted from the works of pioneer girl Laura Ingalls Wilder) follows the family-friendly frontier adventures of the Ingalls clan. A pre—*Highway to Heaven* Michael Landon is Charles Pa Ingalls, an unfailingly moral yet unpreachy farmer; he s married to Karen Grassle s Caroline/Ma, but the real love affair on the show is between Pa and daughter Laura/Half-Pint (Melissa Gilbert). Laura, our ostensible heroine, is kind of a know-it-all tattletale, and yet she is so obviously his favorite child that elder sister Mary (Melissa Sue Anderson) intentionally blinds herself just to get a little attention! (Okay, that s not actually how she goes blind, but it *could* be.) The series lasted long enough for Laura to grow from a bucktoothed geek into an elegant schoolteacher, wife to the totally sexy Almanzo (Dean Butler); and for its waning seasons to have child actors Jason Bateman and Shannen Doherty Cousin Olivered into the proceedings. See also

BATEMANS, JASON AND JUSTINE; COUSIN OLIVER ; and DOHERTY, SHANNEN.

LIVE-ACTION SHOWS, ANIMATED VERSIONS OF Tons of live-action shows in the 70s and 80s rushed animated editions into production to capitalize on their popularity, including *The Partridge Family, The Brady Bunch, Laverne & Shirley, The Dukes of Hazzard*, and *Star Trek*. And when we say rushed, we mean it; the finished product is almost always hilariously bad, with poorly synched voice-overs and animation that resembles a set of Colorforms operated via remote control. Animated *Trek* is so shoddy, it s awesome it features a lot of reaction shots (read: stills), and any scene in which the crew members have to flee an enemy looks like a flock of safety scissors having an epileptic seizure. And seriously, how hard is it to draw a uniform Tribble? Probably not that hard, and yet they biffed it. You don t see live-action shows turned into toons anymore, probably because animated series like *The Simpsons* have made it okay for grown-ups to watch them but in a way, it s a shame. Wouldn t *ER* and *24* work better as cartoons at this point, really? See also *ALIAS*; *BRADY BUNCH, THE*; CARTOONS PRIMARILY DESIGNED AS PROMOTIONAL TIE-INS; *DUKES OF HAZZARD, THE*; *LAVERNE & SHIRLEY*; *PARTRIDGE FAMILY, THE*; *STAR TREK* FRANCHISE; and *24*.

LIVE WITH REGIS AND KELLY Okay, here s the thing about *Live with Regis and Kelly*. It s dumb. It s sappy. It s extremely mawkish. Kelly Ripa needs to quit telling us about how much she and her husband fight and how fat she thinks she is almost as much as producer Gelman needs to come out of the closet. And when it comes to interviewing celebrities, Regis Philbin makes a great game-show host. But despite its many seeming faults, the show is kind of awesome. Regis and Kelly have better chemistry than he ever did with his former cohost, the egregious Kathie Lee Gifford, and watching how flummoxed the stars get when Regis ignores the answers they give to his questions and barrels on, transition-free, to the next one on his card when, that is, he and Kelly aren t bickering like a fond father and daughter is more fun than the manufactured interstar camaraderie of *The Rosie O'Donnell Show* ever was. *Live* gives us a glimpse as to what our lives will be like in twenty years, when we ve stopped going to movies and reading *Entertainment Weekly*, and shows us that it won t be so bad. See also PHILBIN, REGIS; RIPA, KELLY; and TALK SHOWS, DAYTIME.

LONDONS, JASON AND JEREMY, DISTINGUISHING BETWEEN Jason London is the slightly better-looking one who starred in *Dazed and Confused*. Jeremy London, who can't resist a sinking dramatic ship regardless of the medium, starred in *Mallrats*, played Julia's mopey, crappy husband on *Party of Five*, and then filled the role of hapless RevCam second-in-command Chandler Hampton on *7th Heaven*. See also *PARTY OF FIVE* and *7TH HEAVEN*.

LOVE BOAT, THE Allegedly named *The Love Boat* because all the guest-star subplots that took place on the *Pacific Princess* each week would involve the finding or mending of love. We whined and begged to be allowed to watch the comedic interactions with super-famous guest stars of Captain Stubing (Gavin MacLeod), his fat-faced daughter Vicki (Jill Whelan), overly perky cruise director Julie McCoy (Lauren Tewes), nerdy assistant purser and future Congressman Gopher (Fred Grandy), way-too-happy bartender Isaac (Ted Lange), and improbable chick magnet Doc (Bernie Kopell). Looking back, though, it probably had more to do with getting to stay up past 10 PM than with the show itself, which, to tell you the truth, sucked even before Ted "Ace" McGinley showed up and doomed it. Tom Hanks and Nipsey Russell in the same episode *sounds* like a trip, but trust us, the ship

docks at Overactedville. See also BAD SITCOM, SURE SIGNS OF and SHOW KILLERS.

LOVE TRIANGLES Once a couple gets together on a show, that's pretty much that—the sexual tension is resolved and there's no reason to keep watching. Unless the writers cook up a spicy love triangle! The Dylan/Brenda/Kelly love triangle put *90210* on the map, after all, and it wasn't just the sparks that flew between Pacey and Joey that gave us a thrill on *Dawson's Creek*; it was the sucky-baby reaction they could expect from Dawson. And nobody gave a crap about Felicity's art-department travails, at least not compared to all the back-and-forthing between Ben and Noel . . . or Noel waffling between Felicity and Ruby . . . or Ben zigging over to Avery, then zagging back to Felicity. Anyway, every drama worth its salt, from *Melrose* to *Star Trek* (oh, come on—Spock and Bones were totally fighting for Kirk's love), follows the lead of the soaps and peps things up with a love triangle sooner or later. Sooner, if they're smart. See also *BEVERLY HILLS 90210*; *DAWSON'S CREEK*; *FELICITY*; *MELROSE PLACE*; SEXUAL TENSION, RUINATION OF SHOW BY RESOLVING; "SOULMATE"; and *STAR TREK* FRANCHISE.

M

MAD ABOUT YOU Paul and Jamie Buchman (Paul Reiser and Helen Hunt) started out as just your typical New York couple: He's Jewish, she's WASPy beyond belief; he's finicky, she's (adorably) neurotic. At the end of seven seasons, she was a prickly, ball-busting harridan, and he'd had his dignity worn down to a tiny nub. They'd had a child, you see, and just as happens to cute, likable married couples in real life, it changed the Buchmans into screeching control freaks. We'd stopped watching it by then, but will occasionally tune in for the early-years reruns, when their telegenic newlywed antics—Paul lost his ring! Jamie wants to buy a loveseat but Paul doesn't like it!—were sweet and relatable and showed no signs of the horror that was to come. See also BABY, RUINATION OF SHOW BY ADDING and BAD SITCOMS STARRING GOOD COMEDIANS.

MADE Still one of MTV's best reality shows, *Made* takes teenagers who want to achieve some particular goal and unites them with coaches who can teach them everything they need to know. Whatever they want to do—a shallow clotheshorse wanting to become a BMX biker, a metalhead trying to become his school's homecoming king—doesn't really matter; it's all in the journey. And actually, the journey doesn't really matter either, since we're just watching to see them fuck up, complain, and claim they'll never succeed. Half the time, the kids get on the show with projects they have no hope of achieving (like getting into the dancing corps of a Broadway musical). The other half of the time, the kids choose goals that are elaborate smokescreens for their inability to tell the world yet that they're gay (like an extremely tomboyish girl who wants to get made into the star of her school play). Very rarely, the kids just plain wash out, but sometimes even that is character-building and a blessing, like the brainiac boy who realizes when he spends a majority of his football practices running laps that what he really wants is to join the cross-country team. But there's always the promise that they will (awesomely) give up. Oh, and it's also worth watching for the moment in literally every episode where the kid gets discouraged and the producers play Beck's "Lost Cause." (Drink!) See also DRINKING

GAMES and TEENAGERS, BRATTY.

MAGIC SHOWS, TELEVISED Um . . . what's the point? To prove that David Copperfield's thirst for unbuttoned black satin pirate shirts remains unslaked? Because we don't care about that; we care about believing that the magicians didn't fake the tricks, and even though we know they *do*, because they have to, we want to believe that they don't—and the television medium makes that impossible, because the magicians just have too many opportunities to fake us out on TV. Obviously, we watch them anyway, but only to comment aloud on the numerous points in the broadcast at which a cutaway shot would have hidden wires and trapdoors from the curious public. Oh, and to make fun of Copperfield's chest-hair coif. Okay, so apparently we love televised magic shows. Hey, only in America could a nerdlinger in tight pants announce that he wanted to poof the Statue of Liberty and get on TV as a result.

MAIN CAST MEMBER DEPARTURES, NOTORIOUS When a main-credits cast member bolts a show, it often spells doom—sometimes for the show (Clooney bailed on *ER* at the perfect time, really), and sometimes for the cast member (nice movie "career," *Caruso*). Soldiering on without an integral part of the cast can work out for a show; it never hurts *Law &*

Order, and it sort of succeeded for shows like *CHiPs* and *The Hogan Family*, mostly because those shows already sucked anyway. But usually, it's the kiss of death, the moment to which many viewers date a show's demise: Shannen Doherty's departure from *90210* (or Jason Priestley's, or Luke Perry's), Johnny Depp's from *21 Jump Street*, Patrick Duffy bowing out of *Dallas*, Suzanne Somers's contract dispute on *Three's Company* and Farrah Fawcett-Majors's on *Charlie's Angels*. All examples of departures that sent their respective shows spiraling downward. Well, even faster, since we didn't confuse any of those shows with Shakespeare to begin with, but still. See also CARUSO, DAVID, AS GO-TO REFERENCE FOR CAREER SUICIDE; *CHiPs*; CLOONEY, GEORGE; *DALLAS*; DOHERTY, SHANNEN; *HOGANS, THE/HOGAN FAMILY, THE*; *LAW & ORDER* FRANCHISE; RECASTING, NOTORIOUS; *THREE'S COMPANY*; TV LAW OF DIMINISHING RETURNS; and *21 JUMP STREET*.

MAKING THE BAND Few other reality TV shows have offered up such an embarrassment of mockable riches. The original *MtB* attempted to capitalize on the boy-band craze (. . . you heard us) by cobbling together a fivesome of falsettoed *Teen Beat* types, calling it a band, sending it out on the road, and waiting for the pre-pubescent-squeeing-girl-driven bucks to start rolling in. But the world didn't really need the Backstreet Boys it already had, much less twelfth-generation Backstreet photocopy O-Town. The boys of O-Town embarrassed themselves onstage with flat notes and biffed choreography, and embarrassed themselves offstage by . . . well, existing, but also scuffling with each other and crying about their daddies  who didn't love them. O-Town eventually sank without a trace, but MTV continued the show, putting Diddy in charge and assembling different kinds of bands— hip-hop groups, Destiny's Child ripoffs—and *MtB*s 2 and 3 had a job of filling the shoes of O-Town in the dink department. Turns out Diddy isn't just a hip-hop and clothing impresario; he's also a dismissive beeyotch, and when he's telling some sub-stripper from Tampa to do a few sit-ups, it's quite satisfying. Our only complaint: They should just rename it *American Schadenfreudol* already. See also *AMERICAN IDOL*; REALITY TV, HOSTS OF; and *TEEN BEAT*, COVER BOYS OF.

M&Ms, TALKING "Red" and "Yellow," the talking M&M characters, have been enticing us to consume the deceptively simple yet addictively delicious candies since Will Vinton (animator of the California Raisins) and the ad agency BBDO created them in the 1990s. Red (a "milk chocolate" M&M, né "plain") and Yellow (peanut) have since been joined by sassy Green (the lady M&M with the go-go boots) and orange Crisp (personifying the vile "crispy" flavor that Mars just will not give up on). They frequently interact with celebrities such as Megan Mullally and Diedrich Bader. (Okay, fine: "celebrities.") But we love the Ms not just because the candy they shill for is awesome, and not just because Yellow is voiced by J. K. "Vern Schillinger" Simmons, but because they are among the few anthropomorphized food items that know they will soon be eaten, and they're not really cool with that. Which is tough, but, you know, get in our mouths and start melting, guys, prontito. See also CALIFORNIA RAISINS.

MARATHONS It's always the same—you don't set *out* to watch four seasons of *Real World* in a row. You just put on MTV, like, in the background, to keep you company while you tidy up the living room! But then, mid-Swiffer, you realize it's an episode you've never seen before, and maybe that bitchface Flora will get her comeuppance in this one, so you sit down to watch, just in case, and the next thing you know, it's nineteen hours later and you're still slack-jawed on the couch, corneas burning, watching your forty-second straight episode. Whether it's a virtuous *West Wing* marathon on Bravo or an excuse-to-hide-from-your-relatives holiday marathon of *Law & Order* on TNT, the TV marathon is irresistible . . . so don't bother resisting. Line up the Dorito bags, slump on the couch, and indulge yourself in a solid day of *24*. See also BRAVO; DVD, WATCHING AN ENTIRE TV SEASON IN ONE WEEKEND ON; *LAW & ORDER* FRANCHISE; *REAL WORLD, THE*; *24*; and *WEST WING, THE*.

MARIANO, ROB In two seasons of *Survivor* and one of *The Amazing Race*, viewers either loved "Boston Rob" Mariano or hated him. We loooooooved him. Not so much in the first go-round on *Survivor*; he was a punk with an exaggerated sense of his own power and importance in the game. But by the time he returned for the All-Star season, he'd figured it all out. He made a solid alliance with Amber "Whatever You Say, Rob!" Brkich, he performed beautifully in challenges, he knew how to build stuff, he got a nice tan, he kept his shirt off a lot, and he had a hot accent. Er, that sentence kind of got away from us, but the point was that he not only got to the final two with his alliance partner, but he managed to convince Lex not to vote out Amber when it was the smart thing to do, just as a favor to Rob, and to Lex's own disadvantage. Amber won the

All-Star season thanks entirely to Rob's smart game play. The betrothed Rob and Amber then went on, the next year, to rock *The Amazing Race*, playing it harder and more strategically than anyone ever had before. (Throwing a gross food-eating challenge and taking a penalty, *and* convincing two other teams to do the same? Dude!) They came in second in the contest, but first in our hearts.

Well, he did. Frankly—even after watching their nuptialapalooza on CBS in the spring of '05—we don't know what he sees in her. See also REALITY TV, COUPLES ON; *SURVIVOR*; and VAN DEN BERGHE, LEX.

MARIJUANA, CLICHÉS ASSOCIATED WITH Any TV character foolish enough to take a toke, at least on network TV, is doomed to one of two fates: getting "sitcom stoned," with all the overacted paranoia, uncontrollable giggling, equally uncontrollable snacking, and nonsensically loopy deep thoughts that entails; or an inexorable downward spiral from bong hits straight into abuse, addiction, needle-sharing, prostitution, shoplifting, and death (inexorable, and rapid, too—this is usually accomplished in about a week). Very occasionally, a network program will depict getting baked in a way that isn't alarmist and square—the subtle doobie stylings of *That '70s Show*, for instance, or the episode of *Joan of Arcadia* where Luke and Friedman got high and Luke grooved on, then freaked out at, Friedman's screensaver. But usually, a character who smokes up is either evil anyway (Val on *90210)* or done for (the never-before-seen Dead Dick, also on *90210)*, and the effects of pot are inevitably confused with those of much stronger hallucinogens. The TV writers who *have* smoked enough pot in their lives to know what they're talking about are probably required by the Standards and Practices department to make the experience look as hellish and dangerous as possible, but only on *Six Feet Under* could characters get stoned and then just get on with their days—which is, believe it or not, the norm. See also *ABC AFTER-SCHOOL SPECIALS*; *BEVERLY HILLS 90210*; DRUG ABUSE, PORTRAYALS OF; PSAS; and *THAT '70S SHOW*.

MARRIAGE, GREEN-CARD The movie *Green Card* went there back in 1990, but any number of sitcoms had been there already, mining the comic premise of an American marrying a foreigner so that said foreigner can exploit a loophole of immigration law and stay in the country. The variations in the setup are limited: worldly guy marries bumpkin girl; worldly girl marries rube guy; they actually fall in love; they hate each other; one's gay, the other's straight. There's the requisite scene (or montage) of cramming for the test the INS agent will conduct to determine whether the marriage is legitimate, based on whether they know each other's moms' middle names. We can't believe we're about to do this, but we have to give a minuscule amount of credit to *Just Shoot Me!* and *Will & Grace* for changing up the genre: *Shoot* had Rebecca Romijn-Stamos's Adrienne Barker marrying David Spade's Finch because she was Canadian and her visa had run out . . . but she didn't tell him that was why she married him and kept up the fiction for half a season; and *Will & Grace* had Sean Hayes's Jack marrying Shelley Morrison's Rosario and sharing a marital bed with her for a full year. Many seasons hence, she still occasionally calls him "Papi," which is kind of adorable. See also *WILL & GRACE*.

MARRIED . . . WITH CHILDREN See FOX, EARLY YEARS OF.

MARSHALL, GARRY We should probably loathe Garry Marshall; he's responsible for producing several of the more irritating sitcoms in TV history, including *Mork & Mindy* and *Joanie Loves Chachi*. And yet, we kind of love him. First of all, he did have his finger on the TV-viewing pulse of the '70s, and if America took Lenny and Squiggy to its undiscerning bosom, it's not Marshall's fault. Second of all, we're impressed by any genius evil enough to create an animated version of *Happy Days* called *Fonz and the Happy Days Gang*. But primarily, he's so dryly brilliant as an actor in movies like *Soapdish* and *Lost in America* that we totally hope to meet him one day and become his adoptive granddaughters. See also "ARTHUR FONZARELLI"; *LAVERNE & SHIRLEY*; *MORK & MINDY*; and SITCOMS, UNFUNNINESS OF SEMINAL.

MARTINDALE, WINK No other game-show host has ever openly and genuinely enjoyed his job as much as *Tic Tac Dough* emcee Wink Martindale. A lot of game-show hosts start to burn out after a while; they keep smiling, but you can see the crow's feet of despair collecting around their eyes. Not Wink—until the very last episode, he really cared whether you snagged the center square. And he's still grinning it up on Orbitz commercials, although that may be a side effect of the facelifts. We almost feel bad about calling him "Wank Fartindale" when we were kids. Almost. (In case anyone cares, his birth name is Winston.) See also GAME SHOW NETWORK and SCENERY, CHEWERS OF.

MASTERCARD "PRICELESS" CAMPAIGN "[X item]: [price]. [Y item]: [price +/- X]. [Emotionally satisfying result of buying X and Y with MasterCard]: priceless." MasterCard ran about a bajillion different versions of the ad, and its ubiquity got annoying, but now and then they'd come up with a tearjerky one, like Little Leaguers going to a major-league baseball game for the first time, and win us back over. The ad is brilliantly constructed—it's got rhetorical balance, and you can plug in different values endlessly—and it entered the lexicon immediately. Take it from voice-over guy Billy "Left My Very Pregnant Girlfriend for Claire Danes" Crudup: "There're some things money can't buy. For everything else, there's MasterCard." See also CATCHPHRASES, OVERUSED COMMERCIAL.

MATCH GAME There was a time when the naughtiest, most hilarious words you could say on TV were the likes of "tinkle," "doody," "chest," "behind" (or the classed-up French variation, "derrière"), "whoopee," and "pants." That time was 1973, and the show that harnessed all the raw sexual power of those forbidden words was *Match Game*. Hosted by grinning drunk Gene Rayburn and his truly terrifying tar-stained chompers, *Match Game* had contestants fill in the blank in a cute, potentially risqué sentence (for instance, "Dumb Dora is so dumb that instead of filling her tank with gasoline, she filled it with blank") with what they thought the majority of a panel of six celebrities would write; the contestant got a point each time he or she matched an answer with a star's. Some contestants came up with logical or clever answers ("Vaseline?") while others were . . . less gifted ("Tinkle?"). But it almost didn't matter whether they were smart or not— the celebrities were hard to match because they were drunk. Seriously, you see Richard Dawson openly swigging from a highball glass. The show is surprisingly fun to play along with the more you can predict the sort of out-of-left-field answers Fannie Flagg or Orson Bean is likely to come up with. See also *Dean Martin Celebrity Roasts, The,* Commercials for; Game Show Network; Game Shows, Celebrities on; and Rayburn, Gene.

Max Headroom It seemed really cool at the time—a show set twenty minutes in the future, starring computer-generated "host" Max Headroom (a clonkily CGIed version of actor Matt Frewer). And even though it's aged about as well as the movie *Tron*, we still love Max a little bit.

Maximum Exposure One minute it's all fun and games with kids doing stupid skateboard tricks. The next thing you know, that kid's forearm looks like rick-rack. And in case you had your fingers over your eyes, they showed the footage a minimum of eight times. But even when a dude's arm isn't breaking in four places, the show is usually pretty good. The announcer—Cam Brainard, whose credit on IMDb literally reads "Smart-Aleck Announcer Dude"—never varies his jocular cadence, whether he's narrating footage of a kid trying to jump into his pool off his roof (and missing) or of Thai apartment dwellers awaiting rescue from a skyscraper fire on the roof of their building. When the footage happens to come from other nations, the narration is usually a tiny bit racist—not so much that you get offended, but enough that you notice. Like, when Japanese villagers are trying to escape the gushing volcano, the narrator can't resist mentioning Godzilla. But hey, when your show is basically made up of the sort of neo-snuff videos that *Jackass* rejects unopened, why not throw in a few Eisenhower-era racial stereotypes, too? See also *Jackass.*

McG It wasn't enough for him to lower the quality of films with *Charlie's Angels*. He then had to go on to create *Fastlane* (supposedly the new *Miami Vice*, only with a hot chick who sometimes made out with other hot chicks) and produce *The O.C.* (thus making us all pine for *90210* because it was so close, yet ultimately not close enough). But our real problem is obvious. "McG"? Buy some vowels, tool. See also *BEVERLY HILLS 90210* and *O.C., THE*.

MEDICAL DRAMAS, TROPES OF Medical dramas are beloved by the networks for one simple reason: guts. While senators occasionally get all riled up by the amount of violence and gore depicted on TV's many cop shows, showing the goopy aftermath of such implied activities on hospital shows is perfectly kosher. However, the trade-off for depicting all of those complex femur fractures and dislocated eyes is that producers have to come up with dramatically compelling story elements to arrange around them. Frequently recurrent plot devices include: nihilistic gang members who accidentally shoot their own brothers; dying geriatrics who are stoic in the face of imminent death; abandoned newborn babies; patients with DNR orders their doctors brazenly ignore; overwhelmed first-year interns who marvel at how much medical school didn't prepare them for all the chaos; crabby misanthropes leaving the hospital against medical advice; nurses who know more than doctors; shockingly young kids getting pregnant/STDs; ER doctors getting rebuffed by specialists who just don't care about the patients the way the ER docs do; doctors fudging records in order to arrange for costly sur-gery or treatment for patients without medical insurance; and patients who are about to go away on savings-account-draining holidays with their adoring spouses, so you know they're definitely dying from the splinters they just got in their fingers. See also *CHICAGO HOPE*; *ER*; and *GREY'S ANATOMY*.

MELROSE HEIGHTS 90210-2402 See *BEN STILLER SHOW, THE*.

MELROSE PLACE *90210* spin-off *Melrose Place*'s bland first season focused too much on the trials and tribulations of twentysomethings in L.A. and the alleged big-happy-family aspect of the Melrose Place apartment complex. The show needed more conflict, and a second-season retooling added Heather Locklear as mega-bitch Amanda Woodward, rewrote Dr. Michael Mancini (Thomas Calabro) as an erection in scrubs, amped up the soap, and turned *Melrose* into the mustest of must-see TV in the mid-'90s. It had its weaknesses (for example, Josie Bissett's Jane Mancini, aka "The Human Pee Break"), but the good stuff more than made up for them: crazy Kimberly (Marcia Cross) ripping her wig off; Jane's nutbar ex, Richard Hart (Patrick Muldoon), clawing his way out of the grave in which he'd gotten buried alive; unintentionally hilarious treatment of Sensitive Subjects (Courtney Thorne-Smith's Alison remembers her dad bad-touching her and ditches her own wedding by jumping out a window); the acting of Messrs. Jack Wagner and Muldoon, whose scenery-guzzling resembled a pit-bull attack; Billy's (Andrew Shue) dead wife Brooke (Kristin Davis) walking on the surface of the pool and whining, "Billlleeeeee"; and of course the continuing quest of Gay Matt (Doug Savant) to find a boyfriend he could do more than share back-slapping hugs with. The show went downhill in a hurry when a bunch of main cast members left, but in its prime, it was quite possibly the best soap ever. See also "AMANDA WOODWARD"; *BEVERLY HILLS 90210*; CROSS, MARCIA; SCENERY, CHEWERS OF; SHUE, ANDREW; SPELLING, AARON; and SPIN-OFFS.

MENTALLY CHALLENGED PERSONS, ACTORS OF NORMAL INTELLIGENCE WHO'VE PLAYED   Perhaps because actual mentally challenged people are difficult to direct in TV productions—Chris "Corky" Burke aside—the task of portraying characters with developmental delays generally falls to actors without mental handicaps. Larry Drake spent years on *L.A. Law* playing Benny, the office's mentally challenged assistant. Ben Foster had a recurring role on *Freaks and Geeks* as Eli, a mentally challenged student mainstreamed into McKinley High. But mentally challenged adults in TV movies are in a category all their own—much like the

circle of hell we imagine the actors who play them will occupy in the next life. You'd think that *Like Normal People* would have cured would-be producers of TV movies of the impulse to make mawkish treacle out of the lives of mentally challenged people. But nay! 1996 brought us not just two but *four* actors of normal intelligence playing challenged adults in *The Boys Next Door* (Nathan Lane, Robert Sean Leonard, Michael Jeter, and Courtney B. Vance, *all* of whom should have known better). See also *L.A. LAW*; *LIKE NORMAL PEOPLE*; MOVIES, MADE-FOR-TV; and O'DONNELL, ROSIE.

MIAMI VICE   *Miami Vice*, a candy-colored undercover-cop drama heavily influenced by music videos, debuted in 1984, and its effect on the culture was immediate—and rather unfortunate. It was one thing for Sonny Crockett (a stubblicious Don Johnson) to rock the Armani  suit, pastel T-shirt, and manspadrilles with no socks. Dude lived in Miami and had a drug-dealing alter ego to perpetrate. But when Jersey kids sported that look at their bar mitzvahs, it got ugly. The show was produced by Michael Mann, creator of *Vega$* and director of cult films such as *Thief* and *Heat*, and it had a distinctive look and feel—hot cars, tube tops, white-on-white-on-neon décor contrasted with the dark, monosyllabic sulking of Lt. Castillo (Edward James Olmos). And for a few years, we enjoyed watching Crockett and his partner Ricardo Tubbs (Philip Michael Thomas, last seen shilling for a psychic hotline) bust the bad guys, trade quips with foxy Gina "Jean Cusamano" Calabrese (Saundra Santiago) and her giant plastic hoop earrings, and scream through intersections at 123 mph in that rad Ferrari during a Phil Collins music montage. Then Helena Bonham Carter showed up as Crockett's junkie doctor love interest (!), and Sheena Easton came on the show, and then it kind of all went to hell. See also JOHNSON, DON.

MICHELE, MICHAEL Founding member, with Daniel Baldwin, of the *Homicide: Life on the Street* Petrified Forest Players. See also ACTING, WOODEN and *HOMICIDE: LIFE ON THE STREET*.

MICKEY MOUSE CLUB Dear *Mickey Mouse Club*: You couldn't just content yourself with creating a fetish around Annette Funicello's legendary boobies, could you? Ohhhhh no—you had to reincarnate yourself for a new generation of viewers, thereby inflicting such entertainment nonluminaries as Britney Spears, Christina Aguilera, Justin Timberlake, and J. C. Chasez on an unsuspecting world. And what's with giving Fred "*Mouth Sounds*" Newman a job? How many times do we have to tell you not to encourage that guy? We'll give you Keri Russell and Ryan Gosling as mitigating circumstances, but you still have a lot to answer for. *Federline is your fault.* See also *FELICITY*.

MILLER, DENNIS Oh, how we used to love D. Mil, back when he hosted *Saturday Night Live*'s "Weekend Update"—those flowing thinking-man's-mullet locks, that high-pitched cackle after certain punchlines, the wild scrawling sign-off gesture that accompanied his signature "that's the news, and I am outta here." After leaving *SNL*, he did some more standup before landing *The Dennis Miller Show*. Miller had started to believe his own press by that time, though, and while he may in fact have been the smartest guy in the room, *DMS*'s stagy opening "rants" felt canned and smug. He still had the sharpest references in town, and the cackle was still pretty hot, but it's not that fine a line between wiseass and blowhard, and Miller crossed it in the mid-'90s. Why *Monday Night Football* decided he'd make a great color commentator, we have no idea. That failed experiment dragged on for two years and pleased nobody; die-hard Miller fans had to sit through hours of gridiron coverage waiting for some Miller shtick, and football fans didn't tune in to hear Susan Sontag jokes. He got another show on CNBC, and then that got canceled too—maybe he's said everything he's got to say. We can't miss you if you won't go away, Dennis! See also SATURDAY NIGHT LIVE, "WEEKEND UPDATE" HOSTS ON and SPORTSCASTERS, MOST ANNOYING.

MINISERIES, OLD-SCHOOL EVENT EDITIONS "Miniseries" used to mean event programming, at least before the proliferation of cable channels. *The Thorn Birds*, *Roots*, *North & South*, the ludicrous *George Washington* (starring Barry Bostwick as George and Patty Duke as Martha)—the entire country watched and talked about them the next day, even if they were based on a Judith Krantz novel and/or stank, which they usually did, often thanks to the sternly plank-esque "acting" of one Richard Chamberlain, star of both *The Thorn Birds* and *Shogun*. *Roots* got the highest ratings of anything, ever, when it aired in 1977, but nowadays, we don't call multipart movie-quality TV shows "miniseries." We call them "HBO Sunday-night dramas." Despite the best efforts of the producers behind contemporary "special television events" like *Dune*, *Taken*, and *Into the West*, the days of the prestigious, superhyped miniseries are over. See also ACTING, WOODEN and MOVIES, MADE-FOR-TV.

MISTER ROGERS' NEIGHBORHOOD See ROGERS, FRED.

MODELS INC. *90210* begat *Melrose Place* begat *Models Inc.*, the boring little spin-off that couldn't. *Why* it couldn't remains something of a mystery; the cast featured not one but two of the most impressive soap-opera scenery-chewers of all time, Linda "Sue Ellen Ewing" Gray as modeling agency head honcha Hillary Michaels, and—after a futile midseason retool—Emma "Fallon Carrington" Samms. The show aired at a time when model-mania was at its zenith, too; what went wrong? Well, we might politely describe the acting as "dinner theater for the hard of hearing," but that's hardly out of the ordinary on a primetime sudser. The real issue was one of credibility—namely that the actresses were completely unbelievable as models: too short, too thick in the legs, and, in the case of Carrie-Anne Moss, too pocky in the skin. They didn't dress like models, their hair was too poofy and small-town, none of them smoked . . . we just didn't buy it. Only Stephanie Romanov, an actual model, looked right for the part. Most viewers bailed out around the time Sarah Owens developed a drinking problem and actor Cassidy Rae went all "Falstaff meets Cher Horowitz" with it. Sorry, Mr. Spelling. We tried, we really did. See also *DALLAS*; *MELROSE PLACE*; SPELLING,

AARON; and SPIN-OFFS.

MOD SQUAD, THE See SPELLING, AARON.

MOLE, THE Such a brilliant idea for a reality show could, of course, never last on American TV; what's amazing is that they even tried. Contestants compete in challenges—both individually and in teams—of varying inanity (bungee-jumping, pouring red wine without spilling a drop on a white napkin), for which they earn money to go into the pot that will eventually be awarded to the winner. All the while, one of them is The Mole, secretly charged with sabotaging all their tasks—not so much that it would be obvious, but enough that the eventual winner gets screwed over in very small increments. At the end of each episode, contestants take a quiz about who The Mole was; the one with the lowest score is sent home. What made the show so good: The contestants were generally pretty normal, not cast for the drama producers were hoping they'd cause, and in order to direct attention away from their real Mole picks, non-Mole contestants start acting Mole-y, which is entertaining. But the greatest thing about *The Mole* is that since contestants on regular reality shows are all trying to undermine each other all the time, it's awesome to watch it be part of the actual game. Also, host Anderson Cooper is a total bad-ass. See also COOPER, ANDERSON and GAME SHOWS, CELEBRITY EDITIONS OF.

[X] MOMS & DADS Don't understand why stage parents act so crazy? Neither do we—and the first installment in Bravo's brilliant franchise, *Showbiz Moms & Dads*, didn't really help our comprehension. Partly because we spent the bulk of every hour either laughing hysterically or hiding our faces in pillows, but mostly because . . . they're so crazy. Okay, little Jordan (the African-American Jordan, not the bitch-ass white one) and her mom seemed normal, relatively—but everyone else on that show had *serious* problems, starting with the aptly named Duncan Nutter, who dragged his wife and their *seven children* to New York City to live in a *two-bedroom apartment* and pursue acting careers that none of them except him really wanted. Subsequent installments of the series inspired as much squirmy horror—*Showdog Moms & Dads* highlighted the inappropriately close relationship many showdog owners have with their animals, while *Sports Kids Moms & Dads* instructed us all in the concept of dramatic irony with shots of mom Kim worrying about her figure-skater son Bryce's chances at nationals intercut with shots of him skidding on his ass. But nothing will top footage of the Nutter children trying, and failing, to introduce their father to their

friend Mr. Reality. See also BRAVO and REALITY TV, OFF-BRAND.

MONEY, INFREQUENT HANDLING OF BY TV CHARACTERS If TV is a world where documentary filmmakers and record-store clerks and sous chefs can each live in gigantic Manhattan apartments, it's hardly surprising that money is seldom depicted there. When a character loses a job, invests in the stock market, or makes an extravagant purchase, suddenly the economic realities that apply in our world appear in TV Land as well, and we can be sure that financial concerns will be plot elements until, oh, at least the end of the episode. And we know trouble is afoot when someone busts out a credit card, because said credit card will surely be declined for plot purposes. Conversely, it rarely happens that characters have more money than they're accustomed to; occasionally, a distant relative will pass on, leaving an inheritance to be blown through heedlessly so that everything will be back to normal next week, but that's about it. Which, frankly, is fine with us. We have our own real-life financial concerns, so watching them play out all the time in what is supposed to be our escapist entertainment would only depress us. See also REAL ESTATE, VASTNESS OF and WARDROBE, ENDLESSNESS OF.

MONKEES, THE Because, by 1966, the Beatles were too big to star in a sitcom or even to make any more live-action movies, producers Bert Schneider and Bob Rafelson created *The Monkees*. The Prefab Four—simian Micky Dolenz, English Davy Jones, toque-rocking Mike Nesmith, and gormless Peter Tork—had been musicians but weren't a band before they were assembled to star in NBC's sitcom. Each was meant to be an analogue for a Beatle—Davy the cute one (like Paul), Mike the smart one (like John), Peter the tunic-wearing peacenik (like George), and Micky . . . the coked-out drummer (like Ringo). The show—which, to be fair, was for kids—got them into many dumb, cartoonish adventures: The boys are mistaken for spies, get marooned in old-timey Western ghost towns, and fall for socialite girls who are out of their league, but they always have time for a musical number or two. The music is pretty solid mid-'60s bubblegum pop, and it doesn't really matter that they didn't write it or play any instruments on the first few albums. The show lasted two seasons, after which—if VH1's original movie *Daydream Believers: The Monkees Story* is a reliable record of events—Nesmith got pissy about everything. But before then, there was actually a cameo featuring Frank Zappa and Nesmith (playing each other, heh), and the endorsement of no less a discerning fan than John Lennon himself. See also MOVIES, MADE-

FOR-TV and MUSICAL MONTAGES.

MONTY PYTHON'S FLYING CIRCUS For a certain kind of Anglophilic dork, *Monty Python's Flying Circus* is a few sparkling seasons of genius. Dennis Moore, Argument Clinic, the Upper-Class Twit of the Year Awards . . . if you're fortunate enough to see them play out before every nerd you know has had a chance to reenact them for you, they're very funny. And the Pythons also deserve credit for realizing what the writing staff of *Saturday Night Live* never has: that sketches don't need to have endings, and that a sketch show is funnier if one skit segues (or doesn't) straight into the next without a tacked-on punchline. The six members of Monty Python went on to star in four Python feature films, and (among the six of them) a couple of dozen others—one of which (as of this writing) has been adapted into a Broadway musical (*Spamalot*, based on *Monty Python and the Holy Grail*). It's rare for a comedy brain trust to coalesce like that. And it's not their fault that all the biggest losers you knew in college could not stop quoting their work. See also SATURDAY NIGHT LIVE and SKETCH COMEDY ENSEMBLES, FORGOTTEN MEMBERS OF.

"THE MORE YOU KNOW" Like "One to Grow On," but coupled with a little floaty star-of-knowledge graphic and a sing-song tune, aired in primetime, and aimed at adults. "The More You Know" spots always seem to star an *ER* cast member, who always looks vaguely nauseated at having to remind the audience that racism is bad (or whatever . . . we're usually in the kitchen refreshing the Cheeto supply when TMYKs come on). See also *ER*; "ONE TO GROW ON"; and PSAs.

MORIARTY, MICHAEL, BONKERS-OSITY OF After he left *Law & Order*, Michael Moriarty—who played original Executive ADA Ben Stone with idealistic gusto and through several haircuts apparently administered with a blindfold—basically went bonkers, starting with his claim that he got fired from *L&O* for threatening to sue Janet Reno. Moriarty's other big political ideas include running for prime minister of Canada, where he now lives; running for governor of Florida, where he does not live; and petitioning the United States to add Israel as the fifty-first state. The man needs medication, is our point, but we've heard that he likes to medicate himself—with bourbon, at hotel bars in Toronto, which we many times considered visiting to see if we could 1) run into him, and 2) get him wound up on a bonkertastic rant of some kind. Perhaps we need to get a life. See also *LAW & ORDER* FRANCHISE.

MORK & MINDY Some may argue that

Robin Williams's ascendancy as a standup comic and professional irritant would have happened no matter which avenue he took to get there, but that doesn't mean *Mork & Mindy* doesn't bear some of the blame. One of the approximately eighteen spin-offs of Garry Marshall's *Happy Days*, *Mork & Mindy* revolved around the adventures of Mork (Williams), a hirsute immigrant from the planet Ork who lands in Boulder, Colorado (randomly), and attracts the friendship and sympathy of music-store employee Mindy (Pam Dawber). Every episode is essentially the same: Mork's not from Earth, so he has no idea how things work.

This may *explain* why he chooses to go about his terrestrial explorations in rainbow suspenders, but it does not *excuse* it. Eventually, Mindy decides—as Major Nelson did before her—that partnering her life with that of an otherworldly traveler who can barely function in society is a good idea, and she and Mork marry. Shortly thereafter, there arrives a "baby" in the form of Jonathan Winters. (Don't ask; it doesn't matter.) The next time you hear some blowhard complaining about how dumb TV is today compared to the good old days, remind him of this show, because, good Lord. See also *I DREAM OF JEANNIE*; MARSHALL, GARRY; SITCOMS, FISH-OUT-OF-WATER; and SPIN-OFFS.

MOTHER-DAUGHTER RELATIONSHIPS, OVERLY CLOSE There are all kinds of reasons teenagers on TV are rotten jerks. But if the rotten jerks in question are girls, the culprit most of the time is a mother who treats her as more of a friend than a daughter. Maybe if Lorelai Gilmore had kept her daughter Rory on a shorter leash on *Gilmore Girls*, Rory wouldn't have slept with a married man, stolen a boat, or run away from home (twice). *Desperate Housewives*' Susan Mayer is modeling such atrociously clingy behavior in her romantic relationship with Mike that it's a blessing her daughter Julie is about ten times as sensible as her dumb-ass mother. Maxine and Amy Gray, the mother and daughter on *Judging Amy*, may be overly close physically, in that they live together, but Maxine has never ceded her parental duties in favor of friendship and hasn't let the fact that her daughter is in her forties stop her from scolding her for using bad language. Which is one of the eight million reasons Maxine rules. See also *DESPERATE HOUSEWIVES*; *GILMORE GIRLS*; TEENAGERS, BRATTY; and *JUDGING AMY*.

MOVIES, MADE-FOR-TV Watching a TV movie is kind of like watching minor-league baseball: It's definitely baseball, with uniforms and umpires and whatnot, but you've never heard of half the players, and *damn*, do they flail around out there. Occasionally, you'll see real live major-leaguers, guys with actual talent, on a rehab assignment with the lesser team (like Karl Malden and Gary Cole in the Green Beret murder movie *Fatal Vision*), but it's usually no-names like Susan Blakely (*No Child of Mine*) and no-talents like Tori Spelling (*Co-Ed Call Girl*), playing poorly, in movies the Weinsteins wouldn't touch with a ten-foot pole. With that said, if TV doesn't tell *Honor Thy Father and Mother: The True Story of the Menendez Murders*, nobody will, and the scene where Lyle's wig gets ripped off? Priceless. Because that's the great thing about minor-league baseball, too—the slapsticky level of play. If we want to see lofty cinematic product, we'll head down to the cinema—but why bother, when we can pop some corn in the microwave and watch the script of *George Washington II: The Forging of a Nation* inserting a metaphorical umbrella into Barry Bostwick's butt, and then unfurling it? See also ACTING, WOODEN; *ALEX: THE LIFE OF A CHILD*; BAXTER(-BIRNEY), MEREDITH; *BEST LITTLE GIRL IN THE WORLD, THE*; *BOY IN THE PLASTIC BUBBLE, THE*; *DAY AFTER, THE*; DOHERTY, SHANNEN; *KATE'S SECRET*; LIFETIME MOVIES; *LIKE NORMAL PEOPLE*; MINISERIES, OLD-SCHOOL EVENT EDITIONS; and SPELLING, TORI.

MOVIES, TV SERIES ADAPTATIONS OF Movie adaptations of beloved (and not-so-beloved) TV shows practically outnumber original stories at the movieplex—*Starsky and Hutch, Bewitched, The Dukes of Hazzard, Charlie's Angels* . . . we could go on and on. Interesting, then, that so few TV shows get made out of movies these days, especially with the success of *Buffy the Vampire Slayer*, which became a cult hit and critical darling that lasted seven seasons. The '80s definitely saw some bombs in the movies-to-series department, but those projects bombed for good reason. *Diner* should have worked as a sitcom—a bunch of guys sitting around shooting the breeze? It worked out pretty well for that Seinfeld guy later on. But it never saw the light of day, primarily because James Spader and Michael Madsen don't do "shooting the breeze" nearly as well as they do "intense with a side of Manson crazy." *Ferris Bueller* didn't work (Charlie Schlatter as Ferris? Jennifer Aniston in the Jennifer Grey role?), *The Outsiders* didn't work (David Arquette subbing for Emilio Estevez is the least of that project's conceptual issues), but *Clueless* ported over almost the entire original cast, lasted three years, and got the occasional prop from critics. And let's not forget *Fame*, which actually improved on the film over the course of five seasons, and *M*A*S*H*, which took Altman's acerbic commentary on Vietnam and ran with it for over a decade until its 1983 finale, a television event met with genuine mourning in households around the country. We're not saying we'd watch an *Ocean's 11* TV show, but . . . wait. That's exactly what we're saying. Get on that shit, Clooney. See also BEWITCHED; BUFFY THE VAMPIRE SLAYER; CASSIDYS, THE; CLOONEY, GEORGE; *DUKES OF HAZZARD, THE*; *FAME*; *FRIENDS*; MOVIES-TO-TV/TV-TO-MOVIES CAREER PIPELINE/ARC; and WHEDON, JOSS.

MOVIES-TO-TV/TV-TO-MOVIES CAREER PIPELINE/ARC Time was, there were movie stars and there were TV stars, and never the twain did meet. That time has passed. Now, the way it works is that a previously unknown actor breaks out on TV, and movie offers follow. Eva Longoria lands on the buzz-heavy *Desperate Housewives* in 2004, and by 2005 she's filming a political thriller with Michael Douglas and Kim Basinger—that's just one of myriad contemporary examples. Some actors unwisely attribute the movie heat to their own talent and not to their participation in a hit show and decide they no longer need to stay on the TV series that spawned them in case the movie career doesn't pan out. This is how you separate the George Clooneys (those who know when to make the permanent jump) from the David Carusos (perpetrators of premature evacuation). But the pipeline also goes in the opposite direction, which is how you get an actor like Martin Sheen to downshift from *Apocalypse Now* to *The West Wing*. A movie actor who's just sick of the grind of moviemaking may make what is now a perfectly valid decision to take a gig on a comfortable TV series and sleep in his own bed every night. (The validity of the decision doesn't mean we can't still sneer at the failure Michael Rapaport made of his life by appearing on *The War at Home*. Then again, we'd probably be sneering at him regardless.) See also CARUSO, DAVID, AS GO-TO REFERENCE FOR CAREER SUICIDE; CLOONEY, GEORGE; *DESPERATE HOUSEWIVES*; SITCOM, MOVIE ACTRESSES' ATTEMPTS TO PROP SAGGING CAREER BY MEANS OF; and *WEST WING, THE*.

MR. BELVEDERE Once *Benson* and *Who's the Boss?* had piqued America's fascination with the exciting lives of male domestics, the way had been paved for *Mr. Belvedere*, which starred Christopher Hewett as a classically trained British butler working for the Owens family, your standard American boors, headed by patriarch Bob Uecker. Obviously, Mr. Belvedere teaches them some class and manners, but the show is actually only memorable for two reasons: 1) There was a rumor that, under his makeup, Marilyn Manson was actually Rob Stone, who played eldest Owens son Kevin (not true), and 2) on *Clone High*, Principal Scudworth's robot butler Mr. Butlertron was originally called Mr. Belvetron; copyright issues forced producers to change the robot's name, though the distinctive mustache and signature fussy attire—and Mr. Butlertron's habit of calling all characters "Wesley" (a name shared by the youngest Owens child, played by Brice Beckham)—remain the late Hewett's most important and lasting legacy. See also *BENSON*; *CLONE HIGH*; and *WHO'S THE BOSS?*

"MR. FURLEY" *Three's Company*'s original landlord, Stanley Roper, got spun off into his own Andy-Capp-esque sitcom, *The Ropers*, in 1979, thereby making way for '70s fashion's television nadir: Mr. Ralph Furley (Don Knotts). A skinny, irritable, bug-eyed control freak who enjoyed long walks on the beach, lime-green neckerchieves, and bursting in without knocking, Mr. Furley often witnessed things he shouldn't have—or misinterpreted them—and therefore served as the engine that drove the show's wacky-misunderstandings train. See also DORKINESS, TV SIGNIFIERS OF and *THREE'S COMPANY*.

"MR. GREEN JEANS" Many kids liked Captain Kangaroo sidekick Mr. Green Jeans, allegedly a farmer (or an inventor, or something), better than the Captain himself. Green Jeans was a little less . . . *intense*, for starters, but mostly, we loved Green Jeans because he often showed up bearing animals—cool ones, like bear cubs and goats that drank out of bottles, just like babies! Oh, how we begged our moms to get us a giant tortoise, then sulked when told to make do with the prosaic domesticated feline! It seems like Mr. Green Jeans actually wore regular overalls most of the time, but maybe we remember that wrong. See also *CAPTAIN KANGAROO* and CHILDREN'S SHOWS, HOSTS OF.

"MR. HANKEY" Honestly, why *not* create an animated character that's an anthropomorphized piece of poo? Mr. Hankey, the Christmas poo, was introduced in *South Park*'s first Christmas episode in 1997, as a secret friend to Kyle (who reminds us that "it's tough to be a Jew at Christmas"). In classic cartoon style, he only talks to Kyle, so that when anyone else appears, it seems as though Kyle is hanging with and smearing around a chunk of his own feces. After Mr. Hankey brings together a town divided over the religious iconography of Christmas, he returns as the host of "Mr. Hankey's Christmas Classics" (a musical variety show) and in "A Very Crappy Christmas," where we meet the rest of his poo family, including alcoholic wife Autumn and son Cornwallis. Either you think poo is funny or you don't; we do, and are therefore endlessly amused by the poo puns deployed in every Mr. Hankey episode. (Hee! "Cornwallis.") See also HOLIDAYS, "SPECIAL" EPISODES BASED AROUND and SOUTH PARK.

"MRS. FLETCHER" LifeCall, basically a radio transmitter that elderly folks who lived alone could use to call for aid in case of emergency, spawned the infamous "I've fallen and I can't get up" commercial. We're sending help immediately, Mrs. Fletcher! . . . Oh, wait. Lifecall went out of business. Get a cell phone, Grandma. See also "AS SEEN ON TV" PRODUCTS and CATCHPHRASES, OVERUSED COMMERCIAL.

"MRS. POOLE" Mrs. Poole lived next door to the Hogans on *The Hogan Family*, and by the time the series went off the air, the name "Mrs. Poole" had become synonymous with "annoying neighbor." Mrs. Poole bustled in  without knocking, stuck her nose into the Hogans' business, and irritated all and sundry with her gurgly voice and propensity for styling her hair with mane combs. Kudos to Edie McClurg, a battle-tested Hey! It's That Lady! who's never more convincing than when she's bur-bling on about some obscure Midwestern

dessert or hinting that she'd like an invitation to dinner. See also HOGANS, THE/HOGAN FAMILY, THE and NEIGHBORS, INTRUSIVE.

MR. WIZARD'S WORLD Mr. Wizard had a way of performing and explaining his science experiments that made the kids watching at home feel smart—especially compared with the kids who played his assistants. Nobody expected them to understand string theory, but . . . every time with the gee-whizzy "Gravity? Golly, Mr. Wizard, I don't get it!"? See also CHILDREN'S SHOWS, HOSTS OF.

MTV See MADE; MAKING THE BAND; OSBOURNES, THE; REAL WORLD, THE; REAL WORLD/ROAD RULES CHALLENGE, THE; REMOTE CONTROL; RICH GIRLS; and TRL.

MTV VJs Once upon a time, there was a network called MTV. Its initials stood for "music television," and it used to play videos all the time. No, really! The channel debuted with five VJs—Martha Quinn, Nina Blackwood, Mark Goodman, Alan Hunter, and the late J. J. Jackson—and while a few of them had cuteness to recommend them (Quinn *still* looks like she's about twenty), you could tell most of them knew their music and had probably gotten the job on that basis. But the Fab Five eventually got phased out, and successive generations of VJs got more and more underqualified and irritating. Adam Curry had his act together, heee-yuge hair aside, but Downtown Julie Brown didn't seem to know as much about music as she did about wearing big hats and guffawing horsily—not that the odious Kennedy, clearly hired in a misguided attempt to appeal to a "Gen X" audience, was an improvement. By that time, of course, it didn't much matter; MTV had already started to phase out videos in favor of *Real World* reruns, *TRL*, and other traditional programming blocks, so while Ananda Lewis's résumé probably consisted only of "has belly-button ring; can interview boy bands without rolling eyes," MTV didn't need "real" VJs anymore anyway. It needed placeholders to host *Road Rules* reunions and pimp out crappy pop to tweens, and who better for the job than doughy gits like Carson Daly or someone named "La La"? See also *ALTERNATIVE NATION/120 MINUTES*; CAMP, JESSE; CURRY, ADAM; DALY, CARSON; DUFF; HOLMES, DAVE; MUSIC VIDEOS, MEMORABLE; and *TRL*.

MUPPET BABIES   For a brief time in the '80s, it became the vogue to reinvent existing characters in children's programming as, essentially, younger versions of themselves. You may (but probably don't) remember *The Flintstones Kids* and *A Pup Named Scooby-Doo*. (Warner Bros.' *Tiny Toon Adventures* didn't come until later.) But the first installment in this genre-let was *Muppet Babies*. Much as *The Muppet Show* was superior to *The Flintstones* (and, it goes without saying, to that loathsome *Scooby Doo*), *Muppet Babies*—spun off from a segment of *The Muppets Take Manhattan* in which miniature versions of the Muppets sing together in their nursery—was superior to *Flintstones Kids*. It was a perfectly cute look at the imaginative play of . . . well, baby Muppets, overseen by Nanny (voiced by *Leave It to Beaver* mom Barbara Billingsley), of whom all we ever saw was her green-and-white-striped tights. Each episode also included an adorable musical number. Really, as kids' cartoons go, it's one of the best. Excuse us while we go see if DVDs are available yet. See also LIVE-ACTION SHOWS, ANIMATED VERSIONS OF and *MUPPET SHOW, THE*.

MUPPET SHOW, THE   What was basically a showbiz satire—a merry band of puppets who apparently live in an old vaudeville theater and put on a show every week, featuring a special celebrity guest star—managed to appeal to both children and adults. The huge cast of Muppets meant that every viewer, regardless of personality, could have a favorite, and that there was a variety of different character types available to perform the show's quite adorable musical numbers. ("Mahna Mahna" is still a classic among hipsters, and will be in your head all afternoon, we promise.) The show has spawned dozens of feature films, TV specials, toys, books, albums, and the adorable *Muppet Babies* cartoon, and although the franchise hasn't really been the same since Muppet creator and multiple character voicer Jim Henson passed away in 1990, we're glad his vision lives on. One of the few actually entertaining children's shows that *never* talked down to its audience, *The Muppet Show* made primetime safe for puppets . . . in the post–Señor Wences era, anyway. See also *MUPPET BABIES* and TV SERIES, FILM ADAPTATIONS OF.

MURDER, SHE WROTE The premise: Mystery novelist and amateur supersleuth Jessica Fletcher finds herself in the middle of a whodunit each week and solves the case. Of course, everywhere she went, someone just *happened* to get killed shortly thereafter, so the *real* mystery is why the denizens of the show continued to associate with her. Someone turns up dead like seven minutes after she shows up! Every week! Do the math, citizens of Cabot Cove. The show got mocked by critics and standup comedians almost constantly during its twelve-year (!) run, not just for Jessica's bad-luck-charm status but also because it seemed to typify CBS's programming at that time—formulaic, faintly dumb, and aimed squarely at the Metamucil-and-

Polident crowd. With that said, *Murder, She Wrote* is not that bad. It's predictable, but it's not as terrible as it's made out to be. Still: twelve years? Our theory is that

CBS execs would have canceled it, but feared that Angela Lansbury would show up at their offices to protest in person, thus dooming at least one of them to certain death. See also A&E DAYBREAKS and SMALL TOWNS, HIDDEN DEPRAVITY OF.

MURPHY BROWN Like a latter-day *Mary Tyler Moore Show*, *Murphy Brown* followed the backstage antics of a news broadcast, only this time it was a national newsmagazine rather than a local 6:00 news show, and the female protagonist is not a lowly copywriter but a high-powered anchorwoman. Candice Bergen played the titular heroine, a tetchy liberal feminist with huge hair and lockjawed line readings. It was just a run-of-the-mill workplace sitcom—complete with dippy blonde (Faith Ford), stoic old white guy (Charles Kimbrough), working-class kid made good (Joe Regalbuto), and neurotic young boss (Grant Shaud)—until the unmarried Murphy became pregnant in 1992 and Vice President Dan Quayle gave the show a boatload of free publicity by complaining, on the reelection campaign trail, that she was glorifying single motherhood. It made him look dumb and the show look great, and Quayle and his boss lost the election to a guy who had no problem with single moms. Or soccer moms. Or MILFs of any kind, really.

MURRAY, CHAD MICHAEL The archetypal WB teen-drama actor, Chad Michael Murray is almost too pretty, looks good pouting on promo posters and modeling sponsored fashions, and can only muster one and a half emotions convincingly. See also ACTING, WOODEN and *DAWSON'S CREEK*.

MUSICAL MONTAGES In the '60s, when TV shows about pop bands actually constituted a genre, musical montages moved the product. On *The Monkees*, the montage is usually a two- or three-minute lowlight reel of Micky's unfunny chimplike capering, sped up for extra wackiness, but at least you can't *hear* Micky during it, and we like the songs, so it's fine. On *The Partridge Family*, it's generally an excuse for the writers to put a dent in their workload by allowing for several minutes of loving David Cassidy close-ups, which is also fine (or a good time to hit the head). Nowadays, though, the montage uses music by "real" bands, and while it's still the same time-wasting device from a writing standpoint, it's

used to show off the program's hipness quotient, depending on the band doing the heavy lifting during the cross-fades between brooding characters. And for every *Rescue Me* or *The O.C.*, which introduces us to cool new music even if it does so a bit too knowingly, you've got a *Dawson's Creek*, which overlays hideous shots of James Van Der Beek trying to cry with an even more hideous track of Jewel trying to sing and play the guitar. Shut up, Dawson. And Jewel. See also CRYING, FAKE/BAD; *DAWSON'S CREEK*; *MONKEES, THE*; MUSIC CUES, ETHNIC; *O.C., THE*; and *PARTRIDGE FAMILY, THE*.

MUSIC CUES, ETHNIC Because nearly all "exotic" "foreign" scenes are actually filmed on location in exotic Los Angeles, setting a scene in Milan or Shanghai requires deceptive establishing shots, national monuments digitally superimposed behind what's actually Sepulveda Boulevard, and ethnic music to complete the illusion. You're supposed to be on Mykonos? Slap a bouzouki on the soundtrack. Vienna? Why, that's where Mozart's from! *Alias* is particularly guilty of this construction. However, ethnic music cues are also useful when you're staying put at home but are about to run afoul of villains of color: If you can hear maracas and mariachi horns, a Latino gang is definitely gaining on you. See also *ALIAS*.

MUSIC VIDEOS, MEMORABLE Back in the day, almost every song had a video to go with it, and almost none of the videos that came out of the mid-'80s made a lick of sense. The Duran Duran videos, with the body paint and the split screens? The ZZ Top videos, in which the band's proto-PT Cruiser (and enigmatic circular arm gesture) had the magical power to . . . attract women in five-inch hooker heels to the sleeveless-sweatshirted hero? "Sweet Dreams Are Made of This," which prompted endless debate as to Annie Lennox's actual gender? The creepy Genesis video with the rubber Spitting Image masks where Reagan wakes up in a pool of his own sweat? What the? Not that videos of the '90s had a recognizable plot, either, and given a choice, we'd rather watch whatever coked-up directorial vision prompted the J. Geils Band to pour milk onto a snare drum and film it in slo-mo than we would a "Losing My Religion"-era REM spot. Enough with the feathers and Michael Stipe writhing around in an Eames chair like the world's angstiest bisexual pretzel, guys. We get it. . . . Well, we don't get it, actually.

MUSTACHES, GREAT TV Though the old soup strainer has fallen out of tonsorial fashion, some of the greats live on in syndication—the ones you find on the upper lips of Ned Flanders, The Fat Man, the Simon played by Gerald McRaney, Garthe Knight (Michael's evil twin!),

Schneider. We hesitate to name an all-time best, but . . . Magnum. P. I. There are Japanese soldiers in Tom Selleck's 'stache who don't know the war is over. See also AFROS, IMPORTANT TV; *KNIGHT RIDER*; SIDEBURNS, IMPORTANT TV; *SIMON & SIMON*; and *SIMPSONS, THE*.

MY SO-CALLED LIFE On a superficial level, *My So-Called Life* featured all the clichés: bratty teenager, bad-influence friend, nerdy friend with unrequited crush, maybe-cheating dad, leather-jacket-clad laconic love interest, school-play storyline that eerily parallels the events in the characters' lives, Christmas episode featuring a homeless teen angel ghost . . . the usual. But *My So-Called Life* earned its cult status because it only traded in those clichés that had evolved because they're based on truth. It featured some of the most realistic depictions of the life of a high school student, which made it as painful as it was addictive. Whatever shame Claire Danes and Jared Leto have brought upon themselves since, they'll always be able to point to at least one project with pride—coincidentally, the one thing we haven't hated them in. See also

Cool, TV Signifiers of; "Cult Show," Definition of; Dooley, Paul; Holidays, "Special" Episodes Based Around; and Teenagers, Bratty.

N

NEIGHBORS, INTRUSIVE The intrusive neighbor problem is nothing a quality deadbolt wouldn't solve, but TV characters never seem to learn that. It's sort of hard to sympathize with the Hogans when Mrs. Poole comes bustling in, or with Mr. Wilson when Dennis pesters him during his nap. Granted, a lot of TV characters don't seem to mind their intrusive neighbors—Jerry never really felt the need to Kramer-proof his apartment on *Seinfeld*—and others can't really lock the front door, since the boundary-free neighbors are family members (*Everybody Loves Raymond*) or advisees (*Felicity*, which put a running "y'all should lock the door, this is New York City" gag into the third season). Dawson even enabled his intrusive neighbors-slash-friends by putting a ladder against the side of the house. Intrusive neighbors often exist in order to provide "comic" "relief," but still: If you don't want Urkel coming over, throw the bolt, already. See also BAD SITCOM, SURE SIGNS OF; "COSMO KRAMER"; "DAWSON LEERY"; *FELICITY*; *HOGANS, THE/HOGAN FAMILY, THE*; NEW YORK CITY, CLICHED/INACCURATE PORTRAYALS OF; and "URKEL."

NELSON, CRAIG T. Or, as you probably know him, the irascible Coach. That show was on for eight years, people. How? Why? Okay, we watched it a few times, but we weren't proud of having done so, and we didn't know anyone else who did. During the run of *Coach*, Nelson was also able to dabble in his first love: justice-oriented TV movies and miniseries, including *Drug Wars: The Camarena Story* and *Probable Cause*. Post-*Coach*, Nelson went on to play an irascible D.C. police chief on *The District*—or so we hear, not that we've ever seen one second of it. Maybe now that he's had a career renaissance as the patriarch of *The Incredibles*, Nelson can quit playing crabby old yelly guys all the time. See also *ALEX: THE LIFE OF A CHILD*; *COACH*; and MOVIES, MADE-FOR-TV.

NETWORK PROMO BUGS, INCREASING OBTRUSIVENESS OF Like all of the most insidious evils of our world, it started so small, so innocent. In the bottom right corner of the screen would be the network's logo, tiny and semitransparent, so you could still kind of see what was behind it. But over time the bugs got bigger. They were in color instead of that ghostly gray. They became animated with swirls or flourishes so that your eye was drawn to the movement of them. Then there came the promo bands along the bottom of the screen: "You are watching *Lost*." Yeah. WE KNOW. And *then* the networks started cannibalizing their own shows' airtime to advertise other shows, so that we couldn't enjoy a nice quiet episode of *Cold Case* without being informed that there would be an all-new *Survivor* later in the week. You know, networks, we get the TV listings every weekend in the paper, for free.

NEWBORN BABIES, PRODIGIOUS SIZE OF
We understand that it would be challenging to populate a casting call for actual newborn babies; a brand-new infant is fragile and can't be away from his mommy long enough to pretend some other lady just pushed him out of her business. But the workaround most TV shows have come up with—using babies who *are* old enough to work—immediately takes you out of the story, since you know the mother in question didn't just deliver a noggin that huge. Cover them with raspberry jam all you like, we're just not buying these kids as newborns when they look like they can't wait for the director to yell cut so they can go have a latte and a smoke. On the other hand,

using those animatronic baby dolls is an even worse solution—or it will be, until the technology is such that they don't look like AIBOs covered in rubber "skin." [*Shudder.*] See also MEDICAL DRAMAS, TROPES OF.

NEWLYWEDS Why Jessica Simpson is famous is still something of a mystery, but a large portion of the blame probably lies with *Newlyweds*, a reality show that followed Simpson and her erstwhile boy-bander husband Nick Lachey through the early days of their then-marriage. Said marriage's odds of survival never seemed all that great, given that Jessica is a lot younger than Nick (and had stayed a virgin until their wedding night); a lot more famous than Nick, despite having even less talent; and as dumb as a box of hair extensions. Viewers tuned in  hoping that Jessica's functional retardation would humiliate her into oblivion, or at least prompt Nick, after patiently explaining that Chicken of the Sea is in fact tuna for the umpteenth time, to slap her with a divorce filing . . . but it didn't happen. (Well, not on the show, anyway.) On the plus side, we can now report that it is not possible for another human being to annoy us to death, because if the pestilent episode in which Jessica tries to stop saying "oh my God" by instead saying "oh my gaw" didn't do it, it's just plain not possible. See also REALITY TV, COUPLES ON and SIMPSONS, ASHLEEEEE AND JESSICA.

NEWS, CRAPPY LOCAL No matter where on the North American landmass you live, or where else on said landmass you travel, you can rely on one constant: The local news is bad. The average 11:00 broadcast leads with footage of police-car lights flashing while an inoffensive-looking anchor-clone with a bulletproof blow-dry reads sonorously about a shooting, a robbery, or a raccoon knocking over the trash at Wendy's. After the top stories (in order: a tragedy, local or national; something involving local unions, about which nobody cares; footage of the president walking around somewhere; and a nice juicy car wreck or building collapse), the broadcast segues into everyone's favorite local-news staple, the "Something Perfectly Innocent COULD KILL YOU"-slash-"Good God, WON'T SOMEONE THINK OF THE CHILDREN" feature. First comes the assy graphic of, like, a bowl of oatmeal with fangs, subtitled something along the lines of "Quaker? MORE LIKE 'DAMNED LIAR,'" and the revelation that oat bran is not all that good for you *if* you eat nothing but oatmeal, in which case you will get scurvy, which: doy. Or the graphic is a crooked, eeeeevil close-up of a trampoline, which

some Darwin-Award-winning parent allowed her child to play on unattended, and the kid bounced head-on into a tree and broke his neck, which was obviously the trampoline's fault. This is inevitably followed by a clumsy "but kids love basketball, don't they, Bob" transition into the sports segment, and then the weather report (always overhyped, always inaccurate), and then some footage of a pie-eating contest or fun run which nobody in their right mind would have attended. The anchors chuckle and shuffle their papers, and then mercifully it's over.

NEWSRADIO See A&E DAYBREAKS; OFFICE WEIRDOS; and SKETCH COMEDY ENSEMBLES, FORGOTTEN MEMBERS OF.

NEW YORK CITY, CLICHÉD/INACCURATE PORTRAYALS OF The Big Apple of TV Land is, except for the occasional establishing shot of the Empire State Building, almost unrecognizable to the natives, starting with the size of the apartments. Nobody who isn't a DuPont heir lives in a loft the size of the Friends', and they certainly can't make the rent on an Upper East Side one-bedroom on the money from one newspaper column a week like *Sex and the City*'s Carrie Bradshaw. TV people whistle for cabs, or shout "Taxi!" (nobody has actually done this outside of a movie musical since the '50s); the sidewalk is always virtually empty; all the natives are colorfully rude, except for the homeless, who only appear when a bit of homespun wisdom is needed; it's possible for a twenty-year-old to take an apartment in one day, with no deposit or cosignatory or anything, and then "return" it when she and her boyfriend don't like it (one of *Felicity*'s rare  authenticity missteps); the outer boroughs only exist as punchlines; very seldom do characters take public transit, and they'll just . . . show up at their friends' apartments. No doorman, no buzzer, nothing. The shows that got it right were *Seinfeld*, which shot on L.A. sets but at least understood the obsessions of New Yorkers, like parking, cheap food, and Moviefone; *Felicity*, usually, although a real NYU dorm room looks nothing like those Anthropologie-catalog digs; and *Law & Order*, which shoots in NYC. See also *FELICITY*; *FRIENDS*; *LAW & ORDER* FRANCHISE; REAL ESTATE, VASTNESS OF; *SEINFELD*; and *SEX AND THE CITY*.

NICKELODEON "Nick n-nick-nick n-nick-nick-nick / Nick-el-o-dee-ooooon!" PBS had all the good-for-you children's shows like *Sesame Street* and *Mister Rogers' Neighborhood*, but Nickelodeon had the fun stuff: *Mr. Wizard's World*, *Out of Control*, *Double Dare*, and of course *You Can't Do That on Television*. PBS aired what we "should" watch; Nick aired what we wanted to watch—cool sciencey stuff we could try at home, game shows involving obstacle courses, running gags about cafeteria food, and lots and lots of slime and people running around screaming. Nothing against *Electric Company* and its ilk, obviously, and Nickelodeon didn't get it right every time (*Pinwheel*), but it just seemed like the shows came from kids like us, consulting for the network, instead of from some sniffy study about child development. See also *DOUBLE DARE*; *MR. WIZARD'S WORLD*; *OUT OF CONTROL*; *PINWHEEL*; and *YOU CAN'T DO THAT ON TELEVISION*.

NIGHT COURT We get the feeling this show came out of a producers' meeting that went something like this: "How can we get away with making a lot of sex jokes?" "Uh . . . set the show in a brothel?" "Nah, network'll never go for it." "Set the show on . . . Eleventh Avenue in Manhattan?" "Dude, what did I just say?" "Set the show in . . . hell, I don't know, a night court?" The show is sitcom-by-numbers—wacky Mel Torme-obsessed Harry (Harry Anderson), big dumb Bull (Richard Moll), sexaholic Dan (Larroquette), uptight Christine (Markie Post), sassy Roz (Marsha Warfield), dryly reliable Mac (Charles Robinson), and a revolving door of hookers, drunks, and straight-up nutholes. But the premise let them get away with out-of-left-field setups other shows couldn't, so even when the writing stank, it still worked. Everything American children of the '80s knew about whips and chains, they learned from the Dan subplots on *Night Court*. The show dragged on way past its sell-by date and inflicted Markie Post on an unsuspecting nation, but the early episodes starring the late Selma Diamond still hold up pretty well. See also BAD SITCOM, SURE SIGNS OF and "BULL."

NIMOY, LEONARD Though we have no real feelings in either direction about his career-defining work as the Vulcan Mr. Spock in the *Star Trek* franchise, we are grateful that it exists, for one reason: It gave him enough of a profile that he could play very funny fictionalized versions of himself on a couple of episodes of *The Simpsons* and *Futurama*. (Nimoy: "A solar eclipse. The cosmic dance . . . continues." Guy: "Does anyone want to switch seats?") He also did a delightfully campy job as the narrator on schedule-plugging perennial *In Search Of*, managing to sound interested in whether Bigfoot is real. Well done, sir. See also *SIMPSONS, THE* and *STAR TREK* FRANCHISE.

NOID, THE It's really a testament to how dumb we all were in the '80s that the Noid could not only be reproduced in the form of rubber car-window figurines, playing cards, and a videogame . . . but could have been created in the first place. The Noid, for those lucky enough to have forgotten, was the star of a Domino's  Pizza campaign; he wore a bright red suit with bunnylike ears (for no apparent reason), and his project in life was to interfere with the swift delivery of pizzas so that they arrived at their destinations *cold*. Imagine! Anyway, "Avoid the Noid" was the tremendously annoying slogan, and yet because the Noid was a Claymation character and thus the representative of a thrilling new technology, we were enthralled. Although, you know, it's a bit tough to feel *that* superior to everyone who loved the Noid when we live in the age of Shrek. See also CALIFORNIA RAISINS.

NONMUSICAL SERIES, MUSICAL EPISODES OF *Buffy* kicked off the trend with "Once More with Feeling," an operetta-style episode that aired during November sweeps in 2001. Xander summons a demon who makes everyone in Sunnydale sing their most secret thoughts, whereupon the gang finally learns that, before they resurrected her, Buffy was in heaven. There are some actually quite charming little songs, by musical neophyte and *Buffy* creator Joss Whedon. Then, because it never met a gimmick it didn't like, *That '70s Show* did a very pedestrian take on the musical episode in 2002, in which Fez gets a part in the school musical, yawn, and the cast performs covers of such played-out '70s hits as "Shake Your Groove Thing." Fortunately for *That '70s Show*, *7th Heaven* did its own musical episode in 2005, rescuing *'70s* from the title of most awful musical episode of a TV series. Shut up, Camdens. See also BUFFY THE VAMPIRE SLAYER; 7TH HEAVEN; THAT '70S SHOW; and WHEDON, JOSS.

NORTHERN EXPOSURE Quirkiness on a TV show is a delicate proposition. We would say that every would-be quirky show since 1990 has been trying to ape the seemingly organic quirk of CBS's *Northern Exposure*. Brand-new doctor Joel Fleischman (Rob Morrow), having financed his fancy New York education by means of a scholarship from the state of Alaska, has to pay it back by serving as the local doctor in the minuscule town of Cicely, where they've never heard of bagels, there's no Chinese take-out, and the central heating in Joel's cabin is a woodstove. Many episodes hinged on Joel's complete inability to cope outside of Manhattan, but series creators Joshua Brand and John Falsey also created a rich supporting cast—film buff/shaman Ed

(Darren E. Burrows), millionaire former astronaut and aesthete Maurice (Barry Corbin), taciturn assistant Marilyn (Elaine Miles), ex-con philosopher Chris (John Corbett)—so that the town supplied its own storylines and didn't have to focus nonstop on Joel. Joel eventually consummates his love/hate relationship with bush pilot Maggie (Janine Turner); shortly thereafter, Morrow left the show. Joel was replaced by an Italian doctor from L.A. (Paul Provenza) who came with a reporter wife (Teri Polo) in tow, but the two of them didn't add up to one Rob Morrow. Which one doesn't often say about an actor who's about 4'3". See also "CHRIS IN THE MORNING"; SEXUAL TENSION, RUINATION OF SHOW BY RESOLVING; SITCOMS, FISH-OUT-OF-WATER; and SMALL TOWNS, QUIRKINESS OF.

NOTH, CHRIS Bulky, manly frame? Thick ol' head of hair, black as the night? Wolfish grin? Chris Noth had it all. He sailed through the first several seasons of *Law & Order* as Detective Mike Logan, the younger counterpart to a series of ever more aged partners, generally wearing a plaid necktie and brown leather coat or, in summer, a sport coat with an American flag lapel pin. When producers declined to renew Noth's contract in 1995, he ended up on *Sex and the City*, where he played Carrie Bradshaw's white whale, the mysterious businessman known only as Mr. Big. There, he had less to do than he did as Mike Logan—just show up, tolerate Sarah Jessica Parker's whining, and pick up a paycheck—but he seemed to be having a lot more fun. Or, he just got to smile more when he was supposed to be sexing up skinny socialites than he did when he was supposed to be running down perps. See also LAW & ORDER FRANCHISE and *SEX AND THE CITY*.

NUDITY *NYPD Blue* has been credited with breaking down one of broadcast television's most abiding taboos: nudity. Throughout the '90s, as each of *Blue*'s cast members took his or her turn mooning America and America failed to decline immediately into a lawless landscape of Caligulan depravity, other strictures regarding the human body were relaxed: Sometimes you could see a naked boobie on one of the big three networks, if it belonged to a teenager undergoing postmastectomy reconstruction (*Chicago Hope*), or to a corpse (*CSI*). But then there was that whole thing at the halftime show of the 2004 Super Bowl—maybe you heard something about it? That one infamous nork flash set back the cause of birthday-suit broadcasting at least ten years. Once again, a Jackson has to ruin it

for everybody. See also CHICAGO HOPE; CSI; NYPD BLUE; and SUPER BOWL HALFTIME SHOWS, DULLNESS OF.

NUMB3RS What's sexier than math, right? Turns out . . . kind of a lot of things. But that didn't stop director brothers Tony and Ridley Scott from developing *Numb3rs*, a procedural drama about FBI agent Don Eppes (Rob Morrow) and his math-genius brother Charlie (David Krumholtz). Remarkably, Don keeps managing, week after week, to get assigned to cases whose solution depends considerably on math. Enter Charlie, who isn't only supersmart but *also* has impressive security clearances and access to assets in the Department of Defense. He also happens to be a math prof, which is handy for when he has to explain to regular FBI agents (and those of us at home) what the hell it is he does. We're not going to lie: The show is dull, and the addition of Judd Hirsch as folksy Eppes patriarch Alan doesn't really help. But Peter "The Biscuit" MacNicol, as Charlie's physicist colleague Larry, is always amusing in his persnicketiness, and Krummy is so cute, he makes us wish we could do long division in our heads. Maybe Larry can theorize a parallel universe in which that could ever, ever happen. See also SCIENCE, IGNORANCE OF.

NYPD BLUE Also known as *The Thing That Wouldn't Die, Blue* joined the ABC primetime lineup in 1993 amid a firestorm of publicity regarding . . . well, tits and ass, both of which the show planned to bare if a scene called for it instead of pretending that people have sex with their clothes on. This prompted predictable protests from various "pro-family" organizations, but a lot of curious viewers tuned in for the first few episodes, hoping for a cheek shot, and kept tuning in, even though Dennis Franz's were among the cheeks on display. David Caruso caused a kerfuffle by falling in love with himself and leaving after the first season; people kept watching. Resident hottie Jimmy Smits got killed off; people kept watching. Former child star Ricky Schroder, now going by "Rick," replaced Smits; people kept watching. People got used to Schroder and then *he* left and an even funnier thespian punchline, *Saved by the Bell*'s Mark-Paul Gosselaar, tagged in; people kept watching. Sipowicz's (Franz) wife died, he got cancer like twenty times, and his partners either croaked or bailed on him at least once a season, *and* he was kind of a bigot, *and* he did not have a good ass . . . and people. Kept. Watching. It did have a certain appeal—it brought a new level of grit to cop dramas, and at times, between the jerky camerawork and the characters frequently acting like dicks, it felt almost like a documentary. See also BOCHCO, STEVEN; CARUSO, DAVID, AS GO-TO REFERENCE FOR CAREER SUICIDE; GOOD COP/BAD COP; NUDITY; RECASTING, NOTORIOUS; *SAVED BY THE BELL*; SCHRODER, RICK(Y); and SMITS, JIMMY.

O

O.C., THE   Who knew there was such an active rivalry between Newport Beach and Chino? McG, that's who! The micro-named auteur produced *The O.C.* for FOX after his *Miami Vice* update, *Fastlane*, ran out of gas (heh heh). The series revolves around the life of taciturn Chinoan Ryan (Benjamin McKenzie, nicely covering the fact that he was in his mid-twenties when the show began by being about five feet tall). After a minor run-in with the law, Ryan is taken in by his bleeding-heart liberal lawyer Sandy (Peter Gallagher); Sandy's developer wife Kirsten (Kelly Rowan); and their dorky son Seth (Adam Brody). But the ritzy community of Newport Beach isn't prepared to take Ryan's brazen polite behavior and leather-wrist-cuff wearing lying down, and Ryan has a hard time getting accepted by Newport's snobby adults and their bratty kids. Of course, there is a fraught romance between Ryan and the sticklike, alcoholic girl next door, Marissa (a spectacularly unappealing Mischa Barton), and of course Seth lands his dream girl Summer (Rachel Bilson), because that totally happens in real life. *The O.C.* wants desperately to be the new *90210*, but fails because it tries too hard (in vain) to achieve an atmosphere of gritty realism instead of fluffy middle American wish-fulfillment. But, in the absence of any other towering teen dramas, *The O.C.* will do. For now. See also ACTING, WOODEN; *BEVERLY HILLS 90210*; BRODY, ADAM; COOL, TV SIGNIFIERS OF; DORKINESS, TV SIGNIFIERS OF; GALLAGHER, PETER, EYEBROWS OF; McG; *MIAMI VICE*; *O.C., THE*, FISTICUFFS ON; REAL ESTATE, VASTNESS OF; TEENAGERS, BRATTY; and UNIVERSALLY REVILED CHARACTERS.

O.C., THE, FISTICUFFS ON   The series premiere of *The O.C.* got off to a memorable, oft-quoted start by having a crowd of water polo players (guh? This school doesn't have a football team?) beat up Benjamin McKenzie's Ryan, taunting, "Welcome to the O.C., bitch. This is how it's done in Orange County." Yeah, okay, Speedo. Anyway, the formula worked so well that there's been a fistfight in virtually every episode of *The O.C.* Often, the fighting takes place at/interrupts a chichi party or charity event, the better for all of Newport Beach to be scandalized by the local ruffians and their country manners. Also, this allows the writers an excuse to put the girls in gowns and not write dialogue for at least a couple of script pages. See also *O.C., THE.*

O'DONNELL, ROSIE   Rosie O'Donnell has gone through many incarnations in her career—standup comedian; bad film actor; cable host; magazine publisher; memoirist; Broadway star; producer of doomed Broadway musicals—but the one in which she arguably made the greatest cultural impression was in her six-year run as the host of her syndicated daytime talker *The Rosie O'Donnell Show.* It wasn't bad enough that O'Donnell spent her time on TV developing irritating motifs, like flinging Koosh balls into the audience or belting out show tunes with her personality-free bandleader, John McDaniel. After leaving her daytime gig, O'Donnell kind of lost the thread, publishing a free-verse blog, getting into legal disputes with the company that owned the now-defunct *Rosie* magazine, and, most notoriously, headlining the abominable TV movie *Riding the Bus with My Sister* in the role of a mentally challenged adult. If you thought nothing could be worse than watching O'Donnell defend her choice to wear up to forty spritzes of perfume every day (that did happen, and we have not inflated the number for comic purposes), then it's only because your imagination has failed in picturing her with no makeup, a frizzy perm, and a Tweety Bird T-shirt. Inside out. Now, thank your imagination for sparing you that. See also MENTALLY CHALLENGED PERSONS, ACTORS OF NORMAL INTELLIGENCE WHO'VE PLAYED; MOVIES, MADE-FOR-TV; *STAND-UP SPOTLIGHT*; and TALK SHOWS, DAYTIME.

OFFICE, THE   Invading the United States by means of a two-pronged BBC America/DVD attack, *The Office* may very well be the most brilliant comedy British television ever produced. Revolving around the sales office of Wernham Hogg, a paper company in the London suburb of Slough, the series stars Ricky Gervais as David Brent, an incompetent nightmare of a manager cursed (or blessed) with a complete lack of self-awareness. No one in the office respects him at all, which is simultaneously hilarious and painful to watch. Gervais is ably supported by delusional power tripper Gareth (Mackenzie Crook); world-weary receptionist Dawn (Lucy Davis); and Tim (Martin Freeman), the salesman who pines after Dawn in silence. If social awkwardness makes you uncomfortable, then for you to confront *The Office* would be aversion therapy on par with putting a daddy longlegs on an arachnophobe's hand—it will either make you stronger or kill you dead. Series cocreator Gervais wisely ended the series after just two seasons, with an extended Christmas special to tie up loose ends; we in North America could learn something from Gervais's example of leaving on a high note instead of mining a successful vein until it's completely tapped. In 2005, NBC adapted *The Office* with a new American cast, headed by *The Daily Show*'s Steve Carell; it's pretty good, if you can pretend that the British version never existed.

OFFICE WEIRDO   A staple of TV series set in workplaces, the office weirdo may have been accepted into the company of his or her cooler coworkers, but the sense is that it took a lot of time and effort. *Alias*'s Marshall (Kevin Weisman) seems to have desensitized everyone but Sloane (Ron Rifkin) to his mid–op tech briefing digressions; *Gilmore Girls*'s persnickety Kirk (Sean Gunn) is barely tolerated in his workplace of . . . every  place of business in the town of Stars Hollow; *Ed*'s Shirley (Rachel Cronin) is indulged even as she drops such bizarre non sequiturs as "Bendy straws make drinking more pleasurable"; and *NewsRadio*'s Matthew (Andy Dick) is fondly called "Spaz" by all and sundry, despite being what a rather weird temp describes as "the weirdest office weird guy" he's ever seen. Alas, some workplace weirdos are destined never to blend: Let's have a moment of silence for *Six Feet Under*'s Arthur (Rainn Wilson), the cottage cheese–loving, spacey music-composing, off-puttingly cheery undertaker/sometime Fisher love interest, who must take his leave from the mortuary when he is wrongly accused of anonymously leaving his former girlfriend elaborately wrapped pieces of poo. Wilson went on to play another spectacular weirdo on NBC's *The Office*, and though poo showed up in the boss's office there, too, he was not to blame. Perhaps there's something about his presence in a workplace that drives others to acts of fecal terrorism. See also *ALIAS*; DORKINESS, TV SIGNIFIERS OF; *ED*; *GILMORE GIRLS*; and WILSON, RAINN.

OLSEN, MARY-KATE AND ASHLEY   Before they were anorexic, troll-like young adults, the Olsen twins took turns portraying Michelle, the infant daughter on ABC's family-friendly *Full House*. Those who feel the girls' parents are to blame for their apparently troubled personal lives will find some ammunition for their argument in the fact that the Olsens' mother took them to audition for the role when they were only nine months old. Although they shared Michelle, the role that made them famous, the rise, in the '90s, of the "tween" audience provided the Olsens with a market for their straight-to-tape movies (*How the West Was Fun*, *Passport to Paris*, and *You're Invited to Mary-Kate & Ashley's Fashion Party*), videogames, albums, fashion line, bedroom furniture, and short-lived magazine. Between all these product launches, the Olsens also had time to star in *Full House* follow-up sitcoms *Two of a Kind* (see, because they're twins, and . . . oh, you get it?) and *So Little Time*. And because they have been credited as producers on virtually everything they've ever done, they're both millionaires. Which is fortunate, since it has meant that Mary-Kate has been able to check into some of the finest eating-disorder clinics in the nation. Well, theoretically. Really, what it's meant is that both she and her sister can afford to wear seventeen bag-ladyish layers of Marc Jacobs while sucking down twelve Starbucks iced coffees every day they spend in New York. Which is about three days a year, because while at least one of them remains allegedly enrolled at NYU . . . come on. See also ABC's TGIF; *FULL HOUSE*; and TWINS, FORCED HILARITY OF IN COMEDIES.

OLYMPICS COVERAGE   We always look forward to the Olympics—and we always forget, in the years between Olympiads, how jingoistic, schmaltzy, and downright stupid the coverage can be. Never mind the fact that the network, in the interests of equal time for sports nobody cares about, will cut away from a nail-biter of a 1,000 meters to make sure we don't miss a moment of the women's shot put— Olympics coverage also means filling every second possible with mushy behind-the-scenes biographies of the athletes; so-obvious-they're-Zen-koans remarks like "if the U.S. soccer team doesn't score more goals than its opponents, the team won't win!"; and showing the full medal ceremony only when Americans win gold. And we're sure Jim McKay is a nice guy, but . . . enough already. Still, it's worth it— we know it's Smurfy, but we love the figure skating, and we also kind of love how Scott Hamilton pitches a spaz about every single routine. See also SPORTS COVERAGE, FATUOUS and SPORTS COVERAGE, HALL-MARK-Y BACKGROUND STORIES IN.

OMAROSA   Every reality show has to have its villain, and Omarosa Manigault-Stallworth performed the role well enough in the first season of *The Apprentice* that her hatefulness spilled over into the next several casts. Omarosa was imperious, uncooperative, basically incompetent, and impossible to get along with; she had no compunction playing the race card (another contestant's use of the expression "the pot calling the kettle black" struck her as a slur) and used the accidental fall of approximately eight ounces of plaster on her head as a pretext for malingering on a team challenge. Obviously, she didn't win the job of Donald Trump's apprentice, but that didn't mean we were rid of her; she returned for the last challenge of the season, goofing off uselessly around Jessica Simpson—who, and we never thought we'd say this, really deserved better. She also apparently hired a publicist who got her gigs on *Celebrity Poker Showdown, Fear Factor,* and *Dr. Phil,* and in the same *Surreal Life* cast as Janice Dickinson, with whom she instantly clashed. We've never wished so hard for one bitch to scratch another's eyes out, so God bless VH1 for putting them in the same pen and letting nature take its course. See also *APPRENTICE, THE*; *CELEBRITY POKER SHOWDOWN*; DICKINSON, JANICE; *SURREAL LIFE, THE*; and UNIVERSALLY REVILED CHARACTERS.

ONE DAY AT A TIME *One Day at a Time* followed the lives of divorcée Ann Romano (Bonnie Franklin); her daughters Barbara (Valerie Bertinelli) and Julie (Mackenzie Phillips); and their building super Schneider (Pat Harrington Jr.). The show was ahead of its time in focusing on a single mother who actually stayed single for most of the series. Not only that, but feminist Ann had reverted to her maiden name after her divorce—imagine!—and had to work for a living at a typically bleh job. Other than its premise, the show served up standard sitcom fare:

Ann's travails in dating and with her work rival Francine (Shelley Fabares), and Barbara and Julie's sibling rivalry. As the actors playing the daughters realistically aged, they moved on from boy troubles to husband troubles. Toward the end of the show's run, producers Cousin Olivered in Glenn Scarpelli as Alex, son of Ann's boyfriend Nick (Ron Rifkin!), who Ann adopted when Nick was (conveniently) killed in a car accident. The series ran for nine years, ending in 1984 when both Franklin and Bertinelli decided to leave—Bertinelli for dozens of TV movies and Franklin for her first love, the stage. And Phillips? Well, as a recovering cocaine addict, she's presumably taking it . . . one day at a time. See also MOVIES, MADE-FOR-TV; NEIGHBORS, INTRUSIVE; and "SCHNEIDER."

"ONE TO GROW ON" NBC knew it had a captive audience on Saturday mornings, and it took full advantage of that fact by interrupting the frivolous cartoons we'd tuned in for with a series of annoyingly sensible PSAs, narrated by NBC's young stars. "I'm Justine Bateman, and I'll be right back with . . . one to grow on!" We didn't really listen to the perky bromides about the evils of smoking, but watching the actors' attempts to find new ways to inflect the phrase "and that's . . . one to grow on" had its amusements. And it's still fun to say, in response to another person lecturing or correcting you: "I told you we should have taken the Holland Tunnel." "And that's . . . one to grow on." Annoy a significant other with it today! See also BATEMANS, JASON AND JUSTINE; PSAS; and "THE MORE YOU KNOW."

OPENING CREDITS, STYLES OF The job of the opening credits is first and foremost to tell you who's on the show, but the opening credits can multitask. Running a highlight reel of wacky, touching, and/or relevant moments from past episodes can give new viewers an idea of what's in store (Mallory almost knocking Elyse over on *Family Ties*, Buffy dusting vamps on *Buffy*). The credits can also do that work using the theme song (*Clone High*'s is basically the pitch for the show, as is *The Dukes of Hazzard*'s). Sometimes, the producers just want to show off the music they got the rights to (*Rescue Me*, *Joan of Arcadia*, the various expensive Who songs on the *CSIs*), or show you that you're supposed to think the heroine of the show is pretty and awesome (Jennifer Garner's cavalcade o' disguises in the *Alias* credits; Sarah Jessica Parker's jazzy tutu for *Sex and the City*), or make you feel a kinship with the cast as they clown around all BFF (*90210*). Reality-show credits serve as a reminder of the gone-and-totally-forgotten contestants that got das boot in the first few episodes ("ohhhhh yeah, that guy"); *24*'s

credits bring you up to speed on the "previouslies." We like credits in the style of *Lost* the best—just the show's floaty title, and then, the action. Less time on cutesy songs and tricksy editing means more content—in theory, anyway. See also *ALIAS*; *BUFFY THE VAMPIRE SLAYER*; *CSI*, SPIN-OFFS OF; *CLONE HIGH*; *DUKES OF HAZZARD, THE*; *FAMILY TIES*; *SEX AND THE CITY*; SITCOMS, ANIMATED OPENING CREDITS SEQUENCES OF; THEME SONGS; and *24*.

O'QUINN, TERRY Here's what you need to know about Terry O'Quinn, in a nutshell: *He is awesome*. We just could not adore him more. And evidently, we're not alone. O'Quinn has appeared in just about every TV series Chris Carter ever produced (including two different roles on *The X-Files* and a third in the *X-Files* movie), and has since joined J. J. Abrams's repertory company, having played FBI Assistant Director Kendall on *Alias* and Locke (hands down our favorite character) on *Lost*. He's also played a general in a recurring role on *The West Wing*, obviously because he has the look of a man who knows how to dispatch thousands of mothers' sons to war without getting all emotional about it. But we think the fact that O'Quinn's been typecast as a black-ops guy is a pity. Those roles require him to be all steel and bald fury, and deprive those of us in the audience of his lovely, twinkly smile. Really, the best thing about *Lost* is how delighted Locke is by the island, because it means that Terry O'Quinn gets to smile a lot. Which, in turn, makes us smile back. Abrams, if Locke turns out to be evil or a cyborg or something, we're going to kick your ass. See also *ALIAS*; TV BOYFRIENDS AND GIRLFRIENDS; TV SERIES, FILM ADAPTATIONS OF; *WEST WING, THE*; and *X-FILES, THE*.

ORPHANS   A TV writer who wants to make a young character seem deep and soulful has one weapon in his arsenal— killing that character's parents! It accomplishes instant conflict: the kids have a reason to be sad and brood, the kids are loosed from the strictures of parental rules,  the kids are either relocated to a new home or put in the care of an older sibling. *Party of Five* may be the most famous entry in the TV orphan genre (since the death of the titular five kids' parents catalyzed the whole premise of the show), but it's not the only one. *Diff'rent Strokes* and *Webster* upped the ante by putting African-American boys in the custody of rich white people; *Punky Brewster* showed how a poorly dressed young girl could melt the heart of a tight-assed old man; and *Summerland* showed

that it takes a village (of four marginally employed thirtysomethings) to raise three kids transplanted from a Midwestern farm to Malibu. *My Two Dads* killed a young girl's mother so that she could learn, after her death, that her mother had only narrowed down her paternity to two "maybes." *Roseanne* switched it up by having David join the Conner household not because of his parents' death but his mother's abusiveness. And *Growing Pains* brought in an orphaned homeless kid on the theory that he'd be better off with the Seavers than on the street . . . which was debatable, really. See also BAD SITCOM, SURE SIGNS OF; *GROWING PAINS*; *PARTY OF FIVE*; *PUNKY BREWSTER*; and *ROSEANNE*.

OSBOURNES, THE   Never before had primetime heard so much gratuitous F-bombing outside of premium cable. Never before had primetime seen anything quite like the hilariously outré Clan Osbourne, either: Ozzy, the patriarch, made his name as the godfather of heavy metal, biting the heads off bats and drawing the ire of the Moral Majority, but *The Osbournes* presented him as sweat-suited dodderer who couldn't even operate a TV remote without an assist from his deceptively small and baby-voiced wife/manager/in-house battle-axe, Sharon. Sharon is the first to take credit for getting Ozzy off drugs—no easy task given that, according to Mötley Crüe's Nikki Sixx, the guy once snorted *a line of ants*—but based on Ozzy's apparent difficulty staying upright, she should have interceded a lot sooner. And we wouldn't call her spoiled, slobby, substance-abuse-prone offspring a credit to the family, either. *The Osbournes* had its moments, early on, like Ozzy tipping over backward in his makeup chair and Sharon hucking a ham at noisy neighbors, but the show and the family got crazy overexposed in a matter of weeks. The second season flagged somewhat; the family wasn't quite the laff riot it had been, given Sharon's cancer diagnosis 'round about Episode 2, so it had to settle for subplots involving the brood of pets crapping on the rug. Again. We feel like *The Osbournes* is also to blame for the spate of "celebreality shows," like *Fat Actress* and *The Anna Nicole Show*, but that Pepsi Twist ad they did with the Osmonds cracked our shit up, so we guess we can let it go. See also REALITY TV, OFF-BRAND.

OSMONDS OF VARIOUS TALENTS AND TIME SLOTS It all began with *The Osmonds*, an animated series starring the voices of, der, the Osmonds—six singing, dancing, instrument-playing Mormon brothers who served as musical goodwill ambassadors for the United States. (On the show. If they were doing it in real life, it might explain why the Cold War

dragged on so long.) Then came the *Donny and Marie* variety show to capitalize on the tacky sensibility of the late '70s (Bob Mackie designed the costumes, and the siblings often sang while ice skating, accompanied by the Ice Vanities . . . no, seriously). Viewers, mesmerized by the Osmonds' horrifically large teeth, tuned in for several seasons before Marie spun off into her own show and *Donny and Marie* was renamed *The Osmond Family*. But by the early '80s, it seemed like the era of Osmond omnipresence had ended (at least on TV; the Osmonds continued performing in various venues)—until 1998, when misguided '70s nostalgia demanded that Donny and Marie stage a comeback in talk-show form. And so they did, plying their toothy charms on the afternoon audience for two seasons. Donny, who shows up on every single *I Love the '70s*–type program he's invited to, then hosted the game show *Pyramid* for a while. We kind of don't get it, but the ladies seem to love Cool D. See also TALK SHOWS, DAYTIME.

OUT OF CONTROL Before Dave Coulier and his mullet annoyed a nation on *Full House*, he starred in *Out of Control*, the godfather of *Liquid TV*. Nickelodeon only produced a single season, but it seemed like it was on for years—possibly because they kept airing the same episodes until the decade ended, but also because Coulier's Lauper-clone cohost, the never-seen-again Diz McNally, spoke and pronounced words so annoyingly that every minute of screen time seemed like an eternity (even the segments featuring the "Hurry-Up Machine"). "EX-cel-LENT! . . . Booowwwww-riiiiing!" And that squeaky screech of hers . . . argh. Just when you thought you'd have to reach into the television and stuff Diz into a beehive, they'd switch to a skit with "reporters" Hern Burferd and Angela "Scoop" Quigley, who were actually funny, or an animated short. To sum up: cartoons, yay; the little cards Hern put on his fedora that said "pull" instead of "press," yay; Dave and Diz, boo. See also CHILDREN'S SHOWS, HOSTS OF; NICK-ELODEON; and *FULL HOUSE*.

OUT OF THIS WORLD Quite possibly the worst sitcom ever made—it's a complete failure on every level. The premise is ridiculous: The heroine, Evie, is the child of a human mother (Donna Pescow, chewing the cheap scenery like a famine victim) and an alien father (voiced by Burt Reynolds) from the planet Anterias. And as the series went on, she got demi-alien powers . . . so, so stupid. No stupider than *Sabrina, the Teenage Witch*, we guess, but *Sabrina* had production values you couldn't measure in pesos, slightly more professional acting, and a lot less Burt Reynolds. Trivia alert! Maureen Flannigan, who

played Evie, surfaced again as Shana "Chickenhead" Sullivan, one of Matt Camden's girlfriends, on *7th Heaven*; her line readings of horrendous writing had, sadly, not improved. Revenge of trivia alert! The show actually hired an astronaut to "consult." On what, we don't want to know. Oh, wait. We do want to know, because *whaaaaaaat*?! See also ACTING, WOODEN; BAD SITCOM, SURE SIGNS OF; SCENERY, CHEWERS OF; and *7TH HEAVEN*.

OVERHYPED SERIES THAT BOMBED No matter how confident network executives feel about a primetime drama, they should exercise caution before cranking up the Hype-O-Matic 4000. Flogging the hell out of a show often guarantees that the show is going to 1) reek, and 2) get canceled. *Wasteland*, allegedly *Dawson's Creek* creator Kevin Williamson's magnum opus, had its cast plastered on the sides of buses; it lasted only a handful of episodes. CBS thought Darren Star, riding high on the success of *Melrose Place*, would strike gold again with *Central Park West*; didn't happen. *The Contender*, the Sly Stallone reality boxing show that NBC advertised for months in advance, collapsed under the weight of its own publicity (most of it bad—one of the boxers took his own life shortly before the show premiered); Rob Lowe made a big fuss about leaving *The West Wing*, only to find that nobody would be making a fuss, of any size, about

Devil's Advocate rip-off *The Lyon's Den* . . . the list goes on and on. But it's not complete without a mention of the Hype Curse Queen, Gretchen Mol, who appeared on a *Vanity Fair* cover with a big old kiss-of-death lipstick smear on her face, and, sure enough, wound up on the overhyped, undercapitalized David E. Kelley suckfest *girls club*, yanked with dizzying promptness by FOX after only two episodes. See also CENTRAL PARK WEST; DAWSON'S CREEK; KELLEY, DAVID E.; MELROSE PLACE; STAR, DARREN; and WEST WING, THE.

Oz   It's not TV; it's HBOhhhhhh *my God*, he just *yoinked that guy's eyeball*! The soap opera for people who loved gore, hot man-on-man action, and plotting that Tolstoy would have rejected as too convoluted, *Oz* taught us that prison looked a lot like daytime TV—but with many more bare asses. And God bless them, every one (with the exception of Terry "Shut Up, McManus" Kinney's, which we saw way too much of). So, McManus's existence made no sense to us; nor did the fact that warden Leo Glynn (Ernie Hudson) didn't get fired for running the biggest death trap in the prison system, and we needed an Excel file and an algorithm generator to keep up with all the nutty feuds, suballiances, Ryan O'Reily (Dean Winters) double crosses, rapes, drug problems, and theo-ries we had about how Adebisi (Adewale Akinnuoye-Agbaje) affixed that itty-bitty little hat to his bald head at such a disingenuously jaunty angle. Fortunately, writer Tom Fontana threw in plenty of distractions, like the byzantine love affair between Beecher (Lee Tergesen) and Keller (Christopher Meloni), Luke Perry as a preacher (?) who gets blowed up real good, the deliciously evil Schillinger (J. K. Simmons), and Eamonn Walker's fine, fine ass. We would still like an answer to the itty-bitty-hat question, though. See also LAW & ORDER/HOMICIDE/OZ CASTING OVERLAP and NUDITY.

P-Q

"PACEY WITTER"   When The WB's *Dawson's Creek* premiered, it wasn't readily apparent whom ladies (and gay fellows) in the audience were supposed to be rooting for. Neither of the show's male leads—James Van Der Beek as Dawson, and Joshua Jackson as Pacey—held any appeal. As the series wore on, however, Pacey wore us down. He had so little to recommend him, what with the aimless hitting on  every sentient woman around, including Grams, and once he started sleeping with Ta-MAH-ra, his English teacher, his storyline veered uncomfortably into ripped-from-the-headlines territory. But then that ended, and he set his sights on Joey (Katie Holmes), whom we suddenly felt wasn't good enough for him even though we also didn't want her ending up with the insufferable pill that was Dawson. Over time, Pacey became the only character on the show we could stand even a little. He fearlessly defended Jack (Kerr Smith) through his anxious coming-out, reading Jack's "gay poem" in front of the class; he was nice to the McPhees' mentally ill mother; he bought Joey a wall. Most important, he proved himself able to date women without destroying their self-esteem, guilting them into staying with him, or acting as though he thought himself their moral superior. He was, in short, the anti-Dawson. It's also worth noting that Jackson grew up into a very handsome young man—like Kiefer Sutherland's Mini-Me, actually. Many's the thirtysomething woman who's carried a secret torch for him. See also COOL, TV SIGNIFIERS OF; "DAWSON LEERY"; *DAWSON'S CREEK*; "JACK MCPHEE"; and "SOULMATE."

PARENTS/PARENTING, BAD   The majority of bad parenting on TV isn't bad in the abusive sense—unless a Very Special Episode needs fleshing out, in which case a tertiary character's never-before-seen father will turn out to have a drinking problem. No, most bad TV parenting is about laxity. If we'd spoken to our parents the way Dawson Leery spoke to his, our mothers would have killed us and *then* kicked us into next week, and Danny Partridge's know-it-all quips would have earned us an afternoon weeding the yard. Parents on sitcoms and non–cop dramas don't enforce curfews or check homework unless it's expedient to the plot, and they often involve their children inappropriately in their decision-making (the Leerys consulting Dawson on Gale's unplanned pregnancy; Lorelai Gilmore . . . all the time) or overreact in noncredible ways (Joyce Summers kicking Buffy out of the house; the Camdens . . . all the time, but particularly when Mary drank half a beer while babysitting). Of course, on cop dramas, especially the *Law & Order*s, parents bury their infants in coolers, sleep with the same photographers their teen daughters do, sleep with their own teen sons, beat their kids, beat each other at their kids' sporting events, sell their babies to the highest bidder, and so on. But because those aren't recurring characters, we won't count them. See also BUFFY THE VAMPIRE SLAYER; CHILDREN, OVERLY PRECOCIOUS; DADS, TV; DAWSON'S CREEK; GILMORE GIRLS; LAW & ORDER FRANCHISE; PARTRIDGE FAMILY, THE; 7TH HEAVEN; TEENAGERS, BRATTY; and VERY SPECIAL EPISODES.

PARENTS WHO ARE TOTALLY INTO EACH OTHER TO A CREEPY DEGREE   The only thing worse than being a teenager and getting embarrassed by your parents' flagrant PDAs is being the viewer of a TV series featuring teenagers' parents' flagrant PDAs. Because seriously, Cliff Huxtable, keep it in your pants. The biggest joke of the entire first season of *Dawson's Creek* (aside from Dawson's hair) was the fact that Dawson's parents kept getting caught in compromising positions by their child and his friends— and not in their bedroom, either (people put their drinks on that coffee table, so get your bare asses off it!). Similarly, the Keatons were constantly getting booed by their kids for putting the moves on each other. It's rare for us to give credit to Jim and Cindy Walsh, but at least they waited until their kids were out of the house for the evening before WASPily knocking boots. *Off*screen. See also BEVERLY HILLS 90210; COSBY SHOW, THE; DAWSON'S CREEK; and FAMILY TIES.

PARTRIDGE FAMILY, THE   Twinned with *The Brady Bunch* in cultural memory, *The Partridge Family* is a much different show—if by "different," you mean "better." The two shows aired in the early '70s; both families had a blonde matriarch played by an actress with a stage background; both families had about a zillion kids. But that's where the similarities end, as *The Partridge Family* had better, slyer writing; a cuter oldest brother (Cassidy's got Williams beat three ways: better ass, better voice, better comic timing); and chic-er outfits, with Shirley Jones's the chic-est. (No, for real. The mini-dresses she's always in during the first season? So cute!) Also: the bus, which we all dreamed of living on, because it is awesome. Even the ongoing befrazzlement of manager Reuben Kincaid (Dave Madden) by precocious brat Danny (Danny Bonaduce) is played well, and each episode is full of smart asides about everything from Spiro Agnew to Valium. The only down notes were Jeremy "Chris 1.0" Gelbwaks, who had some creepy Manson eyes going on, but recasting the part with less-weird Brian Forster solved the problem; and the prettiness of the cast sometimes interfered with the suspension of disbelief. (Keith having girl problems? Come on.) As for the montages, if you like the Partridges' poppy fake music, you like them; if not, use the time to fix a snack. See also BRADY BUNCH, THE; CASSIDYS, THE; "DANNY PARTRIDGE"; and MUSICAL MONTAGES.

PARTY OF FIVE The ultimate anti–drunk-driving PSA, *Party of Five* tells the story of the five Salinger children—Charlie (Matthew Fox), Bailey (Scott Wolf), Julia (Neve Campbell), Claudia (Lacey Chabert), and Owen (various kids at various ages, since he was an infant when the series began)—who are orphaned when a drunk driver hits their sainted parents, San Francisco restaurateurs. The premise had a high potentiality for schmaltz, and the show sometimes caved to it, but generally it stuck pretty close to real life. Charlie is often resentful at having to become the de facto father to four kids when he's only in his early twenties and had barely even moved out before his parents' death, though he was still able to put aside his personal issues to mack on his alarmingly thin nanny, Kirsten (Paula Devicq). Over the years, the show tackled all the usual issues—teen pregnancy (Julia doesn't end up having an abortion, as planned, due to a conveniently timed miscarriage just as she's about to leave for the clinic); adoption (the search by Jennifer Love Hewitt's Sarah for her birth parents); and domestic violence (committed by Julia's boyfriend Ned, played by Scott Bairstow, who was later accused of a long-term sexual relationship with a twelve-year-old girl—charming). But what everyone most remembers is the multiepisode story arc of Bailey's alcoholism, culminating in his horrifying drunken appearance at Owen's birthday, all done up in creepy-ass clown drag. And if that wasn't scary enough to make a few problem drinkers in the audience reevaluate some of their life decisions, we don't know what possibly could. See also ALCOHOLISM; HEWITT, JENNIFER LOVE; ORPHANS; and TEEN SEX, CONSEQUENCES OF.

PEOPLE'S COURT, THE Cult-of-personality judge shows have spread like kudzu since the '80s—*Judge Judy*, *Judge Joe Brown*, etc.—but none of them can touch the original: *The People's Court*, a small-claims court presided over by grouchy Joseph Wapner, a retired judge with no patience for anyone. Doug "The Court Whisperer" Llewelyn served as narrator/court reporter, and brought viewers up to date on even the most absurd disputes in tones of hushed intensity. An excellent way to fritter away a half hour, immortalized in *Rain Man* by Ray's insistence on watching it. One minute to Wapner!

PERFECT STRANGERS Greece, outer space . . . basically the same thing, right? By which we mean that the premise of *Perfect Strangers* is a rip-off of *Mork & Mindy*: Funny-talking foreigner, played by hammy, hairy loon, descends on an unsuspecting American and ruins said American's life with his inability to fit in and act normal. In *Perfect Strangers*, the foreigner is Balki (Bronson Pinchot), an appalling Mediterranean stereotype from the fictional "Mypos," which was never explicitly identified as a Greek island, but which inspired no end of jokes about sheepherding, so draw your own conclusions. He moves to Chicago to impose himself upon his distant cousin Larry (Mark Linn-Baker), but of course—this being an ABC sitcom of the mid-'80s—the boys end up overcoming their differences and learning from one another. Balki quickly overtook every other char-

acter of the show to achieve Fonz-like levels of ubiquity, assaulting our senses with his "Dance of Joy," his catchphrase ("Of course not, don't be ridiculous"), and his folksy woven vests. *Strangers* spun off *Family Matters*, which makes Bronson Pinchot partly responsible for Urkel. However, getting mauled by Janice Dickinson on *The Surreal Life* is more than enough penance for his crimes against culture. See also CATCHPHRASES, OVERUSED TV; DICKINSON, JANICE; *MORK & MINDY*; SITCOMS, FISH-OUT-OF-WATER; SPIN-OFFS; *SURREAL LIFE, THE*; and "URKEL."

PESENTI, FLO How can *The Amazing Race* possibly be a true meritocracy if someone like *Flo* can win? If, while she scowled, complained, and malingered her way around the globe, Flo had been able to get it up for tasks and participated as an equal member of her two-person team, maybe she wouldn't have been despised so universally. As it was, Flo didn't let the fact that she performed all of *one* Roadblock through the whole length of the *Race* stop her from threatening to quit on a half-hourly basis. All credit goes to her partner, Zach Behr, for basically putting her in a fireman's carry and throwing her over the finish line at every pit stop. At least Flo's time on the show wasn't in vain: Her slackitude may have been part of the reason that more recent seasons require that no one team member do more than six Roadblocks. Sometimes we imagine Flo walking a beam along the top of a bridge or eating a bowl of Tabasco soup, and we smile. See also REALITY TV, QUITTERS OF and UNIVERSALLY REVILED CHARACTERS.

PHILBIN, REGIS You know, there are a lot of celebrities who are spending their careers coasting on past achievements, but maybe none so much as Regis Philbin. Any star who comes on *Live*  should expect that Philbin will have no idea who she is—unless she's over the age of seventy-five. Despite his career as the host of a show about pop culture, Philbin has completely unplugged himself from the world of entertainment, which is good, in a way—it saves us from ever wondering what it would be like if our grandpas hosted a daytime talk show. There's no one stiffer or clumsier in daytime. See also *LIVE WITH REGIS AND KELLY*; RIPA, KELLY; TALK SHOWS, DAYTIME; and *WHO WANTS TO BE A MILLIONAIRE*, REGIS EDITION.

PHONE ETIQUETTE, MYSTERIOUS TV PRINCIPLES OF Television characters are so gosh-dang cool, they don't *need* to say "goodbye"; they just hang up on each other without a sign-off of any kind. But seriously, folks—what's up with that? It's not like a simple "bye" or "talk to you later" takes up much screen time or arouses the ire of the FCC, and you'd think God-fearing types like the Camdens would show better breeding, but they end calls without a sign-off *every time*, and it's rude. Also rude: The tendency of TV characters (like Felicity) to eavesdrop on answering-machine messages not meant for them, and to draw nosily mistaken conclusions. We hope that the advent of voicemail means we'll see less of this impolite contrivance, but the rise of cell phones has done nothing to stop the TV epidemic of just dropping in at people's homes instead of calling first or discussing things on the phone. TV folk don't call ahead—they can't. If they telephoned, we wouldn't get to feast on the marvelous buffet of contrivances that just showing up randomly can serve: running into exes unexpectedly; witnessing or interrupting something they shouldn't have; dumping a wagonload of exposition on another character; hammy eye-rolling in response to yet another barge-in by a detested neighbor or sidekick; giant-armload-of-groceries "humor." See also *FELICITY* and *7TH HEAVEN*.

PHYSICALLY CHALLENGED PERSON/ CHARACTER, CLICHÉS ASSOCIATED WITH According to TV, the physically challenged—usually confined to guest-star slots, so that characters who appear in the credits aren't inconvenienced by having to take the ramp (or use sign language) for longer than one episode—have a lot to teach series regulars about tolerance and overcoming obstacles. Sometimes they impart their lessons via an incessant (and therefore somewhat obnoxious) saintliness, like Mary Ingalls on *Little House on the Prairie*; other times, they do it via a bluntness only they can get away with (Marlee Matlin's Joey Lucas on *The West Wing*, Geri Jewell on *The Facts of Life* and *Deadwood*). And let's not forget Detective Jim Dunbar, hero of *Blind Justice*—he's a cop who lost his sight in the line of duty, but he's not retiring, oh no! He's going back to work! He's still carrying a gun, as stupid from a practical standpoint as it is from a metaphorical one! He's wearing sunglasses indoors, bumping into chairs, and earning his colleagues' grudging respect by solving crimes using his sense of smell! Ron Eldard, call your damn agent! We like it much better when the differently abled just blend, like coroner Doc Robbins (Robert David Hall) on *CSI* and Maya (Kyra Levy) on original *Degrassi*; they've got some issues, but the shows don't condescend to them. See also *CSI*; *DEGRASSI JUNIOR HIGH*; ELDARD, RON; *FACTS OF LIFE, THE*; *LITTLE HOUSE ON THE PRAIRIE*; MENTALLY CHALLENGED PERSONS, ACTORS OF NORMAL INTELLIGENCE WHO'VE PLAYED; and *WEST WING, THE*.

PILOTS Because it is the basis on which a network will decide whether to order a season's worth of episodes, a pilot has to perform many functions: introduce all its characters; make you like them (or at least care what happens to them); establish how they all relate to each other; establish what makes this show different; and plant the seeds for future storylines. This may be why so many pilots are ungainly—that's a lot to pack into twenty-two or forty-eight minutes, which is why you get shorthand exposition such as people calling each other "Sis" (which no one ever does, with the possible exception of Sissy Spacek's family) or reminding each other of things they'd obviously know: "That's why I got fired, remember?" The *Friends* pilot stands as one of the best ever, because it doesn't bother going into elaborate explications of who everyone is or what they do for a living—they're friends, and now you're caught up. *Friends* also deploys a common pilot formula, by bringing a new character (in this case, Jennifer Aniston's Rachel) to a setting to which she's unaccustomed, so that we can be caught up at the same time she is (à la *Northern Exposure*, *NewsRadio*, and *Futurama*). Bad pilots use this gimmick too, and we would list examples if we'd ever watched more than two minutes of any bad pilot. Sorry, *Firefly* and *The Mountain*! Well, actually, we're not. See also EXPOSITION, CLUNKY; *FRIENDS*; *NORTHERN EXPOSURE*; and WHEDON, JOSS.

PINWHEEL "Pinwheel, *Pinwheel*, spinning around!/Look at my *Pinwheel* and *see* what I've *found*!" The *Pinwheel* theme song is so grating *and* so catchy that it sticks in the head for days on end. But the theme song fit perfectly with the show itself, a children's offering on Nickelodeon that featured a large, green, whiny, queeny animatronic monster (read: Oscar the Grouch rip-off) named Ebenezer; two lispy, bungling marionette insects who had this weirdly romantic dysfunctional relationship, even though, if memory serves, they were actually siblings, and whose skits were both endless and pointless; and animated shorts like Simon, the land-of-chalk-drawings kid ("well you know moy name is Soymon/and the things I drawr come trewwwww"—oh, how we longed for him to draw his own death), and the loathsome "Hattytown," in which anthropomorphized hats with British accents . . . had some problems and ran around a lot? We don't know; we only saw it when we were home sick, so some of the stupider aspects of the show could be confusing when we had a fever. Or when we didn't, because did we mention the hats? With British accents? And little felt feet? See also *SESAME STREET* and THEME SONGS.

PIXELATION Apparently, there really is a lot that Big Brother doesn't want you to see—and a lot of it airs on *Big Brother*. Pixelation allows the networks to air all kinds of juicy action, provided the naughty bits are blurred out. You can see Richard Hatch sitting by the fire in the altogether, provided that a dainty cloud of computer-generated smog covers what *a bathing suit really should*. Actually, the pixelation staff on *Survivor*—charged, as they are, with concealing every nipple exposed during a challenge by every errant buff—are probably only the second-busiest in television. The busiest are those who work on *The Real World*, who not only have their hands full with every hot tub orgy, but also must blur out the labels of every soda and clothing brand that hasn't been endorsed by Bunim/Murray Productions. Like we can't tell Cameran's in a Von Dutch hat anyway. See also *BIG BROTHER*; BUNIM/MURRAY; DRINKING GAMES; NUDITY; PRODUCT PLACEMENT; *REAL WORLD, THE*; and *SURVIVOR*.

POLICE VIDEOS, SHOWS RELIANT UPON For real, now—how in the hell do shows like *COPS* and *World's Wildest Police Videos* convince the Taz-T-shirt-wearing nimrods getting arrested to sign the release forms? Do they offer the criminals—excuse us, "alleged criminals"—money? Is it because the alleged criminals are often drunk or high? Because it's one thing if you led half a dozen state troopers on a merry chase for two hours, driving on your rims; we'd be kind of proud of that too. But getting busted for soliciting a prostitute? While wearing Jams? And *your wedding ring*? Why would you let America see that shit? See also *COPS*.

POLITICALLY INCORRECT Once upon a time, it was our fondest dream to get on *PI* and to make some comment so withering that it would permanently wipe the smug grin off the face of Debbie Schlussel, Ann Coulter, or host Bill Maher himself. God knows we certainly screamed enough of them at the TV while the show aired. However, the  show—on which Maher played emcee for a random (and we do mean random) assortment of four guests each weeknight as they discussed politics and the issues of the day—was swept off the air shortly after Maher said, of the September 11 attackers, "We have been the cowards lobbing cruise missiles from two thousand miles away. . . . That's cowardly. Staying in the airplane when it hits the building, say what you want about it, it's not cowardly." Maher dispensed this particular pearl the week of September *17*, 2001. Hey, aren't comedians supposed to have good timing? Yeesh. See also TALK SHOWS, LATE-NIGHT.

POPULAR When *Nip/Tuck* creator Ryan Murphy pitched *Popular* to The WB, he probably described the show as a fairly conventional high-school/blended-family drama. When arch-enemies cheerleader Brooke (Leslie Bibb) and school-paperette Sam (Carly Pope) have to live together because their parents got remarried to each other, adolescent culture clashes ensue at home and at school. And that happened . . . kind of. But it's like the minute the pilot got picked up, every other rule of teen dramas went out the window. The kids didn't look high-school age, and the show didn't bother to disguise that; the "villain," Nicole Julian (Tammy Lynn Michaels), acted more like she'd sprung fully formed from the head of Alexis Carrington than like a sophomore; the so-called nerd, Harrison, was played by hottie Chris Gorham; subplots included Clea DuVall living in a bathroom stall, a cross-dressing teacher, and the incomparable Diane Delano as butch science teacher Chem, who wrote a play about STDs and made the kids perform in it; characters had names like April and May Tuna, Lady T, Sugar Daddy, Emory Dick, and Poppy Fresh; Harrison got cancer, Brooke wound up in an eating-disorders clinic, and all the other characters made horribly crass (and funny) jokes about it. But the best reason to watch *Popular* is, now and forever, the fabulously over-the-top Leslie Grossman as Mary Cherry. Mary Cherry wore an *Electric Horseman* homecoming-queen dress covered with little lights, she had crazy eyes, she played "crabs" in the STD play; she ruled. The show made no sense, and yet, it made perfect sense, but The WB had no idea what to do with it, so they canceled it. Wimps. See also GROSSMAN, LESLIE and HIGH SCHOOL, UNREALISTIC PORTRAYALS OF.

POST, MIKE One of the few brand-name composers in TV, Mike Post is responsible for some of its most memorable music—*L.A. Law*, *The A-Team*, and *CHiPs* are among his more than 150 credits. And while that is a very impressive résumé indeed, the real reason we bring him up is because of a couple of bits of Post trivia we have heard—bits that are substantiated only by anonymous sources, and which you therefore probably shouldn't believe (so if you're reading this, Mike Post, don't sue us). Post Trivia Bit #1: He had a special treadmill made with a keyboard on it; while doing his daily workout, he'll noodle around on the keyboard, coming up with new licks, and make his assistant, standing by, write

them out in musical notation. Post Trivia Bit #2: When a shirt was produced that played on the "Chung Chung!" riff from the *Law & Order* franchise, he demanded a dozen shirts in an assortment of sizes, which he expected to get for free. He gets a residual every time that sound is played—he couldn't just buy them? (That is, if that anecdote were true, which it probably isn't.) See also *A-TEAM, THE*; *CHiPs*; "CHUNG CHUNG"; *L.A. LAW*; *LAW & ORDER* FRANCHISE; and THEME SONGS.

POWERPUFF GIRLS, THE See CARTOONS, HANNA-BARBERA.

POWERS OF MATTHEW STAR, THE The '80s spawned a lot of messed-up shit: Jazzercise, acid wash, and a little show called *The Powers of Matthew Star*, about an alien prince with superpowers who has to hide out on Earth. Peter Barton, so pretty he looked like anime, starred as, well, Star; Louis Gossett Jr. played his minder, Walt, who disguised himself as a high school science teacher. Halfway through the season, the show got rewritten so that Star and Walt both worked for the government, and the whole thing became this weird mishmash of *Superman II* and *The X-Files*. We really only watched it because of pretty, pretty Barton, and because it had the time slot right before *Knight Rider*. As we said: the '80s. Mistakes were made. And, if we recall correctly, Barton's acting coach is not excluded from that statement. See also ACTING, WOODEN; SCIENCE, IGNORANCE OF; and *X-FILES, THE*.

PRACTICE, THE   A legal drama from the "mind" of David E. Kelley, *The Practice* ostensibly revolved around a Boston law firm but was actually devoted to 1) exposing random fetishes, 2) congratulating itself on giving a plus-sized female character (Camryn Manheim) a storyline and a love life, and 3) straining the bounds of credulity on a weekly basis when main characters *and officers of the court* carried on with judges, shot stalkers, sold out clients to the D.A., slept with the D.A., refused to sleep with the D.A., represented themselves during murder trials, halted executions with minutes to go . . . you get the idea. When it premiered, with its propulsive city-streets theme song, the show felt daring and new, and over its run, it had some decent actors: Lara Flynn Boyle, still running a goodwill tab from *Twin Peaks*; Lisa Gay Hamilton and Michael Badalucco; and the three hotties of the apocalypse, Steve Harris, Ron Livingston, and Dylan McDermott. But after only a couple of seasons, the storylines yawed between gratuitous and absurd (and often walked the line of "both"); Lara Flynn Boyle wasted away to nothing but scary grandma-pink lipstick; and McDermott

got that weird Dogboy haircut and started talking like he had a bullet clamped in his teeth. And . . . Larroquette as a serial killer? In 2003, nearly the entire original cast got sacked and replaced with the mainstays of what would become *Boston Legal*, and then, at merciful last, the show got axed. See also KELLEY, DAVID E.; RECASTING, NOTORIOUS; and SPIN-OFFS.

PREGNANCIES, CLUMSY ATTEMPTS AT HIDING ACTORS'   Occasionally, when an actress in an episodic TV series gets pregnant, the writers get enough advance notice to make her character pregnant, too. Brenda Chenowith got knocked up for the last season of *Six Feet Under* because Rachel Griffiths was with child, much as *ER*'s Susan Lewis did when Sherry Stringfield ended up in the same situation. Phoebe agreed to be a surrogate mother for her brother's triplets on *Friends* when Lisa Kudrow became pregnant. And we thought the third-season finale of *90210* was headed toward a long-promised Andrea/Brandon pairing, but we assume Gabrielle Carteris's real-life pregnancy scuttled that storyline; there's no way fair-haired boy Brandon could father a child out of wedlock, so Andrea found a boyfriend who could. But most of the time, if it doesn't fit the show for a character to be pregnant, producers will come up with transparently obvious methods to disguise their leading ladies' circumstances. Julia Louis-Dreyfus spent a season of *Seinfeld* wearing untucked suit shirts or overalls, standing behind Jerry's counter. Debra Messing's Grace was sent off to accompany her husband on a Doctors Without Borders mission on *Will & Grace* when Messing was ordered to take some bed rest. But the most infamous cover-up effort came on *Frasier*: When Jane Leeves's pregnancy started to show, producers thought it would be clever to explain away the thickness in her midsection by crafting a multiepisode arc in which Daphne was compulsively overeating at the start of her relationship with David Hyde Pierce's Niles—and he loved her so much that he didn't even notice her weight gain! Just imagine how blind love could be, that a man wouldn't notice his girlfriend's big fat ass! Shut up, *Frasier*. See also *BEVERLY HILLS 90210*; "BRENDA CHENOWITH"; *ER*; *FRASIER*; *FRIENDS*; *SEINFELD*; and *WILL & GRACE*.

PREGNANCY, CLICHÉS ASSOCIATED WITH
Pregnancy does make women go a bit wacky—on sitcoms, at least. Sitcom ladies have weird food cravings, mood swings, nesting fever, limited choices in fashionable maternity wear, and self-doubt about their fitness as mothers. When it comes time for the blessed event, they forget everything they learned in their Lamaze classes and instantly start screaming for "the drugs," and their labor

is comically protracted, giving the mommy-to-be plenty of time to cuss out both the man who impregnated her and the idiot doctors who can't extract the baby fast enough. On medical dramas, however, pregnancy is an entirely different experience. Mothers go into labor at inconvenient times (while a deck is in the process of collapsing) or in inconvenient places (stopped elevators—okay, those happen on sitcoms as well). Audiences can cluck their tongues disapprovingly at mothers who don't care enough about their children to have stopped smoking and drinking during their pregnancies, mothers who are teenagers and are only carrying to term to get back at their parents or to have one person in the world who'll love them unconditionally, mothers who have been denying their pregnancies and don't want to see their babies before they enter foster care, and mothers who abandon their babies in Dumpsters or toilet bowls. In fact, the worse mother you are, the greater the likelihood that your baby will be born completely healthy; it's the mothers who are most excited about the baby who end up with dead babies and/or dead themselves. Oh, TV irony. You are so very predictable. See also BAD SITCOM, SURE SIGNS OF; BIRTH CONTROL; and ELEVATOR, CLICHÉS ASSOCIATED WITH.

PRESS YOUR LUCK "No whammys, no whammys, no whammys—STOP!!" has become seriously overused as a catch-phrase. Yeah, the contestants don't want the Whammy to show up because he takes all their money and prizes (and to that end, we don't understand why they'd never learn to just  *pass their spins*, hello). But the Whammy is also rash-inducingly annoying—a screechy, poorly animated, bandit-mask-wearing creature, voiced by the restless ghost of Ethel Merman and given to bad puns and breakdancing. We've cracked a number of jokes about how host Peter Tomarken seems coked up most of the time, but if we had to tolerate the squawky Catskills comedy stylings of the Whammy day in and day out, we'd turn to drugs, too. Rest in peace, Pete. See also GAME SHOW NETWORK.

PRICE IS RIGHT, THE, SUCKY PRICING SKILLS OF CONTESTANTS ON Dear contestants on *TPIR*: How do you not know how much toothpaste costs? Do y'all not brush your teeth? Did you come to Studio City from Amish country? . . . No? Then why are you trying to tell my boy B. Bark that you think a tube of Crest is seven bucks? Learn what stuff costs, please. "Love," The rest of the world. P.S.: $2.99. See also BARKER, BOB.

"PRICELESS." See MASTERCARD "PRICELESS" CAMPAIGN.

PROBST, JEFF Possessing the biggest dimples in reality television, Jeff Probst has been presiding over *Survivor* in a succession of crisp safari shirts since its arrival on American TV. We didn't appreciate Probst at first—his unshakably cheery attitude and limited duties on the show made him seem like a simp. But once he started hosting the show's season-ending reunion specials, we realized how wrong we were. Probst pays very careful attention to all the inter-contestant power struggles and uses his time as the moderator of each episode's tribal council to needle them but good. The moment in Season 7 when he disgustedly determined that, by openly asking to get voted out, Osten was really quitting, Probst shamed the malingerer and refused even to snuff his torch. Which was awesome. Probst's starlight dimmed a little when, in 2004, the forty-three-year-old Probst confirmed that he was dating ex-*Survivor* contestant Julie Berry, age twenty-four. On the other hand, given the hot messes that regularly parade through the show's various jungles and forests (Heidi? Elisabeth? Either of the Jennas?), Probst could certainly have done worse. See also REALITY TV, HOSTS OF; REALITY TV, QUITTERS OF; and *SURVIVOR*.

PRODUCTION COMPANY CREDIT SCREENS Once in a while, a TV show's production company tag can become a part of the viewing experience. An episode of *Family Ties* or *Spin City* isn't quite complete without the "Sit, Ubu, sit! Good dog. [Woof!]" tag that accompanies many Gary David Goldberg productions, just like an episode of *thirtysomething* or *My So-Called Life* isn't really over until Bedford Falls's "aaaaaand dance by the light of the moon" sign-off tells the audience it's okay to switch channels. Fans of different shows recognize (and monitor changes in) the different tags—"*I* made this" for *X-Files* enthusiasts, "youuuuu *stinkah!*" for *Practice* buffs, and of course the little monster at the end of any Joss Whedon show that marches past the camera zombie-style, sarcastically growling, "Grr, argh." Whedon, aware of his fan base's . . . er, let's call it "attention to detail," occasionally fine-tuned the tag; following the *Buffy* musical episode, the creature *sang* "grr, argh" instead of saying it, and after the series finale, it turned to face the camera instead of going by in profile as it usually did. See also *BUFFY THE VAMPIRE SLAYER*; *FAMILY TIES*; *MY SO-CALLED LIFE*; *PRACTICE, THE*; *THIRTYSOMETHING*; and *X-FILES, THE*.

PRODUCT PLACEMENT As TiVos and other DVRs have made it easier for us to fast-forward commercials, advertisers have had to get more crafty about where and how they advertise their products. Getting us with the extended-length spots at the movies is pretty clever—we're a captive audience—but the smart advertising money lies in weaving their products seamlessly into the content of TV shows. The *American Idol* winners drink nothing but Coke (and the judges have the cups prominently placed in front of them) and used to sit on a Coke-swoop-shaped sofa. The *Real World* kids guzzle Dr Pepper, and the ones on the *Challenge* get their mission specs on T-Mobile Sidekick phones. *Roswell* went so far as to produce an episode titled "Michael, the Guys, and the Great Snapple Caper." (Guess what? It mentioned Snapple a lot.) This isn't a new idea—back in the day, TV stars commonly did live spots for sponsors like GM (oooh, Pat Boone, you whore), which still sometimes occurs on *Late Night with Conan O'Brien*. And the notion of series fully sponsored by a single company (*Texaco Star Theater*) has been revived with shows like *Pepsi Play for a Billion*. We actually prefer it when shows wear their provenance on their sleeves; don't insult our intelligence by making us think it's an accident that everyone drinks their sodas with the labels turned toward the camera. See also *AMERICAN IDOL*; *REAL WORLD, THE*; and *REAL WORLD/ROAD RULES CHALLENGE, THE*.

PROJECT GREENLIGHT Matt Damon and Ben Affleck certainly meant well when they launched *Project Greenlight*—an Internet competition would yield a winning script, and the author of said script would direct the project for theatrical release—but the movies themselves sucked. (The proof: Three of the four first directors have all but disappeared; it remains to be seen what becomes of "Jabba the" Gulager.) It's a good thing, then, that when you throw cocky but inept first-time moviemakers into the same pot with volcanic executive producer Chris Moore and an anorexic shooting budget, it makes for some tasty reality television. After the first season, the show selected separate writers and directors, which only amped up the conflict. Not that conflict was lacking—what with well-meaning but wooden child actors who had to carry the entire story weight of Pete Jones's saccharine *Stolen Summer*; the self-important *Battle of Shaker Heights* scribe whose previous credits consisted of "craft services"; John Gulager giving himself "whore baths" in the sink at the office; Krista Allen showing up to set drunk; Aidan Quinn's diva trip; and Moore repeatedly bitching out, then firing, his ineffectual, visor-wearing second-in-command, Jeff Balis. See also BRAVO.

PROJECT RUNWAY We really don't want to oversell it. But *Project Runway* just may be the most perfect reality show *ever*. Seriously, *Runway*'s got it all: the tension of short deadlines; psychological warfare; a competition you actually care to watch (outfits!); and plenty of bitchy queens (Santino!). It's edited together with a minimum of voice-overs to goose the action, it requires strangers and competitors to live together (tensely), and most important, everyone always looks fabulous. The contest to discover America's next great womenswear designer is hosted by Heidi Klum, who is lovely to

behold. *Runway* also features Tim Gunn, chair of the Department of Fashion Design at Parsons the New School for Design, who is dry and professional and (as one contestant called him on the first-season reunion episode) a "hot bitch"; he's just as cutting as Carolyn Kepcher and much better dressed. Conspiracy theories abound regarding the show's first season—dominated, as it was, by the bitchiness and crappy designs of Wendy Pepper (one story pegs her as a production plant)—but even if she didn't deserve to be in the final three, the best designer (Jay McCarroll) won. We still pine after one particular brown patterned skirt in his collection. Even if future rounds of would-be designers comprise a show that's only 10 percent as entertaining as the first, it'll *still* be totally brilliant! See also AMERICA'S NEXT TOP MODEL; BRAVO; KEPCHER, CAROLYN; REALITY TV, HOSTS OF; REALITY TV, OFF-BRAND; and UNIVERSALLY REVILED CHARACTERS.

PROMOS, DECEPTIVE How many times has The WB implied that Lorelai Gilmore is right on the verge of hearing a proposal? How often has ABC claimed that this week's is the most shocking Rose Ceremony ever? How many times has NBC promised us that we absolutely will not believe what happens in the last five minutes of *ER*, *Law & Order*, or *The West Wing*? Because Lorelai actually seldom gets proposed to, Rose Ceremonies are basically never shocking, and few of the twist endings on NBC's various dramas actually keep us up nights. We're pretty much at the point that as soon as a network promo primes us to expect something amazing, we reflexively anticipate the opposite . . . which is why we have to commend whoever happened to be in charge of cutting promos for the fourth season of UPN's *America's Next Top Model*. When one "scenes from next week" package showed Tyra Banks totally losing her shit and shrieking at the contestants at panel, we thought for sure it would turn out to be an acting exercise of some kind. So you can imagine our shock when the next episode aired and she actually *did* lose her shit and shriek at

ousted contestant Tiffany, judged by Tyra not to have taken her failure at a modeling contest with the appropriate penitence and shame. So let that be a lesson to the networks' marketing departments: Nothing is more likely to surprise us than to see precisely what you tell us we will. See also AMERICA'S NEXT TOP MODEL; *ER*; *GILMORE GIRLS*; *LAW & ORDER* FRANCHISE; and *WEST WING, THE*.

PROMS Ah, the TV prom: It's a magical night of romance, it's an emotional Hiroshima—on any teen soap worth its salt, it's both at once. Toxic fighting on boats (*Dawson's Creek*), underage drinking (*Dawson's* again) that leads to expulsion (*90210*), missed connections and cleansing bursts of dance (*My So-Called Life* . . . yeah yeah, it was the World Happiness Dance, close enough), three-way dates (*Popular*), the loss of virginity (insert show name here): It's all happening at the prom, which conveniently falls during May sweeps, thus not only permitting but practically requiring all sorts of sex, drugs, and melodrama to occur. Melodrama like, for example, fighting off a gaggle of hell-beasts before the prom, quickly changing clothes, and arriving late to find that your classmates have arranged a sweet send-off for you, and then dancing a bittersweet last waltz with your star-crossed vampire lover, accompanied by a heartbreaking Sundays song

(*Buffy*). See also BEVERLY HILLS 90210; BUFFY THE VAMPIRE SLAYER; DAWSON'S CREEK; HIGH SCHOOL, UNREALISTIC PORTRAYALS OF; MY SO-CALLED LIFE; POPULAR; and TEEN SEX, CONSEQUENCES OF.

PSAS We'd like to dismiss the well-meaning but dorky TV spots with a scoff, but we have to admit that many, many televised public service announcements have lodged in our brains over the years: McGruff taking a bite out of crime; "this is your brain on drugs . . . any questions?" with that Foley-licious shot of an egg frying; the infamous Native American shedding a tear at our littering ways; Reading Is Fundamental (RIF); the talking crash-test dummies; Walter Cronkite urging parents to talk to their kids about crack (. . . you heard us); "give a hoot, don't pollute"; "Parents: The Anti-Drug"; the annoyingly smug agitprop of TheTruth.com; "It's ten o'clock—do you know where your children are?"; the list goes on. And we don't think it's a bad thing to use TV to keep kids from smoking, doing drugs, hating people of different ethnicities, chucking trash on the ground, or driving drunk. If it works, hey, great. We just wish actual programming didn't take on the job of PSAing so often, and so clumsily. *90210* devolved into a PSA on an almost weekly basis. One comical example: the antiviolence episode, which featured David Silver (Brian Austin Green) urging Angelenos of all shapes, sizes, and colors to "squash it" (complete with hand-over-fist signal). If you don't want kids today punching each other, try not making the most punchable one of them all your spokesdweeb. See also ABC AFTERSCHOOL SPECIALS; BEVERLY HILLS 90210; CATCHPHRASES, OVERUSED TV; "ONE TO GROW ON"; and "THE MORE YOU KNOW."

PUBLIC/CABLE ACCESS TV Reserved for community access by order of state authorities, public access is the rambling home of screechy recycling activists, inadvertently hilarious porn, miserably spelled current-events bulletin boards featuring fonts from the Atari era, and frustrated film students who believe simulating train-sickness with a can of cream of mushroom soup is art. See also COMMERCIALS, AMATEURISH LOCAL.

PUCK See RAINEY, PUCK.

PUKA-SHELL NECKLACE The must-have neck-cessory for the '70s teen idol (David Cassidy) and the present-day TIs who emulate him (Barry Watson, Ashton Kutcher). See also CASSIDYS, THE; 7TH HEAVEN; and THAT '70S SHOW.

PUNKY BREWSTER We wouldn't have found Punky so loathsome if the show hadn't tried so hard to make her the sweetest, most heartstring-yanking Pippi Longstocking rip-off who ever lived, but the writers took it too far: She has freckles *and* mismatched shoes *and* wacky stripey socks *and* a preternaturally well-behaved and smart dog *and* everyone loves her. Loves her, dammit! Well, except her parents, who dumped her in a supermarket. And "Punky"? What the hell kind of a name *is* that, anyway? Yeah, yeah, it's short for "Penelope." That's no excuse. We didn't even notice the slight tinge of druncle creepiness in the fact that she got herself adopted by George Gaynes; we just disliked her, and we tuned in every week to roll our eyes at her—until the Very Special Episode about Punky dealing with the *Challenger* tragedy finally put us off our food. Soleil Moon Frye (and what the hell kind of a name is *that*?) got boobs shortly thereafter, which brought an overdue end to the madness. See also BAD SITCOM, SURE SIGNS OF; CHILDREN, OVERLY PRECOCIOUS; ORPHANS; and VERY SPECIAL EPISODES.

QUEER EYE FOR THE STRAIGHT GUY The "five gay men charged with making over hapless, hirsute het guys and their slovenly homes" concept is pretty brilliant—and some of the homes are really, *really* slovenly. When dry wit Thom, the interior design guy, finds pairs of dirty underpants *in the kitchen*, it's fun to feel superior. It's also fun to feel superior to Jai, the culture guy, who is sweet and well-meaning but who really doesn't do anything (besides perpetuate saccharine stereotypes . . . proposing marriage in a Moroccan tent? In the back *yard*? With the ring jammed into a dessert? Dude, come on). The show got overexposed in no time flat, and Carson Kressley's overprocessed hair and painted pants are a puzzle, given that he's the fashion guru. And the single entendres . . . ugh, so painful. We like puerile "hole"-based humor as much as anyone, but boyfriend needs to give it a rest now and then. Anyway, we should be so over the show by now, but it's still a worthwhile hour, and not just because you can get handy home-and-dining tips out of it. Whenever a straight guy walks into his newly painted pad and flips shit at how good it looks, or pulls off a speech or a difficult hors d'oeuvre, or gets all teary thanking the guys for vanquishing his monobrow, it's heartwarming. What? It is! Equally enjoyable: 1) straight guys who resist every single piece of advice, act like dicks, and get ripped on for it by the Fab Five on the Couch of Judgment, and 2) Kyan, who manages to maintain his stone foxiness even when he's wearing bunchy paper tanning-salon panties. See also BRAVO; HOME MAKEOVER SHOWS; and REALITY TV, HOSTS OF.

R

RAINEY, PUCK The Puck wasn t the first *Real World*-er to get kicked out of the house David of *Real World* L.A. holds that honor but he s probably the most memorable. Puck, an abrasive bike messenger who picked his nose and then used the same finger to eat peanut butter straight from the jar, has become something of a reality-TV archetype the personality disorder disguised, unsuccessfully, as an iconoclast. He infuriated everyone in the house with his boorishness, then became the eye of the drama storm when HIV-positive Pedro manipulatively announced that either he or Puck had to leave. The other housemates were not about to put the sainted Pedro out on the curb, so Puck was ejected, via speakerphone (classy, guys), and we never get sick of watching that episode when it airs in reruns not because Puck sucked (although we wouldn t want to live with the dude either), but because the entire house-meeting sequence exposes the *other* roommates as self-righteous whiners ten times more annoying than Puck himself. And by the other roommates, we mean Judd, who is the smuggest pill in the pharmacy. Cram it with walnuts, Cartoon Boy. The vacant housemate spot was filled by Jo, a shrill  vegan and crappy-guy magnet, and Puck s singular ability to annoy doormat Cory and spoiled-brat Rachel was sorely missed. When he appeared on *The Real World/Road Rules Challenge* years later and irritated a whole new generation of Bunim/Murrayers too dumb to see that the best strategy is to ignore him, we couldn t help smiling. See also REAL WORLD, THE; REAL WORLD/ROAD RULES CHALLENGE, THE; and UNIVERSALLY REVILED CHARACTERS.

RAYBURN, GENE Everything about Rayburn is pretty damn creepy: the greasy hair, so thick with pomade that it could deflect a hail of bullets; the big, creepy yellow teeth; the weirdly short torso and extremely long legs, which made Rayburn look like a water bug in a suit; the suit itself, usually polyester and always paired with a hideous tie; the cadaverous cheekbones and ooky piggy nose; the old-school superlong mic that looked like a cattle prod; the rubbery faces he d make;

and let us not forget the flagrant inebriation and boob-ogling. We probably shouldn t speak ill of the dead, especially not one whose unenviable job it was to keep Brett Somers from licking her fellow panelists on *Match Game*, but *damn*, that dude is scary-looking. See also *MATCH GAME*.

READING RAINBOW   Any book can be compelling when it s read by *Rainbow* s mellifluous-voiced host, LeVar Burton. The once (and future?) Geordi LaForge of *Star Trek: The Next Generation* is the perfect host for a slow-paced, chilled-out show like *Rainbow*; he s enthusiastic about the subject matter yet mellow and easy to watch, and by never talking down to his audience, he makes the show entertaining for both kids and adults. The show is just really, really cute. And if it takes a TV show to make kids want to read books well, it s ironic, but so be it. Thanks, LeVar! See also CHILDREN S SHOWS, HOSTS OF and *STAR TREK* FRANCHISE.

REAL ESTATE, VASTNESS OF   It is occasionally useful, in establishing the premise for a TV series, to contrive a reason for characters to cohabitate in unconventional situations in drag (*Bosom Buddies*) or in a sham marriage (*Ned & Stacey*). But normally, TV characters even those who are underemployed, even those in *Manhattan* live in absolutely enormous apartments. Well into the run of the series, *Friends* did offer some halfhearted, grandmother-based explanations for how a sous chef (Monica) and a masseuse (Phoebe) could live so well the former was illegally subletting her grandma s rent-controlled *terrace* apartment, and the latter shared a two-bedroom with her grandma but that still doesn t explain how the series could *begin* with Monica having a whole extra bedroom that she wasn t even using, that Rachel could move straight into. And remember that cavernous apartment Felicity shared with Elena and that English junkie girl in the waning days of *Felicity*? That we were supposed to believe was university student housing?! We realize that the gigantic nature of TV lodgings is due to the necessity of having room enough for cameras to maneuver, but come on. See also *FELICITY*; *FRIENDS*; MONEY, INFREQUENT HANDLING OF BY TV CHARACTERS; and NEW YORK CITY, CLICH D/INACCURATE TV PORTRAYALS OF.

REALITY TV, COUPLES ON   The intensity of the reality-show experience the unfamiliar setting, the isolation from friends and family, the cameras can lead to some instantaneous attachments among people who, under normal circumstances, would barely know each other. It s like when you were a kid and you d go to camp; when the time came to leave, you couldn t imagine living your life without people you d known for all of two weeks. That s the only way we can account for the couplings of *Real World*ers like Amaya and Colin (Hawaii), Landon and Shavonda (Philadelphia), and Danny and Melinda (Austin) never mind all the ones that hooked up during the *Challenge*. And then there s the special case of competitive reality shows, where either latching on to a fellow contestant, or just pretending to, is a strategic move. Rob and Amber partnered up in the early going of *Survivor All-Stars*, got engaged on the show s reunion episode, paired up again for *The Amazing Race*, and even turned their wedding into a CBS special. Now *that's* commitment . . . to maximizing screen time. See also MARIANO, ROB; *REAL WORLD, THE*; and *REAL WORLD/ROAD RULES CHALLENGE, THE*.

REALITY TV, FOX TRAVESTIES OF Every network s come up with an offensive idea for a reality show. In fact, nearly every reality-show idea is offensive on some level. But FOX has distinguished itself as the network that will not scruple to rip off other series ideas and make them even worse. For example, *The Contender* was remade on FOX as *The Next Great Champ*; *Supernanny* as *Nanny 911*; *Wife Swap* as *Trading Spouses*; *Dancing with the Stars* as *Skating with Celebrities*; *The Apprentice* as *My Big Fat Obnoxious Boss*. ABC s *The Bachelor* indirectly spawned FOX s shock-reveal series *Joe Millionaire*. And ABC s *Extreme Makeover* was already exploitative enough, bringing us the *Queen for a Day*-esque sob stories of the unattractive makeoverees; FOX decided to take that already unpalatable premise and morph it into *The Swan*—a *beauty pageant* among the women who went under the knife. Most of the credit for these appalling displays belongs to FOX s reality Svengali Mike Darnell, whose ironic punishment in hell will surely be watching an infinite loop of *Married by America*. See also APPRENTICE, THE and DANCING WITH THE STARS.

REALITY TV, HOSTS OF Given the little they have to do generally, interrupting the action of a show we were following perfectly well in order to tell us what s going on the population of reality TV hosts is just lousy with folks who are . . . just lousy. You can expect inept and rerecorded expository voice-overs from Tommy Hilfiger (*The Cut*), Donald Trump (*The Apprentice*), Jonny Moseley (*The Real World/Road Rules Challenge*), and Heidi Klum (*Project Runway*). Then there are the intrusive types Ryan Seacrest Out! Seacrest on *American Idol* (and his late confr re, Dunky) and Chris Harrison on *The Bachelor*, acting all touchy-feely with the contestants. In a completely separate category are the hosts who attempt to hypnotize us with their terrifying facelifts, and don t think we didn t notice, Kathy Hilton (*I Want to Be a Hilton*) and Claudia DiFolco (*My Big Fat Obnoxious Fiancé*). However, there are some who ve managed the seemingly impossible: Outstanding Achievement in Reality TV Hosting. *Survivor* s Jeff Probst has become increasingly aware of his role as audience surrogate, calling the contestants on their shit at tribal council and in end-of-season reunions. Anderson Cooper never made us feel that he was slumming on *The Mole*, deploying his bone-dry wit at every opportunity and being an impossible act for the dopey Ahmad Rashad to follow. And finally, a moment of silent fantasizing about *The Amazing Race* s Phil Keoghan, possessor of the dreamiest accent and hottest eyebrow-pop in the biz. See also BANKS, TYRA; COOPER, ANDERSON; DUNKLEMAN, BRIAN; HARRISON, CHRIS, INDISTINGUISHABILITY FROM MARK L. WALBERG OF; KEOGHAN, PHIL; PROBST, JEFF; SEACREST, RYAN; and TRUMP, DONALD, HAIR OF.

REALITY TV, "LOYALTY" AND "INTEGRITY" ON Have you ever noticed that the people on reality shows who spend the most time pompously declaiming their own loyalty (to the people in their alliance, at that particular moment) and integrity (as opposed to those they judge to be morally inferior) are losers? If you have too much integrity to poach a cab from a distracted team on *The Amazing Race*, too much loyalty to throw over someone in your alliance if it ll get you one step closer to the final two on *Survivor*, or too much character to temporarily suspend your personal morality to sell overpriced candy on the street on *The Apprentice*, then you re not playing to win. Or you *were* playing to win, but you still lost, so you re spinning your failure as a personal success. Or you re Lex van den Berghe, and you want the world to believe you wouldn t have stabbed Rob Mariano in the *front* if you thought you could get away with it and win a million dollars. Try buying a flat-screen TV with all your integrity, *loser*. See also APPRENTICE, THE; DRINKING GAMES; MARIANO, ROB; SURVIVOR; and VAN DEN BERGHE, LEX.

REALITY TV, OFF-BRAND Reality series like *The Real Gilligan's Island*, *Boy Meets Boy*, and *Outback Jack* may not have the impressive budgets, high production values, and stellar ratings of their broadcast rivals, but what they lack in those areas they make up for in . . . actually, they re just cheap and bad. Never mind.

REALITY TV, QUITTERS OF We acknowledge that *Survivor* is a pretty tough gig, and that we definitely couldn t hack it. But that s why we *haven't gone on it*. What excuse do all these damn *quitters* have? Osten, you think you re going to get *pneumonia*? Janu, you lost all but 2 percent body fat? Suck it up! Especially galling are Jenna Morasca and Sue Hawk, both of whom punked out of the show s All-Star season. Given that they d already been through it once, you d think they d be better prepared. And yes, Jenna s mom was sick, but she was sick when Jenna decided to go on the show in the first place; and yes, Richard Hatch hadn t covered himself with glory when he covered Sue with his naked junk in a challenge, but she d spent a whole season with his obnoxious ass, so she should have shrugged it off. Equally annoying were Marshall and Lance Hudes, who quit *The Amazing Race* in Luxor, Egypt, when Marshall s knees hurt too much for him to continue. First of all, dude was only thirty-one. Second, if he was in such miserable shape, how did he pass the physical to get on the show? Then there s Mario Vazquez, who mysteriously recused himself from *American Idol* s fourth season. Yes, before reporters even had a chance to dig up some hidden arrest record from his misspent youth, as they d done to so many failed Idols before. See also *AMERICAN IDOL*; PESENTI, FLO; and *SURVIVOR*.

REAL WORLD, THE In the early seasons of seminal reality show *The Real World*, you could *sort* of tell yourself that it was good-for-you TV like a PBS *Frontline* documentary, but with more hip-hop on the soundtrack. Seeing what happened when they stopped being polite and started getting real seemed like an interesting sociological experiment in group living and breaking down stereotypes. That didn t last, of course, and as the years went by, the cast members got younger, dumber, and more prone to alcohol abuse and ill-considered hook-ups, both with outsiders and each other. Although maybe it s because *we're* older and more fogeyish now (or, according to San Diego s Frankie, we re not punk rock enough) that today s *Real World*-ers all seem like trashy drunks and camera-whoring dullards, *Trishelle*. And *Melinda*. And . . . um, almost everyone else except Country Jon from the L.A. season. One day not far from now, the show will cast a group that literally implodes from self-absorption, but until then, we ll keep watching, because the whole point of consuming reality TV is to feel superior to its subjects, and boy oh boy does *The Real World* know how to serve up jackasses to that end. Back in the day, we could usually find at least one roommate we didn t want to hit over the head with an angry rattlesnake, but starting with the Boston season, it was all hate, all the time. Matt from the Hawaii cast, if you re reading this: Eat a bee. See also ALCOHOLISM; BUNIM/MURRAY; COOLEY, TONYA, KIDNEY OF; RAINEY, PUCK; REALITY TV, COUPLES ON; *REAL WORLD/ROAD RULES CHALLENGE, THE*; and UNIVERSALLY REVILED CHARACTERS.

REAL WORLD/ROAD RULES CHALLENGE, THE It s like *Circus of the Bunim/Murray Stars*, except that said stars all live together and get in stupid fights while competing in trumped-up events like hanging from trapezes over a swimming pool for long periods of time, eating huge vats of ice cream without hurling, putting together giant puzzles, and so on. Sometimes the theme is a *Fear Factor*—ish mettle test called The Gauntlet or The Inferno, and other times, it s a Battle of the Sexes, and the winners get money and prizes, and blah, but how the game works (and which retired extreme-sports nonentity is hosting) isn t important. The show is a welfare program for past cast members of *Real World* and its bastard cousin *Road Rules* who thought they d surely get acting work in Hollywood once their shows aired. Hollywood, however, isn t looking for r sum s containing sitting around in hot tubs shit-talking each other and getting smashed, so instead of learning to type or going to med school, the BM-ites wind up on the *Challenge*. On the one hand, it s pathetic; some of the Challengers have been on the show

almost every single season (Miami Dan, seriously: It s called temping. Look into it), and they should really get real jobs one of these days. On the other hand, real jobs would expose these narcissistic emotional four-year-olds to innocent people in the American workforce, so it s probably best that they stay quarantined. Who would hire Veronica in the first place? See also *BATTLE OF THE NETWORK STARS*; BUNIM/MURRAY; and *REAL WORLD, THE*.

RECASTING, NOTORIOUS It s reasonably rare nowadays for a show to replace one actor with another in the same role soap operas do it all the time, but you just don t see a Darrin Stephens/Dicks York and Sargent thing in primetime anymore. Even when an actor dies, shows find another way to handle it usually by writing the character off (or using a CGI version of the deceased, a mistake we hope *The Sopranos* doesn t repeat). You do see an occasional recast of, say, a child actor, like the kid who played the second Owen on *Party of Five* and who could not have looked less like the first Owen if he were Asian, but that s about it. See also *BEWITCHED*; MAIN CAST MEMBER DEPARTURES, NOTORIOUS; *PARTY OF FIVE*; and SOAP OPERAS, DAYTIME.

RED HERRING, TOOLS FOR IDENTIFICATION OF ON COP SHOWS Any character acting flagrantly suspicious, getting caught with damning evidence, or even confessing to the crime in the first thirty-five minutes of the episode? Didn t do it. Cop shows have an hour to fill, you see, and any case that may appear closed prior to the second commercial break clearly is not. Think he did it? Check your watch. See also *CSI* and *LAW & ORDER* FRANCHISE.

"REDSHIRT" You know how, on *Star Trek*, a few members of the opening-credits cast would be sent on an away mission to a planet somewhere, and they d always bring along with them a couple of red-uniformed dudes we d never seen before, and coincidentally, *those* dudes were the ones who ended up getting killed? Crazy! Except, not really; since anyone who mattered was never in any mortal danger, there had to be a few tag-alongs who could be sacrificed for the sake of the drama. Contemporary background artists those faceless CIA field agents who get sent out on missions on *Alias*, or offer backup to Jack Bauer on *24* who, unluckily for them, get themselves killed before we ve learned their names or heard their voices, are still called redshirts . . . regardless of what they re wearing. See also *ALIAS*; *STAR TREK* FRANCHISE; and *24*.

REED, ROBERT Yes, Reed fussed at *Brady Bunch* creator Sherwood Schwartz about the writing and directing on the show; yes, he considered the Mike Brady role beneath him not so far beneath him that he wouldn t keep taking Schwartz s money every time the gang got back together for a two-hour movie, but beneath him. Yes, that makes him kind of a git. But the man made a great TV dad, latter-years man-perm and all; nobody rocked a pajama top like our boy Bob, and his death really brought the AIDS crisis home for a lot of people . . . which says a lot about American culture. (None of it good.) But hopefully our favorite TV patriarch taught us all a Very Important Lesson about condoms. See also AFROS, IMPORTANT TV; *BRADY BUNCH, THE*; DADS, TV; REUNION MOVIES; and SCHWARTZ, SHERWOOD.

RELATIVITY This short-lived drama, from the producers who brought us *My So-Called Life* and *thirtysomething*, made two things clear to the viewing public (. . . all fifteen of us): 1) we don t know what Devon Gummersall did to piss puberty off, but man, is payback a bitch, and 2) Adam Goldberg looks super-fine in a wife-beater. *Relativity* is usually considered the *twentysomething* in the Zwick/Herskovitz troika (*Once and Again* is the *fortysomething*), and the show had just really started to get good when it got canceled. Do us a favor, would you? Go nag the production company to put it out on DVD. See also CULT SHOW, DEFINITION OF; *MY SO-CALLED LIFE*; and *THIRTYSOMETHING*.

RELIGION, CLICHÉS ASSOCIATED WITH Perhaps it s because of the secular/liberal media conspiracy the fundamentalist Christians are always bitching about that so many TV portrayals of religious persons directly confront stereotypes we may hold about devotion and piety. *Law & Order: Special Victims Unit* has a recurring character in Charlayne Woodard s Sister Peg, a nun who doesn t wear a habit and works with prostitutes, ensuring their medical care and liaising between them and the cops. *Oz* s Sister Peter Marie (Rita Moreno) ministers to convicts and also happens to be a psychiatrist on the side. Father Ray (Kevin Anderson), the priest at the center of *Nothing Sacred*, was such a renegade that ABC had to cancel the series after hyping the hell out of it (if you ll pardon the pun). Ari (Molly Parker), on *Six Feet Under*, was possibly the most sensuous rabbi in pop culture, all but sitting in Nate s lap as she listened to him drone on about his problems. And *Joan of Arcadia* was chockablock with unconventional religious people and situations, from the seeming advice of our Lord that Joan (Amber Tamblyn) should sleep with her boyfriend Adam (Chris Marquette) to Helen s (Mary Steenburgen) seeking catechism lessons from a

multiply tattooed and pierced ex-nun (Constance Zimmer) who surfs and hits on Helen s son. Fortunately, amid all this heresy, some portrayals of religion are squarely and we do mean *squarely* i n line with our preconceptions of church types: You can always count on the Camdens to be judgmental, close-minded, hysterical, and preachy. Thank God. See also *LAW & ORDER* FRANCHISE; *OZ*; and *7TH HEAVEN*.

REMINGTON STEELE So, Laura Holt (Stephanie Zimbalist) starts a private-detective agency, but she can t get any clients because people don t trust a girl to do PI work (whatever, early- 80s sexism), so she makes up this fake male boss named Remington Steele and starts getting a crapload of work. But *then* this hot British dude shows up and claims *he's* Remington Steele, but he s actually a thief who tried to steal . . . you know what, plot schmot, who cares. We watched it because Pierce Brosnan was a fox, period, especially when he cut like a hot knife through umpteen layers of buttery sexual tension by teasing Laura for getting dithery again. Brosnan went on to star in *The Thomas Crown Affair*, which had a very similar premise and a way cooler heroine (psst, Stephanie Zimbalist: hot oil!), but in the pre-Bond era, we took what Brosnan we could get.

REMINI, LEAH   Let s just get this out, straight up and down: We love Leah Remini. *Love.* We ve loved her since back when she guest-starred on shows like *Blossom* and *Head of the Class*. We thought she was much cooler than Alyssa Milano, whose friend she briefly played on *Who's the Boss?* before getting her own spin-off, *Living Dolls*, playing a teen model alongside a young Halle Berry. We re not going to claim we watched every one of the shows she helped to kill (including *The Man in the Family*, *Phantom 2040*, *First Time Out*, and *Fired Up*), or that we were riveted to *Saved by the Bell* for the season she spent as a Zack Morris love interest. But when she turned up on *The King of Queens* as Carrie, wife of standup comic Kevin James s Doug Heffernan, we were relieved to see that she wasn t playing just a boringly disapproving yet tolerant wifey who was certain not to upstage her onscreen husband. Instead, Remini s Carrie became ever sassier over the course of the series, giving in to her impulse to pick fights with neighbors; forbidding Doug from eating in restaurants where the waiters had slighted her; figuring out an elaborate method of buying expensive clothes and returning them after wearing them once. She s mean, she s defensive, she

can hold a grudge longer than a Mafiosa . . . she s kind of the greatest. See also *BLOSSOM*; FAT GUY/SKINNY WIFE MARRIAGES; *FRIENDS*; *HEAD OF THE CLASS*; *KING OF QUEENS, THE*; *SAVED BY THE BELL*; SHOW KILLERS; SPIN-OFFS; and *WHO'S THE BOSS?*

REMOTE CONTROL   Ken Ober played host on the late- 80s MTV game show in which contestants answered questions about pop culture while nestled in comfy Barcaloungers, eating snacks. The show also featured a then-fetal Colin Quinn as the announcer; a rotating array of hostesses (read: chippies), including Kari Wuhrer, who went on to deflower David Silver on *90210* before eventually disappearing into Straight-to-Video-Land; and Adam Sandler and Denis Leary doing little interactive skits (Sandler was basically the Stanley Spadowski). One of the few game shows that looked more fun to go on than to watch those recliners looked really relaxing. See also BAD SITCOMS STARRING GOOD COMEDIANS and *BEVERLY HILLS 90210*.

RESTAURANT, THE   You can visit every damn Home Depot in North America, but you ll never find a bigger tool than celebrity chef Rocco DiSpirito, proprietor of *The Restaurant*. His doofy Vespa alone probably could have secured him a spot in the Black & Decker Hall of Fame, but the bloated, sulk-prone DiSpirito ensured himself a plaque by: spending more time hawking his line of pots and pans and posing for pictures with the bridge-and-tunnel crowd than he did actually cooking; when he *did* cook, sucking at it; boohooing about his mean old partner, Jeffrey Chodorow, and how Chodorow unreasonably wanted the restaurant to make money; pouting; pissing off the entire staff by never showing up and setting sous chefs against each other; getting puffy; having a whiny model girlfriend; and not understanding basic principles of economics. Chodorow eventually shut the restaurant down and had Rocco barred from the premises, but not before NBC canceled the show apparently, not everyone found Rocco s narcissistic hijinks as amusing as we did. Some viewers complained that the second season tried too hard to create drama, but we loved every minute. Hey, ponytailed manager Shane s trying to talk to Rocco without rolling his eyes again: Drink! See also BURNETT, MARK; DRINKING GAMES; and UNIVERSALLY REVILED CHARACTERS.

REUNION MOVIES A reunion movie is a cynical attempt to capitalize on nostalgia that we, the viewers, do not actually feel; rather, it s the network executives who feel nostalgic for ratings slam dunks. But we always watch the reunion movies

anyway, if only to gossip about which cast members have obviously gotten Botoxed since the original show aired, or to see what contrived excuses they come up with for the absences of key characters (oh, Jo just called to say she s trapped in a cave-in and can t make it). Well, that s not entirely true; we ll watch the first one, *GROWING PAINS*. How many of those movies do they plan to trot out, anyway? We re sorry Tracey Gold has all those legal bills now, but that s not *our* problem. See also *GROWING PAINS*.

REVIVALS Look we liked *The Monkees*. We watched all the episodes; we know all the songs. That doesn t mean that we, or anyone else, wanted to see an updated version of it on MTV that exploited the retro comeback of the original. But an updated version is exactly what the world got, complete with a nationwide search for the next Fab Four (and after all that, it got mercy-killed after only a few episodes). Nobody asked for *The New Gidget*, either, but we got that, too, for three years. *The New Lassie*, *The New Leave It to Beaver* . . . yes, people loved the originals, if by loved, you mean watched, passively, because they had three broadcast channels and no cable, during the dark time in human history when a hula hoop was considered a viable source of entertainment. But that time has ended. If Timmy s down the well again, well, that s his own lookout. Let it go. You too, *Dragnet*. See also BAD SITCOM, SURE SIGNS OF; *MONKEES, THE*; and *TWILIGHT ZONE, THE*, LATER AND CRAPPIER INCARNATIONS OF.

RICH GIRLS   For people who liked *The Osbournes* but felt it would be more entertaining if it featured teenagers who were even dumber, more spoiled, and more poorly socialized, MTV made *Rich Girls*. And God bless them. The show which predated *The Simple Life* by several weeks followed the titular financially well-endowed young women: Ally Hilfiger, daughter of the designer and future wooden host of *The Cut* Tommy Hilfiger, and Jaime Gleicher, Ally s best friend but otherwise a nobody. The show kicked off with Jaime and Ally s prom (featuring a cameo by future wooden *The O.C.* star Mischa Barton) and graduation, and then followed them through a summer of shopping, traveling, loafing in the Hamptons, pining after guys who were obviously not interested in them (Jaime only), moping around England like a tiresome pill (. . . again, Jaime), and whining that they didn t know what they were supposed to do with their lives and that they were forced to grow up too fast (which was news to the viewer, to whom it looked more like they d never grown up at all). Ally, though annoying and cursed with a strangely lockjawed accent,

came across as a basically sweet girl perhaps coddled by her circumstances, but genuinely searching for her purpose in life. But Jaime . . . oy. As sour and unpleasant of personality as she was gargoyle-ish of aspect, Jaime was living proof that, in this life, you get the face you deserve. Rumor has it that the Rich Girls parted ways after the filming of their show s first and so far only season, which is just as well. For Ally. See also *O.C., THE*; *OSBOURNES, THE*; and REALITY TV, OFF-BRAND.

RICHTER, ANDY   At first, no one appreciated him. Andy Richter charged with the unusual task of sidekicking a virtually unknown late-night talk-show host (Conan O Brien) seemed extraneous; guests ignored him, and viewers wondered why he was there. But we had a soft spot for Andy: In *Late Night* s dark first years under O Brien s hostship, some of us even felt he was funnier than Conan. And as the series gradually found its footing, with its weird comedy bits (the plush Conan and Andy, only Plush Andy had Richter s head with the body of a pink dinosaur body; driving Conan s desk; the staring contests), Richter made himself indispensable. When he left the show in 2000, he left a vacancy in the show s repertory company that neither bandleader Max Weinberg nor announcer Joel Godard could quite fill. Fortunately for

Richter, he s having a pretty good career outside of late night. FOX canceled the insanely brilliant *Andy Richter Controls the Universe* far too soon, but put him on another show (okay, it was *Quintuplets*; maybe that was adding insult to injury). He s also having a good run in the movies, costarring in *Elf*, *Scary Movie 2*, and voicing an incredibly adorable baby lemur in *Madagascar*. And as for the villain he played in *New York Minute*, opposite the Olsen twins . . . look, the man has a son. Do you want his kid to have shoes or not? See also FOX, SITCOMS PREMATURELY CANCELED BY; *LATE NIGHT WITH CONAN O'BRIEN*, STARING CONTESTS ON; OLSEN, MARY-KATE AND ASHLEY; and TALK SHOWS, LATE-NIGHT.

RICKI LAKE You know that episode from about ten years ago, the I Have a Secret to Tell You episode, featuring, among other guests, the girl who admitted to her friend that, when the friend asked her to take care of a dying dog because the friend couldn t deal with it, the first girl handed the dog off to her boyfriend, who was supposed to take the dog to the vet and have it put down humanely, but instead he ran over it with a Buick Skylark, kept the money he was supposed to use on the vet and the cremation and whatnot, and took the first girl out to a nice dinner, so the first girl broke up with him but never told the friend

why? And when Ricki started crying and said the ex is the one who should have gotten hit with the car? Yeah . . . that episode? Four out of the five teams of guests on that episode were lying. *Trust us.* Anyway, her staff s gullibility isn t Ricki s fault, and years later, the John Waters heroine and animal activist tried to make her daytime-talk entry less sleazy and more help-y. Okay, the recurring Lie Detector feature was a little sleazy, but in a fun way, and one virtuous Oprah is more than enough. See also TALK SHOWS, DAYTIME and WINFREY, OPRAH.

RIPA, KELLY By all rights, we should hate Kelly Ripa. Not only is she a morning talk-show host, but she s *Kathie Lee Gifford* s replacement. And yet, we think Ripa s kind of cool. Actually, scratch that: In order to maintain some level of dignity and likability despite a job that requires her to sit on one of those ridiculous, teetery stools alongside Regis Philbin, Kelly Ripa must have superhuman reserves of cool. In fact, the more we learn of Ripa s undistinguished roots in the business, the more we love her *Dance Party USA! All My Children* a n d not only did she continue playing Hayley Vaughan Santos months after she landed the *Live with Regis and Kelly* gig, but she s married in real life to the (really hot) guy (Mark Consuelos) who played her husband on the show! On *Hope & Faith*, she plays Faith Ford s flightier sister flightier than Faith Ford! and wears fabulous outfits and gets love interests played by people like Nick Lachey! But really, the place to see Kelly in all her glory is on *Live*: She s always perfectly turned out, without seeming done ; she s obsessed with pop culture, not her kids; and next to Regis Showbizasaurus Rex Philbin, she comes off like she preps for each guest like he or she is the SATs. So she has every job on TV. So what? She s cute. See also ABC s TGIF; *LIVE WITH REGIS AND KELLY*; PHILBIN, REGIS; SOAP OPERAS, DAYTIME; and TALK SHOWS, DAYTIME.

RITTER, JOHN, PRATFALLS AND MUG-GING OF Nobody did slapsticky, non-credible concealment-by-shower-curtain or almost-falling-down spazzy running as well as John Ritter did in seven seasons as *Three's Company* s Jack Tripper. Often, he overplayed it, and that part of the opening credits where he gets hung up on the railing at the zoo isn t nearly as funny as Priscilla Barnes s raging white-shorts wedgie in the next shot . . . but maybe Ritter fell over couch backs and got hung up in revolving doors so effort-lessly that we took him for granted. Cer-tainly we took his acting chops for granted; when Ritter moved into more serious roles (Vaughan in *Sling Blade*, Ben Covington s moistly needy alkie dad

on *Felicity*), his performances were that much more impressive, given how used we d gotten to seeing him launch entire plates of pasta frantically into the air. We miss you, Rittsy, and we re sorry we made fun of *Hooperman*. Sort of. See also BAD SITCOM, SURE SIGNS OF; DADS, TV; *FELICITY*; and *THREE'S COMPANY*.

RIVERS, JOAN AND MELISSA Once upon a time, Joan Rivers was a shticky standup comic who, like Phyllis Diller, got credit in the biz for being every bit as bawdy as her male contemporaries. Her act wasn t really our thing, but whatever. Then her husband killed himself, she apparently ran out of money, and bad things started happen-ing. Like, she started hawking her line of crappy  costume jewelry on QVC. And she got a gig doing red-carpet interviews at awards shows (first for E!, and now for the TV Guide Channel). And she brought in her daughter Melissa her costar in *Tears and Laughter: The Joan and Melissa Rivers Story*, a TV movie about her hus-band s suicide *in which the surviving Rivers women played themselves!!* t o cohost these red-carpet events with her. Joan never knows who anyone is and makes an average of six factual errors per hour in these things, which is sad.

Melissa is similarly unqualified for the job and yet takes it so seriously that it s clear she fancies herself the next Diane Sawyer, which is sadder. If we were Melissa Rivers, seeing the scary-faced showbiz roadkill our mother had become would be inspiration enough to shun the industry and go to nursing school instead; the fact that Melissa wasn t similarly deterred is kind of what makes Melissa Melissa, you know? See also MOVIES, MADE-FOR-TV.

"ROBERT GOREN" The premise of *Law & Order: Criminal Intent* we see the criminals carrying out their nefarious plans, as well as the cops chasing them down doesn t make it the greatest procedural ever, but there is one element that makes it watchable: Detective Robert Goren. Portrayed by Vincent D Onofrio, Goren is the most hilariously over-the-top cop we ve ever seen. Not only does he know everything about *everything* mythology, psychology, German history, architecture, you name it but he s paired with a partner (Kathryn Erbe s Alexandra Eames) who doesn t get to do anything but prompt him for his insights and drive their car. She s also approximately half his height, so she s forced to tip-tap along behind him as he takes his customary nine-foot strides. In fact, Goren uses his prodigious height against everyone, preferring to swoop up behind

a suspect, bend in half, and crane his neck around to stick his nose in the suspect s face. The performance is so delightfully big that it makes the show worth watching just for his histrionics. Or, as we prefer to call them, his D Onofrionics. See also *LAW & ORDER* FRANCHISE and SCENERY, CHEWERS OF.

ROCCO DiSPIRITO See *RESTAURANT, THE* and UNIVERSALLY REVILED CHARACTERS.

ROGERS, FRED Perhaps the most soothing man ever to take to the airwaves, he s remembered with unanimous fondness. Something about the way he came into his little house at the beginning of each episode and changed into a sweater and talked to the kids in the audience like they were his friends set Mr. Rogers apart from most grown-ups, not to mention most children s-show hosts. Watching *Mister Rogers* was like having an auxiliary dad. We miss you, Mr. Rogers. See also CHILDREN S SHOWS, HOSTS OF.

RÖHM, ELISABETH *Angel* s Detective Kate Lockley, a skeptical, vengeful cop who didn t trust Angel but nevertheless believed in the supernatural, was supposed to be a complex, haunted character. She wasn t. She was supposed to have chemistry with Angel. She didn t. What she *did* have was a raging case of bitch-face and exactly one facial expression,

Botoxed goldfish on shrooms because she was played by Elisabeth R hm. And there was much rejoicing when Kate got written off of *Angel* . . . until R hm resurfaced, not on just any show, but on our beloved *Law & Order*. Now, we ve had our complaints about *L&O* replacement staff in the past. Eventually, though, we get used to the new guy or gal and even come to love him or her. But not R hm. Her acting never improved so much as a scintilla; her character grew increasingly snottier and more strident; she had really pretty hair toward the end there, but we only resented her for that. Evidently, the *L&O* writing staff resented her as well, for mangling their carefully crafted lines week after week, *for years*, and when her long-overdue last episode finally arrived, the scribes saddled her with possibly the most out-of-left-field send-off in the annals of drama the bizarre and completely unforeshadowed outing of her character as a lesbian. See also ACTING, WOODEN; *ANGEL*; LAW & ORDER FRANCHISE; and MAIN CAST MEMBER DEPARTURES, NOTORIOUS.

RONCO Among peddlers of as-seen-on-TV products, one man reigns supreme: Ron Popeil, founder of Ronco, which has brought us such fine products as the Pocket Fisherman, Hair in a Can (they call it GLH Formula Number 9 Hair System now, but . . . it s still hair. In a

can), the Inside-the-Shell Electric Egg Scrambler, and many other cabinet-cluttering items for which only the lazy, the insomniac shopaholic, and impressionable children would ever have any use. Ronco ads familiarized generations of TV viewers with the phrases But wait there s more! and It slices! It dices! It juliennes potatoes! (although Ronco reps claim the latter never actually appeared in a Ronco ad). Other commercials and products copied the notorious carnival-barker style of the Ronco ads, but Ron Popeil, extolling the no-more-tears onion-dicing virtues of the Chop-o-Matic, did it first. See also AS SEEN ON TV PRODUCTS.

ROSEANNE Following the hardscrabble working-class lives of the Conner family, *Roseanne* broke ground of all kinds. Sure, there were the episodes everyone remembers, like the same-sex kiss between Roseanne (Roseanne Barr/Arnold/No Last Name Please) and guest star Mariel Hemingway, or the domestic-abuse plotline involving Roseanne s sister Jackie (Laurie Metcalf) and boyfriend Fisher (Matt Roth). But *Roseanne* broke ground in less spectacular ways, too: the house was always an unappealing mess; the kids, when bratty, got disciplined; the lead couple (Roseanne and John Goodman as husband Dan) may have been TV s first fat guy/fat wife marriage, and many episodes involved their struggles with/acceptance of their weight. The show also featured all kinds of loving relationships old guy/young woman (Dan s father, played by Ned Beatty, and Roseanne s friend Crystal, played by Natalie West); young guy/older woman (Fisher and Jackie); guy/guy (Martin Mull and Fred Ward); girl/girl (the especially awesome Sandra Bernhard and Morgan Fairchild). The Conner daughters (Sara Gilbert s Darlene, and Becky played at various times by Lecy Goranson and Sarah Chalke) tried but failed to complete their college educations. Dan dealt, over a long period of time, with his mentally ill mother. The ensemble clicked beautifully, and the writing from a staff that, over the years, included Norm Macdonald (*Saturday Night Live*), Daniel Palladino and Amy Sherman (*Gilmore Girls*), and Joss Whedon (*Buffy the Vampire Slayer*) was always sharp. Toward the end, the show went downhill, but overall, it s a sitcom treasure; maybe Roseanne s lost her mind because she knows she ll never top it. See also *GILMORE GIRLS*; *SATURDAY NIGHT LIVE*; and WHEDON, JOSS.

"ROSS GELLER" Possibly the only fictional paleontologist ever to be part of any TV show s permanent cast, Ross Geller (David Schwimmer) was an unqualified dork. He loved the Osmonds, spent a col-

lege spring break in Egypt with his father, and composed terrible music for his electric keyboard. And yet, we kind of loved him. In fact, our favorite episodes of *Friends* were the ones that revolved

around Ross s nerdish leanings, like the one in which he and Monica performed a childhood dance routine on *Dick Clark's New Year's Rockin' Eve*, and especially the one in which he played quizmaster for a trivia contest to determine whether Joey and Chandler would get to live in Monica and Rachel s apartment, or if the girls would compel the guys to get rid of their noisy rooster. Yeah, yeah, We were on a break bugged after we d heard it forty-three times. But Ross s geeky character details his enthusiasm for saltwater taffy and petty hotel theft make him our most beloved Friend. See also DADS, TV; DORKINESS, TV SIGNIFIERS OF; and *FRIENDS*.

"RUTH FISHER" Ruth Fisher (Frances Conroy), the matriarch of *Six Feet Under* s Fisher clan, is memorable as a TV creation for being so damn weird. She s barely in her fifties, and yet she dresses like she s ignored every fashion advance since 1978. (Pull-on jeans with elastic waistbands?! Ruth, honey: no.)

She was a flower child in her youth, but turned into the most neurotic, tight-bunned lunatic in L.A. County. Her love interests are all over the map from a secretly anarchic funeral director to an outdoorsy hairdresser to a brusque Russian florist to a bizarrely socialized junior mortician to a schizophrenic geologist. She s alternately prudish and way too public about sex. She s extremely judgmental and formal, yet her best friend (Kathy Bates s fabulous Bettina) is mouthy and inappropriate. Ruth is a real quandary, wrapped in a riddle, wearing a long denim skirt with buttons all down the front. See also BRENDA CHENOWITH and DORKINESS, TV SIGNIFIERS OF.

S

SAGET, ROBERT LANE   Yeah, yeah, you know him as Bob, but by using his full name, we re trying to show him the respect he earned for doing surprisingly sharp standup . . . then lost irretrievably by participating in two of the more onerous TV programs in recent

history, *Full House* and *America's Funniest Home Videos*. American audiences probably could have forgiven him for the first one; Saget was the least annoying adult on the show (not that that s saying much, *Coulier*), and the man s gotta eat. But we ve looked for any excuse why Saget might have spent seven *years* as the host and humor-free squirrel voiceover provider on *America's Funniest Home Videos*, and we just can t find a single one. How many times does a guy have to see kids punching their dads in the nuts before he thinks to himself, I ve got to get out ? A lot, apparently. See also BAD SITCOMS STARRING GOOD COMEDIANS and *FULL HOUSE*.

SATURDAY NIGHT LIVE   Consistently entertaining talent factory or lumbering dinosaur of comic irrelevance? You make the call! Since its debut in 1975, the most successful production of Lorne Michaels s career has followed basically the same formula: cold open sketch; monologue in which the guest host clumsily plugs whatever product he or she is there to promote; fake commercial; about fifteen minutes of actually funny sketches, each of which goes on about two and a half minutes too long; musical guest; Weekend Update ; fifty-two minutes of filler. And seriously, why is the show ninety minutes long? The show is only as good as its cast a blessing when said cast includes Will Ferrell or Amy Poehler, and a curse when the best it can muster is Tim Kazurinsky or Ellen Cleghorne. But it s hemmed in by its format, too: The sketches must have one clear premise (in other words, one main joke) and a set conclusion. To see members of its current cast loosed from the confines of Studio 8H and performing improv at New York s Upright Citizens Brigade Theatre is to appreciate how constricting *SNL* can be. And honestly, why even make the show live when there s so little room for improvisation? The show is, by and large, still worth watching, and delivers a couple of sustained belly laughs in each episode. Also, the show eventually figured out that we were all changing the channel after Update and started throwing in one funny but totally out-of-left-field sketch per episode, usually around 12:48 hence, Time-Traveling Scott Joplin. Hee hee hee. See also CHARACTER, BREAKING OF; SATURDAY NIGHT LIVE, FAILED ATTEMPTS TO TURN SKITS INTO FULL-LENGTH FEATURES OF; SATURDAY NIGHT LIVE, FAT GUYS ON; SATURDAY NIGHT LIVE, MOST RELENTLESSLY IMMORTAL CATCHPHRASES OF; SATURDAY NIGHT LIVE, UNFUNNIEST RECURRING SKITS ON; SATURDAY NIGHT LIVE, WEEKEND UPDATE HOSTS ON; and SKETCH COMEDY ENSEMBLES, FORGOTTEN MEMBERS OF.

***SATURDAY NIGHT LIVE*, FAILED ATTEMPTS TO TURN SKITS INTO FULL-LENGTH FEATURES OF** Because it worked out well enough with *The Blues Brothers* and *Wayne's World*, SNL executive producer Lorne Michaels apparently got the idea that *any* skit could sustain a ninety-minute theatrical feature that viewers would actively seek out and pay to watch, quite distinct from something they happen to tolerate because it s being beamed into their homes for free. And when we say that he saw feature-film potential in *any* skit, we mean it: We all remember the

big flops, like *A Night at the Roxbury* (built around those two head-bobbing, club-going cokeheads played by Chris Kattan and Will Ferrell) and *Coneheads* (built around a skit that hadn t actually been seen on *SNL* in about fifteen years). But you may have forgotten about *The Ladies Man*, *Superstar*, *Stuart Saves His Family*, and *It's Pat*, which . . . my God, *PAT?!* A special Killing the Golden Goose award goes to *Blues Brothers 2000* and *Wayne's World 2* for taking our fond memories of entertaining *SNL*-inspired films and crapping all over them. Thank God Chris Farley passed away before they could turn that skit he did with Patrick Swayze about the Chippendales audition into a movie. . . . Okay, that actually might have been pretty funny. Though now that we ve proposed it hypothetically, it s probably being rushed into a production starring Horatio Sanz and Joey McIntyre. See also *SATURDAY NIGHT LIVE* and TV SERIES, FILM ADAPTATIONS OF.

***SATURDAY NIGHT LIVE*, FAT GUYS ON** The Not Ready for Primetime Players, in order to populate the wide variety of sketches they air, require a wide variety of performers men, women, tall, short, white, nonwhite (fewer of them, but still). And although the casts of TV shows are generally made up of conventionally attractive people, no *SNL* cast is complete without one fat guy. But you don t need more than one fat guy at a time, or else people might get confused and put off by the sight of so many Metabolically Challenged Americans on their TV sets. John Belushi, Jon Lovitz, Chris Farley, and Horatio Sanz have each filled *SNL* s fat-guy quota in their eras, ensuring that writers never need worry that there won t be an actor available to play Elizabeth Taylor. See also *SATURDAY NIGHT LIVE.*

SATURDAY NIGHT LIVE, **MOST RELENTLESSLY IMMORTAL CATCHPHRASES OF** The *SNL* catchphrase that you and your friends did the most to drive straight into the ground depends on your generation. From the early years, there was Jane, you ignorant slut ; Candygram ; Cheeseboorger, cheeseboorger, cheeseboorger, no Coke, Pepsi ; and We are from France. The 80s brought us Hey, you: I know you! I know you! ; Man, I hate when that happens ; I m Gumby, dammit! ; Isn t that conveeeeeeeenient ; Choppin broccoli ; We are here to pump [*clap*] *you* up! ; and I m just a simple caveman. Who can forget coasting through the 90s on such borrowed wit as [Name]! Makin copies! ; I live in a van DOWN BY THE RIVER ; That s the way it was, and we *liked* it! ; and I got a fever and the only prescription . . . is more cowbell. In the present day, we may be testing the roadworthiness

of I m just keeeeeding! ; I m rockin *one* leg ; and a heavily Italian-accented GET OUUUUT la Donatella Versace, but it s a little too early to tell which will stand the test of time and endless repetition. See also CATCHPHRASES, OVERUSED TV and *SATURDAY NIGHT LIVE.*

SATURDAY NIGHT LIVE, **UNFUNNIEST RECURRING SKITS ON** We ve never been in the writers room at *SNL,* but we re going to bet there s a sign in there that reads, If it s funny the first time, it ll be twenty times as funny the twentieth time. They may want to check their work on that math problem, because, no. We will confess to enjoying some recurring skits (like Celebrity *Jeopardy!,* Appalachian Emergency Room, *Morning Latte,* and that lady Cheri Oteri played with the weird Bayou accent who kept telling people to Simmer down, now!). But there are dozens more skits that, when they keep showing up, make you wonder what the writers could have possibly discarded. In fact, some cast members should set off alarm bells any time they show up Molly Shannon (Dog Show ; Leg Up ; the Joyologist and the I m fifty! lady basically the same character); Tracy Morgan (Astronaut Jones, Brian Fellow s Safari Planet); and Jim Breuer (Goat Boy, The Joe Pesci Show), though at least in his case we have the consolation of knowing that his career is now well over. We re also not sure how Bear City made it past one installment (bears in clothes we get it), and while the first Debbie Downer skit was moderately amusing in the way that dour depressives always are, it s since become an exercise in making everyone in the scene break character and laugh. Feline AIDS isn t a punchline you really can or should use more than, say, five times. See also *SATURDAY NIGHT LIVE*.

***SATURDAY NIGHT LIVE,* "WEEKEND UPDATE" HOSTS ON**   Ask a hundred different people who s the best Weekend Update anchor (and/or the worst), and you ll get a hundred different answers. Or, actually, about six, because that s as many Update anchors as anyone remembers. We can go backward from the present to Dennis Miller, but then we jump all the way back to the start of the series with Aykroyd and Curtin, and everyone in between is a blur. Gail Matthius? Brian Doyle-Murray? Brad Hall? They all hosted Update, believe it or not. Kevin Nealon was the worst never funny, seldom topical, terrible timing. Norm Macdonald was good weird and non sequitur-y. Tina Fey likes herself an awful lot, which makes her a little hard to take at times. Still, it s all relative. Colin Quinn cracked himself up saying his own name, and while we don t hate that dude as much as some people did, a

self-professed comedian should probably be able to get through *a sentence* without giggling. See also MILLER, DENNIS and *SATURDAY NIGHT LIVE*.

SAVED BY THE BELL   The era of the networks Saturday-morning cartoons was ushered out by two factors: the rise of kid-targeted cable networks that show cartoons 24/7, and *Saved by the Bell*. A live-action sitcom for tweens, *Bell* was every bit as dopey and hackneyed as the primetime sitcoms. The cast was composed of a standard assortment of types alpha male Zack (Mark-Paul Gosselaar); alpha female Kelly (Tiffani-Amber Thiessen); musclehead Slater (Mario Lopez); sexy smart girl Jessie (Elizabeth Berkley); Lisa, the cute girl of color (Lark Voorhies); and Screech (Dustin Diamond), the ber-dork nursing a hopeless crush on Lisa. No one ever remembers anything about the plots, but we do remember Slater s insistence on calling his girlfriend Mama (what?) and Zack s gigantic first-generation cell phone. And we remember where they ended up: Zack somehow landed on *NYPD Blue*; Kelly spent years on *90210* and displayed an amiable comic gift in several sitcoms; Slater entered an ill-advised and very short-lived marriage to Ali Doritos Girl Landry; Jessie did porn (sort of: *Showgirls*); Lisa went on to daytime soaps, we think; and Screech, after growing up reeeeeal ugly and doing an embarrassing cameo in Jon Favreau s *Made*, beat the hell out of Ron Horshack Palillo on FOX s *Celebrity Boxing*. *Saved by the Bell: The College Years* road-tested the gang in primetime, with grim results best left unmentioned. See also *BEVERLY HILLS 90210*; DORKINESS, TV SIGNIFIERS OF; *NYPD BLUE*; REALITY TV, FOX TRAVESTIES OF; SPIN-OFFS; and VERY SPECIAL EPISODES.

SCENERY, CHEWERS OF   Historically, scenery-chewing is not considered a positive; we d like to change that. When you ve consumed the sheer volume of infuriating, dull, stupid, and just plain bad television that we have, you come to appreciate the actors who make up for what they lack in nuance with sofa-gnawing, forehead-artery-bulging enthusiasm it can make otherwise useless TV worth watching. And let s face it: You can whisper *into your wristwatch* to your *talking car* to come *bust you out of jail* as if it s no big thing . . . or you can tear into that line like it s a filet mignon and you haven t eaten in weeks. Hasselhoff went with the steak dinner, and good for him; if you don t have Olivier skills, go for the gusto. In addition to The Hoff, Hall of Fame players on the Well, Points for Effort Acting Team include Jack Wagner, Shannen Doherty, the entire 90s cast of *The Bold and the Beautiful*, Kiefer

Sutherland, Christopher Meloni, and, of course, the Babe Ruth of ham, William Shatner. See also ACTING, WOODEN; *BOLD AND THE BEAUTIFUL, THE*; CRYING, FAKE/BAD; DOHERTY, SHANNEN; HASSELHOFF, DAVID; SHATNER, WILLIAM; *24*; and WAGNER, JACK.

SCHLAMME, TOMMY   If our surname were Schlamme and our parents were shortsighted enough to dub us Thomas, would we decide to go by Tommy ? Tommy Schlamme ?! Yes, we would, because that s awesome. (The dude also directs TV shows, apparently.) See also *ER*; *SPORTS NIGHT*; and *WEST WING, THE*.

"SCHNEIDER"   We have to give it to Pat Harrington Jr., the actor who portrayed building super/friend of the Romano fam-ily Schneider on *One Day at a Time*: He committed to the skeeze 100 percent. The greasy mustache; the denim vest over a Hanes Beefy T with the sleeves rolled up, which was itself stretched over a Schlitz gut; the massive clanky toolbelt dragging down the waist of a large-diameter pair of Wrangler bell-bottoms; the mugging that greeted any euphemism for breasts ; and the ongoing sexual harassment of Ann Romano and her underage daughters all made

Schneider a walking 70s gender-politics pamphlet. We don t endorse his vaguely pathetic brand of sexist leering, but we can live with it. Why? Because it annoyed Ann. See also MUSTACHES, GREAT TV and NEIGHBORS, INTRUSIVE.

SCHRODER, RICK(Y)   He first came to fame in *The Champ*, but not until *Silver Spoons* did The Ricker become a tween-dream household name who graced fully half the covers of *Dynamite* and *Bananas* published between 1982 and 1985. After *Spoons*, he kicked around doing TV movies and miniseries (and, apparently, having some pretty harsh acne), and when he turned up on *NYPD Blue* in the late 90s, we weren t sure what he had to offer (besides insisting that everyone call him Rick instead of Ricky, like, whatever, princess). But he held his own, and his New York accent was actually a lot better than some on that show, *Kim Drunk-laney*. See also *NYPD BLUE*; *SILVER SPOONS*; and *TEEN BEAT*, COVER BOYS OF.

SCHWARTZ, SHERWOOD   Our favorite thing about Sherwood Schwartz is neither the delightful alliterative chewiness of his name nor the shows he produced (although he composed the theme songs for both of his most famous productions, *Gilligan's Island* and *The Brady Bunch*, and while the shows might have sucked, the man could write a catchy ditty). No, our favorite thing about Sherwood Schwartz isn t even about Sherwood Schwartz, really it s about Robert Mike Brady Reed, and how infuriated Reed used to get at the stupidity of *The Brady Bunch* scripts, to the point where he picked fights with Schwartz repeatedly, sent him obnoxious memos on correct dramaturgical structure, and even refused to appear on the *Brady* finale because he hated that episode s premise so violently. Bob, sweetie: You had a man-perm, first of all, and second of all, it s not Shakespeare. See also *BRADY BUNCH, THE*; *GILLIGAN'S ISLAND*; and REED, ROBERT.

SCIENCE, IGNORANCE OF   It s a bit peevish to complain about such things as explosions in space making noise (which they apparently don t) on sci-fi-ish TV series when movies have already primed us to expect them. Still, a defiant ignorance of the laws of biology, chemistry, physics, and, for all we know, math seems to be endemic among TV writers. While the installments of the *Star Trek* franchise have the excuse of taking place in the future to allow us to accept such things as replicators, warp speed, and holodecks, many series set in the present day simply act as though the realities of science just don t exist. So we accept that all manner of gadgets, from biometric recorders to megapixel digital cameras, can be engineered to fit into items as small as rings or lipsticks (*Alias*); that aliens and Native Americans could share a common bloodline (*The X-Files*); and that computers that don t use any operating system you ve ever seen can have their passwords overridden with the greatest of ease and talk to their users (a series we like to call *Every Show That's Ever Been on TV Since Ever*). Apparently the only thing computers *can't* do is basic arithmetic, so genius mathematicians must do their calculations by hand, on chalkboards (*Numb3rs*). We give the *CSI* franchise a ton of credit for showing us how forensic work is actually done, so we know when to call bullshit on other shows although how the LVPD managed to get a multibillion-dollar budget approved is the one mystery the show s never solved. See also *ALIAS*; *CSI*; *CSI*, SPIN-OFFS OF; *NUMB3RS*; *STAR TREK* FRANCHISE; and *X-FILES, THE*.

"SEACREST OUT!" We want to hate the *American Idol* host s goofy sign-off, but we can t. Seacrest is *so* desperate for a patented catchphrase, it s pathetic, and the one he picked is so clearly an attempt to come off like an embedded journalist in occupied territory, it s even *more* pathetic and therefore kind of endearing. Plus, we started saying it in our daily lives as a joke, to make fun of it like when we got off the phone with our friends and stuff, but . . . now we can t stop saying it. So we re left with little choice but to pretend that it rules. See also *AMERICAN IDOL*; CATCHPHRASES, OVERUSED TV; and SEACREST, RYAN.

SEACREST, RYAN He s annoying, no question, but he s on an annoying show, and we can change the channel to get away from it; Seacrest is stuck there. He s got a little too much product going on in the hair and pays a little too much attention to the carefully hip T-shirts and $400 jeans, but if we had to feign caring about Clay Aiken, we d get drunker than Russian royalty before every episode, and somehow  Seacrest gets through it sober. (Well, as far as we know.) We admire him for never cursing, or telling the kids (or Paula) to shut up, and we hate to admit it, but he s . . . actually pretty good at what he does. Or maybe we just *think* he s pretty good compared with Brian Dunkleman. See also AIKEN, CLAY; *AMERICAN IDOL*; DUNKLEMAN, BRIAN; REALITY TV, HOSTS OF; and SEACREST OUT!

SEINFELD We have so much to blame *Seinfeld* for. Like the preponderance of crappy sitcoms built around standup comics (*The Drew Carey Show*, for instance). Like every show about a misanthrope who doesn t get punched in the face all the time (*Becker*). Like every crappy sitcom NBC coughed up for Thursday nights that managed to stay on TV because it happened to air after *Seinfeld* (*Fired Up*, *Suddenly Susan*, that one with Dabney Coleman; remember the episode they did where Jerry was mad that he kept having to open for crappier comics?). But in spite of its many inadvertent crimes against culture, *Seinfeld* deserves its place in TV history. It was sharply written, with complex plot threads that always connected by the end. It had great performances from its four leads as well as its many talented guest stars (like Bryan Cranston, Grace Zabriskie, Wayne Knight, Daniel von Bargen, and our favorite, Patrick Warburton as Puddy). It had characters living in New York who actually acted like they lived in New York, obsessing over real estate and Chinese food. And no show at the time ever concentrated so much on the minutiae of observing the social contract in an urban setting things like who gets to hand over the big salad and how to confront a date about always wearing the same outfit. Of course, since *Seinfeld*, all shows do that, which may be why *Seinfeld* is so painful to watch in syndication. See also CATCHPHRASES, OVERUSED TV; COSMO KRAMER ; and GEORGE COSTANZA.

***SEINFELD*, ALUMNI OF**   *Bob Patterson. Watching Ellie. The Michael Richards Show.* What do all these shows have in common? They were sitcom vehicles for ex-*Seinfeld* stars, and they all got hit by flying truck tires, rolled over, and burst into flames. But although the phrase Seinfeld Curse has been bandied about, it s not exactly accurate. Series cocreator Larry David has been doing just fine on his latest series, the *Seinfeld*-esque *Curb Your Enthusiasm*, and Jerry Seinfeld himself has managed not to embarrass himself by trying, and failing, to recapture past glories. Granted, he s done that by staying out of the spotlight. But think how many other stars you d like more if they did the same. See also BAD SITCOM, SURE SIGNS OF; *SEINFELD*; and SHOW KILLERS.

SELF-REFERENCING BUSINESS, CLOYING
Sometimes, when a show s writing staff has run out of ideas, they ll revert to the one topic they know the best: the show itself. *The Simpsons* can insert characters who will ostentatiously recall the events of past episodes (thanks, Comic Book Guy); *Dawson's Creek* can have Joshua Jackson s Pacey enthuse over the *Mighty Ducks* movie franchise, in which Jackson actually starred; *Seinfeld* can produce a whole season s worth of episodes about the process of getting a show about nothing on the air; and *The O.C.* had its

characters obsessed with a teen melodrama called *The Valley* before its first season was even half over. In fact, *The O.C.* may win the Meta Medal: It s also thrown in references to Benjamin McKenzie s resemblance to Russell Crowe and spent virtually the whole second season having characters complain that things were better last year you know, much as the viewers did. The idea is that we won t bother pointing out a show s shortcomings if the show s already done it first. Nice try, TV writers. Our disses may be redundant, but they re funnier than yours. See also *O.C., THE*; PACEY WITTER ; *SEINFELD*; and *SIMPSONS, THE*.

SENIOR CITIZENS, CLICHÉD PORTRAYALS OF Old people on TV come in two flavors: vibrant, vivacious, and sexually voracious; or crabby, decrepit, and bitter. (Either kind can be senile.) Much as they do when portraying religious persons, today s TV writers usually overcorrect when it comes to creating senior citizens. They make a point of having them live in their own houses, garden regularly, and maintain active social lives, including romantic entanglements, offering TMI about what their girl/boyfriends do or don t like. One scene from *Friends* had Phoebe describing her grandmother, with whom Phoebe shared an apartment, and her grandmother s new boyfriend, who were both insecure in bed and deaf,

so that they always loudly had to reassure each other that they were having a good time. At the other end of the spectrum, we have Arthur Brooks (Harve Presnell) of *Dawson's Creek*, a crotchety curmudgeon not too different from the one he played in *Fargo*. The whole point of Mr. Brooks s character was to show that he was a lonely old crank who just needed the attention of a young person to melt his stony heart, which disappointed us since, until his heart grew three sizes, Mr. Brooks was the only person in Capeside who recognized what a worthless douche Dawson was, and told him so. That was awesome. See also *DAWSON'S CREEK* and *FRIENDS*.

SESAME STREET This most famous of all PBS children s shows had tons of catchy songs and memorable skits: Would You Like to Buy an O, Sing (Sing a Song) as sung by Karen Carpenter, and the ladybug picnic song. *Sesame Street* taught us letters, numbers, and tolerance for imaginary friends, although they kind of sold that storyline out by making Snuffleupagus real after all; about how to deal with grief, when lovable grocer Mr. Hooper died in 1982; and about supporting gay marriage. Oh, please, Bert and Ernie were totally a couple, although what Ernie saw in a guy that anal about his bottle-cap collection, we don t quite see, but anyway. The show s changed a lot in recent times, trying to compete with crap like *Barney* and *Blue's Clues*, and we don t really like Elmo but if that s what it takes to keep future generations of ankle-biters tuning in, okay. We ll always prefer the old-school episodes with spazzy Luis (. . . surpri-i-i-i-i-se!). See also CAPTAIN KANGAROO and CHILDREN S SHOWS, HOSTS OF.

"SETH COHEN" See BRODY, ADAM.

"SEVEN MARY THREE" See *CHiPs*.

7TH HEAVEN A family values —based drama about Rev. Eric Camden (Stephen Collins) and his ever-expanding brood that inexplicably led The WB in ratings year after year, until they euthanized it in the 2005—6 season. Perhaps it was the sweet, affirming moments the show used to feature that made it such a success the diplomatic, unsugary handling of Lucy s (Beverley Mitchell) first period, for example, or Annie s (Catherine Hicks) gender-stereotype-busting household-repair skills. Or maybe it s the resolutely TV-G issues the *7H* crew tackles week after week, reinforcing socially conservative mores in a manner that s safe for the entire family. No, it s that, in its later years, the show turned into a *complete train wreck*, and viewers who despise everything the show stands for still tuned in to see the ham-handed lesson of the week come lumbering in from left field. Nothing about the later seasons makes sense. Ruthie (Mackenzie Rosman) is *obviously* a different ethnicity from the rest of her family; this is never explained. The twins (Lorenzo and Nikolas Brino) suffer from a marked developmental delay and spend most of their time making sandwiches or putting their underwear on over their clothes. Mary (Jessica Biel) toilet-papered the gym, drank a half a beer while babysitting, and got banished to Buffalo to become a flight attendant. Menopause gave Annie a personality disorder. RevCam keeps having heart attacks. Special guest stars have included Richard Lewis and Ed Begley Jr. It s utter surrealist chaos, portrayed via some of the worst acting since Cindy Brady froze up on that kids quiz show. See also BIEL, JESSICA; HAMPTON, BRENDA; PARENTS/PARENTING, BAD; and RELIGION, CLICH S ASSOCIATED WITH.

SEX AND THE CITY If you loved this show, we won t hold it against you. Honest. But we *hated it*, and we watched it every week only *because* we hated it. We didn t hate everything about it; we liked Chris Noth as Mr. Big, and we liked Miranda (Cynthia Nixon). But we hated how the show would always knock Miranda down a peg, making the one noncartoonish character eat cake out of the trash and suffer come-ons from a dude in a sandwich costume. We hated Carrie s (Sarah Jessica Parker) whiny self-absorption cheating on Aidan (John Corbett), sneering judgmentally at Samantha (Kim Cattrall) all the time, whining to Charlotte (Kristin Davis) about how she d gone broke from buying too many shoes and then borrowing money from her and we hated how she lived in a *gigantic* Manhattan one-bedroom *and* had enough money left over for Manolos on her salary from one column a week, and we hated her hair. We hated Charlotte s marriage obsession and prudishness. We hated Samantha s clumsy puns and one-note character. We hated how the girls never took the subway, dumped on Brooklyn and Jersey all the time, and wore heels everywhere without a single shin splint. It had its nice moments Miranda s mother s funeral, the love letters to New York after 9/11 but we knew real women talked like that years ago; we didn t need Darren Star to tell us. See also MONEY, INFREQUENT HANDLING OF BY TV CHARACTERS; NEW YORK CITY, CLICH D/INACCURATE PORTRAYALS OF; NOTH, CHRIS; REAL ESTATE, VASTNESS OF; and STAR, DARREN.

SEXUAL TENSION, RUINATION OF SHOW BY RESOLVING Only in popular culture does boiling hatred (or, failing that, grudging tolerance) between two people *actually* indicate the presence of mutual but unspoken lust. Will they or won t they? They won t until the writers run out of ideas and/or long-term guest stars to play the fated couple s temporary love interests. And then viewers all stop caring. Call it The *Moonlighting* Effect. *Ed* had Ed and Carol (Tom Cavanagh and Julie Bowen) dancing around each other for the better part of three seasons until they both finally just gave in to their throbbing biological urges; shortly thereafter, the show died a swift death. *Northern Exposure* only limped along for a handful of episodes past the long-awaited consummation by Joel and Maggie (Rob Morrow and Janine Turner) of their smoldering mutual dislike. Coy will they or won t they? shows of the future, take a lesson: If the resolution of sexual tension is going to pay off for your series, it needs to happen almost immediately (*NewsRadio*, *Cheers*), happen in one episode and then never get mentioned again (*Seinfeld*), or involve two people who are hot and are totally doing it in real life (*Alias*). See also *ALIAS*; BABY, RUINATION OF SHOW BY ADDING; *CHEERS*; *ED*; *NORTHERN EXPOSURE*; and *SEINFELD*.

"SHA LA LA LA!" What would we dooooooo, baby, without us? Well, apparently, the answer to the musical question that kicked off each episode of *Family Ties* is that we would Sha la la la! And it wasn t just an ad lib, either the male and female singers who duet on the show s theme song sha la la la in harmony. It was part of the song. Why? We don t know. But it s so sappily perfect, somehow. (It also works in real life when you want to take the piss out of someone who s just finished saying something drippy or twee.) See also *FAMILY TIES* and THEME SONGS.

SHA NA NA The 50s nostalgia got a little out of hand in the 70s *Happy Days*, *Laverne & Shirley* but it finally crossed the line with *Sha Na Na*, a half-hour doo-wop variety show (hey, don t look at us). Nobody we know remembers the show fondly, or even remembers watching it, but everyone remembers the distinctive black-sleeveless-shirted Bowzer, given to flexing his biceps at every opportunity and blessed with 1) an elastic *basso profundo,* and 2) a schnozz to rival that of Michael Christopher Moltisanti Imperioli. That dude kind of freaked us out. See also CHRISTOPHER MOLTISANTI.

SHATNER, WILLIAM The man. The myth. The ham that ate Pittsburgh. Yes, we mean The Shat, inaugural captain of the *Star Trek* franchise and famously weird enunciator (what s . . . with . . . the dramatic . . . pausesandthenwordsallruntogether?). Clearly intended as some sort of paragon of masculinity, Shatner s Captain Kirk always got the girl (or the fembot) even though Shatner sported a girdle

and a toupee; Kirk also won most fist-fights handily, despite employing stunt-punching that a fourth-grade talent show would consider amateurish. He always gives his all, whether it s on *T.J. Hooker* or in the *Airplane* sequel, and he s more than willing to bust on himself, like on

those Priceline commercials. We were glad to see him get an unironic lead role on *Boston Legal*; we couldn t think of a better guy to pass all the way through so bad he s good and back around to good again. See also AGING OF MEN ON TV, UNGRACEFUL; SCENERY, CHEWERS OF; SHATNER, WILLIAM, LEGENDARILY AWESOME *SATURDAY NIGHT LIVE* APPEARANCE OF; and *STAR TREK* FRANCHISE.

SHATNER, WILLIAM, LEGENDARILY AWESOME *SATURDAY NIGHT LIVE* APPEARANCE OF On a 1986 episode of *SNL* hosted by Shatner, he played himself in a skit about a *Star Trek* convention and, after a string of questions about *Trek* trivia so obscure that he can t answer any of them, Shatner finally freaks and bellows at the conventioneers to GET A LIFE!, wonders if Jon Lovitz s character (wearing Spock ears) has ever kissed a girl, yells IT S JUST A TV SHOW!, and storms away from the podium. The

Trekkies are horrified, but the emcee forces Shatner to go back to the mic and claim that his outburst wasn t real, but rather a recreation of an episode in which Kirk turned evil. The Trekkies buy it, Shatner is allowed to collect his appearance fee, and everyone s happy, especially the audience at home. And it s a brilliant sketch: It nailed the almost autistic behavior of certain Trekkies (or Trekkers, or whatever we re supposed to call them), and unlike 90 percent of *SNL* sketches, it didn t drag on too long. See also *SATURDAY NIGHT LIVE*; SHATNER, WILLIAM; and *STAR TREK* FRANCHISE.

SHOWBIZ MOMS & DADS. See *[X] MOMS & DADS*.

SHOW KILLERS   Every season, a few show killers get cast again by networks thinking they re going to get lucky, but luck is not a factor when it comes to these remorseless serial killers. (Get it? Serial ? They kill TV series!) We re talking about people like Rena Sofer, who parachuted into *Melrose Place* and *Just Shoot Me!* to reinvigorate them; she didn t, and they both tanked, as did the American version of *Coupling*, of which she was the biggest star. (Which is sad.) Steven Eckholdt has done in a whole pile of shows including, but not limited to, *My Big Fat Greek Life*; *The Monroes*; *It's Like, You Know* . . . but perhaps his greatest feat as

a show killer is to have fatally bludgeoned *Grapevine* not once but twice. (It s a long story.) Breckin Meyer, Danny Nucci, Lenny Clarke, Christine Baranski, Tiffani Thiessen, Ron Silver all have the corpses of former TV series bricked up in their basements. It s not that they re bad actors, or even unlikable ones; they just, for some reason, can t keep shows on the air. However, it is possible for an actor to break a bad streak: Jennifer Garner had two victims on her hands (*Significant Others* and *Time of Your Life*) when she landed on *Alias*; Jason Bateman was a five-time loser when he got *Arrested Development*; and while *Veronica Mars* fans collectively held their breath at the guest-starring arc of one Paula Marshall (late of *Hidden Hills*, *Snoops*, *Cupid*, *Chicago Sons*, *Wild Oats*, and, hilariously, *Cursed*), she failed to work her bad juju, and the show lived to fight another season. See also BATEMANS, JASON AND JUSTINE and GARNER, JENNIFER.

SHUE, ANDREW   It s one thing if a soap opera actor doesn t exactly bring the great Olivier to mind. If, however, said actor *also* looks like a cleaner-shaven *Homo habilis*, you have to wonder if a career change isn t in order. The actor in question is, of course, beady-eyed *Melrose Place* star Andrew Shue. Wooden does not really begin to describe the thespian stylings of Billllleeeeeeee, whose signature facial expression his Blue Steel, if you will was a dopey, open-mouthed duhhhh, which way did he go George affair. And yet, the show asked us to believe that the women of *Melrose* would fight over this doltish tree stump nay, that Alison would mourn his loss by spooning with a quart of vodka every night. When Shue finally bailed on acting in favor of founding a charity organization, Do Something, and pursuing a soccer career, we all breathed a sigh of relief. We hear he s a nice guy and all, but . . . so is Jimmy Carter, and that dude s not going to get it on with Amanda Woodward either. See also ACTING, WOODEN; AMANDA WOODWARD ; and *MELROSE PLACE*.

SIDEBURNS, IMPORTANT TV Luke Perry and Jason Priestley brought sideburns back to facial and cultural prominence in the early 90s, and the sideburn became commonplace once again. But before the dark time the overly clean-shaven 80 s T V actors regularly sported Hell s-Angel-icious pairs of chops, including but not limited to: Doc Baker on *Little House on the Prairie*; Leonard Nimoy s thematically pointy burns on *Star Trek*; Greg Brady s Johnny Bravo jobs; several cast members of *Welcome Back, Kotter*, although the fros often dwarfed the burns; long-suffering *Jeffersons* neighbor Bentley (not to mention long-suffering *Jeffersons* son Lionel); *The Carol Burnett Show* s Lyle Waggoner; Elvis in his 1968 comeback special; and the king of all TV burns, Monkee Mike Nesmith, whose gigantic caterpillars suggested that Neil Young had been shot out of a cannon onto his face. The sideburn is an extremely helpful tool for determining which era a randomly watched rerun falls into. Sideburns, we salute you. See also AFROS, IMPORTANT TV; *BEVERLY HILLS 90210*; *CAROL BURNETT SHOW, THE*; JOHNNY BRAVO ; *LITTLE HOUSE ON THE PRAIRIE*; *MONKEES, THE*; MUSTACHES, GREAT TV; *STAR TREK* FRANCHISE; and *WELCOME BACK, KOTTER*.

SILVER SPOONS Everyone loved this show, back in the day, and we re sorry, but: barf. Ricky Stratton comes to live with his super-rich arrested-development-case dad; treacly father-son bonding and pubescent wish-fulfillment ensue (the dad has a life-size train set running through the mansion, just for starters). Everything about the show is earnest, sticky, and annoying: the leather-lunged theme song, with its promises of tuh-geh-THERRRRR, taking the time each daaaaaaaaay! ; the myriad tight close-ups of squee-magnet Rick(y) Schroder, in all of which he s clearly wearing mascara; the rash-inducing sub-plots involving the dad s love life with pointy-faced Kate (Erin Gray); Ricky s little sidekick, Alfonso (Alfonso Ribeiro), who then went on to play Will Smith s little sidekick on *The Fresh Prince of Bel-Air*; the Michael Jackson outfits; the hyperactive awwww -ing from the audience; and Joel Higgins wearing that stupid engineer hat while driving that stupid train. Indoors. And did we mention the Michael Jackson outfits? Plural? Ah, yes, it seems we did. The show aimed for cute but took a wrong turn at causes cavities, and Schroder did okay with the material, but when he hit puberty, the wheels fell off with a clatter. See also CANNED LAUGHTER, MANIPULATION BY/OF; CHILDREN, OVERLY PRECOCIOUS; SCHRODER, RICK(Y); and THEME SONGS.

SIMMONS, RICHARD   A formerly obese gentleman who worked for a time, in his childhood, selling pralines on the streets of New Orleans, Richard Simmons lost the weight (after, he says, receiving an anonymous note reading Fat people die young. Please don t die) and made it his life s work to help other obese people do the same. Apparently, he felt that the best way to accomplish this was through the sale of videos of extremely low-impact aerobics routines (given a title destined to be ridiculed for eternity: *Sweatin' to the Oldies*) and a diet system called Deal-a-Meal. He also spread the gospel by means of his self-mocking appearances on talk shows: You may recall a string of appearances he made on *Letterman*, until Letter-

man sprayed him with a fire extinguisher. Simmons is also a former daytime talk show host (*The Richard Simmons Show* somehow ran for four years in the 80s, and *DreamMaker* made it one season in 1999). While we may find him grating and queeny, apparently he really does help people, so good for him. But . . . honestly, Rick: pants. Do it for the children. See also CHIA PET; HOMOSEXUALITY, CODED; INFOMERCIALS; and TALK SHOWS, DAYTIME.

SIMON & SIMON   It s standard opposites attract, wah wah fare: Two brothers one who knows about English tailoring and wines (A.J., the blond one) and one who wears cowboy hats and says tarnation a lot (Rick, the Gerald McRaney one) form a private detective agency together. A.J. has to ride in Rick s nonclassy truck! Rick has to go to A.J. s favorite fancy restaurant and eat snails! Har dee har har! Overall, merely inoffensive, although the show s insistence that Rick is a chick magnet is a little confusing. The show s twangy theme song, on the other hand, is an all-time great. See also THEME SONGS.

SIMPSONS, ASHLEEEEE AND JESSICA   It s bad enough that Jessica Simpson has gotten, and stayed, famous merely by being a stupid bimbo. Ashleeeee is famous for being the *sister of* a stupid bimbo, and we don t think Jessica is hot, but we can at least kind of see how other people might. Ashleeeee . . . gosh, no. She s got a beaky nose and a hair colorist who clearly hates her guts (good show, hair colorist!). We don t think Jessica is a good singer; we know for a fact Ashleeeee isn t. She s not a singer at all, suffering as she does from the acid reflux that notoriously interrupted her lip-synched performance on *Saturday Night Live* which is probably fortunate. And she s not an actress, either; do you know how shittily you have to read your lines to rate as *7th Heaven* s worst actor? Neither of the Simpsters has a single thing to offer except to drag the average IQ of *US Weekly* cover subjects down into the *pi* range, and we want them both to go away, forever. But it s like they ve created a perfect sibling storm of unwarranted renown that will inevitably drown us all. See also ACTING, WOODEN; *NEWLYWEDS*; *SATURDAY NIGHT LIVE*; *7TH HEAVEN*; and UNIVERSALLY REVILED CHARACTERS.

SIMPSONS, THE   Because it s been in its death throes for so long, it s easy to forget what a great show *The Simpsons* used to be. Skip its spotty first season when it s on in syndication (or when you re making DVD-buying decisions): The layout of the family home and Homer s voice (Dan Castellaneta) are disorientingly different, plus the episodes move veeery sloooowly. But midway through Season 2, the show finds its footing. It gets more satirical, using the medium of the family sitcom to parody the form, and much quicker, getting off more gags and punchlines per minute than any other show on TV. The show is just . . . good. It s written by people who are literate and smart and who have broad-ranging sources of inspiration, from social hygiene films (Fuzzy Bunny s Guide to You-Know-What) to overly vigilant social workers (But stupid babies need the most love!) to government (This isn t like burying toxic waste. People are going to notice those trees are gone). Its influence is seen not just in its countless imitators but in live-action shows like *Scrubs*, where humor of brows both high and low is crammed into every second of every episode. The bottom line is this: Any fictional family that can so efficiently piss off both George H. W. Bush *and* Bill Cosby must be doing something right. See also CHILDREN, OVERLY PRECOCIOUS; DADS, TV; FAT GUY/SKINNY WIFE MARRIAGES; GUEST STARS, FREQUENT/FAMOUS; and *SIMPSONS, THE*, FAILED CLONES OF.

SIMPSONS, THE, FAILED CLONES OF   Some would argue that *The Simpsons* is itself a nonfailed clone of *The Flintstones*. But that was already a clone of *The Honeymooners*, and both those shows are way old. *The Simpsons* inspired several rip-offs. There were series like *Fish Police* and *Capitol Critters*, which weren t family sitcoms, weren t funny, and tried to build their audiences by mere dint of being cartoons airing in primetime. Neither lasted long. *Dinosaurs* fared somewhat better (though survived long enough to get mocked on *The Simpsons*): It used live-action Muppet-suit . . . things in the form of dinosaurs boorish dad, sensible mom, son, daughter, and baby, in that order. Cynical! Also, it sucked. The longest-running and most blatant *Simpsons* rip-off remains *Family Guy*, which some people like, and since creator Seth McFarlane went on to offer the world *American Dad* a cynical rip-off of *Family Guy* in a roundabout way, *The Simpsons* is partly responsible for that, too. See also *FRIENDS*, FAILED CLONES OF and *SIMPSONS, THE*.

SITCOM, MOVIE ACTRESSES' ATTEMPTS TO PROP SAGGING CAREER BY MEANS OF Once it worked for Candice Bergen, everyone thought they could do it develop a custom sitcom vehicle, make it a hit, and chill out enjoying the family-friendly hours of a multicamera sitcom. The only trouble for the movie actresses who would revitalize their careers this way is that step 2 can t just be willed into fruition, so that step 3 rarely lasts very long before the actress must slink back to making the movies she was trying to

avoid in the first place. Bette Midler (*Bette*), Alicia Silverstone (*Miss Match*), Molly Ringwald (*Townies*), Joan Cusack (*What About Joan*), Teri Polo (*I'm with Her*), Whoopi Goldberg (*Whoopi*) n i c e try, y all, but try again with shows that aren t moronic or boring. See also MOVIES-TO-TV/TV-TO-MOVIES CAREER PIPELINE/ARC.

SITCOMS, ANIMATED OPENING CREDITS SEQUENCES OF We re convinced that the cutely animated opening credits sequences of shows such as *I Dream of Jeannie* and *Bewitched* were expressly designed that way in order to seduce kids into watching shows they think are going to end up being cartoons. Truly, there is no other way to explain the fact that *The Nanny* lasted six seasons. None. See also *BEWITCHED*; *I DREAM OF JEANNIE*; and OPENING CREDITS, STYLES OF.

SITCOMS, FISH-OUT-OF-WATER A lovable character in an unfamiliar setting? What could be more hilarious?! The fish out of water is a tried-and-true sitcom premise, going all the way back to *Green Acres*, *The Beverly Hillbillies*, and *My Favorite Martian*. Taking your protagonist out of his comfort zone leads to all sorts of comic situations. On *The Fresh Prince of Bel-Air*, there was all the (alleged) humor of putting Philly-bred Will Smith in a house with a butler to show how he clashed with his surroundings. The same thing happened with Mypiot Balki in Chicago on *Perfect Strangers*, Orkan Mork on *Mork & Mindy*, and Flushingite Joel on *Northern Exposure*. They mess up idioms, they put their clothes on backward, they ruffle bush pilots feathers when they mistake them for prostitutes . . . and so on. People have a hard time adapting. Add laugh track and stir. See also *MORK & MINDY*; *NORTHERN EXPOSURE*; and *PERFECT STRANGERS*.

SITCOMS, LAVISH SERIES FINALES OF Every show ends eventually. It s a fact of TV life. Now, granted, not every show ends on its own terms or when it intends to that s a privilege extended only to successful shows that pack it in when the show s producers and stars are sick of it. But you d think that the mere fact of escaping cancellation was a feat on par with winning a presidential election, judging by the number of promos, the amount of airtime, and the tearful postshow interviews devoted to sitcoms when they finally end. We blame *Cheers*, which wrapped up its final season in 1993, for establishing the new standard for how a sitcom goes off the air. First, there s a retrospective/behind-the-scenes/clip show; then, there s the final episode, which must be at least an hour long; and then, the whole cast goes on the network s late-night show to drink champagne toasts to their apparently miraculous achievement. In the case of *Cheers*, *The Tonight Show* aired live from the original Cheers bar in Boston. We don t give *Everybody Loves Raymond* credit for much, but the show s producers said upfront that the show s 2005 season finale would be a regular old episode nobody dying or moving away or projected twenty years into the future, and a half-hour long and they stuck to it. Of course, if we d worked with Patricia Heaton for nine years, we d be in a hurry to get away from her, too. See also *CHEERS*.

SITCOMS, UNFUNNINESS OF SEMINAL There s an episode of *Seinfeld* in which Jerry tells one of his many paramours that he s never watched *I Love Lucy*, and she s scandalized and shocked, but guess what? Neither have we, and here s why: If it s in black and white, it s not funny. Black-and-  white dramas from yesteryear can still entertain us your *12 Angry Men*, your *Freaks*. But humor just doesn t age well particularly not humor from the 50s. Never mind all the Bang, zoom to the moon! business on *The Honeymooners*; maybe the implication of domestic abuse would rankle more if it wasn t so cartoonish. But Lucy s attempts at social climbing, Ralph Kramden s many schemes, and Jethro Bodine s borderline retardation are just so witless that now, when we could watch any number of still crappy yet superior sitcoms in syndication or read a book, or go outside, or fall into a coma instead, we just . . . can t. Shut up, slapstick. See also BALL, LUCILLE; MARSHALL, GARRY; and *SEINFELD*.

SITCOM, WORST EVER   See *OUT OF THIS WORLD*.

SIX FEET UNDER   See BRENDA CHENOWITH ; FACINELLI, PETER THE FATCH ; MARIJUANA, CLICH S ASSOCIATED WITH; PREGNANCIES, CLICH S ASSOCIATED WITH; RUTH FISHER ; and WILSON, RAINN.

SKETCH COMEDY ENSEMBLES, FORGOTTEN MEMBERS OF   *Saturday Night Live* has been on since Christ was in short pants, and in that time it has wrung dry approximately eight hundred billion performers of varying degrees of talent and attractiveness. Therefore, most of us have, at our fingertips, the names of a few former cast members who never amounted to anything (Terry Sweeney! Beth Cahill! Gary Kroeger! Danitra Vance!), as well as a few damn, *he* did *SNL*? s (Robert Downey Jr.! Damon Wayans! Ben Stiller! Randy Quaid!). However, smaller sketch-comedy troupes can also include members

no one remembers once their shows go off the air. Terry Jones the screechiest soprano in drag, as well as the Welshiest, among the Monty Python crew is often forgotten as a Python alumnus because he opted for a career as a film director and (seriously) medievalist scholar. And Bruce McCulloch, having failed to follow his fellow Kids in the Hall to fame as a frequent sitcom guest star (like Kevin McDonald), in a brief career on *SNL* (like Mark McKinney), as a bawdy talk-show raconteur (like Scott Thompson), or onto the brilliant *NewsRadio* (Dave Foley), was, as of this writing, last seen directing Tom Green in *Stealing Harvard*. Poor little fella. See also *BEN STILLER SHOW, THE*; *KIDS IN THE HALL, THE*; *MONTY PYTHON'S FLYING CIRCUS*; and *SATURDAY NIGHT LIVE*.

"SKINEMAX"   Cinemax has traditionally filled its late-night schedule with action Z-movies starring Shannon Tweed (read: soft-core porn with a couple of gunfights and some crappy dialogue thrown in). Sure, Showtime had the equally transparent *Red Shoe Diaries*, but if underage boys in the pre-Internet era wanted to see a naked boob, Skinemax was their best bet. See also NUDITY.

"SLIM GOODBODY"   It s a little hard to focus on messages about healthy eating and proper exercise when the messenger is 1) hopping around like the spaz-tastic love child of Richard Simmons and that pinko from the Dr Pepper commercials, and 2) clad in an obscenely tight unitard showing all the body s anatomical structures . . . and we don t just mean the arteries. We mean . . . *structures*. Of the . . . *male* anatomy. Visible . . . uh, *through* the unitard. [*Sigh*] Fine: As kids, we called him Slim Goodboner. It s the same reason we can t watch ballet, and we re not proud of it, but it is what it is. See also PSAs and SIMMONS, RICHARD.

SMALL TOWNS, HIDDEN DEPRAVITY OF
When small towns aren t busy being adorably quirky and cute, they are presenting a placid, conventional front to disguise the roiling corruption beneath the surface. Don t believe it? Watch any true-crime show on A&E. Bill Kurtis is going to kick off the episode by narrating over some B-roll of Buttville, Idaho, where people didn t even lock their front doors that is, until the Buttville Strangler started his reign of terror! (We re paraphrasing.) From *Glory Days* to *Murder, She Wrote*, people are all getting their asses killed outside regions of high population density. And it turns out that fleeing the scary big city can t save honest folks from supernatural horrors, like demons

(*Buffy the Vampire Slayer*, *Point Pleasant*), werewolves (*Wolf Lake*), aliens (*Roswell*), and kryptofreaks (*Smallville*). Small-town kids are also liable to fall in love with their long-lost half-sisters, or what they think are guys but turn out to be cross-dressing girls (*Young Americans*). And don t think the suburbs are any safer; half the time, they re populated by the murderers of junkies and busybodies (*Desperate Housewives*), extremely draconian neighborhood committees (*The X-Files*), Russian spies trying to pass as Americans (*Alias*), or high-class soccer-mom hookers (*Law & Order* Felicity Huffman played one of the part-time whores!). Some people will really put up with a lot just to have a back yard. See also *ALIAS*; *BUFFY THE VAMPIRE SLAYER*; *DESPERATE HOUSEWIVES*; *LAW & ORDER* FRANCHISE; *MURDER, SHE WROTE*; TRUE CRIME SHOWS; and *X-FILES, THE*.

SMALL TOWNS, QUIRKINESS OF Perhaps because they re all forced to live in the decidedly charmless, unquirky metropolis of Los Angeles, TV writers sure do love to romanticize small-town life. There s some cursory effort taken to dramatize what a drag it can be when your options for dating are limited to the three eligible men, and how every person you pass on the sidewalk has already heard all your business before you have a chance to tell your best friend, but that s the downside. As a TV character living in a small town, you can expect to participate in town events ranging from dance-a-thons to snowman-building contests (*Gilmore Girls*) to Founders Day parades (*Northern Exposure*). Though you may have arrived at your small town from somewhere bigger and less quirky, that just means you happen to be the norm that no one else in town conforms to. Even your neighbors legal concerns are adorably quaint, as they sue each other over such things as revealing the secrets of a birthday-party magician s illusions, or giving a bride-to-be a bad haircut (*Ed*). All together now: aaaaaaaaaaw! See also *ED*; *GILMORE GIRLS*; and *NORTHERN EXPOSURE*.

SMALL WONDER *Small Wonder* and *Out of This World* formed a set of who the hell greenlit this cow pie, Judy Garland?

 80s-sitcom book-ends: *OoTW* featured a half-alien, half-human heroine, while *SW* featured Vicki, a robot built by the dad and passed off as a human girl. Tiffany Brissette, who played Vicki, didn t work much after the show went off the air, and she shouldn t have, because sometimes she . . . didn t seem like she was acting like an automaton. Creepy. The show is also at least partially responsible for the career of one Brian Austin Green, which we cannot forgive. See also ACTING, WOODEN; BAD SITCOM, SURE SIGNS OF; *BEVERLY HILLS 90210*; and *OUT OF THIS WORLD*.

SMIGEL, ROBERT If you ve ever watched *Conan* and wondered whose lips they were plugging into the still photos of Bill Clinton, Bob Dole, and Saddam Hussein, wonder no more: They re Robert Smigel s. The brilliant and apparently very busy comic also performs as Triumph, the Insult Comic Dog, and creates cartoons for *SNL* (most famously The Ambiguously Gay Duo) and as if all of that wasn t enough to secure his place in TV history, he also wrote the awesome *SNL* skit in which William Shatner goes apeshit at a *Star Trek* convention. When it comes to TV writing, Robert Smigel is a national treasure. See also *SATURDAY NIGHT LIVE*; SHATNER, WILLIAM, LEGENDARILY AWESOME *SATURDAY NIGHT LIVE* APPEARANCE OF; TALK SHOWS, LATE-NIGHT; and TRIUMPH, THE INSULT COMIC DOG.

SMITS, JIMMY On paper, the dude doesn t have that much going for him. He s got a receding hairline; half the time he s on TV, he s rocking a mullet; and he even has a bit of a lisp. And yet, the total package? So sexy. Jimmy Smits is tall and gorgeous and has an amazing voice. He can make even the least palatable pursuits look right, from defending guilty clients to haunting his old partner from beyond the grave to . . . being on *The West Wing* beyond Season 3. Smit s Matt Santos played the Democratic successor to Martin Sheen s President Jed Bartlet, making the (fictional) world a better and much hotter place, God bless him. See also *L.A. LAW*; *NYPD BLUE*; and *WEST WING, THE*.

SMURFS, THE   For innocent woodland creatures who lived in little mushroom huts and went around topless, the Smurfs sure could put together a merchandising juggernaut Smurf board games, Smurf lunchboxes, Smurf sheets, Smurf cereal (Smurfberry Crunch), and the figurines that everyone collected. We still wanted Gargamel s cat Azrael to eat the lot of them if not for the theme song, which stuck in the brain like a burr in cashmere, then for their cutesy insistence on replacing random words with Smurf. Smurf yourself a grin ? What does that even *mean*? They really needed to knock it the Smurf off with that Smurf. Also: Snappy Smurf. Western culture produced an entity called Snappy Smurf. It s enough to make you want to Smurf yourself. See also THEME SONGS.

SOAP   Every time the networks offer up some weirdo sitcom idea like one built around a Civil War—era butler (*The Secret Diary of Desmond Pfeiffer*) we re sur-prised. But we shouldn t be, because *Soap* is kind of weirder than any of those. It was a hybrid of the sitcom and the daytime soap opera, focusing on two sisters Jessica Tate (Katherine Helmond) and Mary Campbell (Cathryn Damon) their many offspring, and the complicated events of their lives. Some of those were standard soap fare, like affairs, illegitimate children, and alien abductions. But *Soap* also threw us a few curveballs, like one of TV s first openly gay characters (Billy Crystal s Jodie), and a ventriloquist who never seemed to perform, but rather wandered around the house with his dummy. Which no one ever questioned, which is a little awesome. The show also originated Robert Guillaume s Benson, before he went on to his own successful spin-off which was all well and good, but we always loved the chemistry between Benson and Jessica, which Benson just did not have with Governor Gatling. See also *BENSON* and SPIN-OFFS.

SOAP OPERAS, CHARACTER NAMES ON   A soap opera will start out with mainstream character names, but if it stays on the air long enough, the names get really crazy, either because the character in question has gotten married, often to the same person, a thrillion times (viz. Erica Kane Martin Brent Cudahy Chandler Montgomery Montgomery Chandler Marick Marick Montgomery), or the writers have gone straight through the baby-names book and into the Jim Beam. Ridge and Thorne Forrester, Prunella Wither-spoon, Buzz Stryker, Strap Worthbillion, Boobsie Caswell, Brandy Sheloo, Quint McCord we could go on, but kooky soap names based on precious gems alone would take up an entire chapter. Note: One of the names in the list above is fake. And it is *not* Boobsie Caswell. See also SOAP OPERAS, DAYTIME.

SOAP OPERAS, DAYTIME It s easy to poke fun at soaps and at the people who watch them, but when you think about it, the soap opera is probably the most enter-prising medium in American culture. Soaps give you the audacious plots you just won t see in movies or on serious dramas. Soap-opera-ites wear way too much makeup, and it s creepy the way a just-born child will celebrate its third birthday two weeks later, get bundled off to boarding school a week after *that*, and return as a college freshman in time for the holidays. But if you want a Bulgarian prison break, a brain transplant, rapists and their victims getting married to one another, double agents able to disguise themselves with fakey scars, and/or a Gordian knot of step-relatives and exes all scheming at/with/near each other, don t look in primetime; set your TiVo to record a soap. And don t worry time only moves at hyperspeed for kids. For everyone else, a full day can take a week and a half to accomplish (by design, so new viewers can catch up). *The Bold and the Beautiful* debuted almost twenty years ago, and only about a month has passed. See also BOLD AND THE BEAUTIFUL, THE and CHILDREN, OVERLY PRECOCIOUS.

SOAP OPERAS, FAMOUS STORY ARCS OF Oh Mylanta, where to start the *General Hospital* Frisco and Felicia arc *alone* is a book. Possibly in two volumes. The most famous long-term soap plots involved a star-crossed couple or a nutty supervillain,  or both, and man-aged to fascinate and bug the crap out of the audience at the same time. A small cross-section of notorious story arcs might prove illustrative. Let s start with *General Hospital*, which drove us to distraction with the protracted Frisco/Felicia/WSB vs. DVX blathering, the Luke-and-Laura debacle in which he raped her on the dance floor and then they fell in love, blah blah blah, like, we re so sure, and also, we re . . . offended, frankly. *One Life to Live* s Viki Buchanan/Niki Smith split-personality storyline tortured us for *years*; it was ridiculous, and yet we couldn t stop watching the show even when Viki s husband Clint time-traveled to the Old West. (Yeah, you heard us.)

Then there's that stupid Danny Romalotti storyline on *The Young and the Restless*. "Which one?" Exactly. Elsewhere, we barely survived the Patch/Kayla relationship on *Days of Our Lives*, because we felt very strongly that Patch could do better than Kayla. Think you won't get sucked into a daytime serial-killer arc because it's "so dumb"? Think again. See also SOAP OPERAS, DAYTIME.

SOLID GOLD We watched to see the *Solid Gold* top ten, and to see the bands, but especially to gaze upon late great cohost and troubled hottie Andy Gibb. Did you feel so embarrassed for the Solid Gold Dancers and their leotard/braided headband combos that you spent those segments in the kitchen, getting more ice cream? Yeah . . . it wasn't just you. See also GIBB, ANDY.

THE SONNY & CHER SHOW As kids, we thought divorced couples were required to hate each other, so we couldn't figure out how Sonny and Cher could still work together—but then, we didn't watch for the banter. We watched for Cher, whom we longed to befriend because she seemed like the kind of grown-up who wouldn't talk to us like we were babies, and because she had excellent superlong hair and was extremely sparkly. We know it's dumb, but we were, like, four years old, okay? (Call us, Cher!)

SOPRANOS, THE See "CHRISTOPHER MOLTISANTI."

SORKIN, AARON In most industries, getting busted for climbing onto a plane with enough drugs to take down the 2005 Pacers could lose you your job. Fortunately, Aaron Sorkin is in television. The successful playwright and feature-film screenwriter (*Malice, A Few Good Men*) got a taste for palace intrigue, White House–style, with *The American President*, and so he developed the similarly themed *West Wing*, recycling many of the same stars and scores of the same fictional surnames. The famously controlling helmer also wrote most episodes of the show's first few seasons, before either leaving or getting canned, possibly for losing his mind and writing increasingly jingoistic stories post–September 11 (especially the infamous "Isaac and Ishmael," cobbled together in haste in the hours after the attacks . . . and therefore almost certainly *too soon*). Sorkin is also responsible for the much better *Sports Night*, which assembled many of the all-stars of the Sorkinverse, including Felicity Huffman and Joshua Malina. Sorkin has cameoed in several of his projects, always as "Man in Bar." Which we're sure has nothing to do with his personal problems and is just a crazy coincidence. See also HUFFMAN, FELICITY; *SPORTS NIGHT*; and *WEST WING, THE*.

"SOULMATE" A dictionary will tell you it's "one of two persons compatible with each other in disposition, point of view, or sensitivity." However, a *Dawson's Creek* viewer will tell you it's an opposite-sex friend in whom you have no actual sexual interest, yet with whom you are creepily codependent. The show's putative "soulmate" pair were the titular Dawson Leery (James Van Der Beek) and his childhood friend Joey Potter (Katie Holmes). At first, their mutual avowals of soulmatehood constituted denials that they were romantically inclined toward each other, but of course they ended up together at the end of the show's first season. This only kicked off their endless coupling and uncoupling, to the point where one who had only heard the term while watching The WB could be forgiven for thinking that "soulmate" means "person you hook up with when you run out of other prospects." Eventually, the soulmates Joey and Dawson reverted to their original platonic status: Joey ended the series partnered with Pacey Witter (Joshua Jackson), and Dawson ended up alone, proving that cosmic justice is sometimes served, if only fictionally. See also "DAWSON LEERY"; *DAWSON'S CREEK*; LOVE TRIANGLES; and "PACEY WITTER."

SOUND, PHYSICAL PROPERTIES OF You know that old philosophical question about what happens if a tree falls in the forest and there's no one there to hear it? It also works if a tree falls three feet away from a TV character. Only on TV can you have a heated and not especially quiet conversation within arm's length of someone you don't want to overhear it, and do so in complete privacy. How many times did Monica and Rachel argue in the kitchen while guests waited in the living room, on the other side of *no wall*? This principle also applies if you're, say, having a screaming fight in the middle of Nate's birthday party in the hall outside your bathroom, and no one in your tiny bungalow can hear a thing even if there's no music playing. However, when it's convenient to the plot, TV characters can develop superhuman hearing; this is useful to the Camdens, since eavesdropping is their primary mode of receiving information. See also "BRENDA CHENOWITH"; *FRIENDS*; and *7TH HEAVEN*.

SOUTH PARK The profane adventures of four poorly animated Colorado kids and the weirdos who live around them, *South Park* remains one of the best things Comedy Central has ever done. The show's creators have said that the show is meant to counteract all the crap that's taken hold in the popular imagination over the past decade or so—that children live in a Rousseau-ian state of unspoiled innocence until growing up in the world of adults corrupts them. On *South Park*, kids are venal, amoral, opportunistic, and shortsighted—just like kids are in real life. Fortunately, it's very entertaining to watch people living in a consequence-free environment, because it means they do things like hire the local crack whore to give their parents herpes or steal a prehistoric iceman for their own personal gain. In later seasons, the show has become more directly satirical; its apparently extremely short turnaround time allows for whole episodes about such events as the capture of Saddam Hussein or the congressional fight over Terri Schiavo just days after they air on the news. The show is still best when it focuses on Stan, Kyle, Cartman, and Kenny, but we make an exception for "Krazy Kripples," in which local differently abled kids Timmy and Jimmy join the Crips, and Christopher Reeve sucks stem cells out of aborted fetuses. Which you can't say has happened on many other sitcoms, with the possible exception of *Small Wonder*. See also "ERIC CARTMAN"; "MR. HANKEY"; PHYSICALLY CHALLENGED PERSON/CHARACTER, CLICHÉS ASSOCIATED WITH; and *SMALL WONDER*.

SPADER, JAMES Maybe Spader got sick of doing crap movies like *Dream Lover*. Don't get us wrong, that movie is brrrrrilliant, but it probably doesn't cut it for a guy with a Soderbergh movie on his résumé. Spader's first two forays into TV,

blended-family drama *The Family Tree* and the ill-advised TV version of *Diner*, bombed thoroughly, so maybe he thought the third TV show *The Practice* would be the charm. But who cares *why* our favorite shifty-eyed '80s vil-

lain came to the small screen? We're just glad he did, because we love him, and we hope *Boston Legal* is just the beginning. See also MOVIES-TO-TV/TV-TO-MOVIES CAREER PIPELINE/ARC and *PRACTICE, THE*.

SPELLING, AARON For more than forty years, Aaron Spelling has served up a groaning buffet of empty but deeeelicious TV calories, giving American audiences what we apparently hungered for: catfights, nipples, backstabbing intrigue, and shows about nurses who live together and do aerobics in teeny outfits. (Okay, he only did two shows like that, but . . . that's two more than anyone else did.) *Charlie's Angels*, *The Mod Squad*, *Starsky and Hutch*, *Vega$*, *Hotel*, the *90210/Melrose/Models Inc.* troika, *Charmed*—it seems like Spelling's name is on every "name" show produced since the Carter administration, and for every floppy *Queens Supreme* or *Titans*, he's got a hit like *Hart to Hart* or *7th Heaven*. None of his shows qualifies as lofty entertainment, but Spelling's never positioned himself as an Aaron Sorkin or a David Chase, and his most roundly panned production isn't even a show—it's his daughter, Tori, whose mediocre acting and diploma from the Louis Braille School of Plastic Surgery serve as a warning to us all on the dangers of nepotism. See also *BEVERLY HILLS 90210*; *DYNASTY*; *MELROSE PLACE*; *MODELS INC.*; OVERHYPED SERIES THAT BOMBED; SORKIN, AARON; SPELLING, RANDY; and SPELLING, TORI.

SPELLING, RANDY   Aaron Spelling wants his children to succeed, so arranging parts for them on the TV shows he produces is perfectly understandable. *In theory*. In practice, dressing a half-boy, half-frog creature with no discernible acting ability in an oversized polo shirt and sticky Gordon Gekko wig and then casting it as one of Steve Sanders's horndoggily clueless stepbrothers on *Beverly Hills 90210* is just not a wise idea. But that's exactly what happened when Randy Spelling "originated" the role of Ryan Sanders, and while we salute the crafty put-the-bridesmaids-in-ugly-dresses maneuvering that accompanied the move—namely Travis "The Twitch" Wester doing an Eddie Munster homage as other stepbrother Austin—it didn't change the fact that young Randy is *at best* a profoundly average-looking man with a tin ear for line readings. He's still

working, primarily in the deeply compromised *National Lampoon* franchise, which has effectively quarantined him from us, because we wouldn't go to see those stinkers if you paid us. See also ACTING, WOODEN; *BEVERLY HILLS 90210*; SPELLING, AARON; and SPELLING, TORI.

SPELLING, TORI   Next to "nepotism" in the dictionary, you'll find one of those little woodcut illustrations of Tori Spelling . . . although, for a few years there, the publishers kept having to replace the woodcut because Tori kept changing her look. And by "changing her look," we mean "going under the knife." Tori did have a moment there, during the *90210* gang's freshman year, when she kind of had it together appearance-wise. She figured out how to give herself a hot oil, she rocked the supercute space-dyed tops and the little braids . . . she looked good. Then it all went to hell: the offstage hell-raising and Savalas-offspring-dating; the appalling helmet-flip of over-processed blonde hair; the cavernous, keyhole-shaped intra-breast gap; the constant fluffing of her character, Donna Martin, and Donna's fashion-design genius (never made evident to the home audience); the extracurricular appearances in risible TV movies like *Co-Ed Call Girl*, which asked viewers to believe that a girl who looked like a manorexic drag version of Mamie Van Doren and couldn't color inside the lines with her lipstick could cut it as a high-class escort. We must admit that Tori redeemed herself somewhat in later years with roles in *Scream 2* and *The House of Yes*, but she's still got a ways to go. See also BEVERLY HILLS 90210; MOVIES, MADE-FOR-TV; SPELLING, AARON; and SPELLING, RANDY.

SPIN-OFFS We may think of spin-offs—in which a character from one show is transplanted to a new setting and, the network hopes, to new adventures that will keep us *riveted!*—as the relic of a bygone age: *The Mary Tyler Moore Show* begat *Rhoda*, *Lou Grant*, uh . . . didn't Cloris Leachman's character get her own sitcom for a while? Or else you pluck a few character cells from *Dallas* and stick them in a new petri dish—voilà, *Knots Landing*. But spin-offs are still very much with us: Joey moved from New York to Los Angeles, Frasier from Boston to Seattle, Sarah from San Francisco to . . . we don't care, and shut up, Jennifer Love Hewitt. A popular technique for launching a spin-off is to artificially introduce a character into an existing show, so that we're interested in his backstory; then the network conveniently has a whole other series waiting for viewers to check out. This worked well when Jake Hanson (Grant Show) handymanned for Kelly Taylor (Jennie Garth) on *90210,* staying just long enough to make out with her before

repairing to *Melrose Place*. *MP* then turned around and tried to pull the same trick with *Models Inc.*, with less fortunate results. We're now in the era where even reality shows can be spun off: *American Idol* made *American Juniors* possible; *The Real World* and *Road Rules* copulated and delivered the hideous, misshapen love child we call *The Real World/Road Rules Challenge*; and *The Osbournes* was spun off from an episode of *Cribs*. We just wonder how creatively bankrupt a TV producer has to be before he pitches a spin-off for *Designing Women* (in which Delta Burke's Suzanne is a member of Congress) or *Golden Girls* (in which everyone but Bea Arthur's Dorothy is running a hotel and Don Cheadle works there, randomly). And how desperate a network has to be to make those lame-ass ideas into shows they actually think people will watch. See also AMERICAN IDOL; BEVERLY HILLS 90210; BUFFY THE VAMPIRE SLAYER; CSI, SPIN-OFFS OF; CHEERS; DALLAS; DESIGNING WOMEN; FRIENDS; GOLDEN GIRLS, THE; LAW & ORDER FRANCHISE; MELROSE PLACE; MODELS INC.; OSBOURNES, THE; PARTY OF FIVE; REAL WORLD, THE; and REAL WORLD/ROAD RULES CHALLENGE, THE.

SPORTSCASTERS, MOST ANNOYING Which sportscasters you find most irritating depends on which sports you regularly follow on TV. Basketball's got the catchphrase-laden, overcaffeinated bellowing of Dick Vitale; tennis fans cringe when they see a let, because that's Bud Collins's cue to bite off an officious "nnnnet-*CORD*!" And baseball, forget it. We genuinely can't decide who's worse: Joe Morgan, who refuses to accept sabermetrics even though it's been an established part of baseball stat analysis for a decade, and who gets offended at the drop of a hat; or Tim McCarver, whose, er, "admiration for" Yankee shortstop Derek Jeter passed into restraining-order territory in the late '90s. We'll award Howard Cosell annoyance-emeritus status, because he did ask some really stupid questions and he used that weird hitchy Shatner inflection to do it, but that seems almost quaint now—and we'd take it over Jeanne Zelasko's "I'm doing an infomercial voice-over, in 120 mph winds" delivery. See also CATCHPHRASES, OVERUSED TV; ESPN; OLYMPICS COVERAGE; and SPORTS COVERAGE, FATUOUS.

SPORTS COVERAGE, FATUOUS It's safe to assume, at least in our minds, that a viewer who tunes into a televised sporting event actually has an *interest* in that sporting event and its outcome; said viewer does not click over to a football game or tennis match, fold her arms, and say to her television, "Impress me by filling every second of broadcast time with meaningless noise." Odd, then, that sports producers and broadcasters feel compelled to do exactly that, peppering the home audience with whooshy graphics (accompanied by swooshy and/or explode-y noises), meaningless stats (how many left-handed ground-stroke-specialist tennis players have birthdays in February), pester-views with celebs who are in the stands trying to watch the game, "chalk-talk," and dorky CGI characters like FOX's animated baseball, Scooter. All designed to keep us entertained, these ADHD-o-Vision extras just make us more likely to change the channel. Does the observation that "you know what beats good hitting, Jim, is good pitching" really need uttering aloud? See also SPORTSCASTERS, MOST ANNOYING.

SPORTS COVERAGE, HALLMARK-Y BACK-GROUND STORIES IN God forbid coverage of the Tour de France *not* mention that Lance Armstrong nearly died of nut cancer. Heaven forfend a speed-skating qualifying heat take place without a mention of poor Dan Jansen and how his sister died and he fell down a lot, then made a triumphant comeback six years later. And it's very sad how pitcher Jim Abbott was born without a right hand, but he pitched a no-hitter with his *left* hand, so we think he probably did okay for himself. We already like whatever sport it is we're watching, producers; you don't need to braid a heart-tugging tale of triumph over adversity into a redemption arc on the playing field. See also OLYMPICS COVERAGE and SPORTS COVERAGE, FATUOUS.

SPORTS COVERAGE, HORRIFYING CLOSE-UPS IN Randy Johnson is a great pitcher, one of the best who ever lived. We have nothing but respect for his accomplishments on the diamond. That doesn't mean that he's a pulchritudinous individual, however, or that we need a camera angle so tight on his face that we can see split ends in his *mustache*. Just because you *can* push in for a close-up on a bead of forehead sweat that shows the bacteria teeming within doesn't mean that you *should*.

SPORTS COVERAGE, SADLY INEPT USE OF "CHALKBOARD" "TECHNOLOGY" DURING What is the point? Because on the one hand, you've got the guys who use the electric "chalk" to draw, like, a tiny dot that explains exactly nothing, and on the other hand, you've got John Madden crazily Pollocking up a freeze-frame of the offensive line while he's also describing the action he's illustrating. So, we just saw the play, and he's . . . describing it. Again. Maybe we don't so much need the excessive Abstract Fratspressionism on the screen; replaying it in slo-mo and talking over it worked fine for decades, so let's just go back to that, shall we?

SPORTS NIGHT On the subject of Aaron Sorkin's career, most people agree: Whatever horrors *The West Wing* may be guilty of, the man deserves credit for *Sports Night*. And, fair enough. It was a good show. Back in 1998, when the show premiered, we hadn't yet tired of Sorkin's trademark David Mamet manqué dialogue. We also didn't know how much of the second season would be wasted on the self-referential business of CSC, the show's fictional cable network, running into severe financial problems and threatening cancelation of the sports news show—an utterly transparent reference to ABC's threats to cancel Sorkin's sitcom. The show ended after just two seasons, getting killed before it could spin out of control the way *The West Wing* did. We'll consider it euthanasia. See also SCHLAMME, TOMMY; SELF-REFERENCING BUSINESS, CLOYING; SORKIN, AARON; and *WEST WING, THE*.

STACK, ROBERT Stack played Eliot Ness on *The Untouchables*, which allowed him to lend a certain gravitas to his hosting duties on *Unsolved Mysteries*—and as much as we love that cheese platter of a show, it badly needed Stack's solemn intonations and official-looking trench coat to avoid drowning in Lake Campy. Stack got a little freckly and frail toward the end there, but he never once half-assed a line reading of "and she hasn't been seen since," and more important, we felt as if he didn't judge us for watching the show. See also *Unsolved Mysteries*.

Stamos, John   Aw, Blackie. One of the most famous Greek-Americans ever, John Stamos started out as a teen heartthrob/pop star on *General Hospital*, complete with a righteously fluffy mullet. He then trucked that mullet into primetime for *Full House*, on which he played Uncle Jesse. Uncle Jesse, like Stamos, liked singing middle-of-the-road wuss rock, wore tight pants, and was slightly too pretty for a man

. . . none of which is true anymore, thank God. Like many former pretty-boys, Stamos is betterlooking in his forties (!). Post–*Full House* as well as post-marriage to Rebecca Romijn, Stamos returned to the TV sitcom in *Jake in Progress*, a single-camera sitcom in which he portrays the man-slutty title character, a New York publicist whose job gives the show plenty of opportunities to air thinly veiled versions of real celebrity situations. We might sneer at Stamos for making *Jake* his comeback vehicle if we didn't know how much credit he deserved for having a sense of humor about himself. In the series finale of *Clone High*, the man played himself:

As a high-school rival of the show's Principal Scudworth, he selflessly sacrificed his own life to flash-freeze all the clones *and* the Board of Shadowy Figures, and that's after getting a Prom King crown in the eye. *STAMOS!* See also *Clone High* and *Full House*.

Stand-Up Spotlight   A short-lived comedy show that aired during VH1's "damn, we're showing way too many Amy Grant videos, aren't we" era. Rosie O'Donnell, already employing her trademark dying-seagull cackle and terrible hair (in this late '80s incarnation, a tootight perm cut into a mullet-y ziggurat), hosted—but good comedians such as Dave Attell and Margaret Cho made the show worth watching. The trick was to ride the mute button so as to avoid Rosie's shticky interstitial segments, like when she flailed around with the flashlights. Shut up, Rosie. See also O'Donnell, Rosie.

Star, Darren   Everything Darren Star knows about TV he learned at Aaron Spelling's knee: how to stage a catfight; how to contrive reasons to put your female stars in bikinis, including in funeral scenes; how much of your show's plots should revolve around business intrigue (2 percent) and how much around sex (900 percent). *Sex and the City* flourished due to its canny mix of fashion, swearing, and . . . sex, obviously; however, when Star tried to take on the stock market (*The $treet*), the law/matchmaking (*Miss Match*), and Hollywood (*Grosse Pointe*), his golden touch turned to brass. We kind of wish he'd quit trying to make up new shows and just go work on *The O.C.* and make it entertaining—or, failing that, set up a meeting between *O.C.* creator Josh Schwartz and Aaron Spelling's knee. See also BEVERLY HILLS *90210*; CENTRAL PARK WEST; MELROSE PLACE; *O.C., THE*; SEX AND THE CITY; and SPELLING, AARON.

STARSKY AND HUTCH See SPELLING, AARON.

STARTING OVER *Starting Over* premiered in syndication in the fall of 2003. Its inaugural cast of six women included a divorcée trying to lose weight and meet men for the first time since her marriage ended, a widow with a severe and undiagnosed social anxiety disorder, and a self-involved lawyer trying to become "more authentic," whatever that means. The gals are assisted in reaching their various goals by two life coaches: The first season's Rana Walker was replaced in the second by ex-talk show host Iyanla Vanzant, but the producers just could not shake Rhonda Britten, a self-declared "expert in transformative fear" from the "Fearless Living Institute." (Translation: Britten has no professional accreditations.) The show is hypnotically dumb: The life coaches seem to think the best way to make their charges break their bad habits is to put them through extremely literal challenges. For example, a mother and daughter who are codependent must spend a day with their thighs tied together. The idea is that the women achieve their goals (via a series of arbitrary "steps") and then graduate, whereupon a new woman moves in. How successful the show format actually is at improving women's lives is a matter of opinion, of course, though it's no accident that of the original six housemates, two had to come back for tune-ups. See also BUNIM/MURRAY.

STAR TREK FRANCHISE What can we say about the *Star Trek* franchise that hasn't already been said? One of the most successful sci-fi franchises in history, *Star Trek* was the vision of series creator Gene Roddenberry, who saw his baby last just three seasons before it was canceled due to low ratings. Roddenberry basically ignored said ratings and transplanted the original cast—anchored by William Shatner and Leonard Nimoy—into six theatrical features. The culty success of the original series paved the way for four more TV series installments—*The Next Generation*, *Deep Space Nine*, *Voyager*, and *Enterprise*—and made UPN a viable TV network. And despite how annoyingly blinkered its fans can be, the shows are pretty good. The original series was rife with allusions to the classics, and (allegorically) took on social issues of the '60s—when Kirk wasn't busy nailing some green chick with horns growing out of her neck. *Next Generation* had Patrick Stewart to seed the show with Shakespeare references, and it showed us that even physically challenged people (LeVar Burton's visually impaired Geordi, who had a banana clip over his eyes) and cybernetic people (Brent Spiner's endearing Data) can be valuable crew members. *Deep Space Nine* brought us the first ranking Starfleet officer of color (Avery Brooks's Sisko), although it later attracted criticism for the coded anti-Semitism some perceived in its Ferengi characters. *Voyager* . . . was bad. Moving on! *Enterprise* made a bold move: It was set chronologically earlier than all the other *Trek* series, just after the foundation of Starfleet, so that in showing how Earth's comparatively new space explorers related to the inhabitants and governments of other worlds, it could make all sorts of subtextual points about America's relation to older nations. Now may be the right time to bring back William Shatner for a series about the twilight years of James T. Kirk—still autocratically bossing everyone around, still hitting all kinds of alien tail. See also ALIEN SPECIES, DERMATOLOGICAL PROBLEMS OF; "CULT SHOW," DEFINITION OF; FUTURE ON TV, SIMILARITY TO PRESENT OF; NIMOY, LEONARD; PHYSICALLY CHALLENGED PERSON/CHARACTER, CLICHÉS ASSOCIATED WITH; "REDSHIRT"; SCENERY, CHEWERS OF; SCIENCE, IGNORANCE OF; SHATNER, WILLIAM; and TV SERIES, FILM ADAPTATIONS OF.

STAR WARS HOLIDAY SPECIAL, THE You might think *Howard the Duck* is the worst thing George Lucas has ever been attached to. (Or *The Phantom Menace*.) But nay! *The Star Wars Holiday Special* is a supernova of crap the likes of which you *can't even imagine* if you haven't seen it. The story is this: Chewbacca gets detained on his way back to his home planet Kashyyyk, where his father Itchy (okay . . .), wife Malla (Chewie's married?), and son Lumpy (now that's just cruel, and where does Chewbacca get off being a space bandito when he has a family?) are waiting for him to celebrate "Life Day." The first several minutes take place on Kashyyyk, at Chewbacca Manor, with the members of Chewbacca's family carrying an animated conversation . . . in Wookiee. Without subtitles. Over the course of the show, we see phoned-in performances by Harrison Ford, Mark Hamill, and Carrie Fisher (who even sings a Life Day . . . carol?), as well as supporting performances by such random guest stars as Art Carney, Harvey Korman,

Bea Arthur, and Diahann Carroll. It's incomprehensibly bad and excruciatingly boring. See also ARTHUR, BEA and HOLIDAY SPECIALS.

STONERS, TV FOR Not that we'd know anything about such things, of course (hi, Mom!), but certain shows do seem designed for enjoyment under the influence of herb. You can obviously enjoy *Ren & Stimpy*, *Liquid Television*, or an afternoon of kooky Thomas Dolby videos on VH1 Classic without it, and we have done so . . . but we have also theorized that *Teletubbies* is aimed not at children but at the rolling-joints-on-a-Frisbee crowd. One key characteristic of TV for stoners is that it's pretty clearly TV *by* stoners. *H. R. Pufnstuf* is exactly the kind of shit you'd find hilarious—nay, groundbreaking—when you're high off your ass; of *course* it doesn't make "sense," maaaaaaan. That's, like, the whole *point*. See also ADULT SWIM; *AQUA TEEN HUNGER FORCE*; CARTOONS, HANNA-BARBERA; *CHRISTMAS COMES TO PAC-LAND*; and *THAT '70S SHOW*.

STUDS Nestled between *The Dating Game* and *Blind Date* on the timeline of American singles' venues for self-humiliation, there is *Studs*. Two dudes and three ladies are sent on dates with one another, after which all five are reassembled in a studio. Host Mark DeCarlo—recipient of the Congressional Medal of Smarm—then reads off statements the ladies allegedly said about the guys, and the guys have to attribute each assessment to the correct woman; each accurate guess earns him a heart, and at the end, the guy with the most hearts gets to take the woman he likes best on a "romantic" trip, provided that she also chose him. The reason to watch the show (if it could be said there is one) is to parse the obviously scripted statements for their actual meaning: "Jeff really got my motor running" probably means that Jeff jump-started the girl's Civic.

STUNTCASTING TV series use guest stars all the time—that's no stunt, if they're played by anonymous schmoes like Lisa Edelstein or Mike Starr. But when a guest-starring role is filled by an actor of some stature, on the theory that you'll watch the show even if you normally don't, that's *stuntcasting*. It's how Marion Ross, formerly of *Happy Days*, has played main characters' mothers on *Gilmore Girls*, *That '70s Show*, and *The Drew Carey Show*, or how Lindsay Lohan played the love interest for her then real-life boyfriend, Wilmer Valderrama, on *That '70s Show*. Once confined to sweeps episodes, stuntcasting has metastasized and now gets trumpeted in network promos almost every week—and when it gets really out of control, it's usually a sign that a show's writers have lost faith in their cast's ability to generate humor on their own. The fact that *Will & Grace* has played host to Sharon Stone, Matt Damon, Edie Falco, Katie Couric, Jennifer Lopez, Gene Wilder, Alec Baldwin, Janet Jackson, Minnie Driver, Elton John, Madonna, and Cher? That's just a coincidence. See also BAD SITCOM, SURE SIGNS OF; *GILMORE GIRLS*; GUEST STARS, FREQUENT/FAMOUS; *THAT '70S SHOW*; TV LAW OF DIMINISHING RETURNS; and *WILL & GRACE*.

STUNT DOUBLES, SADLY OBVIOUS Nobody expects actors to know karate; damn, David Boreanaz barely knows *acting*, never mind a bunch of convincing Shaolin vampire moves. But when Angel tags out of a fight sequence and his stunt double is obviously a woman—a short, *African-American* woman—it kind of takes us out of the moment. Obvious wigs, differences in build, we can work with that stuff, but when there's a foot difference in height between actor and stunt double? Come on, folks. At least cut to a wider shot. . . . No, wider than that. See also ACTING, WOODEN; *ANGEL*; and BOREANAZ, DAVID.

SUPER BOWL HALFTIME SHOWS, DULLNESS OF We just don't see the purpose of the halftime show. We certainly don't see the purpose of *televising* the halftime show. Maybe it helps pass the time if you're actually *at* the Super Bowl. But for the millions of us watching at home, the combo of overexposed flavors-of-the-week like Ashleeeee Simpson and dinosaurs of rock like Paul "Facelift" McCartney embarrassing themselves with cheesy sped-up medleys is a spectacle we could do without—which is why we always flip to the counterprogrammed *Simpsons*, or MTV's offering. The only people who watch the halftime show: the proud parents of the battalion of interpretive dancers, and folks who missed the Janet Jackson Foil Nip Follies in 2004 and are hoping against hope for more unauthorized boobage. It's a gigantic, boring waste of money; we vote they air a vintage Bugs Bunny cartoon during halftime and give the giant budget to the Red Cross instead. See also NUDITY; SIMPSONS, ASHLEEEEE AND JESSICA; *SIMPSONS, THE*; and SPORTS COVERAGE, FATUOUS.

SUPERMARKET SWEEP God*damn* did we want to go on that show. And by "did," we actually mean "do," because the idea of filling an entire shopping cart to overflowing with snacks and then getting to keep said snacks without paying for them fills our skinflint hearts with joy. It could be a frustrating show to watch, though, because contestants didn't win unless the stuff in their carts added up to the highest value, and when teams wasted valuable time arguing over salsa brands instead of just grabbing cans of salmon, we could never stop ourselves from screaming at the TV: "No no NO no NO, caviar, CAVIAR, you MORONS!"

SURREAL LIFE, THE   What could be funnier than collecting a handful of celebrity has-beens (and, in some cases, never-wases—did Ryan Starr even make *American Idol*'s top five?), having them room together, and forcing them to do silly tasks like bringing cookies to

their neighbors? Well, a number of things, actually, but *The Surreal Life* does have its moments. It's not kidding about the "surreal" part—even René Magritte wouldn't have known quite what to do with the televised romance between Sly Stallone ex Brigitte Nielsen and rapper Flavor Flav. We'd also like to take this opportunity to apologize to *90210* alum Gabrielle Carteris for every mean thing we ever said about her, because she ripped crybaby Corey Feldman about seventeen new ones during the first season, and we love her for it. Later seasons have gotten too reality-"star"-heavy for our tastes, but it's good to know that attention whores without skills or prospects have someplace to go. See also *BEVERLY HILLS 90210*; DICKINSON, JANICE; ESTRADA, ERIK; OMAROSA; REALITY TV, COUPLES ON; and REALITY TV, OFF-BRAND.

SURVIVOR   *The Real World* may have been the first straight-up reality show to take hold in the American culture, but *Survivor* was the one that proved how much better reality TV can be when it literally turns into a popularity contest. An import from European TV, CBS's *Survivor* became an international phenomenon and paved the way for über-producer Mark Burnett's later successes (*The Apprentice*) and failures (*The Casino*). Each season reliably collects a few contestants that you actually like so that you can rejoice when they win (Tom Westman) or, more often, curse the fates when they get booted (Gretchen Cordy, and many, many more). But each season's cast is mostly filled with famewhoring crackpots, which is handy, since the pleasure of watching the show lies in screaming invective at the players you love to hate, whether because they're Machiavellian geniuses (first-season winner Richard Hatch) or crybabies whose rage at their ousters is deliciously satisfying (Lex van den Berghe). Now that the number of seasons is in double digits, the contestants are a bit too savvy and the machinations and alliances and "twists" a little rote. But really, *Survivor* is like pizza: Even when it's bad, it's still pretty good. See also *APPRENTICE, THE*; BONE-

HAM, RUPERT; BURNETT, MARK; HATCH, RICHARD; MARIANO, ROB; PROBST, JEFF; REALITY TV, "LOYALTY" AND "INTEGRITY" ON; *REAL WORLD, THE*; and VAN DEN BERGHE, LEX.

SWEAR WORDS, FAKE, USED TO DUB MOVIES AIRED ON TV We get that when USA airs *The Breakfast Club*, it can't include all of the FCC-baiting language. But honestly, "No, Dad, *flip* you"? Come on. Other variants we've heard include "forget" or "frig" for "fuck," "fakers" for "fuckers," "baloney" for "bullshit," "son of a squid" for "son of a bitch," and both "mother crusher" and (awesomely) "melon farmer" for "motherfucker." But perhaps *Ferris Bueller's Day Off*—which doesn't even contain that many bad words to begin with—deserves a special exhibit in the faux curse Hall of Fame. "Cameron is so tight that if you stuck a lump of coal *in his fist*, in two weeks you'd have a diamond!" and "Pardon my French, but you're an *aardvark*!" Hey, here's an idea: Why not tape over the profanity with silence? See also BASIC CABLE, MOVIES ENDLESSLY AIRED ON.

T

T, MR.   See *A-TEAM, THE*.

TAKING! IT! PERSONALLY!   If real-life police officers, doctors, and lawyers manage to collar criminals, treat the sick, and win cases without overidentifying with the circumstances of a given case, you would never know it from their depiction on television. Apparently, on TV it's not possible to care about a stranger unless his or her situation relates to you directly. TV cops in particular have an alarming propensity to Take! It! Personally! The trope has had its apotheosis in NBC's *Law & Order: Special Victims Unit*—because the show's focus is on "sexually based offenses," and the crimes are therefore especially lurid, each episode is sure to strike a chord with at least one character. Generally, the show's central detective pair Stabler (Christopher Meloni) and Benson (Mariska Hargitay) take turns taking it personally, since he's the father of several daughters, and she was conceived when her mother was raped. Thanks to careful backstory, the odds that any SVU case will fail to engage the emotional overinvestment of at least one character are virtually nil. See also "ELLIOT STABLER"; GOOD COP/BAD COP; and *LAW & ORDER* FRANCHISE.

TALK SHOWS, DAYTIME   When we were kids, daytime television was made up of three kinds of shows: children's programming, game shows, and soaps. But at some point, the balance changed; *Donahue* begat *Oprah*, and both series trafficked in an ostensibly "sensitive" airing of touchy emotional subjects. Some TV producers must have figured that if a soft-focus, balanced approach to topics that had been taboo could attract viewers, then a more sensationalistic take might be even *more* popular! They were right, as along came Ricki Lake, Montel Williams, Geraldo Rivera, and Maury Povich. These bastard children of Oprah and Phil Donahue covered nothing *but* touchy subjects—uncertain paternity, uncontrollable children, those who used to be fat but are now all that. But the mother of all shock talk series is, of course, *The Jerry Springer Show*; we didn't realize that the United States had so many mothers and daughters sleeping with the same guy, Klan members kiting checks, or transsexual Freemasons mistreating their pets, but

Jerry really opened our eyes. Perhaps in reaction to the nadir to which daytime talk shows had descended, the new century years saw the resurgence of happy talk in the old Merv Griffin mold: Both Rosie O'Donnell and Ellen DeGeneres brought successful celebrity chat shows to the air; Oprah spun off *Dr. Phil*; and Oprah herself turned her show into some kind of *Queen for a Day* affair, with guests getting cars and college educations and making us jealous. At least no one ever got jealous watching *Jerry*. See also DR. PHIL; JERRY SPRINGER SHOW, THE; LAKE, RICKI; *LIVE WITH REGIS AND KELLY*; O'DONNELL, ROSIE; and WINFREY, OPRAH.

TALK SHOWS, LATE-NIGHT It's late! The FCC kind of isn't watching! Anything could happen! Or, you might just get soothed into a restful sleep! Such are the promises of late-night talk shows, on which "edgier" comics preside over celebrity interviews and potentially controversial comedy bits. The formula is fairly consistent—monologue; desk piece; celebrity interview; celebrity interview; band or standup comic; "good night, everyone!"—so given the simplicity of its component parts, what's remarkable about the genre is how few people succeed at it. Johnny Carson was the giant in the field, but we grew up on Letterman and Conan. We became familiar with Letterman's flirty manner with his female guests and tetchiness with certain male ones who could give it back as good as they got (as  Charles Grodin and Dr. Phil still do). We chortled knowingly to ourselves when one of Conan's too-Harvard-y jokes failed to land with his studio audience (but *we* got it!), and cackled when he'd underscore the failure by knocking over his desktop microphone. On the occasions when we now DVR Leno—when he has a guest on that we absolutely can't miss—we're amazed at how dead-on every mean impression of him actually is, both of his ear-bleedingly screechy voice and his unshakably sycophantic manner. Frankly, if America really regards him as a bitchin' everyman supported by various African-American bandleaders, then by and large, America is even dumber than we thought. See also *LATE NIGHT WITH CONAN O'BRIEN*, STARING CONTESTS ON and "WILL IT FLOAT?"

TALK SHOWS, NOTORIOUS EPONYMOUS FAILED Actors and comedians do not necessarily make good talk-show hosts. A good talk-show host knows how to put guests at ease and how to conduct interviews in a natural way (or keep them from going off the rails entirely)—there's more to the job than doing the monologue. For every Ellen DeGeneres who understands that, you've got a Whoopi Goldberg who steps on her guests' punchlines, an Alan Thicke whose facelift prevents him from reacting to anything, or a Joey Bishop who probably won the hosting gig at the poker table at 3 AM the night before and has no idea where he even *is*. And who told Pat Sajak that helping contestants with word puzzles qualified him to do anything besides emceeing a charity Scrabble tournament? The celebs keep taking runs at talk shows, though, because a natural-born kiss-ass like Leno makes it look easy, even though it isn't. Matt Lauer can handle a kookoopants like Tom "You Don't Know the History of Psychiatry; I Do" Cruise, but can you imagine Chevy Chase in that interviewer's chair instead? It would have ended in literal bloodshed. (Wow, we said that like it's a bad thing.) See also CHASE, CHEVY, UNMITIGATED LOATHSOMENESS OF; *GROWING PAINS*; *HOLLYWOOD SQUARES*; TALK SHOWS, DAYTIME; TALK SHOWS, LATE-NIGHT; and *WHEEL OF FORTUNE*.

TALK SOUP All the lowlights of daytime talk shows, none of the annoying watching-them-yourself. In fact, you didn't even have to make fun of the shows yourself, because *Talk Soup* did it for you quite well. Greg Kinnear did a creditable job as the inaugural host, but *TS* entered its golden age with the ascension of John "Skunk Boy" Henson to the anchor chair. God, we loved that guy. The sarcastic head twitches, the belly-laughing at his own jokes, the foxy patch of white hair—why'd you ditch us, Johnny? Henson left to . . . do something? We don't really know. All

we know is that he *abandoned us* to successor Hal Sparks, who made *TS* entirely his own by . . . sucking royally. Aisha Tyler was a nominal improvement, but by then, we'd given up on the show. We'll never give up on our dream that Skunk Boy will return to primetime. NEVAH!! See also E! and RECASTING, NOTORIOUS.

TARANTINO, QUENTIN Film not-teur Tarantino is best known for his superbloody Hong Kong–influenced movies— so who better to up the gore factor in an episode of *ER* than Q? And up it he did, when the freshman drama cemented its "It" status with a Tarantino-directed episode during May sweeps of its first season. "Motherhood" featured about eighty-three gallons of signature Tarantino gore splashed all over a girl-gang fight scene that raged between two trauma rooms. Q's next TV trick: a recurring role on spy soap *Alias*. *Alias* creator J. J. Abrams's nutty stuntcasting generally keeps things interesting even when it doesn't quite work, but Tarantino's McKenas Cole came off like a fanboy cross-promotion for *Kill Bill* (and as usual, Tarantino's acting stank up the joint). TV viewers got a brief respite from Tarantino's small-screen aspirations before he came roaring back (as a director, thank God) with the two-hour fifth-season finale of *CSI*, a nail-biter that found Nick Stokes buried alive in a box that was full of fire ants, hot as hell, and rigged to explode. For a blatant, over-the-top ratings stunt that went overboard with kooky camera angles and tricked-up "suspense" (yeah, like they'd kill off a guy in the credits), it was really effective. The verdict: Q on TV's okay, but in small doses, and *behind* the camera. See also *ALIAS*; *CSI*; and STUNTCASTING.

TAXI   It was the show that put diminutive Danny DeVito on the map, constrained the creative genius (whatever) of Andy Kaufman, employed Jeff Conaway after *Grease*, and briefly convinced America that Judd Hirsch could be crush material. The '70s really were a strange time, dude. See also BROOKS, JAMES L.

TEENAGERS, BRATTY   Leaving aside the various sociopathic parent-murdering and mentally challenged teens on *Law & Order*, most TV teens act out way more—and in a way snottier fashion—than we did at their age. True, nobody wanted to televise our teen years,

because we behaved ourselves and were therefore quite boring from a dramatic standpoint, but that's still no excuse for TV teens to break curfew (Julia Salinger), lip off to their parents (all of them, but especially Dawson Leery), go on joyrides (every teenager in California on *CHiPs*), spit on mean teachers (oh, Pacey), stomp off to live with their boyfriends when their dads don't give them their way (Brenda "Stomp! In the Name of Love" Walsh), or, um, be Michael Guerin on *Roswell*. That guy needed a spanking like you wouldn't believe. And some shampoo, but that's another entry entirely. See also *CHiPs*; "DAWSON LEERY"; DOHERTY, SHANNEN; "PACEY WITTER"; PARENTS/PARENTING, BAD; and *PARTY OF FIVE*.

TEEN BEAT, COVER BOYS OF   We don't buy into conspiracy theories as a general rule. But if we found out that TV producers and rags like *Teen Beat* had an "arrangement," whereby actors with sexually unthreatening pretty-boy looks but not much thespian ability get cast in semicrappy shows, and then *Teen Beat*, *Tiger Beat*, *Bop*, and their ilk put said pretty boys on their covers, which in turn drives interest to the semicrappy shows, which in turn drives sales on the newsstand . . . well, it wouldn't surprise us. Finding out that Chad Michael Murray landed the role on *One Tree Hill* because he blew everyone away with a monologue from *Equus* in the audition? *That* would surprise us. Kirk Cameron's teen-dream status makes a lot more sense (and is a lot less upsetting) if it's the result of nefarious kickbacks and not girls actually thinking he's cute, because . . . what? See also CAMERON, KIRK and MURRAY, CHAD MICHAEL.

TEEN SEX, CONSEQUENCES OF TV teens foolhardy enough to have sexual intercourse almost always get pregnant, have a pregnancy scare, come down with an STD, or get ostracized and/or labeled "sluts" by their peers. And of course by "TV teens," what we really mean is "TV teen *girls,*" who suffer the majority of these punishments. Jen Lindley was shunned as a tramp, but nobody said squat to Pacey Witter, and that horndog slept with *a teacher.* Even girls who don't go "all the way" take a penalty—Donna Martin decided to stay a virgin, so David cheated on her. *Degrassi: The Next Generation*'s Emma gave *maybe* two blowjobs and promptly got tagged with throat gonorrhea, followed by a bunch of nasty teasing from her classmates. Did those kids bust on the guy? No, even though he's a juvenile delinquent and she's an environmental activist with straight As. We understand that TV shows can't really send a sex-positive message to a teen demographic without getting in trouble, but they don't have to scarlet-letter the girls every time, or act like it's totally impossible that teenagers can practice safe sex. See also *BEVERLY HILLS 90210*; *DAWSON'S CREEK*; *DEGRASSI: THE NEXT GENERATION*; and TEENAGERS, BRATTY.

TEEN STEAM For about a year back in the late '80s, it seemed as if the *Teen Steam* ad came on during every single commercial break, with Alyssa Milano rocking the mic with only one earpiece of the headphones held up to her head so as not to mar her carefully poofed mane of '80s hair: "Teen steeeeeeeam/Gotta let it out, gottaletitout!" Why anyone thought teenagers would turn to Alyssa for stress relief in the first place escapes us, never mind that said relief came in the form of an aerobics sequence (during which Alyssa blathered about boys and makeup while doing maybe three leg lifts—leaving her video minions to gut out the entire workout) and a music video featuring the then-customary smoke-machined alley and dancers wearing jackets with large buttons randomly sewn onto them, and a . . . rap sequence? Best not to think too deeply about it, probably—or about the fact that a large portion of *Teen Steam*'s customer base probably consisted of pedophiles ogling Alyssa's sweaty-leotard-encased goodies. See also *WHO'S THE BOSS?*

TESH, JOHN John Tesh is like Kelly Ripa, in that we should be very annoyed by him. He is also like Ripa in that he's endeared himself to us against all our better judgment. The nineteen-foot-tall blond got his start in the business as the cohost of *Entertainment Tonight*, where he exchanged stilted banter with Mary Hart for a full decade. He then reinvented himself as a composer and performer of Yannian New Age music and sometime figure-skating commentator while still finding time to write "Roundball Rock," the theme song for *The NBA on NBC*, and to make self-deprecating appearances on *Conan*. Look, the man is a gigantic, cheesy Christian, he knows it, he's cool with it, and we appreciate how good-natured he is about his dorkiness. And if we didn't, he could just crush us under his size 43 wingtips. See also RIPA, KELLY and THEME SONGS.

THAT '70S SHOW How far can a series coast on one joke? Eight seasons, apparently. That's how long *That '70s Show* hung in there, pinning an entire series on . . . funny clothes. GET IT? For God's sake, even the title isn't trying. Fortunately, the producers were smart enough to cast Topher Grace as series protagonist Eric Forman, and he made the show better than it had any right to be; he was skinny and dorky and dry, and had a disgusted, silent stare that even Bea Arthur would admire. But everyone else on that show—shrill brunette Mila Kunis; smug redhead Laura Prepon (Topher's Eric was *way* too good for her); and hard-partying members of the Diddy posse Ashton Kutcher, Danny Masterson, and Wilmer Valderrama—can go die. Grace started getting serious about his movie career in 2004 and left the show the following year, with Kutcher close on his heels; everyone else, with nothing better to do, hung around, all tied for last place in the race to be The Ziering. (Haaaaate!) See also ARTHUR, BEA; MAIN CAST MEMBER DEPARTURES, NOTORIOUS; MARIJUANA, CLICHÉS ASSOCIATED WITH; STONERS, TV FOR; and "THE ZIERING."

THEME SONGS **Type #1**, Show in a Nutshell: The whole premise of the show is spelled out for you in detail in its theme song—*The Brady Bunch*, *Gilligan's Island*, *Clone High*. Never seen the show before? Never mind, you're all caught up. **Type #2**, We Stole a Song, and You're Welcome: Producers found an existing composition and thought, "Why come up with something on our own?" Lazy, but it works—"Where You Lead (I Will Follow)" for *Gilmore Girls* performed by Carole King and her daughter Louise Goffin; "We Used to Be Friends" by the Dandy Warhols for *Veronica Mars*; the Von Bondies' "C'mon C'mon" for *Rescue Me*. (How do we feel about the use of

Who songs for the various *CSI* series? Well, "Who Are You" and "Won't Get Fooled Again" made sense for procedurals, but by the time they get around to *CSI: Provo*, there'll be nothing left but "Squeeze Box.")

Type #3, We Stole a Song . . . Sorry: We realize that Paula Cole may be living off her residuals for selling "I Don't Want to Wait" to *Dawson's Creek*, which is great for her, but bad for us: It's pitched way too high and is so freaking twee. Plus, a time may come when you're induced to perform it at karaoke, whereupon you'll discover that there are all these other verses where people are coming back from war with shrapnel in their skin.

Type #4, From Our Show to the *Billboard* Chart: Sometimes we like TV so much that we turn its theme songs into standalone hits, as we did the theme songs from *Friends*, *Cheers*, and (improbably) *Miami Vice*.

Type #5, The Show's Forgettable; You Only Wish the Theme Was: Some theme songs are so iconic that you remember them even as you forget everything you ever knew about the show, so that someone can sing the first three words and your brain will supply the rest. Examples include the themes from *Welcome Back, Kotter*, *Laverne & Shirley*, *Family Ties*, *The Jeffersons*, *The Facts of Life*, *Jem*, and, of course, *Charles in Charge*.

Type #6, Musical Time Capsule: You

don't need lyrics to make your theme song sound hopelessly dated, as we can prove by reminding you of the instrumental theme songs for *Knight Rider*, *Magnum, P.I.*, and *Beverly Hills 90210*. Both the "outrageous" sax flourish of *L.A. Law*'s theme song and the "sensitive" pan flute tootling of *thirtysomething*'s are so of the '80s, it hurts.

Type #7, Game Show Ear Worm: There's a special place in hell for the composers of game shows' painfully catchy theme songs, which is why we apologize in advance for mentioning *Match Game*, *Jeopardy!*, and *The Price Is Right*.

Type #8, We Might Be Overpromising Just a Little: When you think of *Perfect Strangers*, do you think of it as a show in which people spend much time "staaaaanding tall! On the wings of [their] dream"? No? Because the theme song thinks you should.

Type #9, *The Greatest American Hero*: More like *The Greatest American Theme Song*.

See also BEVERLY HILLS 90210; BRADY BUNCH, THE; CSI; CSI, SPIN-OFFS OF; CHARLES IN CHARGE; CHEERS; CLONE HIGH; DAWSON'S CREEK; FACTS OF LIFE, THE; FAMILY TIES; FRIENDS; GILMORE GIRLS; GREATEST AMERICAN HERO, THE; JEM; JEOPARDY!; KNIGHT RIDER; L.A. LAW; LAVERNE & SHIRLEY; MATCH GAME; MIAMI VICE; PERFECT STRANGERS; POST, MIKE; PRICE IS RIGHT, THE, SUCKY PRICING SKILLS OF

CONTESTANTS ON; "SHA LA LA LA!"; TESH, JOHN; *THIRTYSOMETHING*; and *WELCOME BACK, KOTTER*.

THIRTYSOMETHING   We're thirtysomethings ourselves now, and we have to say, we *still* don't know anyone as overwrought and angsty as the "adults" on *thirtysomething*. TV *infants* don't cry as much as Michael Steadman (Ken Olin) did—he and Hope (Mel Harris) got in a fight, boo hoo! His boutique ad firm failed because he and Elliot (Timothy Busfield) spent their entire operating budget on wacky neckties and Nerfketball kits, boo hoo! Miles Drentell (David Clennon) was mean to him, boo hoo! His friend Gary (Peter Horton) was hotter than him, boo hoo—and now he's dead, *boo hoo*! Dude cried over eeeeverything. But we sniffled a little when Gary died ourselves, and when Hope lost the baby that time, and when Nancy (Patricia Wettig) had ovarian cancer. Wow, we sniffled a bunch of times. The knock on the show—that everyone whined all the time—is valid, and we couldn't really blame Miles for holding them in acidic contempt most of the time—although why he went after Melissa (Melanie Mayron) and her Single Earring of Neurosis, we'll never understand. But it had its affecting moments in spite of all the sulking and the manipulatively whimsical pan flute on the soundtrack. (No offense, Snuffy Walden.) It's the rare show that you can watch either on its own merits or to make fun of, and series creators Marshall Herskovitz and Ed Zwick are our heroes forever for going on to *My So-Called Life*. See also CRYING, FAKE/BAD; *MY SO-CALLED LIFE*; THEME SONGS; and WALDEN, W. G. "SNUFFY."

THREE'S COMPANY   There's really no good reason to watch a *Three's Company* episode for the "plot"—it's nothing you haven't seen a sprillion times before in the wacky-misunderstandings genre, and when Jack Tripper has to pretend he's gay to Mr. Roper so he can keep living with Janet and Chrissy in that "sweet" beach-front apartment, it's kind of offensive. And why is it such a great pad, anyway? It looks kind of run-down to us. Put the show on mute, cue up some old-school silent-movie vaudeville piano on your stereo, and giggle at John Ritter's Buster Keaton impressions—and at the "fashions," including Mr. Furley's numerous silky neckerchieves, the nut-busting white slacks and rugby shirts on Jack, "32 Short Side Ponytails About Chrissy Snow," and coochie-cutter shorts worn over nude pantyhose . . . with sandals. Oh, '70s, you scamp. Better yet, just watch the *E! True Hollywood Story* about the show: 100 percent more Suzanne Somers diva drama, 100 percent less implausible lothario Larry. See also BAD SITCOM, SURE SIGNS OF; *E! TRUE HOLLYWOOD STORY*; MAIN CAST MEMBER DEPARTURES, NOTORIOUS; "MR. FURLEY"; and RITTER, JOHN, PRATFALLS AND MUGGING OF.

3-2-1 CONTACT A favorite of apple-polishers everywhere, *3-2-1 Contact* didn't just teach kids about science—it made study-bugging seem like a career aspiration, thanks to the Bloodhound Gang, a gaggle of kids who solved mysteries using scientific principles. Even those of us who didn't do that well in science as kids liked the idea that we might put our know-it-all-iness to productive use one day, so we stayed glued to the tube whenever this show came on, hoping to pick up a few tips. See also CHILDREN, OVERLY PRECOCIOUS.

TIC TAC DOUGH See MARTINDALE, WINK.

T.J. HOOKER You know Adrian Zmed? Yeah, "the scrawny fifth-generation photocopy of Danny Zuko from *Grease 2*"—that guy? His next role of any consequence: Vince Romano on *T.J. Hooker*. His *last* role of any consequence? Vince Romano on *T.J. Hooker*. Why, you ask? "His blow-dry ate Pittsburgh" is very close, but incorrect. No, it's because,

when the show switched networks before its last season, Zmed would have had to take a pay cut, which he didn't want to do, so he quit, and nobody hired him for a dramatic role again for six years, which, amen, Hollywood. What kind of a crazy mixed-up world do we live in where Adrian *Zmed* thinks he's too good to take a pay cut? We never watched the show—more's the pity, since William Shatner, Zmed, and Heather Locklear sharing a scene in a cop drama sounds like a trifecta of espresso-fueled scenery-gnawing we wish we'd witnessed—but that isn't the point. The point is, shut up, Adrian Zmed. See also SCENERY, CHEWERS OF and SHATNER, WILLIAM.

TNT'S PRIMETIME IN THE DAYTIME Sometimes known as "TNT's Productivity Bane of the Home-Office Worker," Primetime in the Daytime is TNT's fancy name for airing reruns all day. The lineup has something for everyone: fantasy (*Angel*, *Charmed*), hospital suds (*ER*), and the justice system (*Judging Amy*, *NYPD Blue*, and *Law & Order*), all mixed together in a delicious goulash of time-wasting. Thank God for the *Charmed*s, or we would have that station on, uninterrupted, all day. See also A&E DAYBREAKS; *ANGEL*; *ER*; *JUDGING AMY; LAW & ORDER* FRANCHISE; MARATHONS; and *NYPD BLUE*.

TODAY, **WINDOW OUTSIDE**   We don't know what genius thought it was a good idea for *Today* to broadcast from a studio surrounded by windows; more to the point, we don't know why they still do it. Because *Today* is still nominally a news show, and it detracts from the gravity of Matt Lauer's report on casualties in Iraq when he has to intone it in front of a crowd of tourists holding up signs letting us know that "WICHITA FALLS LOVES AL!!!" The show's window-adjacent location also means that Al Roker must deliver his weather updates outside, on the plaza, where he can point out adorable triplets from Arizona and talk to teams of cheerleaders from West Virginia—sweating through his suit in August and huddled into an ineffective wool trench in January. Al deserves better! Also, all of you tourists are in *New York*. You couldn't think of *anything* more fun to do than stand around Rockefeller Center? See also COURIC, KATIE; CURRY, ANN; and LAUER, MATT.

TOM AND JERRY   See CARTOONS, HANNA-BARBERA.

TONYA COOLEY   See COOLEY, TONYA, KIDNEY OF.

TORONTO, FOURTH-TIER SYNDICATED ACTION DRAMAS FILMED IN   You know when you're flipping around the channels on Saturday afternoon and you keep finding these low-budget sci-fi/adventure shows that have no stars (or maybe one, but it's someone like Kevin Sorbo or Richard Dean Anderson), and all the supporting cast looks weirdly milk-fed, and they keep saying "aboat" when they mean "about"? It's because they're filmed in Toronto, Ontario, Canada. The city can be (and has been) dressed to look like Chicago, New York, Pittsburgh, and Washington, D.C.; the crews are experienced and efficient; and best of all, the Canadian dollar is weak, so filming a series there is an easy way of keeping production costs down. Dick Wolf's various productions don't have to concern themselves with such matters as how much gets spent on craft services, but when you're working on the likes of *Adventure, Inc.*, *Earth: Final Conflict*, *Forever Knight*, *Once a Thief*, *Relic Hunter*, or *TekWar*, every cent you can save on M&Ms makes a difference. Only you're in Canada, so you'll actually be serving Smarties. See also CABLE CHANNELS, UNWATCHED.

TRADING SPACES   See "CRYING PAM" and HOME MAKEOVER SHOWS.

TREBEK, ALEX   Whether Alex Trebek was a know-it-all before he started hosting the long-running syndicated game show *Jeopardy!* or whether the show turned him into one is unknown. One thing is certain: His tone of mock-apology when he tells contestants their answers (or "questions," because it's *Jeopardy!*) are wrong must be maddening if you're on the receiving end. If we were Mrs. Trebek and he tried that crap on us ("Ooh, no, the correct answer is, What is *right* on Elm Street?"), the only question he'd be asking is "Where are my teeth?" Still, Trebek generally does a good job interacting with the Asperger's cases that make up the *Jeopardy!* contestant pool; one of the greatest pleasures of Ken Jennings's 2004 winning streak was the way Alex and Ken's relationship evolved into fond bickering, as though they were the game-show version of an old married couple. See also JENNINGS, KEN and *JEOPARDY!*

"TRIUMPH, THE INSULT COMIC DOG"
Look, we don't claim to understand the genesis of a rubber hand puppet of a dog (we think it's a boxer) that is also an insult comic, in the manner of Don Rickles, with a Russian accent. But ultimately, it doesn't matter *how* such a random idea originally evolved: We have it now, and it's hilarious. First spotted in a comedy bit on *Late Night with Conan O'Brien*, Triumph has gone on to harass celebrities in such locales as

the MTV Video Music Awards, where even a bad-ass like Eminem couldn't withstand the onslaught of abuse from what is, at the end of the day, *a hand puppet.* What a baby! See also CATCHPHRASES, OVERUSED TV; SMIGEL, ROBERT; and TALK SHOWS, LATE-NIGHT.

TRL It actually stands for "Total Request Live," not "Teenagers, Really Loud," although you could be forgiven for thinking so. This MTV afternoon staple has become synonymous with the sheeplike, high-pitched-squealy cultural tastes of adolescent girls. Okay, not all adolescent girls, obviously—just the sign-waving ones who block the sidewalk outside the show's Times Square studios every day and think Hilary Duff is awesome. (For purposes of clarity: Hilary Duff is no such thing.) TV, movie, and music stars important to the "squeeeee!" demo appear on *TRL* to perform (or just endure the supersonic wailing of their fans) and shill their product. *TRL* is also responsible for foisting Carson Daly on the viewing public—feel free to insert your own acidic remarks about the wheels of karmic justice. We'll be over here, continuing to ignore the show and most of the folks who appear on it in the hopes that it, and they, will go away. See also DALY, CARSON and MTV VJs.

TRUE-CRIME SHOWS Surely a fancy

theory exists as to why we find true-crime programming so fascinating; perhaps it's the same reason we enjoy other, less gory "reality" TV, namely that true-crime shows allow us to feel superior to others—but while *Survivor* merely lets us feel smug about how we could totally eat a disgusting bug or stand on a pole for six hours without whining, shows like *American Justice*, *COPS*, and *City Confidential* feed a much more visceral sense of self-righteousness, because 1) we would never drive drunk or beat up our significant others; 2) if we *did* do that stuff, we would make sure to wear pants; 3) we would definitely never kill someone; and 4) if we *did* kill someone, we would never get caught like those boneheads on *Forensic Files*, who don't watch *CSI* and therefore don't know that merely washing bloodstains off the floor is no match for luminol. And seriously, what is with all the people who think hiring a hit man is a viable solution to marital problems? It's called "getting a damn divorce," people. Look into it. See also BUNNELL, SHERIFF JOHN; *COPS*; COURT TV; *CSI*; KURTIS, BILL; SMALL TOWNS, HIDDEN DEPRAVITY OF; *SURVIVOR*; AND *UNSOLVED MYSTERIES*.

TRUMP, DONALD, HAIR OF Here's what's going on, as near as we can figure it. Donald Trump still has some coverage on the sides, but he's bald on top, and his hairline actually starts around the middle of the back of his head. So he grows *that* part *really* long, and then he combs that all forward, over the top of his head, and then *folds* it back onto itself. So essentially, it's a two-ply comb-over. But that's just a theory; it's not like we've gotten close

enough to get a good look. One thing is for sure, though: He lives in New York, and whether he's a billionaire or a mere millionaire, the man is comfortable. Therefore, he has both access to and the means to afford some of the best hair stylists in the world. Yet he walks around looking like that. It's weird. See also *APPRENTICE, THE* and REALITY TV, HOSTS OF.

TV BOYFRIENDS AND GIRLFRIENDS With so many actors on TV who either play characters we hate or just play characters hatefully, we cling to the few actors we like and make them our TV boyfriends and girlfriends. It's not a sexual thing, necessarily; we don't want to sleep with Angela Bassett's bad-ass CIA division head on *Alias*. We just love her because she could punch a hole in a car. On the other hand, Greg Grunberg, who played Eric Weiss on *Alias*, couldn't punch a hole in a pancake, but we'd still marry him. (Hey, love is a mystery.) *Scrubs*'s rageaholic Dr. Cox (John C. McGinley) wouldn't really make a good partner, but it's fun to imagine sparring with him. Similarly, Leah Remini's Carrie Heffernan on *The King of Queens* would be supremely hard to be friends with on a long-term basis, but we'd enjoy having lunch and getting our nails done with her, while we bitched about inferior customer service and made fun of people behind their backs. Very few of our TV boyfriends would make good *real* boyfriends, in fact, but it's still fun to daydream about dating a Fichtner look-alike. See also *ALIAS*; ELDARD, RON; FICHTNER, WILLIAM; FIGHTING, FEMALE CHARACTERS WHO ARE GOOD AT; GRUNBERG, GREG; *KING OF QUEENS, THE*; and REMINI, LEAH.

TV CATCHPHRASES, OVERUSED See CATCHPHRASES, OVERUSED TV

TV LAW OF DIMINISHING RETURNS The TV Law of Diminishing Returns states that a serial drama will begin to decline precipitously, both critically and in the ratings, when one or more of the following events occurs: 1) the show has aired for three seasons (*The West Wing*); 2) the show's creator turns over the reins to subordinates, or senior writers move on to other projects (*Angel*); 3) the show spawns a spin-off while the show itself is still on the air (*Buffy*, *The X-Files*); 4) the contrivance that the central characters would all have stayed together is too great a burden for the premise to bear (*Buffy*, *90210*); 5) the premise itself is too frail to sustain (*Twin Peaks*); 6) main cast members leave (*7th Heaven*, *ER*, *The X-Files*); 7) more than half the main characters have dated/slept with one another (*ER*, *Felicity*). Procedural dramas aren't usually subject to the Law of Diminishing Returns, because they rely primarily on plot to remain compelling, but high school shows and workplace dramas fall prey to it all the time—the high school shows become college shows, thus losing the drama inherent in the setting; the workplace dramas eventually run out of ways to exploit the job for crises and fall back on soapy intra-workplace snogging. Producers seldom acknowledge or obey the Law, choosing instead to drive the show until it breaks down on the shoulder completely. The one exception: *Felicity*, which actually could have gotten away with keeping all the central characters in one place (they did live in NYC, after all), but chose not to ping-pong Felicity between Ben and Noel *again* and bowed out gracefully. See also *ANGEL*; *BEVERLY HILLS 90210*; *BUFFY THE VAMPIRE SLAYER*; *ER*; *FELICITY*; *7TH HEAVEN*; SPIN-OFFS; *TWIN PEAKS*; *WEST WING, THE*; and *X-FILES, THE*.

TV NATION A decade ago, Michael Moore didn't cut quite the controversial figure he does now; he really only had

Roger & Me on his résumé when he took his agitprop act to TV with *TV Nation*, a show that functioned a lot like those segments on *The Daily Show* where they make fun of people by pretending to do an investigative report. *TV Nation* sent respected African-American actor Yaphet Kotto (of *Homicide*) and Caucasian-American ex-con Louie Bruno onto the streets of New York City to see who'd have an easier time catching a cab; got the head of the Michigan Militia, which spawned Timothy McVeigh, to sing "Kumbaya"; tried to hug all fifty governors; and drove its anticorruption poultry mascot, Crackers the Corporate-Crime–Fighting Chicken, to different cities in a big old RV. It might sound kind of dumb and attention-whory, and then as now, Moore went for a lot of cheap shots at middle management's expense. But before Michael Moore had bought his own hype, it worked: The stories usually had a serious message (racism is still a huge problem; Americans have too many guns; Jack Kevorkian is creepy), but the show didn't take itself too seriously. And when Moore & Co. set off a bunch of car alarms in front of a car alarm company CEO's house, oh, how we laughed. There wasn't really anything like it on TV until *The Daily Show* debuted in 1996. See also "CULT SHOW," DEFINITION OF and MOVIES-TO-TV/TV-TO-MOVIES CAREER PIPELINE/ARC.

TV, PEOPLE WHO ARE SMUG ABOUT NOT WATCHING/OWNING When you ask them whether they saw *Survivor* last night, they can't just say they don't watch it and let the conversation move on; they always have to make a huge effing deal of explaining that they don't even *have* a TV. And then it's like you have to defend your decision to watch reality TV instead of spending a productive Thursday evening curing cancer or reading to the blind, which they totally didn't do either, anyway.

TV PRODUCERS, UNQUALIFIED CELEBRITIES AS This isn't about an actor developing a project with the express purpose of starring in it, as William Petersen did with *CSI* or Lisa Kudrow with *The Comeback*. And it's not about those times when an actor suddenly gets promoted to producer status in Season 5, as happened to Helen Hunt late in the run of *Mad About You*. This is about celebrities who think the sheer magnitude of their stardom can make any show a hit. This is how, we assume, Ashton Kutcher was able to parlay his limited notoriety from *That '70s Show* into series deals for the likes of *Punk'd* and *Beauty and the Geek*. But it's not only in the realm of reality shows that actors overreach: George Clooney's fingerprints are all over *K Street* and *Unscripted*, produced through the company he runs with Steven Soderbergh—a noble idea, to be sure, but maybe we'd admire it more if it yielded some watchable series. There *are* actors who should give up acting entirely to concentrate on making good TV, like Shaun Cassidy did, on a nice run with *American Gothic* and *Cold Case*. And although *Push, Nevada* was a bust for their production company, LivePlanet, Matt Damon and Ben Affleck more than bounced back with *Project Greenlight*. See also CASSIDYS, THE; CLOONEY, GEORGE; *COMEBACK, THE*; *CSI*; *MAD ABOUT YOU*; *PROJECT GREENLIGHT*; and *THAT '70S SHOW*.

TV SERIES, FILM ADAPTATIONS OF It's hard to identify a successful formula for movie versions of TV shows. Why does a live-action version of *Inspector Gadget*, which really should not work at all given that the show relied heavily on Gadget's animated extend-a-legs, do okay, when classic cartoons like *Rocky and Bullwinkle* bomb horribly? "Um, because *Rocky and Bullwinkle* was never that great to start with?" Oh, we agree—but neither were *Charlie's Angels* or *Starsky and Hutch*, and those movies turned out pretty well. And *The Brady Bunch* is really a pretty terrible show, but we liked those movies, primarily because they sent up the series at every opportunity. *The X-Files* movie succeeded because it had something to add to the series canon; meanwhile, the *Star Trek* movies (all umpteen of them) succeeded because America loves a Shatner. See also *BRADY BUNCH, THE*; MOVIES-TO-TV/TV-TO-MOVIES CAREER PIPELINE/ARC; MOVIES, TV SERIES ADAPTATIONS OF; *STAR TREK* FRANCHISE; and *X-FILES, THE*.

24 Do you enjoy nuclear bombs? Weaponized viruses? Cougars? FOX has just the show for you. *24*—a terrorism drama that hit the zeitgeist by premiering in November 2001—follows Jack Bauer (Kiefer Sutherland, who graciously used his time out of the public eye to become very sexy), an agent of the government's fictional Counter Terrorist Unit. Each episode takes place in "real time," so a twenty-four-episode season comprises one exceptionally bad day in Jack's life. Jack's had to kill his ex-mistress, a persnickety apparatchik, and countless bad guys, assisted by variously capable desk agents, dubious feats of computing, and extremely favorable L.A. traffic. What started out as a suspenseful, unpredictable thriller has metamorphosed into a standard procedural veering ever more sharply to the right of the political spectrum. Still, there's the fun of a largely conscienceless hero, in a show in which literally anything could happen. See also *ALIAS*; COMPUTERS, CLICHÉS ASSOCIATED WITH; "JACK BAUER"; and "KIM BAUER."

21 JUMP STREET The time: the late '80s. The place: FOX, a network still so new it has afterbirth clinging to it. The premise: baby-faced cops go undercover in schools to solve crimes and address Important Issues like crack, unsafe sex, drunk driving, and, um, running a car-theft ring out of your auto-shop class. *Jump Street* catapulted its stars—Johnny Depp as the sensitive one; Peter DeLuise as the meathead; Dustin Nguyen as the foxy Asian; and Holly Robinson as . . . well, the girl—onto teen-mag covers and locker doors. Richard Grieco joined the cast later as so-called bad-ass and spin-off victim Dennis Booker, but only Depp had a career of note afterward. Painfully written, hammily acted, and splattered with acid wash, the show dated horribly, but is still amusing as a time capsule (one episode features Pauly Shore and a splendidly mulleted Jason Priestley *in the same scene*). See also CANNELL, STEPHEN J. and FOX, EARLY YEARS OF.

***TWILIGHT ZONE, THE,* LATER AND CRAPPIER INCARNATIONS OF** Famous original *Twilight Zone* had people with pig snouts and William Shatner hallucinating a creature outside his airplane window ("there's something! on! *the wing*!"). The *Twilight Zone* movie had sweaty, freaky John Lithgow in the Shatner role, and that superdisturbing girl with no mouth. No wonder *TZ* as a franchise idea seems like a fertile resource to TV producers—but with every successive version, it loses a little something. We liked the '80s version okay, when we couldn't find anything else to watch, and it had good guest stars and directors; so did the 2002 version (hosted, inexplicably, by Forest Whitaker). But shot in color, without Rod Serling, the whole thing just seemed sort of halfhearted. See also REVIVALS; SHATNER, WILLIAM; and STONERS, TV FOR.

TWIN PEAKS It doesn't happen often that the sort of person who'd go into episodic television has an imagination too big for the medium. Then there's David Lynch. Superficially a murder mystery about all-American girl Laura Palmer (Sheryl Lee), *Twin Peaks* took several detours on the way to solving the crime—abusive husbands, one-eyed inventors (who also happened to be housebound, just for fun), identical cousins, soulful bikers, and one broad who carried around a log as though it were a baby all showed up along the way. The investigation also embroiled FBI Special Agent Dale Cooper (Kyle McLachlan), from whose by-the-book, big-city perspective we, the viewer, discover the seemingly placid town of Twin Peaks—both its surface quirkiness and its secret corruptions. The show became an enormous cult phenomenon, spinning off related products like Laura's secret diary and the tapes Agent Cooper was always recording for his assistant, Diane. The show may have become *too* popular, though, as Season 2 arrived and proved with each episode that Lynch had no idea how to wrap things up, and finally Laura's killer turned out to be . . . her dad? But when he was possessed, or something, by this gray-haired freak named Bob? It was all  extremely unsatisfying, and the companion feature film *Fire Walk with Me* didn't really answer any of our lingering questions. It's not surprising that, when Lynch turned in a meandering, impenetrable pilot for a new series called *Mulholland Drive*, ABC decided not to pick it up; what's surprising is that they ordered another show from him in the first place. See also "CULT SHOW," DEFINITION OF; SMALL TOWNS, HIDDEN DEPRAVITY OF; and TV SERIES, FILM ADAPTATIONS OF.

TWINS ON COMEDIES, FORCED HILARITY OF On sitcoms, twins are either so much alike that they finish each other's sentences and are frequently mistaken for one another because they dress alike, or else they share the same face but are precise opposites in every other way! Ironic! See also BAD SITCOM, SURE SIGNS OF; *DOUBLE TROUBLE*; OLSEN, MARY-KATE AND ASHLEY; and TWINS ON COP SHOWS, DASTARDLINESS OF.

TWINS ON COP SHOWS, DASTARDLINESS OF Okay, *Without a Trace* is an FBI show, but whatever, same difference—it's the dastardliness of twins we're concerned with, specifically identical twins played by Tony Goldwyn, one of whom lets the other take the fall for his serial killings . . . over the course of two different episodes! Twice the evil, twice the fun! It's just never good news for the white hats when twins show up on an investigative drama, because it means their identical looks, fingerprints, or DNA are going to confuse witnesses, foul up evidence collection, and make it hard for jurors to turn in accurate verdicts. It's great news for the viewer, though, because the same actor usually has to play the "twins," and it's fun to see how the director deals with that. Or not. . . . Oh, look, the director cut between them again instead of using a two-shot—drink! See also DRINKING GAMES; RED HERRING, TOOLS FOR IDENTIFICATION OF ON COP SHOWS; and TWINS ON COMEDIES, FORCED HILARITY OF.

227 The notably unfunny sitcom responsible for kicking off Jackée Harry's reign of primetime terror (and continuing that of humor-impaired former *Jeffersons* maid-kick Marla Gibbs).

The only mitigating factor: Regina King, the best "girl, please" eyebrow in the business, making her debut as teen daughter Brenda. See also JACKÉE.

U-V

UNIVERSALLY REVILED CHARACTERS
We hate you, Rupert Boneham, Lex van den Berghe, Dawson, Omarosa, Dawn Summers, Cousin Oliver, Phoebe Halliwell, Sydney Andrews, Ray Pruit, Marissa Cooper, Kim Bauer, Wendy Pepper, Gamblin' Gabe, Dawson, Clay Aiken, Julie Emrick, Horatio Caine, Serena Southerlyn, Ann Romano, Jeff Balis, The Puck, New Becky, Poochie, Skippy, Carrie Bradshaw, Dawson, Ruthie Camden, Michael Guerin, Max Greevey, Nate Fisher, Duncan Nutter, Micky Dolenz, Rocco DiSpirito, Dawson, Tim McCarver, the Dr Pepper guy, Jennifer Love Hewitt, Jessica Simpson, Chevy Chase, and Dawson. And yet, we love you, because nothing but *nothing* is more exciting than rooting for, nor more satisfying than witnessing, your inevitable comeuppances. Julie and Serena: written off! The Puck and Lex: voted out! Dawson: shanked for another guy! Rocco: locked out of his own restaurant! Clay Aiken: second place! Balis and Omarosa: you're fired! *You're all fired!* Except Rupert. Like fuckin' herpes, that one. See also AIKEN, CLAY; *APPRENTICE, THE*; *BEVERLY HILLS 90210*; BONEHAM, RUPERT; *BUFFY THE VAMPIRE SLAYER*; CHASE, CHEVY, UNMITIGATED LOATHSOMENESS OF; "COUSIN OLIVER"; "DAWSON LEERY"; *FAMILY TIES*; HEWITT, JENNIFER LOVE; "HORATIO CAINE"; *INTERVENTION*; "JULIE EMRICK"; "KIM BAUER"; *LAW & ORDER* FRANCHISE; *MELROSE PLACE*; *[X] MOMS & DADS*; *MONKEES, THE*; *O.C., THE*; OMAROSA; *ONE DAY AT A TIME*; *PROJECT GREENLIGHT*; *PROJECT RUNWAY*; RAINEY, PUCK; *RESTAURANT, THE*; RÖHM, ELISABETH; *ROSEANNE*; *7TH HEAVEN*; *SEX AND THE CITY*; SIMPSONS, ASHLEEEEE AND JESSICA; *SIMPSONS, THE*; SPORTSCASTERS, MOST ANNOYING; and VAN DEN BERGHE, LEX.

UNSOLVED MYSTERIES   Kind of an Ann Rule book, but in TV form, *Unsolved Mysteries* presented . . . well, exactly that, but "that" covers a lot of ground—mostly unexplained disappearances and cold missing-persons cases, but also ghosts, UFO sightings, the Beale Cipher, conspiracy theories, and fugitives from justice. The show relied heavily on portentous narration from host Robert Stack (trivia alert: before Stack, Karl Malden and Raymond Burr both served as the hosts), interviews with family and law enforcement, and "recreations" of various crimes and hauntings whose production values approached Ed Wood levels in the low-budget department. It's also worth noting that we have watched, no kidding, *hundreds* of *UM* reruns in syndication, and not once have  we spotted an actor in said re-creations who went on to do anything of note (except Virginia Madsen, who did a turn as the cohost for one season). In spite of the amateurish nerdiness, it did have a way with a chilling setup, and *Unsolved Mysteries* actually solved a ton of these cases by getting people to call the toll-free number. See also *AMERICA'S MOST WANTED* and STACK, ROBERT.

"URKEL" Urkel, a ridiculously over-the-top caricature of terminal nerdiness, somehow became the Cosmo Kramer of the *Perfect Strangers* spin-off *Family Matters*. In fact, Steve Urkel wasn't even on the show until episode 9, when producers apparently figured out that what the show needed was a dork in suspenders to live next door and pine after the family's elder daughter. And they weren't wrong, apparently, because America was captivated by "Did I do thaaaaat?" for eight more years. In the show's final season, Jo Marie Payton—who played Harriette Winslow, the character from *Perfect Strangers* who'd spawned *Family Matters* in the first place—declined to return, reportedly complaining that the series had begun to rely too much on Urkel for its humor. We can't imagine what gave her that idea, unless it was that in addition to Steve Urkel, Jaleel White played *six* other roles on the show: Myrtle Urkel, Elvis Urkel, Steve Winslow, Original Gangsta Dawg, Bruce Lee Urkel, and Stefan Urquelle, a suave alter ego of Steve Urkel who turned into a separate person when . . . Urkel cloned himself? A writer actually wrote that, and one of the big three networks filmed it, and *people watched it*. See also ABC's TGIF; BAD SITCOM, SURE SIGNS OF; CANNED LAUGHTER, MANIPULATION BY/OF; CATCHPHRASES, OVERUSED TV; "COSMO KRAMER"; DORKINESS, TV SIGNIFIERS OF; NEIGHBORS, INTRUSIVE; *PERFECT STRANGERS*; and SPIN-OFFS.

V It was probably some kind of allegory about Communist nonparanoia—rat-eating aliens come to Earth asking for human help, but are they being sincere?—but we didn't care about that when the original *V* miniseries aired in 1983 (followed by a series the next year). We didn't care about all the business with the government and the resistance and blah blah blah. All we cared about was being allowed to stay up and watch when the lady gave birth to her half-human, half-alien baby. And then the baby came out! And looked totally human! Phew! But then! It had a lizard tongue! And then the babies were twins, and the second baby looked like it was *all* lizard! (With a human tongue? We can't remember; we watched the second baby's birth only through our fingers.) *V* is probably the sort of thing that seems extremely scary when you're a kid but would be laughable if watched now. Unfortunately, we're still too creeped out to put that theory to the test. See also MINISERIES, OLD-SCHOOL EVENT EDITIONS and MOVIES, MADE-FOR-TV.

VAN DEN BERGHE, LEX When he was first on *Survivor*—back in the show's third season, set in Africa—Lex van den Berghe was okay. A little intense, maybe a little too obvious in his attention-seeking, what with the tattoos and piercings, but a good player and a real threat in the game who made it all the way to the final four. But in the All-Star season, a few years later, Lex was reborn as an annoying, judgmental, humorless sore loser. Getting outplayed by "Boston Rob" Mariano apparently short-circuited something in Lex's brain, and once he was voted onto the jury, he devoted himself to shaking his head disgustedly at everything Rob said at tribal council. And (when not on TV) to drafting the speech he would make to the final two, in which he accused Rob of selling out their friendship for "a stack of greenbacks." As though that were not *the*

entire point of the competition, and as though Lex—like so many sore losers before and after him—wasn't just bitter that he hadn't been able to screw someone else over before getting screwed over himself. It made Lex the undisputed love-to-hate contestant of the All-Star season—no small feat, considering that he was sharing a beach with Rupert Boneham. The one tattoo he *doesn't* have, and should, is the word "Chump." See also BONEHAM, RUPERT; MARIANO, ROB; REALITY TV, "LOYALTY" AND "INTEGRITY" ON; and *SURVIVOR*.

VERY SPECIAL EPISODES Prohibited by Jerry Seinfeld on *Seinfeld* ("no hugging, no learning"), parodied by *The Simpsons* and *Clone High*, a Very Special Episode is an episode that feels more like school than like escapist entertainment—a social hygiene film with Tide ads. If it's got a lecturing tone, feels like a PSA, and presents an overly simplistic picture of a complex issue, it's probably a Very Special Episode—and if it's an episode of a sitcom in which any of the main characters is crying, throwing plateware, or otherwise chumming the Emmy waters with bait, it's definitely a Very Special Episode. VSE topics often include drug or alcohol abuse; bad touching; war, death, and grief; homosexuality; depression; smoking; shoplifting; secret cutting; and eating disorders. They customarily conclude with a Very Valuable Lesson. And said episodes almost always conclude neatly: Characters who need to go to rehab agree to do so; characters who have body-image issues cheerfully order a plate of onion rings; child abusers get arrested or beaten up. Ambiguity has no place in a VSE. Patronizing, oversimplified lessons rule the day. See also *BLOSSOM*; *CLONE HIGH*; "THE MORE YOU KNOW"; "ONE TO GROW ON"; PSAS; *SEINFELD*; and *SIMPSONS, THE*.

VH1 See *BEHIND THE MUSIC*; *STAND-UP SPOTLIGHT*; *SURREAL LIFE, THE*; and *VH1 LEGENDS*.

VH1 LEGENDS Sort of like *Behind the Music*, but more reverent toward its subjects (Marvin Gaye, Janis Joplin) and with different famous folk taking narration voice-over duty (Steven Tyler, Kris Kristofferson). Where *Behind the Music* seems to enjoy dishing the dirt, *Legends* takes a more elegiac tone. We never burst into tears during a *BtM* the way we do during the *Legend* episode featuring Queen, which sounds really pathetic, and kind of is, but the section about Freddie Mercury's death is just really sad. Oh, shut up. The world is a poorer place without Freddie and his satin jumpsuits with little wings on them, and you know it. Who would make a more fantastic *American Idol* judge than that guy? Nobody, that's who. See also *AMERICAN IDOL* and *BEHIND THE MUSIC*.

VIEIRA, MEREDITH Meredith Vieira started out as a serious journalist. No, really: She was a correspondent on *60 Minutes*. But then she agreed to be on this new panel-style daytime talk show with Barbara Walters, and the wheels came off the bus. Vieira is the best of *The View*'s five hosts—which, we know, is like saying she's the prettiest turd in the toilet bowl—but she's still a loon. As long as Walters is around, her niche on the show can't be as the gravest and most distinguished stately newswoman, so instead, Vieira made herself the most inappropriate, discussing such matters as her digestive processes, her disinclination to wear panties, and the time her husband had sex with her when she was asleep. And yet, she still outclasses Katie Couric, her predecessor on Viera's gig, as of 2006, on *Today*. See also TALK SHOWS, DAYTIME; *VIEW, THE*; and *WHO WANTS TO BE A MILLIONAIRE*, SYNDICATED VERSION.

VIEW, THE When people complain about what's wrong with talk shows, we're guessing that "not enough hosts" is seldom among their grievances. And yet, that's exactly what sets *The View* apart from every other happy-talk daytime show—five times as many hosts. Built around Barbara Walters—the one with the most gravitas, to give you a chilling sense of what the show is like—the idea behind *The View* is to bring to the proceedings the perspectives of women from all different walks of life. When the show started, it had a working mother (Meredith Vieira), a divorced woman in her fifties (Joy Behar), a single professional (Star Jones), and a young woman "just starting out" (Debbie Matenopolous). But now Jones is married (perhaps you heard something about it?) and having realized that Matenopolous was an incompetent moron, they wrung out Lisa Ling, who was too good for the show. Then the youth slot was filled by Elisabeth Hasselbeck, a barely informed Republican and former reality-show contestant who is *also* married. As a talk show, *The View* is fairly unsuccessful. Celebrity guests come out only to be set upon by all five women at once, talking over each other and shrieking like the harpies they are. But it is worth watching for the trainwreck value of "Hot Topics," in which the ladies discuss the issues of the day with greater and less degrees of intelligence and usefulness (. . . *Elisabeth*). See also *BARBARA WALTERS SPECIAL, THE*; TALK SHOWS, DAYTIME; and VIEIRA, MEREDITH.

VIGODA, ABE   Abe Vigoda has been moping through character roles like pop culture's depressive grandfather since *The Godfather*, but it's on TV that he reached his biggest audience—on *Barney Miller* and its spin-off, *Fish*; on *As the World Turns*; and in countless *Conan* walk-ons, in which his main purpose is to prove he isn't dead. (Of course, if he's passed away by the time you read this: R.I.P., Viggie! You always looked like you needed a hug.) See also SPIN-OFFS and TALK SHOWS, LATE-NIGHT.

VILA, BOB   See HOME MAKEOVER SHOWS.

VIVA VARIETY   "Vivaaaaa vaaaarietaaaaaaaay!" This parody of '70s-era glitzy variety extravaganzas started off with a delightful bellow but never really caught fire, perhaps because the concept might have worked for a single sketch but came off limply as a continuing series. Several veterans of *The State*—Thomas Lennon as Meredith Laupin, Kerri Kenney as the former Mrs. Laupin, and Michael Ian Black as the slow-witted Johnny Bluejeans—made up the main cast, and the show incorporated celebrity appearances with *Gong Show*–style novelty acts. It should have worked (what better models than Sonny and Cher?), but it couldn't decide whether it wanted to make fun of variety shows or become one. Michael Ian Black can really wear a pair of hot pants, though, we'll give the show that much. See also BLACK, MICHAEL IAN and *SONNY & CHER*.

W

WAGNER, JACK Just thinking Wagner's name can make us blush, because not *only* did we follow every single twist and turn of Frisco's romance with the insipid Felicia (played by Wagner's later real-life wife Kristina), but we *also* bought his adult-contemporar-Brie albums, and whenever "All I Need" came on the radio, we would *shush people*. Wagner had a deliciously evil turn as DOC-tor Peter Burns on *Melrose Place*, slummed in a series of husband-and-wife tooth-whitening-systems ads (which is kind of weird, given that he seems to have lost a bottom tooth at some point), and now he's chomping the curtains on *The Bold and the Beautiful*. He's aged pretty well (except for that no-tooth thing), and nobody can whittle a living-room set down to a pile of sawdust faster than the Wag. Our dream: He turns up on *Dancing with the Stars* and does the lambada. See also *BOLD AND THE BEAUTIFUL, THE*; *DANC-ING WITH THE STARS*; SCENERY, CHEWERS OF; SOAP OPERAS, DAYTIME; and SOAP OPERAS, FAMOUS STORY ARCS OF.

WALBERG, MARK L. See HARRISON, CHRIS, INDISTINGUISHABILITY FROM MARK L. WALBERG OF.

WALDEN, W. G. "SNUFFY" He's probably most famous for scoring the Zwick/Herskovitz constellation of shows —*thirtysomething, Once and Again, My So-Called Life*—but he's also scored the constellation of shows known as "practically all of them." *The Wonder Years, The West Wing* theme song, the Roe v. Wade TV movie . . . you name it, he's composed interstitial music for it. It's harder to identify a signature Snuffy music break these days, now that he seems to have weaned himself off that fey flute nonsense, but if you're watching a rerun, here's how to tell if it's Walden on the soundtrack: twangy flamencoid guitar accompanying wacky/humorous moments (viz. Hope and Michael trying to find a time to have sex on *thirtysomething*); poignant scenes underlaid with a harmonic hum and a simple, high-pitched plinky piano melody; and the aforementioned overly whimsical wind instrumentation. We don't know why he's called "Snuffy"; "William" seems like a perfectly serviceable first name to us. But he made his television debut as a member of the Squigtones on

Laverne & Shirley, which is a pretty rad credit for a composer, so we'll let it go. See also *LAVERNE & SHIRLEY*; MUSICAL MONTAGES; MUSIC CUES, ETHNIC; *MY SO-CALLED LIFE*; THEME SONGS; *THIRTYSOME-THING*; *WEST WING, THE*; and *WONDER YEARS, THE*.

WALTERS, JAMIE   Okay, obviously we set out to make fun of Jamie Walters, very meanly and at great length, because he's not just Donna-abusing, pumpkin-vending Ray "With One T" Pruit from *Beverly Hills 90210*, who acted out every viewer's fantasy by pushing Tori Spelling down a flight of stairs—he's also one of the screamy plaid-shirted faux-grungies that infested the early to mid-'90s like termites. He starred in a short-lived show about a band of those very pests, *The Heights*, and sang the crappy Top 40 theme song, "How Do You Talk to an Angel?" . . . if you can call that "singing" and not "breathy grunting." Walters had the worst case of eyes-too-close-together bitchface we've ever seen on a dude, but! It turns out that Walters is *also* a recently minted LAFD firefighter, and before that, he worked as a paramedic. Not only did he take a hint and bail on the fame trip, but he's out there helping people, so now we kind of have to like him—or at least respect the fact that he's a better person than we are. Damn you, Walters! See also *BEVERLY HILLS 90210* and SPELLING, TORI.

WARDROBE, ENDLESSNESS OF   We know that TV series productions keep vast racks packed to the gills with all the accumulated clothes their actors have worn. So why don't they conserve that space by having characters wear their outfits more than once? The lowliest TV waitresses, social workers, and record-store clerks have apparently unlimited apparel budgets—each new episode finds them rocking outfits we've never seen before. And not that we expect documentary-level realism from the likes of, say, *Friends*, but good God, how did Monica and Rachel store all those pairs of jeans, even in their absurdly giant apartment? We must give props to the shows that bucked this TV trend: *My So-Called Life* frequently recycled clothing—realistic, given that the show featured teenagers, who not only have to shop on their allowances but will wear only the few articles of clothing they think are sufficiently cool; and the ladies of *Law & Order* frequently show up in suits we've seen before—which we knew for a fact in the case of Claire Kincaid and Jamie Ross, because many of said suits were memorably ugly. See also *FRIENDS*; *LAW & ORDER* FRANCHISE; MONEY, INFREQUENT HANDLING BY TV CHARACTERS OF; *MY SO-CALLED LIFE*; and REAL ESTATE, VASTNESS OF.

WEAKEST LINK, BRITISH-LADY EDITION   The hour-long original version of *Weakest*

Link has more filler, and host Anne Robinson has a scary witch mouth (and scary witch outfits . . . what's up with those magician frock coats?), but she's quite satisfyingly mean to the contestants when they biff the answers, and the questions are a bit harder than the half-hour version, so home viewers can feel more  superior about getting them right. See also GAME SHOW NETWORK; *WEAKEST LINK*, GEORGE GRAY VERSION; and *WEAKEST LINK*, HIP-HOP CELEBRITY EPISODE.

***WEAKEST LINK*, GEORGE GRAY VERSION** Half an hour; sucky. See also *WEAKEST LINK*, BRITISH-LADY EDITION.

***WEAKEST LINK*, HIP-HOP CELEBRITY EPISODE** It's hard to explain why the hip-hop ep stands out among the myriad celebrity episodes *Weakest Link* aired, but Young MC's shameless flirting with Anne Robinson (you heard us) might have something to do with it. Or perhaps it's Nate Dogg, clad in a fawn-colored leather fedora and an "I'm-a KILL YOU" scowl and laying waste to the geography questions (not to mention dissing Da Brat, repeatedly). And if loving Reverend Run's hat and wanting to borrow it is wrong, we don't want to be right. Try to catch it on GSN sometime, but wear sun-glasses; Da Brat is wearing a metric ton of gold necklaces. See also GAME SHOWS, CELEBRITY EDITIONS OF and *WEAKEST LINK*, BRITISH-LADY EDITION.

"WE ARE OUT OF SWEET ROLLS!!" See also *ELECTRIC COMPANY, THE*.

WEBSTER Eventually, Gary Coleman just wouldn't do anymore—America needed an *even teenier* wisecracking African-American youngster with chubby cheeks and big brown eyes. Enter Emmanuel Lewis as Webster, an orphan adopted by retired gridiron meat-wagon George Papadapolis (Alex Karras) and his Fraggle-esque wife Katherine (Susan Clark). Laughing, loving, and diabetic comas ensued; we would go into more detail, but we don't want your kidneys to shut down. See also BAD SITCOM, SURE SIGNS OF; CHILDREN, OVERLY PRECOCIOUS; and ORPHANS.

WEDDINGS, FAMOUS TV If a TV wedding aims to lodge itself in the cultural memory like popcorn in a molar, it's best if something goes horribly awry. Do you remember the Bradys' wedding for Carol's fetching mod-yellow second-marriage outfit? No. You remember it because Tiger and Fluffy threw down and Mike pitched face-first into the cake. Other popular methods of making a TV wedding unforgettable include: the bride ditching the groom (Alison defenestrates herself on *Melrose Place*); the groom ditching the bride (Xander wimps out on Anya on *Buffy*); the mutual "wow, we don't even like each other" ditch moments before the ceremony (Brandon and Kelly on *90210)*; the groom says the wrong name at a key moment in the ceremony (Ross on *Friends*); and the always popular real-life wedding, featuring a cavalcade of freakish celebrity attendants, that is revealed as a sham barely a year later (Liza and David Gest . . . and ew). Or you can always go the British royalty route and stage a spectacular wedding that lasts for hours, thus filling the heads of impressionable little girls with crazy ideas that blossom into Bridezilla madness twenty years later . . . although "horribly awry" really doesn't begin to describe what became of Charles and Diana. It's wise for TV shows to halt a wedding at the altar instead of letting the characters go through with it; that way, viewers get all the drama of the wedding planning and the cold-feet subplots and the flashback/reunion episodes, but by calling it off at the last minute, the show can avoid killing the sexual tension and create even more drama in the aftermath. See also *BEVERLY HILLS 90210*; *BRADY BUNCH, THE*; *BRIDEZILLAS*; *BUFFY THE VAMPIRE SLAYER*; *FRIENDS*; and *MELROSE PLACE*.

WELCOME BACK, KOTTER Yet another instance of '70s culture not translating very well to the present day. We understand the premise—Mr. Kot-tair returns to his old high school to teach/inspire the underachieving Sweathogs; cue laugh track—but we don't understand why Kotter's antique Catskills quips get laughs or help him relate to urban youth. (Not that Vinnie Barbarino's rejoinders are any better. "Up your nose with a rubber hose"? *This* was his signature punchline?) We also don't get why Horshack is even *in* the Sweathogs; isn't it supposed to be a gang, basically? And isn't Horshack 1) tiny, and 2) kind of queeny? The show's just not very good, and it didn't get any better when Travolta's movie career blew up and the show turned into a Barbarino vehicle. But the luxuriantly poofy hair on almost everyone in the cast is well worth tuning in for, and if you can't remember why Fat Travolta of today is famous, well, this is why. He used to be a fox. But . . . that was a long time ago, before *Swordfish*, for which that tub still owes us eight bucks. See also CATCHPHRASES, OVERUSED TV; MOVIES-TO-TV/TV-TO-MOVIES PIPELINE/ARC; and TEENAGERS, BRATTY.

WEST WING, THE Long hours, backstabbing coworkers, behind-the-scenes maneuvering, ingratiating yourself to the boss—just your typical workplace drama.

Except the workplace is the White House. Aaron Sorkin's drama series started off in 1999 with a bang, earning critical praise, excellent ratings, and a staggering four consecutive Emmys for Outstanding Drama Series. Which is kind of shocking, since that includes two Emmys past "Isaac and Ishmael," the notoriously terrible episode that kicked off the show's third season in 2001. Sorkin wrote the episode as a direct and immediate response to the September 11 attacks. Little did we know then, but "I&I" was the beginning of the end for *The West Wing*.

The show had held it together through Sorkin's struggle with drugs and through the actions of its money-grubbing supporting cast, but Sorkin's jingoistic reaction to 9/11 alienated even the show's most devoted fans. When he and fellow executive producer Tommy Schlamme left the show in 2003, it was too late to stanch the bleeding. The greatest tragedy, though, is that some of the best actors of our time—Bradley Whitford, Richard Schiff, Stockard Channing, Martin Sheen, the late John Spencer, and Allison Janney, among others—were being wasted speaking lines like "Can we get this godforsaken event over with so I can get back to presiding over a civiliza- tion gone to hell in a handcart?" Shame, really. NBC euthanized the show in 2006, coincidentally just as actual America was starting to seem ready again for a progressive White House filled with bright-eyed do-gooders burning with the righteous flame of public service. For a change. See also PROMOS, DECEPTIVE; SCHLAMME, TOMMY; and SORKIN, AARON.

WHEDON, JOSS   Joss Whedon is a cult idol for creating *Buffy the Vampire Slayer* (and its successful spin-off, *Angel*)—he created one of the all-time outstanding TV heroines, a high school girl who could fight like an aikido master, but who also had relatable problems with boys. In the early seasons of that show, Whedon was working at the height of his powers, writing outstanding dialogue for strong, nuanced characters and setting up suspenseful season-long story arcs. But not long after souled vampire Angel spun off into his own show, the wheels started to loosen on the Whedonmobile. He got distracted, running two shows, and entrusted key plotting duties on *Buffy* to writers like Marti Noxon, who ignored the show's carefully constructed internal mythology. He started making arrogant remarks about viewers needing him to tell them what they wanted to see. He got the mistaken idea that people would give a crap about a space western (the flawed and short-lived *Firefly*) just because he'd written it. Whedon is a perfect illustration of the Elvis-Eggers Principle of Effective Writing, to wit: No matter how much talent you've got, you need an editor or some other advisor who will tell you sugar-free when you're screwing up, and get you to hear it. Joss: You've got the skills to pay the bills, and "Once More with Feeling" is literally the only musical of any kind that we can stand, but you completely biffed the Slayers-in-waiting, the Buffy-Spike relationship, Pylea, and the River Tam sub-"plot." Find yourself a sensei who will tell you the truth about your blind spots. See also *ANGEL*; *BUFFY THE VAMPIRE SLAYER*; NONMUSICAL SERIES, MUSICAL EPISODES OF; and SPIN-OFFS.

WHEEL OF FORTUNE "Dear *Wheel of Fortune* Contestants: Look. It's a glorified game of Hangman. How many times does one of you dolts have to pick 'K' first before you figure out that *that's stupid*? You want the car, you buy an 'E.' It's having to smile through idiotic letter choices like yours that gave me an ulcer that ate through my entire rib cage. I hope a giant Q falls out of the sky and squashes you. 'Love,' Vanna White. P.S. Yes, Sajak is a host-bot. He prefers to be called '5.0.' P.P.S. I am drunk right now." See also STONERS, TV FOR.

WHERE IN THE WORLD IS CARMEN SANDIEGO? This venerable kids' show let kids track the mysterious Carmen Sandiego through various locales worldwide. The final round presented the last remaining contestant with a huge, unmarked map of a continent; host Greg Lee would call out the names of countries (or, in the case of the United States, states), and the kid would have to run all over it and put light poles in the appropriate spaces on the map. Occasionally, the kid would luck out and get South America, but if he got Europe or Africa, he would not be taking home the most fabulous prize PBS could afford, and therefore would have to buy his own used Atari 2600.

WHO'S THE BOSS? *Who's the Boss?* continues in the long tradition of incredibly sappy ABC sitcoms—this one revolving around single mother Angela Bower (Judith Light) and her brat Jonathan (Danny Pintauro), who advertise for a live-in housekeeper and get more than they bargained for in retired baseball player Tony Micelli (Tony Danza) and his tomboyish daughter Samantha (Alyssa Milano). The show perpetrated several great fictions on the American public: 1) that Tony Danza could act, despite evidence to the contrary on an existing previous sitcom (*Taxi*) in which his character was *also* named Tony, as though producers couldn't be sure that he would be able to stay in character otherwise; 2) that

Judith Light was a great beauty, despite four-inch black roots in her fake-blonde hair, and that she was . . . not that attractive; 3) that sexually inappropriate senior citizens like Angela's mother, Mona (Katherine Helmond), are *hilarious*. The show stayed on the air for eight long seasons, in which time Angela and Tony danced around each other for a while and then finally did it, which was . . . weird. And then the show ended, scattering the cast to the four winds. Light made eight million Lifetime movies, Danza did a few more series and a daytime talk show, Milano made an exercise video awesomely titled *Teen Steam* and then bimboed her way through *Charmed*, and Pintauro came out of the closet and tried to make us all call him Dan (which we will not). See also DADS, TV; LIFETIME MOVIES; SENIOR CITIZENS, CLICHÉD PORTRAYALS OF; SEXUAL TENSION, RUINATION OF SHOW BY RESOLVING; TALK SHOWS, DAYTIME; *TAXI*; and *TEEN STEAM*.

WHO WANTS TO BE A MILLIONAIRE, REGIS EDITION *Millionaire*, an Americanized version of a British game show, took off like a shot in 1999 and saturated the culture almost immediately. Even people who watched perhaps five minutes knew all about the show: the host, the irrepressible Regis Philbin; the structure of the show, in which contestants could win a million bucks if they answered fifteen progressively more difficult multiple-choice questions correctly; and the catchphrases the show spawned—"Final answer?" "I'd like to use a lifeline." ABC should have reacted to *Millionaire*'s unexpected success by saying, "Hmm . . . the show premiered in August, maybe we should wait and see if it maintains its ratings level." Instead, the network rearranged its entire schedule in order to quintuple-burst episodes almost every night of the week in primetime, and the show managed to stagger along under a huge burden of overexposure for about a year. Eventually the ubiquity of the show proved too much, and it got sacked. We'd give the show itself a solid B, but it just aired too often and had too many celebrity episodes. See also CATCHPHRASES, OVERUSED TV; PHILBIN, REGIS; and *WHO WANTS TO BE A MILLIONAIRE*, SYNDICATED VERSION.

WHO WANTS TO BE A MILLIONAIRE, SYNDICATED VERSION How to make yourself feel smart: Turn on the soothing, Regis-free version of *WWTBAM*; answer all the questions easily; point, laugh, and feel superior when the contestant biffs an easy eighth-grade-English question. How to make yourself feel very very dumb: Point, laugh, and feel superior when the contestant uses a lifeline to answer a $400 question; announce to everyone within earshot that "this one is so cinchy, God"; get it wrong; and check yourself into assisted living facility for thinking Hemingway wrote *The Nanny Diaries*. Our point? Most questions on the syndicated *WWTBAM* really are easier, but beware—now and then they slip in a *Jeopardy!*-level question about botany to keep you from getting cocky. See also *JEOPARDY!*; VIEIRA, MEREDITH; and *WHO WANTS TO BE A MILLIONAIRE*, REGIS EDITION.

WILL & GRACE   Did Debra Messing make us hate *Will & Grace*, or did *Will & Grace* make us hate Debra Messing? No matter, really; the point is that we're not wild about either of them. *Will & Grace* made one positive step: It depicted gay characters who were actually gay instead of just hinting around about it. But then it took two steps backward by making its gay characters perfectly stereotypical—Eric McCormack's Will is a persnickety neat freak who wears women's jeans and has a whole drawer full of "delicates," while Sean Hayes's Jack is a promiscuous, high-talking himbo—so that the full effect of the show isn't too far off from a homosexual minstrel show. And the ladies aren't much better: Megan Mullally's Karen is a rich, amoral slag (. . . actually, she's kind of awesome), and Debra Messing's Grace is a needy, selfish hag. The show has attempted, over the years, to distract us from how noxious the cast is by employing a phalanx of famous guest stars—it's not enough that Jack has to have a relationship with the son he fathered by artificial insemination, the child's mother has to be played by Rosie O'Donnell. Exactly when and how the show jumped the shark is a matter of debate (we say that Jennifer Lopez's appearance as herself was an especially egregious low point), but the show started with a sharp and sparkling pilot, and that was a long, long time ago. See also O'DONNELL, ROSIE; PILOTS; and STUNTCASTING.

"WILL IT FLOAT?"   Late-night talk shows are characterized by their dippy and inane comedy bits, and while *Late Show with David Letterman*'s "Will It Float?" is not the dippiest or most inane (that "honor" probably belongs to *Conan*'s Masturbating Bear), it's right up there. The premise is this: They wheel out a huge tank of water, present an item (a folding vinyl lawn chair, a glass bottle of linseed oil), bandleader Paul Shaffer and Dave debate whether it will float or sink, the thing is dumped in the tank, and the results are noted. It sounds dumb because it *is* dumb, and yet you might be surprised by how anxiously you argue your prediction against that of your spouse. Because 316 Cadbury Eggs *should* float, and if they *don't*, they must have been tampered with in some way, right?! See also *LATE NIGHT WITH CONAN O'BRIEN*, STARING CONTESTS ON and TALK SHOWS, LATE-NIGHT.

WILSON, RAINN We're not saying Rainn Wilson is ugly, in the least. We would *never* say that, because we love him. But he *is* odd-looking. He's got a big, round forehead—like a baby's!—and small, suspicious eyes. Time was, when he turned up on a show (like *Law & Order: Special Victims Unit* or *Dark Angel*), we could be sure either that he *had* done something really bad, or that we were supposed to think he did so we wouldn't suspect someone who was more conventionally handsome. But Wilson's role as Arthur on *Six Feet Under* expanded, if only a little, the range of roles he could play. We realize that others found him annoying, but we thought his particular brand of intensely controlled emotion brought a new energy to the show. Wilson now plays Dwight Schrute on the American version of *The Office*; Dwight is obsessive, power-mad, and—like all Wilson characters—profoundly weird. Which is why it's so delightful that a significant portion of each episode is taken up by his officemates' teasing him. But the difference between Dwight and most TV joke-butts is that his reactions are even funnier than the teasing, like when he was convinced that he needed to form an interoffice alliance to protect himself from downsizing and dyed his hair blond to disguise his identity. Why? Look, with a Rainn Wilson character, you can never ask why. See also DORKINESS, TV SIGNIFIERS OF; *LAW AND ORDER* FRANCHISE; *OFFICE, THE*; OFFICE WEIRDO; and "RUTH FISHER."

WINFREY, OPRAH How long is it going to be before Oprah starts her own religion? Think about it: She's *way* more famous than L. Ron Hubbard ever was. And her followers are at least as devoted to her as Scientologists are to their late spiritual leader. In her many seasons as the host of her eponymous talk show, Winfrey has gone through several incarnations—exploiter of sensitive emotional issues; fat-positive media star; tight-jeans-clad liquid-diet success story; bringer of literature to America's housewives; fat-positive media star; starfucker; diet and exercise guru; sainted distributor of material goods. It's probably in this last capacity that Winfrey is most well known these days. She kicked off her nineteenth season by giving a car to each member of her studio audience, and her annual "Favorite Things" episodes—in which she runs down a list of holiday gift ideas, giving one of each item to the screaming women in her studio—are legendary. We're as apt to take a swipe at Winfrey's earth-mother-ishness as anyone, but folks like her, and she's not hurting anyone. Except James Frey. See also TALK SHOWS, DAYTIME.

WINGS *Wings* was actually . . . kind of not that terrible. It was a standard workplace sitcom, set in a tiny Nantucket airport. But its cast, Crystal Bernard aside, was stronger than you might remember: Tim Daly and Steven Weber, as pilot brothers Joe and Brian Hackett, had real comic timing and were dreamy, Tony Shalhoub did a great job with very little material as cab driver Antonio, and we liked Thomas Haden Church as dopey mechanic Lowell waaaaaay back before his Oscar nomination for *Sideways*. Look, we're not saying we're running out to buy the DVDs or anything, but it's fine on in the background. *Please* stop judging us. See also BERNARD, CRYSTAL.

WKRP IN CINCINNATI Sitcoms of the '70s and '80s generally don't age well; *WKRP* is an exception. Covering the backstage shenanigans at the titular radio station, the show covered all aspects of the business with its cast of lovable weirdos, from newscasters to DJs to ad salespeople to the station manager. Everyone remembers the Thanksgiving episode where the station dropped turkeys from a helicopter over the city of Cincinnati (with predictably disastrous results), but for us, the show was an introduction to how stoners might behave and to the idea that a woman could be smart and nerdy and still be gorgeous, and not only when she took off her glasses (and thank *you*, Jan Smithers, for Bailey Quarters). For years, *WKRP* reigned as the best sitcom set in a radio station, until *NewsRadio* came along and unseated it. Still, it remains one of the all-time great workplace sitcoms. See also STONERS, TV FOR.

WOLF, DICK You might think, based on the kudzu-like properties of the *Law & Order* franchise, that everything Dick Wolf touches turns to gold. Not so! His very first producer credit is on Leif Garrett film vehicle *Skateboard: The Movie*. (Oh, how we wish we were making that up.) He's also responsible for such TV bombs as boring newspaper drama *Deadline*; not one but two shows about con artists helping the government (*Players*, starring Ice-T and Costas Mandylor, and *South Beach*, "starring" Eagle-Eye Cherry. We don't make the news, we just report it); seventeenth-generation *West Wing* photocopy *D.C.*, which featured former *Real World*-er Jacinda Barrett; true-crime selection *Arrest & Trial*; and the *Dragnet* revival, which wasn't terrible, but which gave Eva Longoria the leg up into primetime she needed prior to becoming the most overexposed TV star of the decade. With that said, if Wolf produces it, and Oliver Platt *doesn't* star in it, we'll usually watch it. See also *LAW & ORDER* FRANCHISE; OVERHYPED SERIES THAT BOMBED; *REAL WORLD, THE*; and *WEST WING, THE*.

WONDER YEARS, THE Oh, this show is

cute. Maudlin and overly nostalgic? Sure. Also? Cute. Suburban kid Kevin (Fred Savage) grows up in the bucolic late '60s and early '70s with nerdy best friend Paul (Josh Saviano) and dream girl Winnie (Danica McKellar), while his adult self (Daniel Stern) narrates the proceedings. Kevin's also got a gruff, taciturn dad (Dan Lauria), a chirpy mom (Alley Mills), a hippie-ish older sister (Olivia d'Abo), and a bullying older brother (Jason Hervey). Kevin's childhood is typical in every way: He attends public school, where he's an average student; he plays sports and watches TV; he's solidly unspectacular. But  the genius of the show was in finding the humor in banal but recognizable situations, from navigating the confusing world of girls' mixed signals and muddled communication to appreciating a tough math teacher only after the man suddenly passes away. Once sister Karen got married to Michael (a fetal David Schwimmer) and Kevin got a driver's license, we lost interest, but the early episodes make us nostalgic for an era we didn't even live in and make us wonder if we could pull off wearing an itty-bitty little New York Jets jacket. See also DORKINESS, TV SIGNIFIERS OF and WALDEN, W. G. "SNUFFY."

WOOLERY, CHUCK Woolery started out on *Your Hit Parade* and *Wheel of Fortune* and is probably best known for hosting *The Love Connection* for more than a decade, but regardless of the show, he's one of the best sports in the business. *Lingo* is so down-market, they can't afford to replace burned-out bulbs on set, but Woolery soldiers on in the mood lighting, chuckling at his own jokes and popping the occasional eyebrow at the home audience. Nobody really watched *Greed*, but everybody loved the promos, with Woolery bursting into rooms and popping out of money piles and the other people in the shot looking at the camera all, " . . . Bitch crazy." He looks like he's had about a hundred face-lifts (and he also starred in a reality show about his daily life called *Naturally Stoned*—hee), and he's sort of like Hasselhoff in that he doesn't think he's better than anyone and is more than willing to make fun of himself. See also *LINGO* and *WHEEL OF FORTUNE*.

X-Y-Z

X-FILES, THE We loved *The X-Files*, for a while, but then it went on for a skrillion seasons—long past the point where any of us believed that series creator Chris Carter could link up the neck implants, the boxcar full of dead aliens, Scully's (Gillian Anderson) Jesus baby, that shapeshifter dude with the neck poker deal, Fox's (David Duchovny) sister, Fox's father, the Cigarette Smoking Man, the State Department, the—well, you get the idea. Each season he'd just slap on another layer of exposition. But! The episodes that had nothing to do with the show's central "mytharc" were quite enjoyable—like the episode where Scully meets a dude whose tattoo talks to him (guest-voiced by Jodie Foster), or the one where Jesse L. Martin plays a kickass baseball player who happens to be an alien in disguise. Eventually, Duchovny figured out the series was going downhill and quit, and then *Anderson* left, leaving the series in the capable hands of Robert Patrick and the incompetent hands of Annabeth Gish. And then it ended, and no one missed it. Rumor has it that there may yet be a theatrical sequel to *The X-Files* movie, and God knows it's not like anyone involved in the series has anything better to do now. See also ACTING, WOODEN; ALIEN SPECIES, DERMATOLOGICAL PROBLEMS OF; BABY, RUINATION OF SHOW BY ADDING; "CULT SHOW," DEFINITION OF; DUCHOVNY, DAVID; GUEST STARS, FREQUENT/FAMOUS; MAIN CAST MEMBER DEPARTURES, NOTORIOUS; SCIENCE, IGNORANCE OF; SMALL TOWNS, HIDDEN DEPRAVITY OF; TV SERIES, FILM ADAPTATIONS OF; and *TWILIGHT ZONE, THE*, LATER AND CRAPPIER INCARNATIONS OF.

YOU CAN'T DO THAT ON TELEVISION We probably saw every episode of *YCDTOTV* that aired between 1979 and 1986, aka "The Christine Years"; we don't really remember Alanis Morissette, but we did cherish an embarrassing crush on cutie Kevin Kubusheskie, and back then, popping in and out of a row of lockers with all our friends cracking jokes looked like the best job in the world. The show didn't have all that much to it, in retrospect: running gags involving saying "I don't know" and getting slimed, or mentioning water and getting drenched; recurring skits about disgusting cafeteria food and over-the-top mean/drunk parenting;

catchphrases that we can still find ourselves busting out now and then, like Barth's notorious "Dzhhhaaiii heard that!" and the gnatlike Alasdair's "sometimes it's so easy, I'm ashamed of myself"; horrible puns and Catskills wordplay; and the announcer's fake "preemption" notices involving *Mr. Rogers Vandalizes the Neighborhood*. But just browsing through the show's IMDb entry gives us a giggle twenty years later. D-V-Ds! D-V-Ds! See also TV BOYFRIENDS AND GIRLFRIENDS.

YOUNG AMERICANS That this show ever came to exist in the first place is a testament to The WB's commitment to locking up the youth demographic. Technically a spin-off of *Dawson's Creek*—a backdoor spin-off, in that the *YA* protagonist, Will Krudski (Rodney Scott), appeared in a few episodes of *DC* and then was never mentioned again—the series followed the class conflicts in and around private school Rawley. And even though Will was the ostensible star of the show, we can't remember anything he ever did. Will couldn't possibly compete with the somewhat gay love between long-eyelashed Hamilton (Ian Somerhalder) and "Jake"/Jacqueline Pratt (Katherine Moennig). You'd think there would be no reason for a girl to pose as a boy in order to attend a private school that was actually *coed*. Oh—and the entire enterprise was sponsored by Coke, which you'd think

would have more of an interest in using its clout to promote wholesome family values and not the alternative sexuality that we always assumed was going on at private schools anyway. See also *DAWSON'S CREEK*; HIGH SCHOOL, UNREALISTIC PORTRAYALS OF; HOMOSEXUALITY, CODED; PRODUCT PLACEMENT; and SPIN-OFFS.

YULE LOG, THE No, not Harry Hamlin in a Santa hat. For fireplaceless city dwellers (and pyrophobes), TV's Yule Log is the perfect holiday companion. Instead of messing around with kindling, just turn on this televised loop of a fire, complete with traditional brass andirons, gentle crackling, and muted Christmas carols. The Log originated on New York City's WPIX in the '60s and ran until 1990, when PIX realized it could wring more revenue out of an overaired holiday movie like *Miracle on 34th Street*, and canceled The Log (which ran commercial-free). Outraged Log fans launched a Bring Back the Log Web site and petitioned station management until The Log was allowed to make its triumphant return in 2001. And lo and behold, The Log won its time slot that year. See also HAMLIN, HARRY; HOLIDAY SPECIALS; and RÖHM, ELISABETH.

"THE ZIERING" It was 2004 when we coined the term "The Ziering," in an article for msnbc.com, to describe the one actor on a long-running show whose career will most likely die upon its series finale. As a service to those actors who may now be contemplating a future in which they can no longer count on their longtime meal ticket, we have compiled some markers for potential Zieringhood down the road: you're the title or main character of your show; you've never exceeded sidekick status; you were on the show the entire time it was on the air; you're a junkie; you're famously "difficult"; you get more attention for your off-screen shenanigans than for your work on the show; you're fundamentally untalented and/or unattractive. "But America loves me!" say these Zierings-to-be. "My show is a cultural touchstone, and I, a cultural icon. Everyone wants me now—they'll want me forever!" That's what Philip Michael Thomas thought, too. And do you really think you're any better than the cop of color from *Miami Vice*? See also BAD SITCOM, SURE SIGNS OF and ZIERING, IAN.

ZIERING, IAN We understand that when it comes to pop-cultural objects of desire, the tastes change with the times. We're not going to act like we expect the alleged hunks of *90210* to look attractive to us *now*. But we were teenagers when Ian Ziering played West Beverly poon hound Steve Sanders. Dude was fugly then, and he's probably fugly now, assum-

ing he's still alive. Ziering wasn't the first twentysomething to be cast as a high-schooler, nor the first with a rapidly receding hairline. But Ziering's choice to camouflage his male-pattern baldness by growing out his blond, curly hair made him look like the third groomsman at every wedding between 1977 and 1981.

 And it helped matters not a whit that his character was a douchey boob who hit on everything with a pulse and put the "frat" in "fratty bubbe-latty." Ziering later proved his judgment to be as peerless as his character's when he married Playmate Nikki Schieler, who had sense enough to divorce him after five years but too little to realize that keeping the "Ziering" on the end of her name was not a positive. Also? He pronounces his name "EYE-an," and God help you if he hears you pronounce it wrong. The prosecution rests. See also AFROS, IMPORTANT TV; AGING OF MEN ON TV, UNGRACEFUL; BELT, WHY MEN ON TV WEAR A TUCKED-IN SHIRT WITHOUT A; and *BEVERLY HILLS 90210*.

ZOBOOMAFOO Lord only knows why we started watching a children's show about animals cohosted by a lemur puppet named Zoboomafoo and set in an imaginary neighborhood called Animal Junction. But we know why we *kept* watching: The puppet's human cohosts, enthusiastic zoologist brothers Chris and Martin Kratt, who really look good in cargo shorts. Er, "share many interesting facts about exotic species." It's probably really wrong that we developed crushes on the hosts of a children's show, but you have to make your own fun in this life. See also CHILDREN'S SHOWS, HOSTS OF.

Acknowledgments

Tara and Sarah would like to thank our wonderful staff on TWoP, past and present; our enthusiastic and supportive site readers; our partners at Yahoo!, who bailed out our listing ship when we were taking on a lot of water (if by "water," you mean "crippling debt"), and haven't asked a thing in return except for us to keep doing what we do; our agent, Rick Broadhead; our smart and intuitive editor Melissa Wagner; Erin Slonaker, Doogie Horner, and everyone else at Quirk Publishing; the Buntings: Barbara, Dave Sr., Mr. Stupidhead, and Sam; the Arianos: Carol, Louis, and Leah; and finally Tara's infinitely patient, supportive, and talented husband David T. Cole, who told us in the first place that we should find other people to recap shows that aren't *Dawson's Creek* and turn it into a Web site. That worked out pretty well!